D0161154

MISPLACED OBJECTS

JOE R. AND TERESA LOZANO LONG SERIES IN
LATIN AMERICAN AND LATINO ART AND CULTURE

MISPLACED OBJECTS

Migrating Collections and Recollections in Europe and the Americas

SILVIA SPITTA

UNIVERSITY OF TEXAS PRESS ◆ AUSTIN

This book was made possible in part by the generous support of
The John Sloan Dickey Center for International Understanding
and the Office of the Dean of Faculty at Dartmouth College.

Copyright © 2009 by the University of Texas Press
All rights reserved
Printed in China
First edition, 2009

Requests for permission to reproduce material from this work should be sent to:
    Permissions
    University of Texas Press
    P.O. Box 7819
    Austin, TX 78713-7819
    www.utexas.edu/utpress/about/bpermission.html

♾ The paper used in this book meets the minimum requirements of ANSI/NISO
Z39.48-1992 (R1997) (Permanence of Paper).

LIBRARY OF CONGRESS CATALOGING-IN-PUBLICATION DATA

Spitta, Silvia, 1956–
    Misplaced objects : migrating collections and recollections in Europe and the
Americas / Silvia Spitta. — 1st ed.
        p.   cm. — (Joe R. and Teresa Lozano Long series in Latin American and
Latino art and culture)
    Includes bibliographical references and index.
    ISBN 978-0-292-71897-5 (cloth : alk. paper)
1. America—Relations—Europe.   2. Europe—Relations—America.   3. Accultur-
ation—America—History.   4. Acculturation—Europe—History.   5. America—
Emigration and immigration—Social aspects—History.   6. Europe—Emigration
and immigration—Social aspects—History.   7. Material culture—America—
History.   8. Material culture—Europe—History.   9. Collectors and collecting—
Social aspects—Europe—History.   10. Museums—Social aspects—Europe—
History.   I. Title.
    E18.75.S66   2009
    305.9'06912097—dc22
                                                                        2008042051

To Gerd, Lou, and Sean

TABLE OF CONTENTS

PREFACE   ix

INTRODUCTION: Misplaced Objects and Subject Matters   3

PART I: THE OBJECT AS SPECIMEN   25

1. Misplaced Objects from the Americas and the
Emergence of the European *Wunderkammern*   27

2. Transatlantic Subject Matters and Big Bones:
The Real Gabinete de Historia Natural de Madrid   49

3. Writing the Natural History of Our Destruction: From P. T. Barnum's
National Histrionics to Contemporary, Post-Apocalyptic *Wunderkammern*   67

PART II: MIGRATING ICONS AND SACRED
GEOGRAPHIES IN THE AMERICAS   95

4. GuadalupeNation: Disappearing Objects, National Narratives   96

5. Guadalupe's Wheels: Runaway Image, Undocumented
Border Crosser, Miracle Worker   117

6. The New Mexico/New Mestizo Effect:
Enchanted and Otherwise Enacted Spaces   139

PART III: FOUND OBJECTS AND RE-COLLECTING SUBJECTS   161

7. Re-Collecting the Past: *Latinidad*'s Found Objects,
Photographs, and Home Altars   163

8. Sandra Ramos and the Cuban Diaspora:
La vida no cabe en una maleta   181

EPILOGUE   199

NOTES   209

WORKS CITED   245

INDEX   259

PREFACE

THE CONTINGENT, not-searched-for-but-found book, exhibition, or object sometimes gives rise to unexpected ideas. Who hasn't searched for a book in a bookstore or a library, only to find another one? A well-designed cover or an intriguing title catches our eye and, curious, we pick it up. A friend or a student will tell us about something they think might interest us, and indeed it does. Before we know it we are onto a project very different from the one we had originally envisioned. I am both humbled and awed by the realization that many of my intellectual endeavors have arisen from chance encounters and random discoveries that upset my intentions and the order of things. What in retrospect looks like a coherent academic or life project has, in fact, often depended upon the types of incongruous meetings and unsought juxtapositions that delighted the surrealists. If this is so in one's private life, how much more so must it be in the lives of cultures and the making of history? We like to forget that, much like the workings of a kaleidoscope, meanings arise from the continually changing and rearranging patterns of things.

Having written a book on the dynamics of transculturation in Latin America, I was intent on working through the theoretical differences between transculturation and mestizaje. While transculturation refers to the layered processes of cultural destruction and re-creation in the Americas after 1492, mestizaje focuses on the racial mixture brought about by the arrival of Europeans, Africans, and Asians in the Americas. Muddying the waters further, mestizaje, of course, also covers cultural forms of miscegenation (as in "mestizaje cultural"). I was in search for a clearer distinction between them, when in conversations with Carol Bardenstein I learned about her work on the Palestinian-Israeli conflict, which she tells through the uprooting and planting of trees and the fight over key symbolic objects such as the Jaffa orange and the prickly pear. Her construction of the history of that region caused me to begin to shift my emphasis away from subjects and onto objects. Indeed, I began to suspect that mestizaje cannot be separated from the objects that serve to mark identities—whether national or personal. The story of the Virgin of Guadalupe as a national symbol of mestizaje, her border-crossing capacity, and the multiple appropriations to which she has been subjected, reflected in radical shifts in her iconography, make this very clear.

It was only natural, then, that I should "find" *Imaginary Parents: A Family Autobiography*, co-authored by the Ortiz Taylor sisters. I picked up the book, struck by the title and the cover photograph of a miniature installation. Daughters of an Anglo father and a Mexican mother whose family had been in California long before the establishment of the U.S.-Mexico border in 1848, theirs is a family story that highlights the dynamics of "brown" as it is intervening in the United States, dominated by the black/white divide. Sandra and Sheila visited Hanover and asked to visit Varujan Boghosian, a colleague of mine whose work I had seen around town but whom I had never met. During our visit to his studio I understood how seemingly random objects are harmoniously held together by an underlying narrative that the viewer often only intuits.

The sisters also brought one of the miniatures from *Imaginary Parents* with them. As I held that small object in the palm of my hand, I was overcome by the intense loving care that had gone into its making, and was suddenly reminded of my mother Mayvor's love of objects and the awe with which she held them. When I happened on Cuban artist Sandra Ramos's *La vida no cabe en una maleta* [*Life Does Not Fit into a Suitcase*] at the Museum of Latin American Art in Los Angeles (MOLAA), the relation between objects, identities, and memory became clear to me. The suitcases and trunks in her installation poignantly represent the Cuban Diaspora. Objects drive the trajectory of these exiles: the longing for the "consumer paradise" that they believe the United States to be leads many to abandon Cuba despite the terrible loss experienced by exiles. Yet Ramos's mostly empty suitcases and trunks also inscribe the sorrow of those who are left behind. When I visited the artist in Havana, she received me warmly and explained how her installations served as a metaphor for the loss she had personally experienced.

The impression these visits with artists left were reinforced by a postcard from London from my student Dorothy Karlin, mentioning Mark Dion's "cabinet of wonders," a contemporary archaeology made up of trash dredged from the bottom of the Thames and displayed at the Tate. Dion's work cued me in to the tendency of contemporary artists to juxtapose high and low, art and trash, and to recycle found objects. That postcard turned my attention away from the personal, memory-anchoring function of objects that originally inspired this study, and toward the great transatlantic displacements of people and objects that have shaped our modernity. The Hood Museum's exhibition of the "Age of the Marvelous" in 1991, curated by my colleague Joy Kenseth, provided a historical context for this early compulsion to collect and display. Although quite accidental then, it no longer seemed that way when I encountered Rosamond Purcell's installation "Adam and Eve" in Madrid's Museum of Natural History. Fascinated, I went on to study her work. Her stunning photographs initially arrested my eye, but it is her collaborative work with the late Harvard paleontologist Stephen Jay Gould that underpins this study. Their questioning of our modern conceptions of rationality and order, combined with the musty objects that natural history has left in its wake, sparked my interest in early cabinets of wonders and my desire to understand how profoundly the exotic objects arriving from the Americas after 1492 had destabilized certainties in Europe. And in Vermont, David Fairbanks's Main Street Museum in White River Junction tickles Upper Valley residents with exhibitions such as those of Daniel Webster's socks (bought at K-Mart), the "monster" that he and his mother dredged out of the Connecticut River, and other such precious rarities. Thanks to David, a frequent visitor to my classes, I have become aware of the whimsical collections of the Museum of Jurassic Technology in Los Angeles, and Josh Polon, my former student and now an aspiring filmmaker, photographed them for this book.

Topping this lucky series of finds and friends, Annelise Orleck and Alexis Jetter suggested that we stay at the Mabel Dodge Luhan House in Taos when my family and I traveled to the Southwest in search of anachronistic representations of the Virgin of Guadalupe that persist there despite her changing iconography elsewhere in the Americas. There we found representations of the mestizo Virgin before she had become a Mexican national symbol, and we also unexpectedly encountered a different form of patronage. Our stay at that famous house helped me to understand how collections of Indian and Hispanic arts by New York socialites such as Mabel Dodge Luhan had subsumed the racial and cultural alterity of the region. With their collections, they transformed the Southwest into a "land of enchantment" distant in time and space, yet popularized across the United States as a "look," alluring and fashionable.

I thank Rosamond Purcell, Mark Dion, Cristóbal Toral, Fred Wilson, Max Aguilera-Hellweg, Meridel Rubenstein, Fazal Sheikh, John Valadez, Mirta Kupferminc, Pedro Meyer, Charles Mann, Marion Martínez, Sandra Ramos, Sheila and Sandra Ortiz Taylor, Yolanda López, Luis Tapia, and all the artists included in this book for their incomparable generosity and fearless spirit.

Lois Parkinson Zamora, inordinate friend, taught me to overcome my horror of the Baroque, and to appreciate its infinite play of folds and the power of whimsy. Alberto Sandoval, the bravest of my friends, has survived AIDS for almost twenty years and has inflected every line of this book. While I doubt that he will ever convert me to Broadway musicals, I owe him many things, including my growing appreciation for freaks and monsters. Keala Jewell's work on the de Chirico brothers and her perverse sense of things has deepened my interest in the weird and quirky. During our trip to Philadelphia to the conference on the role of curiosity in early American science, Kathleen Corrigan taught me the profoundly democratic and utopian intent of botanical gardens. Marianne Hirsch and Leo Spitzer's friendship and work on the Holocaust, memory, and photography have been a continual source of inspiration. Roxana Verona has misplaced all of her books, but has survived exile with incredible talent. She and her sister Manuela Holban first showed me Joseph Cornell's magical boxes. I also thank the Hemispheric Institute of Performance and Politics, a floating archipelago of friends across the Americas, in particular Diana Taylor, Marlène Ramírez-Cancio, Tomás Ybarra-Frausto, Teresa Ralli, Miguel Rubio, Guillermo Gómez-Peña, Susana Baca, and all the Hemi participants. They have made me experience disciplinary boundaries as constraining, and hence inspired me to transgress them.

At Dartmouth, Provost Barry Scherr and Deans Lenore Grenoble, Carol Folt, and Kate Conley, as well as Ken Yalowitz and the Dickey Center for International Understanding, supported my work most generously. Mary Coffey, Agnes Lugo-Ortiz, Annabel Martín, Lois Parkinson Zamora, Don Pease, Ivy Schweitzer, and Christianne Wohlforth participated in the Dickey Center's review of the first draft of my manuscript. Their helpful comments and suggestions contributed much to this book. Mary Jean Green's support throughout the years has been invaluable. Campus conversations with Anne Weatherman, Klaus Milich, Melissa Zeiger, and Bruce and Emily Duncan are reflected on many of these pages. Barbara Thompson at the Hood Museum and Jay Satterfield at Rauner Special Collections contributed much fun and quirkiness. Laura Braunstein revised the manuscript, Sarah Slater bravely tackled getting the rights to many of the images, and Mikel Valladares, who embodies better than anyone I know the accumulative, all-embracing spirit of libraries, tracked down arcane sources. Humanities Computing and Otmar Foelsche, Susan Bibeau, and Thomas Garbelotti and Jason Nash saved me on many a day when everything seemed lost.

At the University of Texas Press, Theresa May has unfailingly been there for me, and the two readers for the Press, Tripp Evans and the reader who preferred to remain anonymous, gave the manuscript much of their time, and hopefully caught all of the embarrassing mistakes.

Last but not least, Gerd has read each successive draft of this book and has always commented wisely. He is my luckiest find and the one that has allowed everything else to fall into place.

MISPLACED OBJECTS

LAS COSAS

El bastón, las monedas, el llavero,
la dócil cerradura, las tardías
notas que no leerán los pocos días
que me quedan, los naipes y el tablero,
un libro y en sus páginas la ajada
violeta, monumento de una tarde
sin duda inolvidable y ya olvidada,
el rojo espejo occidental en que arde
una ilusoria aurora. ¡Cuántas cosas,
limas, umbrales, atlas, copas, clavos,
nos sirven como tácitos esclavos,
ciegas y extrañamente sigilosas!
Durarán más allá de nuestro olvido;
no sabrán nunca que nos hemos ido.

—Jorge Luis Borges, *Elogio de la sombra*

PLAIN THINGS

A walking stick, a bunch of keys, some coins,
a lock that turns with ease, useless jottings
at the back of books that in the few days left
me won't be read again, cards and chessboard,
an album in whose leaves some withered flower
lies pressed—the monument of an evening
doubtless unforgettable, now forgotten—
and in the west the mirror burning red
of an illusory dawn. So many things—
a file, an atlas, doorways, nails, the glass
from which we drink—serve us like silent slaves.
How dumb and strangely secretive they are!
Past our oblivion they will live on,
Familiar, blind, not knowing we have gone.

—Jorge Luis Borges, *In Praise of Darkness*

Todos los años, por el mes de marzo, una familia de gitanos desarrapados plantaba su carpa cerca de la aldea, y con un grande alboroto de pitos y timbales daban a conocer los nuevos inventos. Primero llevaron el imán. Un gitano corpulento, de barba montaraz y manos de gorrión, que se presentó con el nombre de Melquíades, hizo una truculenta demostración pública de lo que él mismo llamaba la octava maravilla de los sabios alquimistas de Macedonia. Fue de casa en casa arrastrando dos lingotes metálicos, y todo el mundo se espantó al ver que los calderos, las pailas, las tenazas y los anafes se caían de su sitio, y las maderas crujían por la desesperación de los clavos y los tornillos tratando de desenclavarse, y aun los objetos perdidos desde hacía mucho tiempo aparecían por donde más se les había buscado, y se arrastraban en desbandada turbulenta detrás de los fierros mágicos de Melquíades. "Las cosas tienen vida propia—pregonaba el gitano con áspero acento—todo es cuestión de despertarles el ánima."

—Gabriel García Márquez, *Cien años de soledad*

Every year during the month of March a family of ragged gypsies would set up their tents near the village, and with a great uproar of pipes and kettledrums they would display new inventions. First they brought the magnet. A heavy gypsy with an untamed beard and sparrow hands, who introduced himself as Melquíades, put on a bold public demonstration of what he himself called the eighth wonder of the learned alchemists of Macedonia. He went from house to house dragging two metal ingots and everybody was amazed to see pots, pans, tongs, and braziers tumble down from their places and beams creak from the desperation of nails and screws trying to emerge, and even objects that had been lost for a long time appeared from where they had been searched for most and went dragging along in turbulent confusion behind Melquíades's magical irons. "Things have a life of their own," the gypsy proclaimed with a harsh accent. "It's simply a matter of waking up their souls."

—Gabriel García Márquez, *One Hundred Years of Solitude*

MISPLACED
OBJECTS
AND
SUBJECT
MATTERS

THIS STUDY IS DRIVEN by the Melquíadesque assertion in the opening pages of *One Hundred Years of Solitude*, also echoed in Borges's poem "Las cosas," that things have a life of their own. Not necessarily tricked by a gypsy, I have always suspected this, and I have watched things happen with a sense of wonder somewhat akin to that which determines the lives of the inhabitants of Macondo. José Arcadio Buendía sold his family's last means of livelihood, trading a mule and a pair of goats because he was convinced that the magnets of the gypsies possessed magical alchemical powers to also attract gold. While I do suspect that things have a life of their own, and while that suspicion partially underlies my interest in and fascination with objects, I won't make that assertion here. *Misplaced Objects* is driven, however, by the underlying notion of misplacement and the paradoxically simple thesis that when things move, things change. While literary fiction and films like to play with these forms of dis- and misplaced objects (think of the monolith that suddenly appears in *2001: A Space Odyssey*, the Coca-Cola bottle thrown out of a plane in the African desert and found by a Bushman in *The Gods Must Be Crazy*, the role of the ring in *The Lord of the Rings*, the function of "clues" in detective fiction, etc.), I am interested in tracing the kinds of epistemological, cultural, and geographical shifts that had to take place for the myriad objects that migrated between Europe and the Americas to find their new place within altogether alien contexts.

The (il)logic of misplacement drives this book in its attempt to highlight those moments when objects enter a new cultural context. Initially, the new objects are incongruous; suddenly, quotidian space looks different. In order to understand the effects and theorize the dynamics of misplacement that underlie and structure this book, I borrow Foucault's explanation in *The Order of Things*—modeled on how archaeology constructs both its subject and its object—of a culture's epistemology as the *table* on which things are ordered. Applying Foucault's notion quite literally, in my mind's eye I see an object such as Montezuma's headdress (Figure 0.1) suddenly appearing around 1500 on the table on which Europeans had, until then, ordered the things that structured their world. A "history of things," George Kubler writes, includes "both artifacts and works of art, both replicas and unique examples, both tools and expressions—in

short, all materials worked by human hands under the guidance of connected ideas developed in temporal sequence."[1] But in 1500 an object such as Montezuma's head-dress was not yet archaeology's object. That is, it was not yet an "artifact"—it was simply exotic and soon considered the signature piece of a culture never heard of before. Appearing on the European "table," what could Montezuma's headdress do, but desta-bilize the existing order of things? Forcing a profound reshuffling of the known, it could stand only for the image of "America" that would gradually take shape: indeed, what could it do, to continue with Kubler, but change the "shape of time"?

Juxtaposed with "normal" things, objects arriving from afar were greeted with a sense of wonder, leading Descartes to posit that it was "the first of all passions."[2] Won-der was Europe's first response to the newness of the New World following Columbus's 1492 voyage because wonder steps in when the table of our culture gets messy, when logic and order fail. During this initial, sudden, pre-logical, pre-reflexive phase—whether seen as a rush of intense emotion to the blood and heart (Albertus Magnus) or to the brain (Descartes), the object stands utterly alone, decontextualized, untamed by any classificatory system, "unmoored and unmooring" the rapt observer. Wonder, according to Stephen Greenblatt, causes a "rift" and a "cracking apart of contextual understanding," and thus constitutes "an elusive and ambiguous experience."[3] While

0.1. *Feather headdress*
Museum für Völkerkunde, Vienna

0.2. *Curiosities Shop*
Taormina, Sicily
Photo Spitta 2006

illuminating, analyses like Greenblatt's quickly slip away from the wonder-arousing object to the awed subject. If we focus differ-ently, and stay with the object rather than highlight the emotion of the observer, the enormous role of misplaced objects in the formation of our modern epistemology comes fully into view. Indeed, as I argue throughout, it is not the awed subject, but rather the misplaced object, that causes a rift in understanding. We find a clue to the unsettling of the subject/object binary that structures our certainty and that I am attempting to undo in this study when consid-ering the words *marvel*, *wonder*, and *curiosity*. All three function both as verbs and as nouns, simultaneously designating an object and a state of mind and thus underlining those moments conjoining the object and the subject.[4]

Allowing both Foucault and myself to indulge in our desire to be literal, of course, is the ongoing critique of how museums construct and anchor national and private mean-ings in the things they opt to collect and contain. Displaced, Montezuma's headdress should have served as an index to the violence and probable theft that had led to its mis-placement. That it did not is clear from the lack of any mention in the writings of discov-erers and conquerors, and of many travelers, scientists, and collectors regarding the cor-rectness of appropriating the native objects and specimens they were "gathering" for the emergent science of natural history.[5] Set amid things altogether alien to it, having lost its place in the culture that created it and that anchored its meaning and whose meaning it in turn anchored, Montezuma's headdress was disorderly on every level and misplaced in every sense of that word. Since there was no epistemological table on which it could find a place, what work could it do, then, other than upset European certainties? Indeed, the emergence of modern science, natural history, and Europe's first museums—that immense epistemological shift that we call modernity—gives witness to the sheer force of misplaced objects to destabilize certainties and rearrange cultural tables.

MISPLACED AMERICAN OBJECTS

Unclassifiable by any known standard of the time, the objects arriving in Europe from the Americas were organized next to one another in what were called cabinets of wonders, or *Wunderkammern*. Shells, beads, tusks, coins, feathers, coral, archaeological artifacts, jewelry, weapons, precious stones, and animal and botanical specimens gathered from across the Americas, as well as objects arriving from the East, were *all* set together *on the same plane*. Haphazardly assembled in what to us today look like messy and illogical collections, those exotic objects were displayed for their wonder-inducing powers, yet they put an entire period's epistemological "table" into disarray. This process ultimately restructured the West's knowledge systems and led to the emergence of European museums (of art, science, and natural history), botanical and zoological gardens, and thus increasingly to the distinction between art and science that marks modernity. Indeed, European Wunderkammern—the focus of the next chapter—make visible the extent to which the arrival of strange and marvelous objects from the Americas brought about the European epistemological sea change that has shaped our time.

No one has better described the experience we have today when confronted with the cabinets of wonders than Jorge Luis Borges. In his oft-quoted story "The Analytical Language of John Wilkins," he reports having stumbled upon a certain "Chinese encyclopedia" (the *Celestial Emporium of Benevolent Knowledge*), which classified animals in an order completely alien to our modern taxonomic imagination and sense of rationality (by grouping them as tame, embalmed, stray dogs, sirens, the Emperor's, fabulous, innumerable ones, drawn with a very fine camelhair brush, others that from a long way off look like flies, etc.). While Wilkins did indeed exist and write in the 1600s, no one to date has found the "Chinese encyclopedia." Borges's completely deadpan tone describing these incongruous groupings, indeed, his assumption of extreme disorder as something absolutely normal (and hence his reflection that what for other cultures constitutes order may seem utterly bewildering to us), so surprised Michel Foucault that, "out of the laughter that literally shattered" him, he was led to write *The Order of Things*—his archaeology of the human sciences.[6]

Borges's story had the same effect on Foucault as Marcel Duchamp's 1917 placing of a urinal in a museum ("Fountain," Figure 0.3) had on our understanding of the politics of display.[7] What both works immediately make evident is the otherwise invisible ordering of things. Without referencing the transformative effect the arrival of exotic objects such as Montezuma's headdress had in Europe, "Fountain" and its placing highlight how incongruence leads us to the limits of our imagination, to a space where we must question our own sense of order. As Foucault recalls, his laughter shattered all his assumptions about "*our* thought, the thought that bears the stamp of our age and our geography—breaking up all the ordered surfaces and all the planes with which we are accustomed to tame the wild profusion of existing things, and continuing long afterward to disturb and threaten with collapse our age-old distinction between the Same and the Other." *The Order of Things*, then, is the necessarily failed attempt of thinking our way into an altogether different rationality: "the stark impossibility of thinking *that*."[8] What better illustration of what Foucault meant by "that" than to recall the unease that Europeans must have felt as ships laden with strange objects arrived on their shores? What did they make of them? How did they place them? Others who played with this type of strangeness were the surrealists. They understood the epistemology of a period as consisting of all the things that "fit" together on an imaginary table, and they realized how our mindset mirrors the table on which we organize things. They delighted in jarring our consciousness and never tired of the perverse thrill that came with confronting us with all sorts of misplacements (think of Méret Oppenheim's fur teacup, for example, or the adoption of Lautréamont's "encounter of a sewing machine and an umbrella on a dissecting table" as the symbol for their movement).[9] Our discomfort when faced with such juxtapositions gives us an idea of what Europeans must have experienced with the discovery of the New World. And while we cannot repro-

duce the effect that the presence of unknown objects must have had, we nevertheless do not tire of endless variations on the theme of "aliens" in fiction and films.

More importantly, despite the fact that Foucault based his analyses in *The Order of Things* on the works of three Hispanic writers and artists (Cervantes's *Don Quixote* as the first modern novel, Velázquez's painting "Las Meninas" as the beginning of new forms of representation, and the passage in Borges's Chinese encyclopedia as the possibility of a radically different order of things), it is not inconsequential that he *completely* bypassed the question of the impact that the conquest and colonization of the New World had on the great epistemic shifts that transformed Europe and that shaped our modernity. The Americas fell off Foucault's own epistemological table as they often have, in fact, since 1492, when they were misplaced in world history and geography by Columbus (as the "Indies"). We all know that you sometimes lose things when you misplace them, and much has been lost as a consequence of the rise of Eurocentrism since 1492.

0.3. The Fountain, *1917*
Marcel Duchamp
Photo Alfred Stieglitz
© 2008 Artists Rights Society (ARS), New York/ADAGP, Paris/Succession Marcel Duchamp

While my first chapter charts the breakup of the cabinets of wonders and the emergence of Europe's first museums and scientific academies, my second chapter focuses on Madrid's Wunderkammer, the Real Gabinete, or Royal Cabinet, and its important, yet marginalized, contribution to Europe's scientific preeminence in the nineteenth century. Madrid's Real Gabinete was crucial in transforming the Americas from the paradise Columbus and others thought they had found to a naturalist's paradise, and thus transforming marvelous objects into ethnological artifacts. Intuiting its role in the emergence of modern science and the consequent parting of the ways between Latin and Anglo America, U.S. President Thomas Jefferson felt that the science arising in Europe was deeply Eurocentric and in need of revision. The exchange between him and Bru, the official dissector of the Real Gabinete in Madrid, is only now being studied. This little-known correspondence illustrates how the United States—in contrast to the rest of the Americas—emerged as an important scientific center increasingly in competition with Europe, thanks in part to Jefferson's collaboration with Madrid's Real Gabi-

Ioan: Stradanus inuent.
Theodor. Galle sculp.

AMERICA.

Americen Americus retexit, &   *Semel vocauit inde semper excitam*.

0.4. Vespucci Discovering America, *1589*
Giovanni Stradano (1523–1605)
Bibliotheque Nationale, Paris
*Photo credit: Bridgeman-Giraudon/Art
  Resource, NY*

nete in his search for "big bones" that would prove that species in the Americas were superior (not inferior) to those in Europe. Jan van der Straet's (Stradano) representation of the encounter of Vespucci, standing in full regalia and holding an astrolabe, in front of a naked "America" (nature and woman), reclining in a hammock while members of her tribe are shown roasting a human leg, would prove strangely prophetic—if not paradigmatic—of the epistemological divide that would arise between the West and the rest.

Chapter Three pursues the divide (science/nature) between Anglo and Latin America and the United States by turning to P. T. Barnum's massive collections of specimens and exotic objects, which were deployed in an increasingly histrionic center-staging of science for a mass audience. It ends with contemporary cabinets of wonders such as those created by Mark Dion and Rosamond Purcell and alternative museums such as the Museum of Jurassic Technology in Los Angeles and the Main Street Museum in White River Junction, Vermont, which shift the focus away from the marvelous creations of artists and nature and instead work to salvage—as if writing the natural history of our destruction[10]—the refuse of our society. The post-1492 period that saw its culmination in the Enlightenment has seemingly run its course, as is becoming evident in the current questioning of museological practices. Indeed, we have come full circle: from objects displayed as marvelous in the early Wunderkammern to objects salvaged from the trash and exhibited in modern cabinets as the "marvels" of the world.

MISPLACED AMERICAN SUBJECTS

As the three chapters in the first part of this study show, the objects that arrived in Europe from the Americas led to the enormous sea change we call modernity, even as the impact of the Americas, constitutive of modernity, was erased.[11] Indeed, through misplacement, Europe was able to convert the destabilizing effect of strange and exotic objects into emerging technologies of power as they undertook the colonization of the Americas and much of the rest of the world. In a parallel, yet profoundly asymmetrical way, in the second part of this book (Chapters Four, Five, and Six), I discuss how the objects that arrived in the Americas from Europe in turn destabilized certainties there. Of course, the most obvious strange objects to reach the Americas were guns, gunpowder, the wheel, the Bible, and horses. With "Germs, Guns, and Steel,"[12] the conquistadores literally leveled indigenous cultures. Nowhere is the devastating potential of migrating objects more apparent than in the Americas, post-1492—indeed, in any scenario, what is more violent and more misplaced than a bullet?

When thinking about misplacement, it is important to remember that the exchange of objects between Europe and the Americas occurred under the sign of Conquest and colonization, and hence occurred in profoundly uneven ways, other than, perhaps, the exchange of plants and animals.[13] Objects from Europe arrived under the banner of imperialism and thus were imposed in the interests of domination, whereas indigenous objects entered the European Wunderkammern and taxonomies as strange and exotic. Indeed, in European intellectual history, the Americas are misplaced in a fundamental way as a source of specimens (plant, animal, mineral, human)—rather than as a subject or a producer of knowledge.[14] Incorporated into European epistemology as objects of study, then, how else could indigenous Americans respond to colonization but from a position of weakness (as specimens) and by employing what Josefina Ludmer has called "tactics of the weak"?[15] Furthermore, while objects from the Americas arrived in Europe without a concomitant migration of people (other than the occasional Indian to be displayed as a rarity), European objects arrived in the Americas *along with* successive waves of Europeans, Africans, and Asians. Cultural change has therefore been most often theorized in terms of *mestizaje*, or race mixture (inscribed as the birth of the mestizo bastard out of the rape of indigenous women by Spanish conquistadores).[16] In coming to terms with this long colonial legacy of violence, Latin America has produced a prolific if not wild and unruly intellectual corpus of texts. Concepts such as hybridity, *métissage*, creolization, syncretism, colonial semiosis, coloniality, etc., all, in one way or another, attempt to theorize the multifaceted ways in which first indigenous communities and then emergent nations reacted to and subverted colonial impositions. However, these concepts run the danger of simply proliferating further, since they reiterate essentialist notions of racial and ethnic identity. More importantly, their focus on identities circumvents the crucial role played by objects in delimiting them.

Dirt is "matter out of place," writes Mary Douglas.[17] That most basic definition of how we define the boundaries between the pure and impure, of what is in place and what is out of place, is inextricably linked to the history and development of the concept of mestizaje. *Leed's Shoes 1983*, painted by the Mexican-American John Valadez, represents one of the fundamental ways of thinking about the dynamics of what is

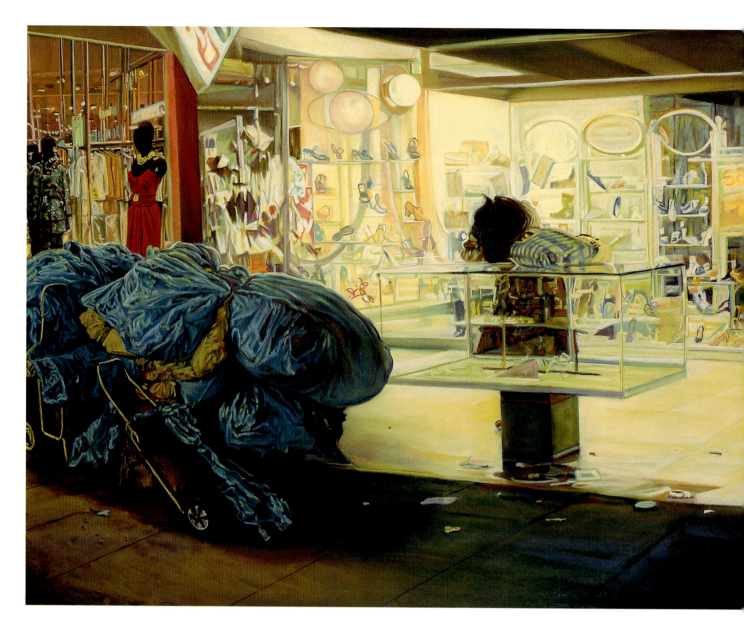

treated as dirt: the homeless person huddled at the entrance of Leed's department store is literally dirt poor and visually equated with the trash (or is it the homeless person's belongings?) piling up at the foreground of the store. While this painting could serve as a jolting reflection on contemporary race relations and the marginalization of poverty in the United States, and while this reading could be extended to encompass an implicit critique of the way colonialism relegated Americans to the margins of history, science, and modernity, it also suggests the hierarchies of race in Latin America. Nowhere is this structure of inclusion and marginalization better illustrated than in the caste paintings (or paintings of miscegenation or mestizaje). These series, consisting usually of sixteen individual paintings, purportedly represented all the different possible racial combinations that arose during the colonial period. Each painting depicts a couple with their mixed-race child. While many of these series were "mass" produced as ethnographic documents and of little artistic value, in the better-executed series, the upper castes are marked as wealthy, whether by the sumptuous clothes they wear or by the space they inhabit. The first paradigmatic mixture is identified with the label "Of Spaniard and Indian, Mestizo" (Figure 0.6). Directly proportional to degrees of racial mixture, the most mixed castes are increasingly darkened and shown peddling their wares in the streets. The most mixed castes then are treated like matter out of place, and

0.5. Leed's Shoes 1983
2004 John Valadez
Courtesy of the artist

labels such as "Tente en el aire" or "Hold Yourself Up in the Air,"
"No te entiendo" or "I Don't Understand You," and "Torna atrás"
or "Throwback" reflect this marginalization (Figure 0.7a). Most
telling is the association of racially mixed individuals with zoological taxonomies and their labeling as "coyote" or "lobo" (wolf).
Toward the end of the series, and with the inclusion of Africans into the racial mix, the
couple (particularly the black or mulatto woman) is represented as prone to violence.

Created to satisfy European curiosity regarding indigenous American populations,
the caste paintings are witnesses to the taxonomic drive of the eighteenth century, and
are but one example of the myriad ways in which Europe—and particularly Spain—
"mapped" the Americas in terms of natural history (botany, zoology, mineralogy,
archaeology) and, most pointedly, biology: the different races the encounter produced.
The caste paintings trace how the Enlightenment, which literally means "shining a light
upon," shone a light upon nature. They also show, however, how that light increasingly became distorted by colonialism into the pseudo-science of eugenics—thus, the
progression from rich to poor and from "pure" to mixed is seen in terms of increasing
degeneration of the "species." As in Valadez's painting, people are misplaced objects—
viewed as out of place, yet all the while they are being violently placed within a tax-

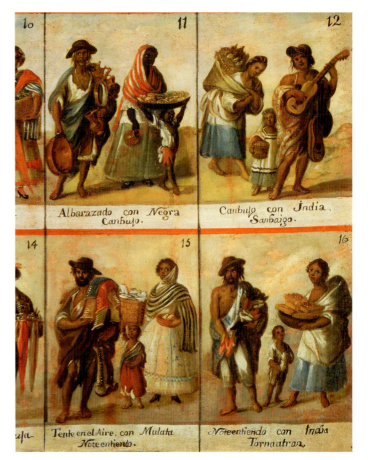

De Español y Mestiza, Castiza.

10 11 12

Albarazado con Negra Canbujo.

Canbujo con India Sanbaigo.

14 15 16

Tente en el Aire con Mulata Noteentiendo.

Noteentiendo con India Tornaatras.

0.6. De espagnol y Mestiza: Castiza
Miguel Cabrera (1695–1768)
Museo de América, Madrid
Photo Credit: Scala/Art Resource, NY

0.7a. Human Races/Las castas, *detail*
Anonymous, eighteenth century
Museo Nacional del Virreinato, Tepotzotlan,
   Mexico
Photo Credit: Schalkwijk/Art Resource, NY

onomy. Moreover, when Americans are inserted into taxonomies, that is, as they become objects of knowledge, they are elided as subjects. Some of the paintings in these series, which were included in the collections of Madrid's Real Gabinete, serve as mute witnesses to the perceived need to control unruly populations by "framing" and displaying them as objects of study.[18] Foreshadowing and also embodying the pigmentocracies that ensued in Latin America, it is ironic that the caste paintings also show, first and foremost, that "race" is unrepresentable other than as rough (and random) gradations in color. Indeed, culture, economic status, place, and occupation, that is, the placement of individuals within a certain material context, serve as the culturally accepted, highly coded way of "seeing" race. Within this extremely hierarchical system, the independence movements of the 1820s brought together deeply divided communities by mobilizing ideologies of mestizaje as the harmonious coexistence of different races and cultures. These national imaginaries would paradoxically go on to deploy mestizaje both to underpin a sense of commonality *and* to serve as a mechanism of exclusion. Mestizaje was mobilized to locate a privileged national subject so that colonized forms of disidentification and caste privilege would dominate at the expense of democratic forms of inclusion. This legacy has had lasting effects. Even today, poverty or wearing native dress invariably serves as an index of marginality, despite any and all claims of mestizo commonality.

This ongoing stratifying and divisive ideology is illustrated at work by haunting photographs that appeared in the news in the 1980s during the dirty war in Guatemala and other parts of Central America. They often showed one man, in military uniform, pointing a machine gun at Indians (maybe his friends and family) in Maya-Quiché villages in the highlands (Figure 0.7b). What mechanisms had made it possible for one Indian to be placed on one side of the social divide and the other on the other, I wondered? And what did mestizaje have to do with this violent cultural and personal divide? As we know, the military is one of the most effective hierarchy-imposing and socially leveling mechanisms in the world, and in Latin America it functions as a veritable mestizo-making machine. The military, in Erving Goffman's words, is a "total" institution, and total institutions strip individuals of their "identity kit."[19] In Latin America, too, Indians' "identity kit" is taken away from them when they enter the military.[20] Forced into military service—"caught" walking on the side of the road by military patrols—the Indians' hair is shorn, their traditional dress and personal belongings are confiscated, their native languages are forbidden, and a profound sense of cultural and racial shame is instilled. Before long—through the various mechanisms of policing the body, the imposition of an "other" sense of authority and hierarchy—they stop dressing and identifying as Indian. After military service, what remains of an Indian? And what is a "mestizo" in this context other than a lack? Conversely, what is a mestizo other than his or her "identity kit"?

Despite the importance of objects to mark identities, few critics (excepting those who study religious syncretism) have focused on the fact that the cultural changes that ensued during the colonial period were mediated by and through the dis- and misplacement of objects. If racial mestizaje is intimately—in every sense of the word—linked to migration, the condition that makes transculturation possible is the reconfiguration of people (racially) and objects in a new context. Indeed, how is the "mixing" of races

0.7b. La cruz de la violencia *[The Cross of Violence], detail*
Nicario Jiménez
The scene at the foot of the cross represents the brutal way in which the Peruvian army and Sendero Luminoso pitted Indians and campesinos against one another.
Photo Lou Gemunden

or mestizaje marked but through culture: art, music, foods, literature, religious icons and practices, and the different cultural geographies that emerge? Mestizaje, then, is framed by these objects and practices and cannot be represented other than through them. National belonging is affirmed by highly visible images and syncretic religious and national symbols, as well as collections of objects in national museums. Telling in this respect are the murals of the great Mexican artists Rivera, Orozco, and Siqueiros commissioned by Minister of Culture José Vasconcelos to paint the epic of mestizaje in Mexico. Nowhere is the racial unrepresentability of mestizos more evident, paradoxically, than in Orozco's famous "Epic of American Civilization"—which could equally well have been called "Epic of Mestizaje" (Figure 0.8). Painted on the walls of the Reserve Room in the basement of Baker Library in the 1930s at Dartmouth College, it is both thematically and aesthetically an oddly misplaced object. While it draws visitors from far and wide, the unsuspecting visitor happening upon the mural feels suddenly as if he or she had stumbled into another space and time. As I was writing this book, I often studied Orozco's "Epic" in search of the way in which he had represented mestizaje, but I was invariably at a loss, for in this fabulous mural Orozco seemed to be unable to represent mestizaje other than through depictions of degenerate generals, corrupt military leaders, and valiant revolutionaries, contrasted to historic Aztec leaders. Is this because it is ultimately impossible to represent mestizaje per se? As in the casta paintings, is it because mestizos are only representable through their circumstance and their "identity kit": the dress they wear, the space they inhabit,

0.8. The Epic of American Civilization: Hispano-America *(Panel 16), Fresco, 1932–1934*
Jose Clemente Orozco
Commissioned by the Trustees of Dartmouth College, Hanover, New Hampshire
Courtesy of the Hood Museum of Art

the objects they possess, and always in contrast to marginalized indigenous peoples? Or is it because everyone is mestizo and there is no "outside" of mestizaje?

While mestizaje remains largely unrepresentable, then, as an ideology it does privilege the female body as *the* site of mestizaje.[21] It should therefore come as no surprise that the most visible symbol of mestizaje in the Americas is the Virgin of Guadalupe. Indeed, the Virgin of Guadalupe has played an indispensable role in the foundational hagiography of Mexico. Brought to Mexico by Cortés and his men, the Spanish Virgin of Guadalupe fast subsumed the apparently eradicated pre-Columbian Aztec cult of the goddess Tonantzin, thanks to a series of miracles that took place (according to Guadalupan accounts) only ten years after the fall of the great Aztec city of Tenochtitlán, and moreover, *on the very site* where the Aztec goddess's temple had formerly stood at Tepeyac on the outskirts of Mexico City. Crucial to how fast the cult spread was the Virgin's dark color, obviously identifying her with Indians and mestizos alike. In a world devoid of hope, her color transformed her into their "mother" and "patroness." When Father Hidalgo started the move toward independence in the early nineteenth century, he rode under her banner, brilliantly understanding that the only ideology that would unite such diverse populations against the Spaniards was that of mestizaje (as utopian ideal of racial unity), and that the only symbol under which he could rally the very populations marginalized by that ideology was the Virgin. For how is it possible for an ideology to persist in the face of deep discrimination against a majority indigenous population? Rebellion would have followed rebellion—and it did in countries such as Perú and Bolivia, which were not dominated by ideologies of mestizaje.[22] Indeed, while mestizaje is present across Latin America as a utopian ideal of racial harmony, few nations, other than Mexico, have so successfully integrated that ideology into their foundational national imaginary. And it probably is not altogether accidental that Mexico, of all Latin American countries, would be the one most successful in promoting the conjoining of the Virgin of Guadalupe with the ideology of mestizaje. Given its closeness to the United States (so far from God, so close to the United States, in Porfirio Díaz's words), the celebration of racial heterogeneity and harmony could be read as a reaction to and critique of the black/white racial divide operant here.

While mestizaje (the "cosmic race," in José Vasconcelos's coining)[23] arose in Latin America as the result of mass migration of people across the Atlantic, we are seeing today another migratory wave worldwide, and scientists predict that with global warming this tendency will only increase exponentially. Helping to explain contemporary artists' obsessions with suitcases and trunks of all sorts, estimates set total numbers of migrants worldwide as high as 50 million. With these migrants, as I show in Chapter Six, the Virgin, once carried across the Atlantic, is on the move again and "on wheels," this time crossing into the United States from Mexico. Hence, while I could have chosen almost any other religious icon from Latin America to discuss the misplacing of objects, the increasing reach of the Virgin of Guadalupe across this country, and into Canada as well, triangulates nicely with the transatlantic migration of objects studied so far. Simultaneous with the Virgin's arrival in the United States, the politics of "brown"[24] (as mestizaje is translated, intervening between black and white) are arriving too. Indeed, increasingly visible as an icon, the Virgin of Guadalupe is now bridging cultural and religious divides. A multiply misplaced object, she is appearing not only on Catholic altars and in churches, but has also become a fashion statement and part of the "identity kit" marking *latinidad* in the United States. Tattooed on bodies, spray painted on lowriders, she also appears on posters, candles, and other religious paraphernalia sold at supermarkets across the country. Miracles, formerly alien to an Anglo-American cultural context, are more and more frequently reported. As a religious cult, Guadalupanism is also being mobilized in the interests of defending the rights of migrant and undocumented workers—be they Mexican, Dominican, Salvadoran, etc. Concomitant with the migration north of this predominantly Mexican religious icon and its commodification, then, is its increased significance as an index of *latinidad*[25] across the differences that divide Latin Americans in the United States—hence, *translatinidad*.

Significantly, the Virgin's trajectory north from Mexico traverses the U.S. Southwest, a region that before 1848 and the signing of the Treaty of Guadalupe Hidalgo belonged to Mexico, and before that to Spain. Known as New Spain, this region preceded and then coexisted in uneasy tension with New England during the colonial period. In this multiply traversed and multilayered region, archaic representations of the Virgin coexist with modern ones that originate in Mexico. Important as a middle ground and immense borderland—simultaneously separating the United States from and joining it to Mexico—this important region invariably falls off the table in the construction of the U.S. national imaginary, which grounds itself in the original thirteen colonies and cannot (yet) embrace the many parts out of which it is constituted—and particularly not its Hispanic colonial legacy. As Chapter Seven shows, the alterity of this land in the middle has been marked by New York socialites who settled there between the two world wars and created fabulous collections of Southwestern arts, and through them, an "enchanted" space outside history. In the 1960s and 70s, this same space would be appropriated by the Chicano movement as Aztlán—an imaginary homeland from where the tribes that settled Tenochtitlán and the Valley of Anahuac (what is today Mexico City) originated. While still an imaginary homeland "somewhere" in the U.S. Southwest, Aztlán has been mobilized by Latinos to underline migration as a historically grounded continuous back-and-forth across the border that allows them also to critique the increasing militarization of the border region as a process that instantly transforms New Mexicans, Californios, and other longtime borderland dwellers into wetbacks and illegal aliens.

*I come to the fields and spacious palaces of memory (*campos et lata praetoria memoriae*), where are the treasures (*thesauri*) of innumerable images . . . When I enter there, I require instantly what I will to be brought forth . . .*

—St. Augustine, *Confessions*

RE-COLLECTING SUBJECTS

As is clear from the examples by means of which I discuss the dynamics of misplacement in the first two parts of this study, catastrophic historical events often underlie the misplacement of objects. With migratory waves, objects become detached from the spaces and memories to which they are and were anchored, even if only through unconscious and unacknowledged associations or dissociations. Having lost some of their

meaning, they are reconfigured in new spaces and acquire different meanings. A stunning depiction of this process of uprooting is artist Mirta Kupferminc's engraving "En camino" [En route], sometimes also titled "Nuestros árboles" [Our Trees] (Figure 0.9). Born in Argentina, the daughter of Holocaust survivors, she represents migration as people literally uprooting themselves. With all their belongings on their backs, along with branches and tree canopies, they are set in motion despite deep inner resistance that pulls them back to their origin.[26] In my final section, I therefore turn to objects as vehicles of intimate and inward narratives.

0.9. En camino *[En route], aka* Nuestros
árboles *[Our Trees]*
2001 Mirta Kupferminc
Intaglio 27.3 × 23.4 inches
Argentina
Courtesy of the artist

The profound connection between objects, identity, and memory was brought home to me when I found myself helping the daughters of dear friends move their belongings out of the family home. As I was carrying some of the boxes they had stored in their parents' attic, I found one on which the eldest had written VERONIKA'S MEMORIES. I was somehow sure that it contained photos, letters, souvenirs, ticket stubs, concert programs, and the bric-à-brac that young girls everywhere endow with magical value. Remembering that, as a consequence of the importance of these memory-embodying dimensions of objects, losing one's possessions to a fire is ranked, along with the death of a loved person, divorce, and exile, among the major stressors of the modern world, I wondered what would happen to my friends' daughter's memories if that box were lost. Or if Veronika, after having stored it in her parents' attic for years, opened it to find objects that she revisited lovingly—maybe nostalgically—only to decide she no longer needed them, that they had become disposable.

At different times of our lives, most of us clear out our houses and throw away some of our "memories," and this may have been the fate of Veronika's box too. Chinese popular wisdom embodies this impulse as the need to make room for new energies in the many rules elaborated in feng shui manuals in vogue today. What we consider "normal,"

"sane" behavior is clearly linked to the ability to maintain a balance between order and disorder. The inability to throw things away is often seen as a symptom of emotional imbalance; conversely, too clean a desk is said to be the sign of a sick mind. Sometimes when we throw things away, we do so simply to make room for new things; at other times we feel the memory-object has served us long enough, much as the silent partners that accompany us throughout our lives yet do not mourn our passing alluded to in Borges's poem "Las cosas." Despite these important memory-anchoring functions, and despite the fact that we are all determined by material things in countless ways, we nevertheless refuse to acknowledge—much less theorize—the full extent of the power of objects over us. "[F]or us, to love things is something of an embarrassment. Things are, after all, mere things," writes Peter Stallybrass in his moving essay "Worn Worlds," where he reflects upon his relationship to the things—particularly an old frayed jacket—left him by a close friend who had passed away.[27] Indeed, it may be that nowhere is the power of objects more evident than in their ability to mediate between the living and the dead. The things in a person's life suddenly acquire immense power to recall that person. When friends or family pass away, their things pass into our lives and occupy a special place, usually in altars of sorts—whether a person is religious or not, and whether the "altar" is acknowledged or not.[28] As Stallybrass concludes, asserting the mediating function of his friend Allon White's jacket: "I cannot recall Allon White as an idea, but only as the habits through which I inhabit him, through which he inhabits and wears me. I know Allon through the smell of his jacket."[29] While death triumphs over the sheer materiality of the body, the objects that had made

(above) 0.10a and b. *Expressions of gratitude*
Afro-Peruvian singer Susana Baca's altars in her home in Lima
Courtesy of the artist
Photo Spitta 2006

(opposite, top) 0.10c. *My altar*
*The space in my home study in New England where I
originally put photographs of my husband and children
became an altar when I added photos and things of
friends and family who had passed away. In the foreground is my colleague Christina Dupláa's necklace with
a stone she had found on a beach. A jeweler in Barcelona
turned it into a precious piece with a silver half-moon and
a star in honor of Joan Miró.*
Photo Spitta 2007

(opposite, bottom left) 0.10d. *Alberto's altar*
*During many years of teaching at Mt. Holyoke College, and
battling AIDS since 1990, Alberto Sandoval-Sánchez
started a collection of sculptures of virgins as a way of
contesting the repressive dogma and homophobia of his
Catholic prep-schooling in Puerto Rico. This eclectic collection, both beautiful and utterly kitschy, became part
of an imposing altar in his home in South Hadley upon
his partner's unexpected death of a massive heart attack
in 2003.*
Photo Spitta 2007

(opposite, bottom right) 0.10e. *Guadalupe altar.*
Taxi stand, Puebla
Photo Spitta 2007

up a life become animated with memory-imprints. More recently, Joan Didion writes that the alarm clock she had received from her husband for Christmas and that stood on her nightstand stopped working one year before his death. After he died, the wafer-thin, black alarm clock had a mind of its own and "could not be thrown out. It could not even be removed." And the same thing happened with the colored Buffalo pens that had long since "gone dry, but, again, could not be thrown out."[30]

Despite the fact that we all have had and often continue to have real boxes or places where we "store" our memories or that "hold" our memories in place, few of us know today why we do this and why we learn the quotidian mnemonic of switching rings from one finger to another or putting something out of place to remind us of that which we wish to remember. Frances Yates's *The Art of Memory* traces the development of "the art of memory" not as we have come to practice it but as it was developed by the poet Simonides of Ceos (ca. 556 to 468 B.C.). Indeed, Simonides taught orators to "pin" memories to places (e.g., the entrance to a cathedral, the columns, the statues, the paintings, and so on), thereby allowing them to memorize literally thousands of speeches.[31] He derived his immensely effective mnemonic technique thanks to a tragic personal experience. He left a dinner party for a few minutes, called outside by someone who turned out not to be there, and this alleged call (by an angel? A premonition?) saved him, for, while he was gone, the ceiling of the building collapsed, killing all the guests at the dinner table. As one of the survivors, Simonides

0.10f. *Ground Zero altar*
The Ground Zero Cross was found a few days after September 11 in the rubble of the World Trade Center. It was apparently formed out of beams from Building One crashing into Building Six. Construction workers erected an altar with it and inscribed the names of fallen police officers and firefighters. There is now a "Ground Zero Cross Petition" on the Internet to raise money to maintain this altar and save it from attacks by atheists. See http://www .conservativealerts.com/cross.htm.
Photo Spitta 2006

was faced with the gruesome task of identifying the severely dismembered bodies. He was able to do so only because he had memorized where everyone had been seated. He learned firsthand not only that place and identity often coincide, but also that memories can be attached to places, and indeed, that it is easier to remember things when one trains one's memory to do this consciously and systematically. Not interested in personal memory, but in creating a system that would allow orators to remember vast numbers of speeches, Simonides invented a system of artificial memory upon realizing that "orderly arrangement is essential for good memory."[32]

While few of us learn his technique, we are all subject to forms of involuntary memory that function, for all practical purposes, in a similar but unconscious manner. In the course of living our lives, we all "pin" our memories—however inadvertently—to the houses and cities we inhabit and to the objects with which we surround ourselves or that surround us. Simonides's observations prove illuminating to my discussion of the losses incurred by migration, because he shows how much we depend on *order* to hold our thoughts (and identities) in place and why it is significant that dirt is matter out of place. With migration, the cultural order is undone and experienced as a *radical undoing*. Much is lost and misplaced in the transition from one place to another, and much work needs to be done in order to create and attach new memories to new places. While there is loss, nostalgia, and disorientation, however, much that is new, vibrant, and creative also emerges from the reshuffling of things in new contexts. Therefore, the focus of my last two chapters is on the works of the Ortiz Taylor sisters and on Sandra Ramos's installations, which inspired me to write this book. That is, as I mentioned in the preface, I end with the Latinization being effected gradually by the private, familial, laborious, and loving cultural and memory work of the millions of Latinos in the United States. While Latinization is reflected in the current boom of Latino art and literature, it is also evident in the Virgin of Guadalupe's exponentially growing capacity to embrace Latin American immigrants. The Ortiz Taylors' *Imaginary Parents,* with its accompanying miniatures, as well as Ramos's suitcases and trunks, remind us that the work of the great collectors, which often resulted in the establishment of museums and other such examples of national showcasing, most often started out as a private obsession.

SUBJECT MATTERS

Every new cultural configuration and therefore every subject position depends upon transcultural processes: the uprooting of objects, the loss of place and memory that such uprooting entails, the reconfiguration of objects in foreign spaces, and the concomitant reorganization of the epistemological table of the receptor culture under the impact of those objects. The notion of *misplacement*, then, underlines my entire project. We create narratives of the past based on the shards, the fragments of things, the texture and design of pottery and textiles that cultures leave in their wake. This connection between objects and cultural narratives leads James Clifford and other ethnographers to assert that cultures are "ethnographic collections."[33] While this statement may sound apodictic and even hyperbolic at first, and despite the fact that some cultural forms may survive embodied in the internalized repertoires of dance or performance,[34] it is clear that cultures that leave no material traces irremediably disappear. Indeed, in most cases we only "know" defunct cultures through the memories embodied in the objects that survived them. Objects' inability to mourn does not mean, however, that they do not carry a "memory," an imprint of the action of human thought: and in Kubler's words, that they allow us to intuit an emerging shape in time.

The late Harvard zoologist and geologist Stephen Jay Gould explains how this shape in time is to be taken quite literally, since it is constituted as a complex totality through numerous overlyings of objects and human action. He shows this interpenetration of subject and object at work in the famous fossil fish embedded in Solnhofen limestone that has allowed the soft parts of the fish (fins and body outline) to be preserved along with the fish fossil's bony skeleton. The surrounding rock in which the fossil is embedded has cracked and been stapled together. This suture is the youngest stratum, and it in turn is marked by penciled numbers and corrections in classification written directly on the rock, a piece of paper with notes attached, and two words seemingly printed on the rock: Gold and Oesterr. These, it turns out, were from the Austrian paper wrapping used when the fossil was transported to the United States. In Gould's reading, the top layer is the most recent, and the bottom layers are the oldest. Geologists uncovering amalgamations of this sort are "quite literal about 'overlying'" because they reveal something about time, but also because they show us that what emerges out of the shards of the past is always a multilayered complex totality. Indeed, nothing comes to us unmediated. Crucial in this respect and underlying all of Gould's own famous interventions, especially his lifelong collaboration with photographer and installation artist Rosamond Purcell (indeed, their attraction to the early Wunderkammern), is the recognition that science and art have remained deeply implicated with each other despite all notions to the contrary. Studying the artistic rendering of Purcell's photograph of the overlayered fossil fish, Gould left us with the injunction that intellectual life "should not be construed as two cultures of science and humanities at war." Just as art and science are inextricably linked, Gould asserted that so, too, the subject and the object are indistinguishable from each other despite traditional cultural accounts. He concludes that the sequence of superposition on the Solnhofen fossil fish shows "an unbroken transition from things of nature to things of art, flesh to rock to paper to ink," and that this "illustrates the embedding of mind in nature."[35]

In his meditations on mind, memory, and matter, the early twentieth-century French philosopher Henri Bergson collapses the opposition between mind and matter in a different way. He writes that one can perceive the world only through the body— that object-image par excellence—and that as a consequence, every time one moves, "everything changes, as though by a turn of a kaleidoscope."[36] Bergson is not thinking of a subject (like the Enlightened Eurocentric subject) situated at the center, spinning around an axis and surveying the world. More radically, in the kaleidoscope, he seems to have made the subject and the object indistinguishable from each other, for am "I" not the kaleidoscope in his phrasing? Extending his metaphor a bit further to help clarify my own growing unease with conventional distinctions between subject and object, I assume that I am immersed in materiality and can only articulate my "I" through the materiality of my body. In the chapters that follow, I therefore assume an "I" that is distinguishable from a world of materiality (things) only at those moments of attention and tension between "I" and "it" that I call the "object." This "I" emerges much as the reconstituted image emerges after the turning of the kaleidoscope. *Misplaced Objects* is, then, my attempt to think through the object, and as such it is the attempt to think through the subject/object divide that structures our thinking.

In much the same manner as a photograph invariably disappears as an object when we focus on its referent (the photographer's object), objects, too, prove to be endlessly elusive and singularly ungraspable.[37] They do seem, however, to become of concern to us at moments of crisis.[38] The surrealists' fanciful playing with incongruous juxtapositions emerged in the time of political instability between World Wars I and II, and more recently, the narratives of Holocaust survivors, Vietnam veterans, political exiles, and migrants all privilege objects in their construction.[39] Important for challenging the subject/object divide in the 1960s is the so-called "knowledges reconstruction project." European and U.S. intellectuals at the Institute for Policy Studies in Washington, D.C. (Marcus Raskin, Joseph Turner, Susan Buck-Morss, Ann Wilcox, and Herbert Bernstein, among others), came together to critique our epistemology. They started out with the premise that the modern forms of rationality, science, technology, and the subject/object binary have to be rethought in the interests of saving a planet many felt was doomed, particularly after the failure of leftist revolutionary ideals. They argued in different joint and individual publications that our epistemology is colonial, that our "knowledges define the character of modern life and are presently used for colonizing and controlling purposes," indeed, that "much of our inquiry system sustains racism, sexism, and classism."[40] Their call was to create a general awareness of the colonial and colonizing underpinnings of our "rationality" and a "reconstructive knowledge" that would allow for a more humane, ethical, and ultimately sustainable world. Their ideal was to create the conditions of possibility that would allow for dialogue on and across many of the divides that currently hinder the free exchange of ideas and positions. Appealing to the more utopian moments in Marx's thinking, they envisioned creating the possibility of having everyone involved first take "turns of participating in what is eaten, what is to be grown, and how to take out the garbage" and then sitting down at the same table to negotiate.[41] Their group's proposed democratization of work and space would undo the situational politics of the museum panopticon that has structured our certainties for so long. The work of this group is echoed in contemporary artists' reclaiming of the messiness of the early Wunderkammern and in feminist, queer, and much postmodern and border criticism. While the "knowledges reconstruction project" is now defunct, it has reverberated provocatively across the academic and artistic spectrum and was capped—in what could constitute a rough periodicity—by Susan Stewart's marvelous *On Longing: Narratives of the Miniature, the Gigantic, the Souvenir, the Collection,*[42] and more recently still, by Bill Brown's *Things*. To cite the words with which Brown ends his introduction (and which outline his intellectual project by aligning it with Bergson's), we need to undermine "our very capacity to imagine that thinking and thingness are utterly distinct."[43]

Finally, as studies such as Brown's, Stewart's, and others show, any attempt to undermine hierarchies between subject and object, that is, any attempt to shift the focus away from the subject and to *think through the object* necessarily breaks down disciplinary boundaries because disciplines are both formed and hence constrained by the object they study.

PART I

THE OBJECT AS SPECIMEN

Premios literarios contantes y sonantes me ayudaron a adquirir ciertos ejemplares a precios extravagantes. Mi biblioteca pasó a ser considerable. Los antiguos libros de poesía relampagueaban en ella y mi inclinación a la historia natural la llenó de grandiosos libros de botánica iluminados a todo color; y libros de pájaros, de insectos o de peces. Encontré por el mundo milagrosos libros de viajes; Quijotes increíbles, impresos por Ibarra; infolios de Dantes con la maravillosa tipografía bodoniana; hasta algún Moliere hecho con poquísimos ejemplares, "Ad usum delphini," para el hijo del rey de Francia.

Pero, en realidad, lo mejor que coleccioné en mi vida fueron mis caracoles. Me dieron el placer de su prodigiosa estructura: la pureza lunar de una porcelana misteriosa agregada a la multiplicidad de las formas, táctiles, góticas, funcionales.

Miles de pequeñas puertas submarinas se abrieron a mi conocimiento desde aquel día en que don Carlos de la Torre, ilustre malacólogo de Cuba, me regaló los mejores ejemplares de su colección. Desde entonces y al azar recorrí los siete mares acechándolos. Mas debo reconocer que fue el mar de París el que, entre ola y ola, me descubrió más caracoles. París había transmigrado todo el nácar de las oceanías a sus tiendas naturalistas, a sus "mercados de pulgas."

Más fácil que meter las manos en las rocas de Veracruz o Baja California fue encontrar bajo el sargazo de la urbe, entre lámparas rotas y zapatos viejos, la exquisita silueta de la Oliva Textil. O sorprender la lanza de cuarzo que se alarga, como un verso del agua, en la Rosellaria Fusus . . .

Algunos de estos trofeos pudieron ser históricos. Recuerdo que en el Museo de Pekín abrieron la caja más sagrada de los moluscos del mar de China para regalarme el segundo de los dos únicos ejemplares de la Thatcheria Mirabilis. Y así pude atesorar esa increíble obra en la que el océano regaló a China el estilo de templos y pagodas que persistió en aquellas latitudes.

—Pablo Neruda, *Confieso que he vivido*

Ready cash from literary prizes helped me to buy some editions at outlandish prices. My library grew to a considerable size. Antique books of poetry brightened it, and my bent for natural history filled it with magnificent books on botany, illustrated in full color, and books on birds, insects, and fish. I found wonderful travel books in various parts of the world; incredible Don Quixotes, printed by Ibarra; Dante folios in exquisite Bodoni type; even a Molière from a very limited edition prepared, "Ad usum Delphini," for the son of the King of France.

But, actually, the loveliest things I ever collected were my seashells. They gave me the pleasure of their extraordinary structure: a mysterious porcelain with the purity of moonlight combined with numerous tactile, Gothic, functional forms.

Thousands of tiny undersea doors opened for me to dip into, from the day Don Carlos de la Torre, the noted Cuban malacologist, gave me the best specimens from his collection. Since then I have crossed the seven seas, wherever my travels took me, stalking and hunting down shells. But I must confess that it was the sea of Paris that, wave after wave, washed ashore most of my shells for me. Paris had transported all the mother-of-pearl of Oceania to its naturalist shops, to its flea markets.

Finding the exquisite contours of the Oliva textilina under the city's Sargasso, among broken lamps and old shoes, was easier than plunging my hands in among the rocks of Veracruz or Baja California. Or catching the spear of quartz that tapers off, like a sea poem, into Rostellaria fusus . . .

Some of these trophies may have had a historic past. I remember that in the Peking Museum the most sacred box of mollusks from the China Sea was opened to give me the second of the only two specimens of the Thatcheria mirabilis in existence. And thus I was able to own that remarkable work of art in which the ocean gave China the style for temples and pagodas that still survives in those latitudes.

—Pablo Neruda, *Memoirs*

CHAPTER ONE

MISPLACED OBJECTS
FROM THE AMERICAS AND THE
EMERGENCE OF THE
EUROPEAN
WUNDERKAMMERN

The Wunderschrank . . . [T]his combinatorial cabinet reminds us of the long cultural conversation objects have had, and will continue to have, with one another and with us.

—Barbara Maria Stafford, *Devices of Wonder*

For what else is this collection but a disorder to which habit has accommodated itself to such an extent that it can appear as order?

—Walter Benjamin, "Unpacking My Library"

. . . through collecting, the passionate pursuit of possession finds fulfillment and the everyday prose of objects is transformed into poetry, into a triumphant unconscious discourse.

—Jean Baudrillard, *The System of Objects*

Curiosity resists control, both as an appetite and as a material object [it is] imperialistic and aggressive. A product of the age of discovery, it vibrates between the spectator and the spectacle, the possessor and the possession.

—Barbara M. Benedict, *Curiosity: A Cultural History of Early Modern Inquiry*

WHILE MOST HISTORICAL STUDIES focus on the logistics and violence of the colonization of the New World, few mention the profoundly destabilizing effect of the arrival of massive numbers of objects from the Americas in Europe.[1] Having traditionally underpinned cultural memory in specific ways, set adrift by conquest and plunder and radically unanchored and displaced, these objects were first collected in European cabinets of wonders or cabinets of curiosities. These spaces, the forerunners of our modern museums, were created to contain, in both senses of the word, the alterity of the objects arriving in Europe in a steady flow after 1492.[2] Having lost the personal, social, and symbolic values that had embedded them in indigenous cultures, and contrary to all expectations, indigenous objects would literally overcome Europe's ability to order things. The words "marvelous" or "exotic," with which these objects were greeted,

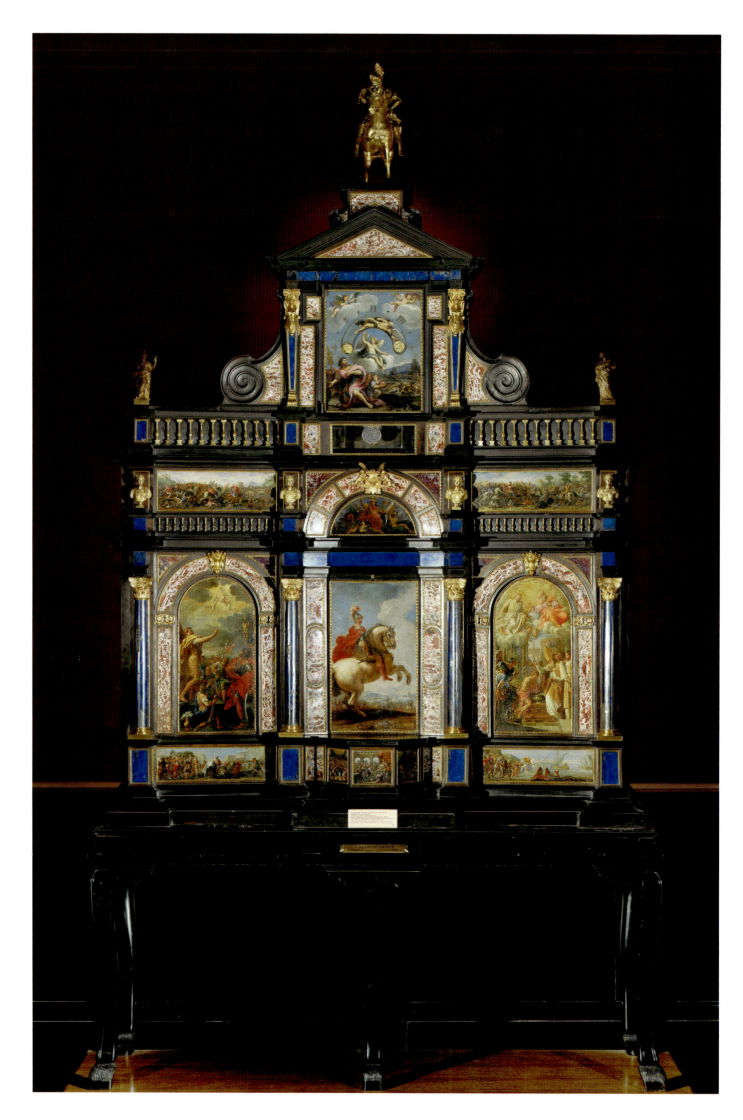

never quite cloaked their sheer incongruity, the distance they had traveled, and thus the distance that separated one cultural system from another. As Barbara Benedict points out, curiosities resist curiosity. Displacement, then, does not result in the complete and successful assimilation of the displaced object; misplacement always invariably results and is never fully canceled or corrected by time or strategies of containment. The continued need throughout modern western history for museums, dioramas, exhibits, and other forms of interpretive control makes clear the extent to which the radical alterity of American objects was never completely assimilated.[3]

What we see from the Renaissance onward, then, are two moments in the life of an American object: the first is its violent deracination from the originating culture and displacement into a world to which it is alien (which forces a reorganization of that world); the second is a reorganization of European collections of objects under the impact of a changed consciousness. As I will show below, at times it is not quite clear which comes first. While today many collections are reorganized according to critiques of Eurocentrism and the politics of display, in the case of the Wunderkammern it seems evident that at that first moment of cultural contact, the displacement of objects from the Americas to Europe was responsible for a radical epistemological shift in the receptor-culture.[4] For, what work could misplaced objects do other than signal the destruction of indigenous cultures and at the same time throw the thinking of early modern Europe into question?[5] Robbed of their meaning and "collected" in the cabinets of wonders, indigenous objects slowly acquired value through metonymy, as the Bambara mask came to stand for or become an "ethnographic metonym" for the whole of Bambara culture[6] and a privileged object such as "Montezuma's headdress" came to signify the wealth and splendor of the entire (conquered) New World, and thus the power of Europe over the world. The development over the last centuries of natural science and modern science, contrary to overarching claims of rationality, has thus been closely linked to allegory and emergent forms of colonialism.

1.1. Roman cabinet with clock
Giacomo Hermann (1668)
Painters: Guglielmo Cortese, Carlo Maratta,
   Pietro del Po
Clockmaker: Pietro Tommaso Campani
Kunsthistorisches Museum, Vienna, Austria
Photo credit: Erich Lessing/Art Resource, NY

The cabinets of wonders were distinguished in German as pieces of furniture used as display cases and works of art in their own right (*Kabinettschränke, Kunstschränke, Wunderkabinette,* or *Wunderschränke*),[7] or as entire rooms known as *Wunderkammern,* harmoniously conjoining art and science (Figures 1.2, 1.3, 1.4, 1.13, and 1.14). Since all these wonderfully bizarre spaces were ultimately dismantled, today we can only get a glimpse of what they looked like from two engravings, that of the Italian Ferrante Imperato's "museum" and Ole Worm's famous Amsterdam cabinet[8] (playfully re-created from recycled objects by installation artist Rosamond Purcell, as we will see in Chapter Three). The Wunderkammern were most often described as collections of "curious objects, displayed for ostentation or for the study of some art or science" ["objetos curiosos, para ostentación ó para estudio de algún arte o ciencia"].[9] From their inception, cabinets of curiosity were caught between wonder at the marvels of nature, man, and God, yet they oscillated also between the fear of and the desire to transgress God's secrets. Over time, therefore, curiosity began to be understood as "imperialist and aggressive,"[10] even as it continued to drive scientific and artistic endeavors. Barbara Benedict argues that curiosity, understood and defined as "seeing your way out

of your place," peaked between 1660 and 1820.[11] Simultaneously a noun (a curiosity), an adjective (a curious man), and an adverb (curiously yellow), curiosity helped Europeans see their way out of their place by impelling them to provide new places, and hence a new epistemology, for strange things.[12]

In the early days of the Wunderkammern, extreme contrast dominated the aesthetics of display: the miniscule was placed next to the enormous, the monstrous next to the beautiful.[13] Rarity and exoticism were at a premium: embryos, fetuses from illegal abortions, livers of alcoholics, enormous pearls, exquisite artwork and trompe l'oeils, shells, tusks, archaeological and ethnographic findings, scientific objects, mirrors,[14] and miniatures of all kinds were grouped together in collections of things that look to us today as messy, haphazard, and bewilderingly Baroque.[15] Three main categories in dynamic tension initially underpinned the organization of these wonder-containing and wonder-provoking spaces. Objects were classified as *Naturalia* (zoological, botanical, and mineral natural wonders) and *Artificialia* (rare and illuminated manuscripts, and scientific and art objects). A third category, which could be called *Naturficialia*, was an important intermediate form conjoining the marvels of nature (coral embedded in jewelry, carved tusks and shells, etc.) with marvelous feats of

1.2. The Sciences and the Arts
Adriaen Stalbent (1589–1662)
Museo del Prado, Madrid
Photo Credit: Erich Lessing/Art Resource, NY

(opposite, top) 1.3. *Title copper plate of Ole Worm*, Musei Wormiani historia, *Lugd. Batavorum, Ex Officina Elseviriana*
Leiden, Elsevier, 1655
Courtesy Smithsonian of Institution Libraries, Washington, DC
Ole Worm's museum served as the founding block of Denmark's modern museums. The oak root (mounted upside down) growing around the lower jaw of a horse in the background is apparently the only zoological survivor of the collection and has been of particular interest to artists like Rosamond Purcell.

(opposite, bottom) 1.4. *Frontispiece, interior of Ferrante Imperato Collection, woodcut*
From Dell'historia naturale, libri XXVIII, Naples: Costantino Vittale, 1599
Courtesy Smithsonian of Institution Libraries, Washington, DC
Notice the central positioning of the visitors in all of these representations of the Wunderkammern as well as in Figures 1.13 and 1.14.

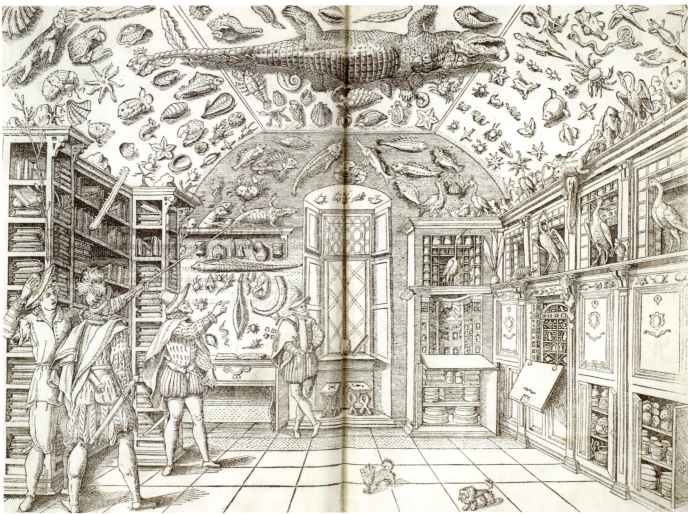

craftsmanship that rivaled those of God.[16] Not articulated but nevertheless implicit in these works, as in early natural history's fascination with the tension between the monstrous and the beautiful, is the underlying notion of the perfectibility of nature (and God's handiwork). Famous throughout Europe for these kinds of Baroque allegorical dramas and highlighting of the scientists' progressive unveiling of the workings of nature, man, and God was Frederik Ruysch's (1638–1731) Cabinet in Amsterdam.

1.5. *Quartz, example of* Naturalia
Vienna Naturhistoriches Museum
Photo Spitta 2006
Natural history museums attempt to awe the
visitor in the spirit of the Wunderkammern
in their attempts to possess and display the
biggest and rarest specimens.

This collection, which ultimately served as the cornerstone for Peter I's *Kunstkamera* in St. Petersburg, spilled into five rooms filled with specimens that the famous anatomist had preserved through the invention of intravascular injections of fixatives and dyes.[17] Ruysch combined his important scientific invention with macabre theatrics (Figures 1.7, 1.8, 1.9). With the help of his daughter (a famous artist in her own right), he assembled fetuses, mummies, and skeletons as tableaux, making them look as lifelike as possible. His creations were dressed in pearls and shown playing violins made of dried tissues that look like lace. In one tableau the skull of a syphilitic prostitute was placed in the same jar with a baby's leg shown kicking it. Ruysch's exhibits were displayed to friends and the public not only to show off the anatomist's scientific innovations; they were also reflections on the transitoriness of life and the perils of *vanitas*. Interesting in and of themselves, Ruysch's work makes evident the allegory and theatricality of the early Wunderkammern that also underpins the emergent scientific order and modern forms of rationality.

1.6. Daphne
Abraham Jamnitzer (1555–c1600)
Silver statuette, with coral; late sixteenth
* century*
Nuremberg, Germany
Photo Credit: Erich Lessing/Art Resource, NY

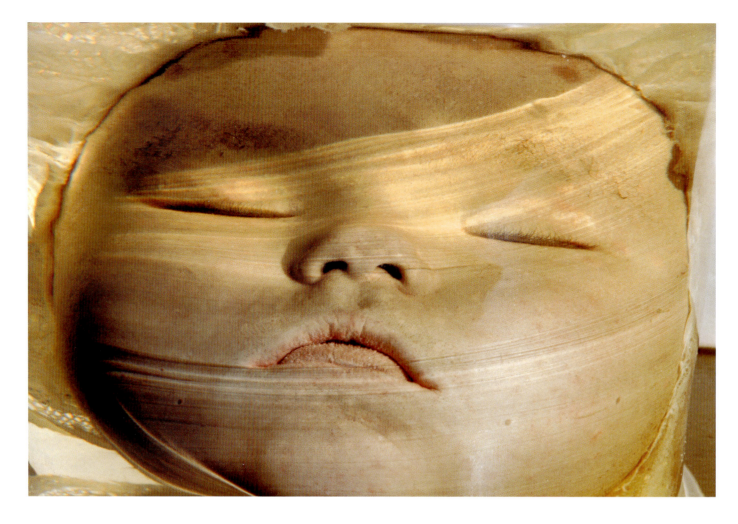

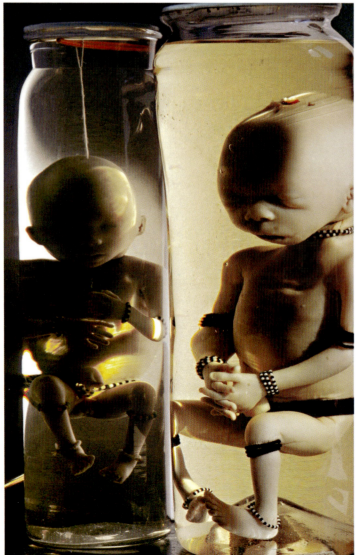

1.7. *Baby in jar*
Fredrik Ruysch, Leiden
Peter the Great Museum of Anthropology and Ethnography
(Kunstkammera), St. Petersburg
Photo © Rosamond W. Purcell 2007
Courtesy of the artist

1.8. *Baby with beads*
Fredrik Ruysch
Peter the Great Museum of Anthropology and Ethnography
(Kunstkammera), St. Petersburg
Photo © Rosamond W. Purcell 2007
Courtesy of the artist

1.9. Allegory of the Transitoriness of Life
   with "Music" as a Theme
Federici Ruyschii
Thesaurus Anatomicus Octavus
Amstelodami
Courtesy Rauner Special Collections Library,
   Dartmouth College
Photo Spitta 2006

As early as the sixteenth-century New World chronicles, as in seventeenth- and eighteenth-century natural history writings, and certainly in the Wunderkammern, we witness the Baroque impulse to overarch and include, just as we witness the related themes of abundance and ownership. The cabinets of wonders embodied this Baroque sensibility and considered themselves not only as visual encyclopedias but, as in Ruysch's works, also simultaneously as privileged performative sites—that is, as theaters of the marvelous. Indeed, anatomy was studied in highly performative anatomical theaters.

The same gaze that was turned outward to study the world was turned inward to study the body. The anatomist Vesali shows a macabre progression as a body is stripped of skin to reveal the underlying musculature and then stripped of muscles to show the bone structure underneath, until it can no longer hold itself up;[18] abnormalities and diseases were displayed in medical museums,[19] and memory theaters[20] created encyclopedic and mnemonic spaces purported to contain, in highly coded form, all that was known, past and present, about the earth, the heavens, and God.[21] Cabinets of wonders were therefore thought of not only as archives, but equally as living theaters of memory.[22] Emphasizing the inseparable connection between display and spectacle, and underlining the spatial dynamics I have been outlining, the Wunderkammern have been variously described as "miniature houses of images," "spectacle-enclosing boxes," "universes-in-a-box," and "encyclopedic chests." The notion that a space could encompass and contain the whole world can perhaps be attributed to the con-

1.10. Anatomy amphitheatre, Padua, Italy
Photo Credit: Erich Lessing/Art Resource, NY
The earliest demonstrations in anatomy took
    place here.

1.11. Frontispiece, anatomy lesson
Andrea Vesalii, De humani corporis fabrica
    libri septem
Basileae [Ex officina Ioannis Oporini,
    MDXLIII], 1543
Notice the throngs watching the demonstration,
    the skeleton as allegory of the transitoriness
    of life overlooking the lesson, and the naked
    sculpture clinging to the column and seem-
    ingly coming alive.
Courtesy Rauner Special Collections,
    Dartmouth College
Photo Spitta 2007

vergence of the ancient art of memory with Gutenberg's invention of moveable type in 1450 and the publishing of the Bible—a "holy" book that unites print and materiality with the idea of God and the nonmaterial world. Of all books, the Bible would lend itself most prominently to miniaturization, since miniature books call attention "to the book as total object," in Susan Stewart's words.[23] The West, forty-odd years after the

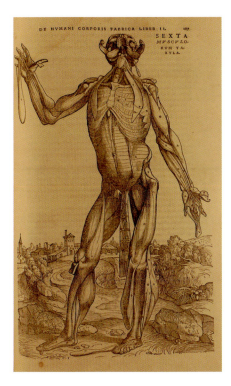

1.12. The Human Body

Andrea Vesalii, De humani corporis fabrica libri septem

Basileae [Ex officina Ioannis Oporini, MDXLIII], 1543

This engraving is part of a series showing the human body progressively stripped of skin and muscles until it can no longer hold itself up. This engraving shows the body's musculature and underlying skeleton. It is propped up by a pole.

Courtesy Rauner Special Collections, Dartmouth College

Photo Spitta 2007

publication of the first Bible, saw the first mass printing (2,500 copies) in Latin and German of the *Liber cronicarum,* or *Nuremberg Chronicle,* which claimed to be a compilation of the entire history of humanity—that is, a book of the world or, conversely, the world as a book.[24] Less than a hundred years later (ca. 1569), Flemish geographer Gerhardus Mercator (1512–1594) mapped the entire world and coined the term "atlas" with his publication of the *Atlas, sive cosmographicae meditationes de fabrica mundi* (1585).[25] Paralleling the Bible's collapse of all meaning and knowledge into one text, the space of the Wunderkammern aspired to the status of a Gesamtkunstwerk,[26] or complete work of art, coupling visibility with knowledge, theatricality, and power.

As historians and art critics have pointed out, in the Wunderkammern the macrocosm literally irrupted in the microcosm: the world, suddenly, almost overnight it would seem, was "in der Stube" (in the home).[27] Entitling the subject to a central, privileged, voyeuristic space, the operating assumption of the cabinets of wonders therefore was that in their wild, exuberant, encyclopedic inclusiveness, they laid bare the marvels of the entire world. The Spanish naturalist and explorer Antonio de Ulloa wrote of his visit to the famous British cabinets of wonders (while a prisoner receiving very gentlemanly treatment) that they were spaces in which all of nature was transplanted, spaces where the visitor encounters "a live, general, and complete history of everything hidden under the waves, produced by the earth, animal and vegetable in all the regions and elements" ["una historia viva, general, y completa de quanto encubren las Ondas, produce la Tierra, y se cría viviente, vegetable, y particular en todas las Regiones, y Elementos"].[28] Wonder is by definition erratic and enthusiastic, but seventeenth-century European science was harnessing the chaotic energy of wonder in the service of knowing, and thus controlling, the world. Indeed, Ulloa's wording anticipates the discovery of X-rays, and highlights the notion of history as *natural* history.[29] Moreover, facilitating the transition between "discovery" and "empire," the central position of the royal visitors of the cabinets allowed them to survey marvelous objects collected from far and wide and thus to feel that they had the world within arm's reach. Engravings and paintings of early cabinets of wonders, as well as paintings of Kunstkammern, significantly, *all* position the visitors to those spaces at the center of the room, and by extension, also at the center of the epistemological system that was taking shape under the impact of the objects at hand. Jan the Elder (Velvet) Brueghel's

Allegory of Sight (1617) illustrates the emerging equation of sight and knowledge, while Frans Francken II and Jan Brueghel II's *The Archdukes Albert and Isabella in a Collector's Cabinet* (ca. 1626) represents the Archduke and Isabella exercising that equation (Figures 1.13 and 1.14).

Despite the collecting frenzy that overtook the continent, the most rare and exotic objects that arrived in Europe entered the princely Wunderkammern as symbols of wealth, fashion, and cosmopolitanism and thus also served to show off the worldliness, connections, and acquisitive power of individual rulers.[30] The acquisition of exotic objects and luxury items from far and wide, however, soon became the driving force that shaped the lives of many of their creators.[31] In turn, frenzied acquisition drove many collectors into bankruptcy, sometimes repeatedly. The story of Rembrandt is paradigmatic of the extremes to which sheer wealth, acquisitive drive, and human frailty could combine into full-blown obsession. Indeed, his collection of artworks is unparalleled even by today's standards of extreme wealth.[32] (His spectacular bankruptcies, however, seem vaguely familiar.) As I will show in the next chapter, the insatiable appetite for the new resulted in the establishment of what eventually became important worldwide networks of connections and the sharing of information created for the amassing of things. More importantly for my argument here, the exuberance of the collections subverted attempts to contain their wildness, but other forces undermined the ordering principle of the Wunderkammern, for, as any collector knows, the "logic" and driving force behind every collection is that it is by definition always incomplete. Collections therefore tend to grow exponentially and threaten every collection with the specter of chaos.[33] Indeed, many Wunderkammern soon exceeded not only the spaces designed to house them but also the ordering capacities of their owners; many simply became massive accumulations of random things, mere storage spaces for stuff.

1.13. Allegory of Sight
Jan the Elder (Velvet) Brueghel (1568–1625)
Museo del Prado, Madrid
Photo Credit: Erich Lessing/Art Resource, NY

1.14. The Archdukes Albert and Isabella in a Collector's Cabinet
Frans Francken II and workshop with Jan Brueghel II, ca. 1626
Photo Credit: Walters Art Museum, Baltimore

This cumulative, imperialistic, and out-of-control impulse to collect is consonant with the rhetorical figure of the polysyndeton, that is, with the "use of multiple conjunctions or coordinate clauses in close succession," most often resulting in seemingly endless lists of accumulated objects connected by an "and" that initially acts as the mirage of a connection between one thing and another.[34] The cracks in the scientific edifice that was being erected under the sign of colonialism had already begun to emerge in this form of accumulation and in these lists.[35] Despite the ever-present threat of chaos, however, as misplaced objects rapidly accumulated and overflowed the rooms and cabinets designed to hold them, they began to be reorganized according to increasingly sophisticated classificatory systems. Refusing the apparent ordering of the polysyndeton, coins were collected in one room, botanical specimens in another, technological inventions in yet another, and so on. Taxonomies were invented and successively fine-tuned. The Wunderkammern therefore served as the foundation of our modern museums, botanical gardens, zoos, and scientific and university academies. The Danish Royal Kunstkammer established around 1650 by King Frederik III, for example, was dispersed in 1825, as is shown in the graph (Figure 1.15).[36] (It is now being re-created as a virtual museum, allowing visitors to the site to play with the collection and create their

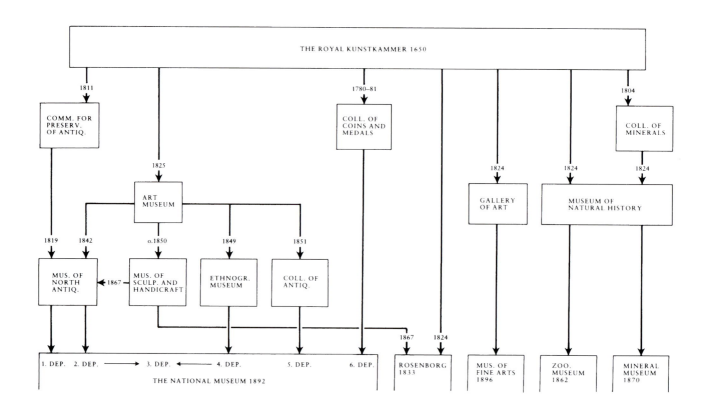

1.15. *Schematic representation of the breakup of the Royal Kunstkammer into various museums*

Images from O. Impey & A. MacGregor (ed.), The Origins of Museums: The Cabinet of Curiosities in Sixteenth- and Seventeenth-Century Europe, *2nd edition, London: House of Stratus 2001. Reproduced with permission of Jane Mellanby.*

own order of things.)[37] In the transition from the Wunderkammern to the museums shown in the graph, we can trace the continued need for a series of increasingly rigid forms of housing for, and differentiation of, collections. In line with this need to order, and written against what was perceived as the chaos of nature, the first modern classification system, Linnaeus's 1735 *Systema naturae: Creationis telluris est Gloria Dei ex opere naturae per hominem solum* (*The Earth's Creation is the glory of God, as seen from the works of Nature by Man alone*), was soon further refined and expanded by Count Buffon's thirty-six-volume *Histoire Naturelle, Générale et Particulière*, which he began to publish in 1749.[38]

It is striking to notice how often the eminent French naturalist and superintendent of the Royal Garden and Cabinet, George-Louis Leclerc, better known as Count Buffon (1707–88), and other scientists of his time use the word "disorder" in their texts. Despite Buffon's description of his life's work as the endeavor to find a place for everything and to put everything in its place, the fear of disorder continually overcomes him. He is afraid, in particular, of those objects and specimens that "belong in-between" and therefore "tend to upset the whole general system" ["objets mi-partis qu'on ne sait où placer, et qui dérangent nécessairement le projet du système general"; translation mine].[39] Another element that threatens the system is quite mundane: it is simply the lack of space to contain all the objects that belong together in one space ["[O]n est souvent obligé d'interrompre l'ordre des suites, parce qu'on ne peut pas concilier l'arrangement de la méthode avec la convenance des places"].[40] The inability to find a place for everything and to put everything in its place helps to explain the successive decentering revisions and expansions of Buffon's work in particular, and scientific knowledge in Europe in general.[41] It also helps to explain Europe's fascination with the monstrous evident especially when confronted with racial mestizaje and mixtures of all sorts.

Intent upon order, Europe continued to be obsessed with disorder, because while there is danger in the unruly, there is also freedom. Buffon knew this very well, playing as he did with combinations of all kinds. The objects that belonged together but did not "fit" together in one place because of their size were rearranged in displays that grouped things in such an unorthodox manner that their essence "shone forth unconstrained by any imposed order" ["C'est-là que les objets les plus importants de l'Histoire Naturelle sont présentés à leur avantage: on peut les juger sans être contraint par l'ordre méthodique parce qu'au moyen de cet arrangement, on ne s'occupe que des qualités réelles de l'individu sans avoir égard aux caractères arbitraires du genre et de l'espèce"].[42] It is to Buffon's credit that this arrangement and poetics of display foregrounds the tension between the desire to archive, survey, classify, and document, and the desire to look closely at things. Like many scientists of his time, he was enough of an artist to intuit the freedom inherent to disorder. His attempt to negotiate between order and disorder suggests that his account of natural history was necessarily incomplete and arbitrarily determined by the holdings of the Royal Garden and Cabinet. Ultimately dooming his project, Buffon's ambition to embrace "all the objects that the Universe provides us with" ["tous les objets que nous présente l'Univers"] is also what constitutes its greatness.[43]

Buffon never tires of advising aspiring naturalists to look at things carefully, without prejudice, without ascribing to objects qualities that are not theirs or putting them hurriedly into a place and system where they do not belong. In Buffon's insistence on patience and diligent observation, he may be said to belong to a long tradition of poets, novelists, and artists whose lives and works revolved around the careful observation of nature. That is, he insists on letting the system emerge by itself. His concern points to the underlying foundation of modern scientific empiricism, but it also betrays the deep anxiety of misplacement. So he instructs his reader "to look, and look again, and look often" ["On doit donc commencer par voir beaucoup & revoir souvent"]. Given the difficulty of undoing the rapid and unrelenting labor of prejudice so evident in the science of the time, attention, he insists, must be scrupulous in order to avoid arranging things into false taxonomies.[44] Buffon was right to fear the power of fixed taxonomies. He was also right in warning against the nefarious effects that misplacing could have on the system in general. However, he was not immune to national pride. Leaving himself and his system open to criticism, he placed European species at the top of his hierarchy, and, as we will see in the next chapter, it was on this point that Americans contested European science as Eurocentric.

As their placement within taxonomies suggests, objects arriving in Europe from the Americas were transformed into specimens (biological, botanical, mineral, and human) and studied, not only for their wonder-provoking capacity but increasingly as objects of scientific inquiry.[45] Central to their double misplacement, that is, displacement to Europe and then transition from exotic object to specimen, then, is the gradual transformation of the Wunderkammern from wonder-containing spaces to scientific ones; concomitantly, the emphasis shifts away from the object treasured as marvelous to the object viewed with scientific curiosity. This shift can be explained in part if we consider that indigenous cultures were to a great extent destroyed during the European conquest and colonization of the New World: many of the great objects of native civilizations were made of stone monoliths and thus could not be easily transported, and many spectacular gold and silver objects were melted down to facilitate transport as bullion. It is therefore no surprise that botanical and zoological specimens from the Americas tend to dominate European collections. (Indeed, as the archaeologist W. J. Rathje points out in his discussion of the Taliban's destruction of the colossal Buddhas at Hazara, this type of iconoclasm is so pervasive worldwide that "of the Seven Wonders of the Ancient World, only the Great Pyramids of Egypt still survive." And he wonders if even the pyramids would have been destroyed by now if it weren't for the fact that they were "so hard to destroy.")[46] Thus, not only did the specimens arriving in Europe post-1492 allow for the emergence of the all-seeing subject and knowledge-producing individual invariably represented at the center of the Wunderkammern that I have been discussing, but the focus on specimens also turned the Americas into a naturalist's paradise. Concomitant to the emergence of science and modernity, indeed, underpinning them both, lies the transformation of the Americas into an object of inquiry. Indeed, it would not be altogether hyperbolic or inaccurate to say that the Americas are "framed" (in both senses of the word) by natural history museums. However, the logic of museums obscures, and often erases altogether, the violence of misplacement through its aesthetics of orderly display. Eurocentrism, then, can also be explained as the tension between the centripetal centering of the cabinets, the condensation of knowledge in the I/eye (which can also be seen as an enduring provincialism), and the immense centrifugal extension of the known world implicit in those containing spaces.

The privileged vantage point of the European subject and the increasing emphasis on the total visibility of the world produced by the Wunderkammern shaped the nature of inventions that followed. Technologies of "augmented vision" such as panoramas, dioramas, the camera obscura, the camera lucida, and mirrors were invented. By the early seventeenth century, Galileo had built, used, and rebuilt the first telescopes and turned them upward to study the heavens. The telescope, whose most important function is its "light-gathering power," allowed Galileo to see the "shockingly pocked, imperfectly spherical moon and other blemished moons orbiting Jupiter," and more importantly, of course, to see the "vast extension of the bounds of the visible universe."[47] Conversely, the invention of the microscope by the Dutch lens grinder Hans Lippershey in 1608 expanded the known world effected by telescopes, only in reverse.[48] "The daydream of the microscope," as Stewart points out, is "the daydream of life inside life, of significance multiplied infinitely within significance."[49] Artists, in turn, experimented with augmented vision technologies both to study and to represent the world in greater detail and clarity. Tellingly, the etymology of "perspective"—seeing through— aptly encodes the artist's aim to represent the inner workings of art and nature from a single, central point of view.[50] It is no wonder, then, that all of this would culminate in a period that would call itself "the Enlightenment."[51]

A recent exhibition at the J. Paul Getty Museum, "Devices of Wonder: From the World in a Box to Images on a Screen," focused on the development of modern media technologies such as the Internet, video games, IMAX movie screens, photography, film, eBay as a modern Wunderkammer,[52] and the long line of "mesmerizing optical appliances that paved their way: mirrors, pinhole images, magic lanterns, flip-books, peep-show boxes, panorama theatres and the phantasmagoric wonder chambers that contained them all."[53] These new technologies share the privileging of the visual, and the condensation of the world in the eyes of the observer that the Wunderkammern first made possible. Yet growing certainty about the visibility of the workings of the world brought with it growing uncertainty as to what remained invisible and unknown. Sir Isaac Newton embodied the persisting tension between Baroque and Enlightenment modes of being in the world: a physicist, he was also a theologian and an alchemist. He straddles the scientific revolution of the seventeenth century, delving into the obscure, invisible properties of objects and, yet, along with Leibniz, he invented calculus in order to map the workings of the universe. His life endeavor was a personal quest to rival the marvels of nature (Naturalia) with his own creations (Artificialia).[54]

The capacity to bring the outside world into the inside, the privileging of sight, and the conflation of augmented visibility with surveillance and colonial control can be traced in the development of the camera obscura. A precursor to photography, the camera obscura initially consisted of an entirely darkened room in which a small hole had been made that allowed light to filter in. The light rays projected an inverted image of whatever was outside onto a wall in the room. Leonardo da Vinci described it in his notebooks in 1490. Giovanni Battista Della Porta, in his book *Magiae Naturalis* (1558)—inspiring generations of artists to follow—recommended it as a drawing aid.[55] Once the device became widely known in the late nineteenth century, it was used in amusement parks in Europe and the United States (Central Park, Santa Monica, and Coney Island). A device that allowed people to "spy on the unaware," it became a metaphor, like photography, for voyeurism. These "cameras" were therefore strategically located. One on the Isle of Man was placed on a cliff walk favored by couples. A postcard titled "Magic Mirror of Life" advertised a camera obscura on the Santa Monica pier (installed at the end of the nineteenth century): it showed a couple embracing next to the small building. Those inside the camera obscura overhear the young man saying to his girlfriend: "Ah, Alicia, at last we are by ourselves, far from unsympathetic and prying eyes."[56]

These new technologies of augmented vision not only made possible the mapping of the entire world but also enhanced the articulation between visibility and imperialism, and implicated geography and empire building. Indeed, in Jonathan Lamb's ironic words, the "empire of science is the human eye."[57] Paintings of geographers and rulers, often with the globe at their fingertips, affirm the privileged vantage point of the European subject in Cornelis de Man's *Geographers at Their Work* (Figure 1.16). In the first image the geographers' collusion with empire is made very clear, while in the second, Queen Elizabeth I is shown after her defeat of the Spanish Armada. She is made up almost as a Wunderkammer, and she literally has the world (shown as tiny in relation to her size and importance) at her fingertips (Figure 1.17). One map of Spain's colonies, undertaken by the official Spanish geographer Tomás López, was so small that all Spanish functionaries could carry it comfortably along with them on their incursions into the New World,[58] as if the empire were literally in their pocket.[59] The fascination of the period with miniatures is anything but accidental, for, as Stewart has noted, miniatures expand time and thus allow the imagination to travel farther in history as well as in space.[60] The drive to enlighten the world, then, depended upon the privileging of the European eye/I, and the result was imperial expansion. The mapping of extensive new territories and the banishment of the monsters that had until then inhabited the fringes of maps led to the shift, as some traditional philologists would have it, from a God-centered to a man-centered world and from the Middle Ages to the Renaissance. All orders—natural history, geography, the classification of human "types"—were thus subsumed by a visual regime, and in the transition from Wunderkammer to museum, as we have already seen, the status of objects also changed. With the development of natural science, the search for *curiosities* gave way to the search for *specimens*, valued for their potential uses and commercial value.[61] In transforming the Americas into a naturalist's paradise devoid of any knowledge-producing potential, Europe positioned itself as the center of all that was enlightened, scientific, rational, and secular.

1.16. Geographers at Their Work
Cornelis de Man (1621–1706)
Hamburger Kunsthalle, Germany
Photo Credit Bildarchiv Preussischer
Kulturbesitz/Art Resource, NY

1.17. The Armada Portrait of Queen Elizabeth I,
    ca. 1588
Coll. Duke of Bedford, Woburn Abbey
Bedfordshire, Great Britain
Photo Credit Snark/Art Resource, NY

As in Foucault's *The Order of Things*, despite the crucial role the Americas played in the inception of modernity, western scientific thought ignores, or disavows if necessary, the role that objects from the Americas played in its constitution. We have come to call this type of epistemic violence Eurocentrism. The term might have served to elucidate the matter, but in fact it has become merely a heuristic device, describing *what* is at work but not *why*. In typical solipsistic fashion, critics and historians insist that the erasure of the Americas in constituting modern European thought happened primarily because Europe was *not interested* in the impact of the Americas. And Europe was not interested, because 1492 and all subsequent discoveries, in J. H. Elliott's words, "were incorporated into an essentially Eurocentric conception of history."[62] But *why*? Why the enormous worldwide impact of Eurocentrism, considering that every culture situates itself at the center? The global reach of Eurocentrism—indeed, the Hegelian notion of progress as the development of a world spirit culminating in Europe—becomes really comprehensible only when we consider how the cabinets of wonders positioned the European subject in a privileged vantage point with respect to the marvels of the world that lined their walls.

Telling of the insurmountable technology/nature binary that has characterized the divide between Europe and the Americas since the Enlightenment is the oft-repeated lament, echoed recently in Maria Helena Machado's words:

> To Brazilians, nothing sounds more familiar than statements that Brazil has been blessed in terms of nature. Indeed, from our earliest childhood, we learn to identify our country through enthusiastic manifestations about the wonders of our geography, not to mention the flora and fauna whose extraordinary diversity and wealth comprise the treasures that God generously bestowed upon us (of course, while all other nations have had to work hard to amass wealth) (13–15, 13).

J. H. Elliott corroborates Machado's words when he argues that "Brazil has proven to be a source of wonder and fascination to foreign observers [. . .] ever since the Huguenot pastor Jean de Léry recorded his impressions of the Tupinamba Indians in 1578" ("Snakes in Paradise," 40–42, 40). The implicit critique in Machado's and Elliott's statements, of course, is of the centuries-long relegation of the Americas (and particularly Brazil and the Caribbean, perhaps because of the history of slavery and the export of carnival)[63] to the status of a naturalist's paradise and by extension a place to be plundered. In Eduardo Galeano's shorthand, "We Latin Americans are poor because the ground we tread is rich."[64] The image that would drive the unequal, skewed economic exchange system that Mignolo has called "coloniality," as I mentioned in the Introduction, was already represented in Stradanus's engraving in *Nova reperta* of the "encounter" between Vespucci (dressed, and holding magic technology) and America (naked, and lazily swinging on a hammock) while cannibals delight in roasting a human leg (see Figure 0.4). A how-to book of sorts, the *Nova reperta* (with a mass printing) included a series of engravings that served as "windows" into workshops, studios, and laboratories to aid in "shaping the 'vision' of a mass audience."[65]

Finally, despite the fact that we are all more or less aware that in the eighteenth and nineteenth centuries the world looked to Europe for scientific knowledge and innovations, indeed, that Europe far surpassed the United States until well into the twentieth century in this respect, Spain's crucial contribution to the emergence of western science continues to be overlooked.[66] As if only to prove the colonial underpinnings of our certainties, Spain repeatedly falls off the epistemological table that constitutes modernity. While this could be attributed partially to Spain's exit from the stage of history as a consequence of the nineteenth-century independence movements in the Americas, that is, to its status as an empire on the wane, it is also the result of Spain's lack of a sustained coherent government policy with respect to science. Unable perhaps to imagine itself out of colonial dependence on mining, or to see the potential profitability of science, Spain buried its magnificent scientific archive in the dark and musty bowels of its Museum of Natural Science. Were it not for the zealous efforts of María de los Angeles Calatayud, the museum's current curator, that story might have been destroyed by moths and dampness (and the chapter that follows might not have been written). Indeed, the history of Spain's Wunderkammer, the Gabinete Real de Madrid, established in the late eighteenth century, explains how Stradanus's "America" would become the operative image for an entire continent for centuries to come, and even long after the end of colonial rule.

But ranking requires a criterion for assigning all individuals to their proper status in the single series. And what better criterion than an objective number? Thus, the common style embodying both fallacies of thought has been quantification, or the measurement of intelligence as a single number for each person. This book, then, is about the abstraction of intelligence as a single entity, its location within the brain, its quantification as one number for each individual, and the use of these numbers to rank people in a single series of worthiness, invariably to find that oppressed and disadvantaged groups—races, classes, or sexes—are innately inferior and deserve their status. In short, this book is about the Mismeasure of Man . . . determinist arguments for ranking people according to a single scale of intelligence, no matter how numerically sophisticated, have recorded little more than social prejudice. . . . We pass through the world but once. Few tragedies can be more extensive than the stunting of life, few injustices deeper than the denial of an opportunity to strive or even to hope, by a limit imposed from without, but falsely identified as lying within.

—Stephen Jay Gould, *The Mismeasure of Man*

Así fueron los grandes museos que se desarrollaron durante el siglo XVII, como el famosísimo de Atanasius Kircher en Roma; o el de Fernando Cospi en Bolonia; el de Hans Worm en Copenhague o, ya en España, el que tenía Vicencio Juan de Lastanosa en Huesca, tan alabado por Gracián en sus escritos. A partir de aquí se irá desarrollando lentamente el museo como concepto, incorporando los matices que cada momento histórico iba aportando, hasta convertirse en el siglo XIX en una institución pública cuya misión esencial sigue siendo la de clasificar la realidad, la cual aspira a contener, fragmentada en millares de objetos, dentro de sus almacenes y salas.

   —José Ramón López, "La fábula del tiempo," in *Richard Ross: Historia natural*

This is what the great museums that developed during the 17th century such as Atanasius Kircher's in Rome, or that of Fernando Cospi in Bologna, or Hans Worm's in Copenhagen or, now in Spain, that of Vicencio Juan de Lastanosa in Huesca (so praised by Gracián in his writings) were like. From then on the museum would slowly continue evolving as a concept, incorporating the nuances of each historical period, until it became in the 19th century a public institution whose essential mission is that of classifying reality, which it aspires to contain, fragmented in millions of objects, within its storage spaces and halls.

   —José Ramón López, "The Fable of Time" (Translation mine)

. . . we Latin Americans are poor because the ground we tread is rich . . .

   —Eduardo Galeano, *Open Veins of Latin America:*
   Five Centuries of the Pillage of a Continent

CHAPTER TWO

TRANSATLANTIC
SUBJECT MATTERS
AND
BIG BONES

The Real Gabinete de Historia Natural de Madrid

THE HISTORY OF THE Real Gabinete de Madrid (Royal Cabinet) is a case study for a number of developments that are the focus of this study: the speed with which once-private collections were bought up in order to found royal and public "cabinets of wonders"; the rapid transformation of these wonder-containing spaces into natural history museums, botanical gardens, and scientific academies; the eighteenth-century transition from natural history (natural philosophy) to natural science; the parallel emergence of the important distinction between science and philosophy (and that of the scientist vs. the philosopher/poet/artist); the linking of scientific and economic concerns, and finally, the intersecting of modern rationality, science, and the dominance of the visual and colonialism in the colonization of knowledge. While Spain has played a crucial role in establishing the underpinnings of modern science, that role and the role of the Americas in general has been consistently overlooked in accounts of the inception of modernity.[1] The waning of Spain as a colonial power and the rise of the British Empire in the nineteenth century and the shift from Spanish to English as a dominant world language are partially to blame; Eurocentrism, as we saw in the previous chapter, *is* to blame. Yet the skewed picture we have inherited of the rise of modernity and scientific understanding is also due to Spain's lack of a coherent, sustained scientific agenda. Indeed, as the history of the ups and downs of the Real Gabinete show, the Gabinete and its scientists were subjected to the whimsy of individual rulers and "enlightened despotism"[2]—their important and laborious scientific findings were repeatedly brushed aside or buried in musty storage rooms.[3]

The Gabinete underwent serious and rather sudden mutations, reflecting the interest or lack of interest of individual rulers: after originating as a mere storage space for the rare and marvelous objects arriving from the Americas, it rose to great heights in the late eighteenth century, only to revert back to obscurity in the early nineteenth century. It sponsored costly expeditions to Perú and Chile, Nueva Granada (Colombia), and New Spain (Mexico) in 1777, 1783, and 1787, respectively. An expedition around the world led by Tuscan-born scientist Alejandro Malaspina was undertaken in 1789. It left Cádiz en route to the Pacific Northwest and mapped the region and gathered botanical and ethnographic information along the way.[4] Another expedition was sent to Perú and

Chile to collect mineral samples in 1795; Juan de Cuéllar went to the Philippines in 1785, and there was also the famous scientific voyage to the Pacific in 1862.[5] The Gabinete also sponsored the publication of important scientific works such as Buffon's *Histoire Naturelle* (a translation was commissioned by José Clavijo y Fajardo in 1785). Perhaps even more stunningly, in 1803 Spanish physician Francisco Javier Balmis developed the means of successfully transporting the newly discovered smallpox vaccine. Between 1803 and 1806, with the support of Charles IV and the Real Gabinete, Balmis organized the first large-scale public health inoculation campaign in the Americas and the Philippines (in the process of which he also circumnavigated the world and reached China).[6] According to Mexican physician Ignacio Chávez, this expedition was "one of the cleanest, most humane, and most authentically civilized pages ever written in history."[7] (Dominican writer Julia Alvarez has recently published the novel *Saving the World,* based on this expedition.) Despite these achievements, the fate of the Gabinete as a museum continued to mirror that of the nation: its subsequent downfall ("decaimiento") between 1787 and 1813 closely matched that of Spain.[8] Visitors to the Gabinete lamented its sad state; scientists Christian Herrgen and Carl Erenvert von Moll bemoaned the lack of a coherent Spanish scientific policy as well as the neglect of the marvelous collections at the Real Gabinete.[9] Alexander von Humboldt, one of whose expeditions to Mexico (which he famously described as "the more rare and transparent region") was generously funded by King Charles IV of Spain, remarked that "no European government has invested a larger amount of money to advance the knowledge of plants than the Spanish government." Moreover, he wrote the king: "None of the monarchs who have occupied the Castilian throne have contributed more liberally than your Majesty to the obtaining of accurate information regarding the state of that valuable portion of the globe, which in both hemispheres yields obedience to the Spanish laws." Three botanical expeditions to Perú, New Granada, and New Spain "have cost the Spanish state around two million francs" and yet, despite numerous and heavy investments of this kind, Spain had little to show.[10]

These ups and downs in Spanish support for the Gabinete reflect the country's ambiguous relation to science portending its relegation to the margins of Europe, whereas the U.S. would rise as a world power precisely thanks to President Jefferson's promotion of science not only for commerce but also as an intellectual front with which to undermine the colonial forms of knowledge being produced in Europe about the Americas. Oddly enough, a shipment of "large bones" from Argentina to Madrid would provide a link between Jefferson and the Real Gabinete. This finding would be mobilized by Jefferson to argue against European notions of the time that viewed the Americas as a continent not only where species were smaller, but also as a space that would lead to the eventual "degeneration" of Europeans transplanted there. Jefferson's focus on "big bones," as we will see below, was a strategic ideological intervention and effort at decolonization. It has resulted in the lasting fascination with dinosaurs in the American imaginary. Paradoxically, despite moments when American policies fluctuated just like Spain's, lasting support for science was obtained, thanks not only to Jefferson's efforts and his promotion of the Lewis and Clark expedition, but also, oddly enough, through the histrionics and flair for the spectacular of P. T. Barnum's American Museum that is the focus of the next chapter. In contrast, in Latin America, visionaries such as Jefferson may not have had the transcendence and reach that he possessed; moreover, given that the continent became increasingly important as a source of natural history specimens for the Real Gabinete, individual countries were unable to shake the colonizing forms of self-knowledge that it was producing. To this day, local, indigenous epistemologies all across the Americas are still fighting an uphill battle to be recognized as such.

While throughout Spain, as in the rest of Europe, there had been numerous collections and cabinets of wonders, and while King Philip II's library and collection at El Escorial were quite fabulous,[11] by the eighteenth century, Spain had fallen behind the rest of Europe and lacked a royal, public cabinet that would serve as the nexus of scientific lines of force that were beginning to converge in the rest of Europe.[12] The way for Spain to reinsert itself into the dominant world order, as understood at the time, was through the creation of a Wunderkammer. As a consequence, the Real Gabinete was first constituted in 1752 (one year after the publication of the *Encyclopédie*) at the urging of the Spanish naturalist and scientific traveler Antonio de Ulloa (1716–95). Ulloa, as we saw in the previous chapter, was a functionary of the Spanish government, a naturalist, and an explorer who had taken part in the famous scientific voyage to the equator organized by the Academy of Sciences of Paris and directed by Charles-Marie de la Condamine.[13] He very clearly understood that in order to sustain and enrich itself, the Spanish Empire depended on two things: the mapping and surveying of its colonial territories, and, given the decline in the production of silver at Potosí (Bolivia), the continued identification of possible mine-sites for the extraction of minerals. In 1772, in his now famous *Noticias americanas* (the account of his travels and scientific explorations), Antonio de Ulloa lucidly wrote that the acquisition of wealth, particularly precious metals, was the main incentive of any nation because with these materials everything else could be acquired ["El incentivo mayor de las Naciones ha sido en todos tiempos las riquezas y metales preciosos, que son los medios de adquirir las demás cosas"].[14] Despite its promotion by Ulloa, however, the Real Gabinete did not flourish in the first years of its existence. Subject as it was to the vagaries of the Crown, the Gabinete suffered the fate of many collections. For a period it became a mere storage space for the massive numbers of objects arriving from the New World. At one particularly low point it even lost its name, reverting back to being called *Casa de Geografía*—the original name of the building in which it had been housed on Alcalá street in Madrid.[15]

The Real Gabinete's foundational date now stands as 1771, when it was finally and lastingly constituted under the auspices of Charles III of Spain (1757–88), who convinced Pedro Franco Dávila (after much prompting by Dávila himself) to donate his private cabinet of wonders. A wealthy Ecuadoran naturalist based in Paris, Dávila used the fortune he had inherited to travel across Europe in his search for objects for his famous Gabinete de Historia Natural y de Curiosidades del Arte y de la Naturaleza. It was considered vaster than any private collection of the time, its fame rivaling even that of the King of France.[16] Dávila himself was known throughout Europe and beyond from his extensive correspondence. He was such an unrestrained, obsessive collector that in some circles he had become notorious, and it is reported that he literally grabbed things he desired out of the collections and even the hands of friends and acquaintances.[17] Like so many avid collectors before and after him, he collected objects faster than he could organize them, and he, too, repeatedly had to sell several cabinets of wonders in order to avoid imminent bankruptcy.[18] At one of these junctures, he was convinced to move to Madrid and, in return for the donation of his famous cabinet to the Crown, was named the Real Gabinete's lifetime director. The aim of transferring Dávila's collection to Madrid was driven by the Crown's desire to regain its standing in Europe through the display of its power and worldliness in a Wunderkammer replete with rare and marvelous objects and naturalist specimens from far and wide. Dávila himself repeatedly expressed his interest in moving from Paris to Madrid; he also repeatedly bemoaned the fact that—as was clear from the glaring lack of a public, royal cabinet—the very country that had once stood at the forefront of scientific discovery under Philip II had fallen so far behind the rest of Europe in his time.[19]

After relocating Dávila's entire cabinet of wonders, and after years of negotiations and renovations, the Real Gabinete opened its doors to the public on November 4, 1776, in the same building that had formerly housed the Casa de Geografía. Dávila had expected massive public attendance and had 300 invitations printed for the opening, but only 200 people came. However, word of the magnificence of the collection quickly spread throughout the city and aroused the curiosity of thousands of people. The result was that a crowd of over 3,000 people stormed the Gabinete a few days later. It is reported that in their eagerness to admire the magnificent and exotic objects on display, the crowd broke the doors and almost trampled the Gabinete's sole watchman underfoot. He left his post, refusing to return for fear of his life ["diciendo que por ninguna manera lo ejecutaría más, pues exponía su vida"].[20] That very night Dávila asked for six military personnel to substitute for the watchman. This stormy opening makes it clear that Dávila had been quite astute in manipulating the Crown's need to display its "enlightenment" by possessing a marvelous cabinet *and* in reading the public's thirst for knowledge and desire for curiosities.[21]

Signaling also how right he was in his emphasis not only on the cabinets as public spaces of learning but also as spaces of scientific inquiry, by 1815—that is, less than fifty years after its establishment—the name of the Gabinete had been changed from Real Gabinete de Historia Natural (Natural History) to Real Gabinete de Ciencias Naturales (Natural Science). This renaming saw a shift in self-definition: the collector/connoisseur, and largely self-taught and curiosity-driven naturalist and savant (or sabio) of the early years of the Wunderkammern (1500–1700), had been transformed into the scientist (or "Académico") associated with one or more European institutions of learning spawned by those very spaces. Indeed, Dávila not only arrived in Madrid with his famous collection: he also lent the court his name and impressive worldwide network of connections. A member of the Academia de Historia of Madrid and of the Scientific Academies of Berlin, St. Petersburg, and Kassel, Dávila had been distinguished by King Frederick of Prussia, and his prominence had even been recognized by Buffon, who recommended him as a Fellow of the Royal Society of London.[22] Dávila's correspondence poignantly illuminates the close association between the *housing* of the different branches of science that he was instrumental in bringing about, the creation of that type of learned scholar and scientist, and the growing distinction between art and science.[23] In sum, Dávila belonged to an emerging cosmopolitan, enlightened, and academic elite.[24] His extensive correspondence, recently published by María de los Ángeles Calatayud of the Museum of Natural Sciences, demonstrates four points in the development of modern, western scientific rationality: first, the cabinet-driven emergence of a European-wide learned circle; second, the importance of translation in the ensuing inter-European scientific dialogue; third, the establishment of a worldwide network of connections for the gathering and exchange of objects crucial to the collection; and finally, the promotion of a series of scientific voyages to the Americas.

During the early years of the Gabinete's second and final establishment under the stewardship of Dávila, the distinction *between* things (taxonomies) had not yet been firmly established, and the Gabinete, like the early Wunderkammern, housed what to us would seem an undifferentiated jumble of things (several Velázquez paintings, Amerindian archaeological remains, mineral samples, animal and botanical specimens, etc.). In this sense it was no different from the many privately owned cabinets full of wonders from the Americas that had been established all over Spain since Columbus's voyages.[25] Dávila's extensive correspondence shows that the collection, like all collections, was by definition incomplete. As a consequence, his search for new wonders and botanical and animal specimens was insatiable. Having the Crown's full support and a compulsive, unrestrained collector at the helm, the collection grew exponentially and Dávila repeatedly ran out of space. He therefore began a series of successive reorganizations. Alongside his collectionist obsession, then, and crucial to the success of the venture was his understanding of the importance of *order*—an understanding that mirrors the impending shift from collector to scientist that I have been outlining. In his praise of a fellow collector's zeal, and echoing Buffon's fear of disorder, Dávila criticizes his friend's inability to order things, "recognizing that he was more adept at collecting than knowing objects and hence has marvelous things but everything is utterly disorganized" ["reconociéndole más habilidad para recogerlas que para conocerlas, cree que tiene bellísimas cosas pero muy desordenadas"].[26] Dávila clearly understood the danger his Gabinete faced: that it could again become a haphazard storage space of the rare and marvelous like its famous predecessors. Following Buffon's taxonomy, therefore, he created separate rooms to house animal, mineral, and botanical specimens; bronzes, medals, engraved stones, and other monuments; a gallery of paintings; a stamp collection and the library; a mineral-polishing facility, and last, a special room for duplicated items in the collection. In this Dávila again followed in Buffon's tracks, since the order laid out in the *Histoire naturelle, générale et particulière avec la description du cabinet du roy* (1750) was based on the collection at the Parisian Royal Garden and Cabinet, which Buffon had amassed himself. Buffon did this by establishing, like Dávila after him, an extensive network of worldwide sources meant to provide him with the things necessary to complete the collection. Buffon's pursuit became so famous that one biographer recounts how objects arrived for him from all over the world and, "when taken at sea, [the specimens] were respected even by pirates, and forwarded, unopened, to Paris."[27]

By 1867—not even a hundred years after its foundation—Madrid's Gabinete (now the Museo de Ciencias Naturales) was forced to relocate entirely. As was the case with cabinets of wonders all over Europe, the museum's collection too was broken up, and its holdings were further divided. Some of the caste paintings, Amerindian vases, earrings, and religious icons in its holdings were transferred to the Museo Arqueológico Nacional; the sections pertaining to ethnography were moved to the Museo Etnológico Nacional; artworks went to the Prado,[28] and botanical samples to the Botanical Gardens.[29] In 1941 the Museo de América was created from the ethnographic holdings pertaining to the Americas still in the possession of the Museo Nacional de Ciencias Naturales. The Amerindian ethnographic holdings, caste paintings, "emplumados" (paintings made of feathers), and other objects obtained during the various scientific expeditions funded by the Gabinete are housed there now. More recently, and signaling a further subdivision and more precise classificatory system, some of the holdings have gone to the Museums of Decorative Arts and the Museum of Science and Technology. Indeed, the holdings of the Gabinete were so vast, Calatayud contends, that they contributed to the foundation not only of these institutions but to almost all centers of learning and museums across the continent. She writes that it is "rare to find a museum or a centre of learning not only throughout Spain but also in all of Europe that does not possess some of the collections that initially enriched the Real Gabinete de Madrid" ["Raro es el Centro destinado a museística o el dedicado a la enseñanza en toda España, incluso en Europa, que no posea algunas [colecciones] de las que en un principio enriquecieron un solo Gabinete: el Real de Madrid"].[30]

Dávila not only continually reorganized the Real Gabinete but even more importantly, perhaps, he instructed that all new items be accompanied by precise and detailed labels. Indeed, Dávila's appointment was strengthened by a letter sent by the Crown to all colonial administrators requiring them to meticulously collect, preserve, and whenever possible draw plant, animal, and mineral samples and send all of these specimens to the Gabinete ["Instrucción hecha de orden del Rey N.S. para . . . los Virreyes, Gobernadores, Corregidores, Alcaldes Mayores e Intendentes de Provincias," 1776]. Dávila predicted that if promoted far and wide across the Spanish Empire, these "Instrucciones" would very shortly transform the Gabinete into Europe's most important collection ["se expidarán órdenes por todos los dominios del Rey para que envíen colecciones de los tres reinos y pronto ser, el de España, uno de los mejores de Europa"]. While the eighteenth-century questionnaires emphasized the identification of minerals and mines, they nevertheless also required extensive documentation regarding fauna, flora, and cultural manifestations.[31] As has been highlighted repeatedly, as a result of this vast archival effort, the number of specimens arriving in Europe from the Americas was so immense that it overwhelmed not only available space but even linguistic capacities for naming them.[32]

Signaling continued shifts in imperial designs as well as the more transcendent change in the way objects were valued (once for their wonder-arousing capacity, then increasingly for their scientific value), the royal questionnaire formulated under Dávila followed a long line of *informes* and *instrucciones* that had been successively emitted by the Crown throughout the colonial period. Indeed, the first questionnaire, containing fifty sections ("Instrucción y memoria"), began to circulate in 1577. While the emphasis of the questionnaires shifted over time, the breadth and scope of the requests for detailed geographical and historical information from Spanish functionaries must have been overwhelming if not daunting. The staggering number of questions included the name and exact location of the area administered, the name of the settlement in the native tongue, the reasons for the name, who the "discoverer" and conqueror of the area had been, the circumstances of the conquest, the quality and temperament of the water and the wind, whether the earth was fertile or infertile, flat or mountainous, the rivers that crossed it and their quality, how many Indians lived there, the reasons why the population diminished (if it diminished), what language or languages were spoken, what the Indians knew, how they behaved, to whom they paid tribute, what their rites and customs were, how they governed themselves, how they dressed, what they ate, what trees and grains brought from Spain grew there and how much they produced, what herbs and medicinal plants grew there, what animals there were, how animals imported from Spain were faring, what mines, precious stones, and salt deposits were to be found, the form of the houses, the building materials employed, the distance to other settlements, the location of the town, a map of it with the streets drawn in, what Spaniards lived there and where, etc., etc. As if this were not enough, and in order to counter any potential blind spot in the questionnaire, the last item asked the chronicler to comment on anything *else* worthy of note ["Con todas las demás cosas notables en naturaleza y efectos del suelo, ayre y cielo que en cualquiera parte huviere y fueren dignos de ser savidos"].[33] As María del Carmen González Muñoz comments rather wryly, "One notes the extraordinary complexity of the document and the inclusion of historic, geographic, ethnographic, zoological, botanical questions and even of questions prompted by pure curiosity" ["Se observa la extraordinaria complejidad del cuestionario y la inclusión de materias históricas, geográficas, etnográficas, zoológicas y botánicas y hasta de pura curiosidad"].[34] Additionally, if we consider the intrusive questionnaires formulated by the clergy to detect idolatrous practices, which included yet another long list of questions ranging from the convert's dreams to his or her sexual practices and postures,[35] the "mapping" of the Americas covered not only the material but the spiritual realm as well, and attempted, quite literally, to leave no stone unturned.

The impressive heterogeneous corpus of texts produced, known as the "chronicles of the New World"—despite including also secondhand accounts that spread myths of Amazons and other such monsters—displays an unprecedented amount of detailed information about all aspects of life in the Americas.[36] Indeed, many of the chronicles stand today as the first extant examples of careful observation, natural history, and ethnographic writing. Fray Ramón Pané's 1493 account of the islands of the Caribbean may be the West's first ethnographic text.[37] It was followed, among others, by the almost epic, twenty-one-volume *Historia Natural y General de las Indias* (from 1535 on), written by Gonzalo Fernández de Oviedo, Governor of Cartagena de Indias and Santo Domingo, who had been named the Crown's official chronicler, or Cronista de las Indias. His monumental text, with its excruciatingly detailed descriptions of the flora, fauna, and ethnology of the Americas, makes Oviedo, along with Jesuit José de Acosta and his equally important *Historia natural y moral de las Indias* (1590), one of the West's first naturalists.[38] Alongside them, prominent physician Francisco Bravo, who finally settled in Mexico, published his *Opera medicinalia*—"the first book on medicine ever produced in America"—in 1570.[39] A bit later, royal doctor Francisco Hernández—with the aid of a very precise and detailed Informe—was commissioned in 1576 to travel to Mexico to compile an ambitious work on its flora. His work is the "largest natural history written in the Renaissance"; its botanical section alone consists of 893 text pages and includes more than 2,071 illustrations. It carefully describes more than 3,000 plants, 40 quadrupeds, 229 birds, 58 reptiles, 30 insects, and 35 minerals. Overwhelmed by the data and the impossibility of classifying such an enormous amount of new information, and faced with the impossibility of European science to assimilate the vast number of new species, Hernández tried to invent a new naming procedure, "devising a hybrid system that combined Mexican terms with the European alphabet classification tradition."[40] Unfortunately, his radically new terminology was not accepted, and one can only surmise how different science would have looked to us today had it been. Having completed his magnum opus, he went on to write his *Antigüedades de la Nueva España*, in which he recounts the history and culture of the Nahuas, particularly the Mexicans and Tetzcocanos—another milestone as it is one of the first historiographies based on firsthand indigenous testimonies [una "historiografía apoyada en testimonios indígenas de primera mano"].[41]

With Spain's growing dependency on mineral extraction, for a time the identification of potential mine sites dominated the questionnaires—particularly in 1752.[42] This almost exclusive interest shifted to the 1776 questionnaire and its much more all-encompassing, natural history–inclined interest in essentially *everything* (plants, animals, peoples, etc.).[43] Formulated by the Crown in order to support Dávila's work at the Real Gabinete, the 1776 questionnaire demonstrates the increasing interdependence between commerce and science. Indeed, the collection of specimens and information required was designed to promote scientific knowledge *and also* to detect any potentially useful and exploitable properties in things. As Don José Celestino Mutis writes in a letter to the King in 1764, curiosity is fast becoming subservient to the commercialization of nature:

> The America in whose blessed soil God deposited an infinite number of things most admirable does not stand out only because of its gold, silver, precious stones, and any other treasures in its bowels. It also produces for use and commerce exquisite dyes that industry will continue to discover in its plants; cochineal is abundant here although the natives do not grow it because they are indolent. There is also the precious wax of a bush called Laurelito and that of the Palm; many glues that could be used by the Arts, admirable wood to make musical instruments and furniture. They also produce many other trees, herbs, resins, and balsams for the good of humanity. . . . The traveler should collect, describe, and conserve such things and deposit them in the Real Gabinete and other public spaces so that our wise men get to know them and thus excite their curiosity so that someday they be useful to mortals.

> [La América en cuyo afortunado suelo depositó el Criador infinitas cosas de la mayor admiración, no se ha hecho recommendable tan solamente por su oro, plata, piedras preciosas, y demás tesoros que oculta en sus senos; produce tanbien en su superficie para la utilidad y comercio esquisitos tintes, que la industria iria descubriendo entre las plantas; la cochinilla de que ai abundancia en este Reyno, aunque no la cultivan por su indolencia los naturals de estas Provincias; la preciosa cera de un arbusto llamado Laurelito y la de Palma; muchas gomas, de que pudieran hacerse algunos usos ventajosos en las Artes; maderas mui estimables para instrumentos y muebles; produce finalmente para el bien del género humano muchos otros árboles, yerbas, resinas, y bálsamos. . . . Un viajero deberia ir recogiendo, describiendo, y conservando semejantes producciones, para que depositadas en el Gavinete y otros lugares públicos las conocieran los Sabios, excitaran su curiosidad, y se hiciera de ellas util aplicación en algun dia para bien de los Mortales.][44]

Here we see foreshadowed the way in which science would increasingly become subjected to the economy. This subjection has grown exponentially, as is seen most recently in the controversial practice of European- and U.S.-based pharmaceutical companies' attempts to copyright the DNA of *all* potential medicinal plants in Latin America. In a similar vein, while earlier questionnaires requested mainly written descriptions, the new imperative implicit in the Instrucciones asks the colonial administrator to *collect*, label, preserve, and/or draw anything of interest ["cuanto de curioso ó notable hallaban en los Estados que gobernaban"]. Reminding us of Wordsworth's famous dictum that "we murder to dissect,"[45] overwhelming numbers of plant, animal, and mineral specimens and Amerindian cultural artifacts arrived at the Gabinete precisely tagged, described, drawn, and preserved. The same fate befell no small number of unfortunate indigenous people who themselves were used as spectacular exhibits. As if all these information-gathering mechanisms were not enough, the Real Gabinete also funded the important exploratory and scientific expeditions to the Americas listed above.[46]

The Instrucciones's detailed questionnaires illustrate the simultaneous telescoping and microscoping process I have been highlighting throughout: one single precious stone that came from the New World would arrive in Spain "tagged" with all the information that the Crown (i.e., Hacienda—Public Treasury) needed in order to uncover a whole system (the mine where the gem was found, the mechanism of extraction, how much was extracted, who owned the mine, and other details, down to the day and hour when it was discovered)—indeed, all the pertinent information that made that specific area and mine eminently knowable, exploitable, and taxable. The massive transcontinental and transatlantic archival process undertaken under the auspices of the Real Gabinete therefore served not only taxonomic and scientific purposes; the "memoria" or "memory" of the specimen (that is, its provenance and biography) enabled colonial functionaries to administer, tax, and exploit the colonies as well.[47] If we imagine that the same was done for all the plants and animals and peoples of the New World (as is evident from all the labeled drawings of plants, animals, and different indigenous peoples extant in Dávila's catalogues), what we have before us is an unprecedented, immensely efficient mechanism of gathering information and hence of surveying and surveilling a vast territory. When we consider, additionally, that the Spaniards founded most of today's cities in the Americas within one hundred years of the continents' "discovery," the immense cabinet-driven archival and scientific information-gathering enterprise unsettles traditional historical explanations that contrast English and Spanish colonialism to the detriment of the latter. In contrast to these stereotypes (that pit English industriousness against Spanish greed) and seriously challenging them, the development of the Real Gabinete shows the extent to which the continued Spanish presence in and colonization of the Americas came to be understood and theorized by the eighteenth century as a scientific and economic enterprise. Also, and perhaps more importantly yet, these crude oppositions overlook the extent to which the Real Gabinete's findings served as a crucial underpinning of western science and the inception of modernity.

Indeed—given colonial relations, circuits, and power differentials, and additionally, given the erasure or submersion of native epistemologies—the museums and institutions of learning spawned by the Real Gabinete became the filter through which Americans

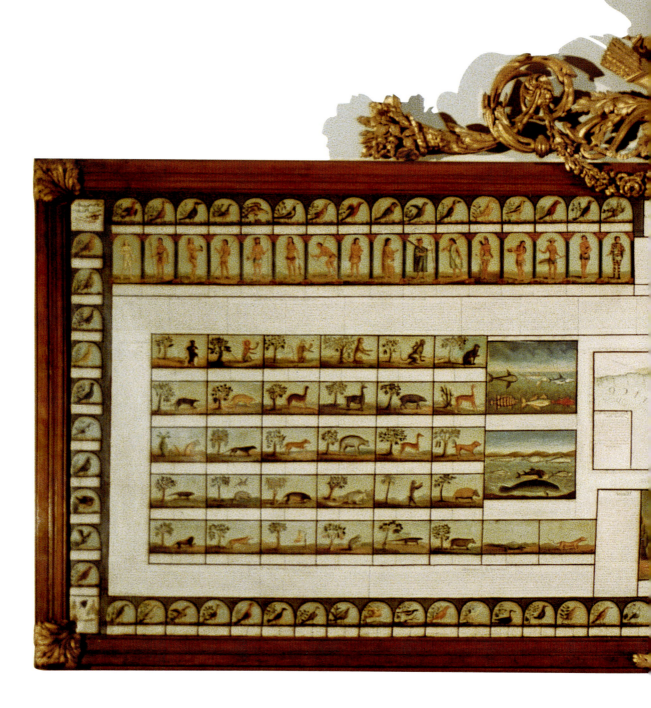

came to know themselves.[48] Nowhere is the thorough, ant-like mapping and "framing" (in both senses of the word) of the Americas better illustrated than in the little-known but fabulous painting *Quadro de Historia natural, civil y geográfico del Reyno del Perú, año 1799.* Envisioned as well as commissioned by José Ignacio Lequanda, an imperial administrator of the Andean city of Huamanga,[49] the painting was created by Luis Thiebaut in order to satisfy the "curiosity" of Spaniards with as full an account as possible of the kingdom of Perú (about which little factual information was available). A very large canvas, measuring 3.25 × 1.15 meters, this painting centers around a map of the colonial Kingdom of Perú with a map of the mine of Gualgayoc (or Chota), underneath which Lequanda labeled the different areas of the mine. Surrounded by larger and smaller squares, each representing either the fishes of the sea (seen through the waters

2.1. Quadro de Historial Natural, civil y geográfico del Reyno del Perú, año 1799
Luis Thiebaut
3.25 × 1.15 meters
Museo de Ciencias Naturales, Madrid

as if with X-rays), or the animals and plants and peoples of the land, and further elaborated by Lequanda's written history on all sides, the painting epitomizes the immense epistemological shift that had taken place in Europe since the inception of the Wunderkammern. In its broadest strokes, the painting represents the colonial economy and geography of Perú, the history of the Incas, and the Spanish Conquest of Perú, as well as ethnographic data and detailed paintings of botanical and zoological specimens, highlighting their uses, pharmaceutical properties, and myths and stories enveloping them. This painted history understands "history" as natural history in both the traditional and the emergent sense of the word that I have been outlining. It also very clearly shows the collusion of surveying/surveilling and seeing/overseeing mechanisms with imperial economic concerns. This painting was therefore appropriately dedicated to and hung in the Suprema Secretaría de la Real Hacienda de Indias until it passed to the holdings of the Museo Nacional de Ciencias Naturales de Madrid, where it hangs today in the Director's private office.

Thiebaut, like many chroniclers who popularized the Americas and spread fantastic myths about the region, had never left Europe. He nevertheless executed the painting, basing his work on sketches and written descriptions of plants, animals, and inhabitants in the Gabinete that were provided to him by Lequanda. Lequanda himself, stationed as he had been in the Andean city of Huamanga, constructed his natural, civil, and geographic history of Perú from different sources: oral histories, hearsay, Inca quipus ("El Libro augusto de los Yncas"), the census of 1791, etc. If ekphrasis refers to the written description of a visual image, then this is a case of what could be called reverse-ekphrasis. Animals, plants, and peoples are painted quite accurately, using the preserved specimens, sketches, and labels referring to them in the collection of the Real Gabinete.[50] While mines continue to be described in great detail (number of mines, number of miners, location, volume and value of extracted minerals, etc.), they form only one rather minimal element of the painting's composition. The greater part is dedicated to the drawings and accompanying descriptions of people, animals, and plants. The written text highlights pharmacological properties and native beliefs regarding their uses—all outlined with an eye to their com-

2.2. *Detail, two Indians*
Quadro de Historial Natural, civil y geográfico del Reyno del Perú, año 1799
Luis Thiebaut
3.25 × 1.15 meters
Museo de Ciencias Naturales, Madrid
Photo © Rosamond W. Purcell 2007

2.3. *Detail, two animals*
Quadro de Historial Natural, civil y geográfico del Reyno del Perú, año 1799
Luis Thiebaut
3.25 × 1.15 meters
Museo de Ciencias Naturales, Madrid
Photo © Rosamond W. Purcell 2007

mercialization.[51] The merits of quinine are discussed (as they are discussed endlessly across different natural histories), as is the fast and wasteful overharvesting of the tree from which it is derived; sinamon [cinnamon] is praised for the color of its wood and for its leaves which, when applied to the head, cure headaches; etc.[52] In Lequanda's work the ideological justification for the perpetual despoilment of Latin America (bemoaned in Machado's lament of the exoticization of Brazil, with which I ended the last chapter) continues unabated.

It is appropriate that this painting was initially hung at the Secretaría de Hacienda, because it is, beyond the common platitudes about God and Church in Lequanda's introduction, above all an homage to the rarely highlighted fact that the Spanish Empire was a *commercial* venture. Lequanda in fact regrets that the painting is incomplete, since it lacks a breakdown of crucial economic information—taxes, incomes, expenditures, etc.[53] A strategic attempt to curb the growing creole desire for independence from Spain, the text contrasts the Indians' "phlegmatic" character and the "creoles' love of luxury and ostentation" (so often stressed in caste paintings) with the industriousness of colonial administrators like Lequanda himself, on whose crucial contributions the colonies depended for survival and economic well-being ["El Español Peruano es idólatra de fausto y ostentación. Sólo apetece la opulencia en quanto se proporcionan medios para lucir: prefiere los honores á la utilidad"].[54] More importantly, composed simultaneously for the curious and the scientific gaze, the painting with its bird's-eye perspective presupposes that the world has become visible, knowable, exploitable.[55] Seeing is overseeing. Unlike the initial justification of the Conquest as the exchange of native wealth for religious salvation, Lequanda justifies colonialism here as the fair and necessary exchange of European industriousness for native raw products and minerals ["El Perú deve pagar con sus riquezas metálicas y otros preciosos frutos con que brinda la feracidad de su terreno, los afanes de la industria Europea . . ."].[56] Predictably, he lauds his own endeavors as a colonial administrator of the city of Huamanga, arguing that the area was very poor when he arrived but became industrious, commercial, and opulent as a result of his administration ["Esta Ciudad era muy pobre; pero desde que se erigió la Yntendencia, y el presente Autor estableció en ella Caxas de Real Hacienda, extinguiendo las de Guancavelica se ha hecho industriosa, comercianta y opulenta."][57] Foreshadowing Jane Jacobs's fundamental observation that cities are above all else centers that *create* wealth, Lequanda emphasizes the economic development of Huamanga with the foundation of the Yntendencia that he oversaw as a colonial administrator.[58] Appearing as it was at the end of the eighteenth century, Lequanda's insistence on the "industriousness" of the conquistadores has to be placed in implicit dialogue with England's justification of its own imperial ventures and increasing encroachment on Spanish-held territories. Indeed, Lequanda's insistence on the notion that the Spaniards created wealth by their industriousness, inventiveness, and commercial experience and always, of course, *in spite of* the natives' indolence, has to be read in this light. The *Quadro*, among other things, therefore also reproduces Lequanda's duplicitous argument: as a producer of wealth for Spain, he claims that he is a producer of wealth for the area under his supervision.

In an important aspect of how the Americas were created as a naturalists' paradise, and reflecting Gould's observations on the violence inherent in ranking, human groups become classified *in the same manner and on the same plane* as animals and plants. In this respect, the painting reproduces the practice of many cabinets of wonders: specimens are organized in a gradually ascending order that reflects their growing importance with portraits of important men dominating the upper levels.[59] Likewise, in the *Quadro* on the top row, two series of sixteen different human "types" are set on either side of the composition and divided into two groups: "naciones civilizadas" and "salvajes." Their placing on one or the other side depends on whether or not these indigenous peoples were urbanized, whether or not they lived in a "state of nature," and finally, whether or not they practiced cannibalism. Lequanda's description of the "civilized" peoples of Perú depends on both class and racial distinctions that were becoming increasingly widespread through the period's famous series of caste paintings, discussed in the Introduction. In fact, six of these were in the holdings of the Real Gabinete and have recently been passed to the Museo de America. Valued not as art objects but as ethnographic documents, these series reproduce European ideas associating the Americas and particularly race mixture with degeneration.[60] As the couples represented become increasingly mixed, therefore, they begin to show signs of poverty and degradation. As I pointed out above, European naturalists—particularly Buffon—had written that only smaller and inferior animal species existed in the Americas. Thus, they raised the specter that the fate of degeneration would befall Europeans transplanted there. Since powerful arguments against this thesis had been leveled by Bru (the Gabinete's official dissector) and Thomas Jefferson, among others, the fear of degeneration now reappears as Europe's fear of disorder and of the in-between, the unclassifiable hybrid, and the throwback. Thus, while the original mestizaje that serves as the cornerstone of Colonial Latin America is represented as the harmonious marriage between two elites, the series gradually turns away from racial harmony, as it represents ever more mixed and impossible-to-classify groups. While Lequanda mentions many different kinds of Indian tribes, he also typically highlights the mixture of Spaniards and Indians,[61] despite the fact that in the written section he stresses that mestizaje

2.4a. *Sculpture of "native" woman in the Butterfly Pavilion*
Vienna
Photo Spitta 2004

in Perú was mostly derived from the mixture of "blancos" and "negros." Blacks and mulattos are the ones who most mix with Spaniards ["es la casta que más se une al español"].[62] The *Quadro* itself, however, does not represent mulattos in any way, underlining the fact that black/white miscegenation was viewed as too messy and has been submerged repeatedly in favor of a genealogy tracing the harmonious mixing of two aristocracies (one Spaniard, the other Indian).[63]

As we saw in the previous chapter, the names given very mixed couples in the casta paintings (such as "tente en el aire") not only show a great lack of classificatory subtlety, but serve as an index to the precarious, in-between, unclassifiable position in the representation of mestizaje. More important for my argument, however, is the fact that the caste paintings, as well as the *Quadro*, subsume humans under the logic of the specimen by putting animals, plants, minerals, and humans on the *same plane*. People

2.4b. *Frisco Native American Museum and Natural History Center shop*
Frisco, Outer Banks, North Carolina
Photo Spitta 2004

2.4c. *Frisco Native American Museum and Natural History Center*
Frisco, Outer Banks, North Carolina
Photo Spitta 2004
The announcement posted at the entrance reads: "A far cry from your early movie and TV exposure to THE ORIGINAL AMERICANS! *We know you will truly enjoy your trip back in time."*

are distinguished from plants and animals only by virtue of their position higher in the visual hierarchy. Making representation destiny, from this moment on, American culture would become part of nature. In Vienna's "Butterfly Pavilion," a sculpture of a native woman inhabits the same space as the birds, and in natural history museums in the United States, natural history and Native American history continue to be confused. To a great extent, this conflation continues today in the practice of displaying American Indian artifacts and remains in natural science exhibits or in equating American Indians with natural history. As installation artist Fred Wilson observes, in New York City you see "native" artifacts in the American Museum of Natural History on one side of Central Park, then walk across to see similar objects displayed as art at the Metropolitan Museum.[64] This relegation of the Americas to the status of an object of study and a naturalist's paradise—indeed, the power dynamics involved in colonialism and the colonization of knowledge that stripped indigenous Americans of subjectivity by treating them as so many objects—helps explain why historians of science tend to entirely dismiss Latin America's and Spain's contribution to the sciences. Arguing that there were "few if any scientific contributions of any importance made during the eighteenth century by Spaniards in Spain," they conclude that it is therefore "not surprising that Spanish-Americans did not accomplish very much for the progress of science."[65] While Latin America has not yet managed to come into its own in this respect, calls to establish native universities taught in indigenous languages and focusing on indigenous epistemologies are gathering momentum. And while the United States mirrored Latin America's scientific backwardness in the nineteenth century, seeming very "unproductive" when compared to Europe,[66] it would gain its intellectual independence thanks to the Real Gabinete and the political savvy and flair for the spectacular of President Thomas Jefferson. Oddly enough, the story is that of the transformation of a specimen of big bones, which made its way from Argentina to the Real Gabinete. The extant correspondence between Jefferson and Juan Bautista Bru (1742–99), the Real Gabinete's official painter and taxidermist, shows that Jefferson had heard of a newly discovered mastodon (a fossilized skeleton of the *Megatherium americanum,* a ground sloth known as the megaterio) found by naturalists in 1787 on the shores of the Luján River in the vicinity of Buenos Aires. In 1788 (in keeping with Charles III's instructions to his colonial agents), the bones were sent to the royal cabinet in Madrid, where Bru assembled them the following year in what constituted the first reconstruction anywhere of a fossilized mammal. Bru prepared and mounted the skeleton on all fours rather than upright as it should be, and he also made 22 drawings and 5 plates of it.[67] It still stands on display in the National Museum of Natural Sciences in Madrid. The information was passed on to Georges Cuvier (1769–1832) in Paris, and through him word got to Jefferson, who lost no time in contacting Bru.

Crucial to establishing the United States as a modern scientific center was Jefferson's growing realization that the knowledge about the Americas that was being produced in Europe was faulty, detrimental to the Americans' self-understanding, and in need of serious revision. Jefferson correctly surmised that science was being enlisted to promote colonial hemispheric cultural and economic imbalances. Enlisting the aid of Bru and the Real Gabinete, Jefferson strategically contested Buffon's assertion that the climate of the Americas invariably led to the degeneration of European species (and people, as we saw in the *Quadro* and the caste paintings) transplanted there and, worse yet, that American species overall were deficient and smaller when compared to European ones. Jefferson therefore was intent on proving that the Americas surpassed Europe in every way possible. Within this scientific debate, bigger was literally better, and the search for larger animals and species became imperative. When scientists found enormous bones in Kentucky, Jefferson was predictably excited. He immediately requested from Bru a detailed description and drawings of the megaterio in the Gabinete and only then, having compared notes and ascertained his findings, sent his samples of the American mastodon to Paris.[68] As if to illustrate the importance of spectacular visibility for the promotion of science, W. J. T. Mitchell's *The Last Dinosaur Book* tells the story of the emergence of and continued fascination with dinosaurs in the United States, but is completely unaware of the important role Bru and the Real Gabinete played in helping Jefferson to critique Buffon and other naturalists' Eurocentric taxonomies. As Mitchell writes, "America's big bones were a demonstration of its 'natural constitution,' its virility, potency, and dominance in the Darwinian struggle among nations."[69] If in Jefferson's time Native Americans had been largely marginalized and written out of history as lacking a great civilization, natural history

2.5. *Harvard Mastodon*
Museum of Natural History
Photo Spitta 2005

2.6. *"Toys 'R' U.S. (When Dinosaurs Ruled the Earth)"*
Mark Dion 1994
Courtesy of the artist and Tanya Bonakdar Gallery, New York

and in particular dinosaur-worship made up for this lack of a great past.[70] Installation artist Mark Dion never tires of playing with this fascination instilled in children.

It is noteworthy that Jefferson, a member of the American Philosophical Society founded by Franklin, saw himself forced to turn to Spain for scientific information and dialogue.[71] Jefferson was frustrated with the fact that—unlike in Europe—there was an almost complete disregard in the United States for the value of science. He succeeded in using economic arguments to promote the Lewis and Clark expedition (in line with the expeditions promoted by Spain's Gabinete Real and other European scientific academies), but was never able to repeat the feat again. Unable to gather funds and support to re-create the magnitude of the Lewis and Clark expedition in his lifetime, the discovery and mapping of the Northwest territories by and for "Americans" nevertheless became the foundational narrative of the United States. Mirroring Columbus's rhetoric of the "discovery" of then-unknown lands, Lewis and Clark viewed the regions they traversed as a paradisiacal botanical garden. Throughout their expedition, they took great care to send back to Philadelphia specimens that they gathered along the way, paralleling the methods used by the Real Gabinete. Thus, Lewis and Clark aided Jefferson in his endeavor to educate society and to make the general public understand the importance of science for industry, the creation of wealth, and the narrative underpinning a national identity.

In contrast, Spain's scientific ventures lacked a prominent and outspoken spokesman like the United States had had in Jefferson. As we saw, science continued to be subjected to the personal whimsies of successive administrations and never had a coherent, sustained policy. At the end of the famous scientific expedition (Comisión Científica del Pacífico) that took place between 1862 and 1865, Spanish naturalists, having traversed South America from the Pacific to the Atlantic, met up with Louis Agassiz and his North American expedition, funded by a Boston millionaire. To Don Francisco de Paula Martínez, traveling in the cheapest of berths, the difference in the funding between both expeditions was telling: while Agassiz (first winner of the Nobel Prize in the Americas) and his men traveled by steamboat, dressed well, and kept clean, the Spaniards had traveled by foot overland, without clothes or shoes, their beards long and unkempt. From Don Francisco's description it would seem as if the humidity had rotted the Spanish explorers' belongings and even their whole beings ["Ellos comenzaban su viaje por medio de vapores y con todos los recursos necesarios; así es que estaban bien vestidos y arreglados. Nosotros estábamos derrotados completamente, sin ropa, sin zapatos, con largísimas barbas, y otras circunstancias hijas de un viaje tan dilatado, cuya última parte había sido hecho a pie y por ríos, donde la temperatura y la humedad había podrido los pocos efectos que traíamos"]. Having spent three years at the mercy of indifferent administrators, suffering from perpetual lack of funds and support, and traversing a continent where anti-Spanish sentiment reigned supreme, Don Francisco de Paula Martínez—invoking the conquered-conquistador trope—concludes that his whole group looked more like a group of beggars than a scientific expedition commissioned by a European government ["todo nuestro conjunto, parecía más de mendigos que de comisionados de un gobierno europeo"].[72]

As if only to prove him right, Don Francisco de Paula's diary itself lay for one hundred twenty-five years gathering dust in the National Museum of Natural Science. Were it not for the zealous industriousness of curator María de los Ángeles Calatayud, who was instrumental in telling the history of the Real Gabinete and its famous founder, the diary would never have seen the light of day. Using its fate as an example of Spain's continued disregard of the groundbreaking endeavors of the Gabinete for western science, Miguel Angel Puig-Samper ruefully comments in the Prologue to the recently published diary that, as with so many other instances, Don Francisco de Paula's work was fated to remain forgotten on the shelves of the museum. It is as if the fatal destiny of the great labor of the Spanish scientific expeditions were to be shoved aside in some musty and dark cellar waiting to be devoured by time ["Como en tantas ocasiones, su obra permanecía olvidada en los armarios de un Museo, como si el fatal destino de la gran labor desarrollada por las expediciones científicas españolas fuera, casi siempre, estar arrumbada en algún oscuro sotano a la espera de ser devorada por el tiempo"].[73] This state of affairs is particularly troubling given how much Spain invested in scientific endeavors in the New World. In stark contrast to Spain's negligence of its scientific discoveries and their relegation to the dustbin of history, then, stand Jefferson's spectacular displays of mastodon bones in the White House (leading to his inauguration as the "Mammoth" and "Naturalist" president);[74] the fanfare with which the Lewis and Clark expedition was advertised; and the instrumental role their journey had in the founding of the nation. I can think of no more apt symbol of the exchange of information and transatlantic dialogue between Jefferson and Bru of the Real Gabinete that would lead to this parting of the ways than the enormous dinosaur that oversees passenger traffic from nebulous heights in a concourse at Chicago's O'Hare Airport.

2.7. *Dinosaur towering over passengers United Concourse, Chicago O'Hare Airport Photo Spitta 2007*

As we will see in the next chapter, while Spain has yet to come to terms with the important role the immense archival efforts of the *informes* played in the production of modern science, science in the United States survived for a period after Jefferson by being coupled almost entirely to spectacle, thanks to P. T. Barnum's national histrionics and his massively appealing, moralizing, and spectacular shows at the American Museum (sited on Broadway in New York City, quite appropriately). Given Jefferson's emphasis on big bones, the continued focus on dinosaurs in museum displays and the magical fascination with dinosaurs fostered in children across the United States are understandable. However, this emphasis also serves as an index of the different trajectories followed by Latin America and the United States.

CHAPTER THREE

WRITING THE NATURAL HISTORY OF OUR DESTRUCTION

From P. T. Barnum's National Histrionics to Contemporary, Post-Apocalyptic Wunderkammern

Sweet is the lore which Nature brings;
Our meddling intellect
Mis-shapes the beauteous forms of things:
—We murder to dissect.

—William Wordsworth, "The Tables Turned"

But the closer I came to these ruins, the more any notion of a mysterious isle of the dead
receded, and the more I imagined myself amidst the remains of our own civilization after its
extinction in some future catastrophe.

—W. G. Sebald, *The Rings of Saturn*

La naturaleza real palidece ante el platonismo del museo [Real nature recedes before the
Platonism of the museum].

—Pere Alberch, "Más Africa que Africa: Richard Ross y la poética de los museos" [José Ramón López, *Richard Ross: Historia natural*]

I understand all too well the impulse to Joseph Cornell-box the world.

—Rosamond Purcell, *Owl's Head*

The Musée de l'Homme—the Museum of Man—is one of the world's most important muse-
ums devoted to anthropology, ethnology, and prehistory. Its collections are arranged—by in
large [sic]—according to geographical region, and includes the Inca mummy (in fetal posi-
tion) which inspired Edvard Munch's painting The Screem *[sic].*

—Description of the Musée de l'Homme on the Paris.org website

THE CREATION OF BOTANICAL, ZOOLOGICAL, and human taxonomies framed the Americas primarily in terms of natural history.[1] Indeed, as the *Quadro* and the vast archival work of Madrid's Real Gabinete make clear, by the end of the eighteenth century the logic of natural history had pervaded all aspects of life, allowing most things—if not *everything*—to be reduced to the logic of the specimen. The meticulous collecting, labeling, and cataloguing of nature transformed sight into oversight, while the distinction between surveying and surveillance collapsed with mechanisms of colonial control. Paradoxically, the creation of increasingly sophisticated classificatory systems was coupled with the placing of non-European people and nature on the same plane. Theoretically this lack of distinction is for us, today, shocking. Yet it is not unusual for many of us to have, until quite recently, seen indigenous peoples exhibited in museums as living dioramas; and we still remain largely immune and immured to the reduction of indigenous peoples to natural history. This process, which originated with the live exhibits of native Arawaks that Columbus took to Queen Isabella's court (where they were displayed for two years), continues largely unquestioned in the conflation of indigenous peoples with natural history in natural history museums. Today, many museums worldwide still hold native remains, despite growing uncertainty as to their status and despite the public's increasing unease when confronted with these displays. Indeed, Maria Pearson, the Lakota leader instrumental in the 1990 passing of the Native American Graves Protection and Repatriation Act (NAGPRA), began her crusade twenty years earlier as a consequence of the differential treatment accorded human remains. It is generally understood that when white remains are accidentally found during construction, graves are being violated, and the remains are therefore immediately reinterred. In contrast, Native American graves are seen as potential sources of valuable archaeological artifacts, and the remains are automatically boxed up and sent to the Office of the State Archaeologist as scientific specimens.[2]

Worse yet, Africans have been framed quite literally as taxidermied specimens. Among the most notorious cases is that of the *Negro de Banyoles*, a Southern African tribal leader who had been taxidermied and displayed in a Catalan museum until 2000, when public uproar forced the "dismantling" of that exhibit at Madrid's National Museum of Anthropology and the repatriation of his remains to Botswana.[3] Another well-known case is that of Saarjite Baartman, a Khosian woman from Cape Town, disparagingly referred to as the Hottentot Venus, who served much of her life as a live exhibit in France and England (where she was exhibited naked in a cage at Piccadilly in the early nineteenth century), and whose brains, skeleton, and a wax model of her genitals were displayed in the Musée de l'Homme in Paris until 2002, when her remains, too, were repatriated after many years of protest from the South African government.[4] Despite this, the Musée de l'Homme, as is evident from the epigraph to this section, continues to advertise spectacular human remains in its collection. The numerous misspellings in the advertisement, however, may be due not only to the translator's inadequacy, but also, as we will see below, to the current identity crisis of natural history museums.

More popularly still, curio shops across the world continue to traffic in human remains, thus manipulating people's credulity, gullibility, and suspension of disbelief, and playing their desire and nostalgia for the marvelous off against their incredulity. Ye Olde Curiosity Shop on Seattle's waterfront, originally established in 1899 as Stand-

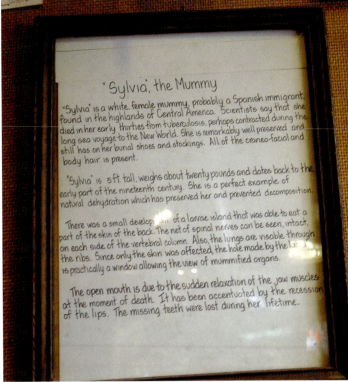

"Sylvia', the Mummy

"Sylvia" is a white, female mummy, probably a Spanish immigrant, found in the highlands of Central America. Scientists say that she died in her early thirties from tuberculosis, perhaps contracted during the long sea voyage to the New World. She is remarkably well preserved and still has on her burial shoes and stockings. All of the craneo-facial and body hair is present.

"Sylvia" is 5 ft tall, weighs about twenty pounds and dates back to the early part of the nineteenth century. She is a perfect example of natural dehydration which has preserved her and prevented decomposition.

There was a small develop... of a larvae island that was able to eat a part of the skin of the back. The net of spinal nerves can be seen, intact, on each side of the vertebral column. Also, the lungs are visable through the ribs. Since only the skin was affected, the hole made by the la... is practically a window allowing the view of mummified organs.

The open mouth is due to the sudden relaxation of the jaw muscles at the moment of death. It has been accentuated by the recession of the lips. The missing teeth were lost during her lifetime.

3.1a and b. *"Sylvia" the Mummy*
Exhibit at the Ye Olde Curiosity Shop, Seattle
This exhibit is apparently the skeleton of a Spanish immigrant to Central America in the nineteenth century. She stands close to a collection of indigenous shrunken heads.
Photo Spitta 2004

ley's Free Museum (an Indian trading post), today advertises itself as containing "amazing oddities" and having "everything in the world sardined into one fantastic shop." Inspired by a gift of *The Wonders of Nature* from his third-grade teacher, Joe Standley became a passionate collector of nature's curiosities and owner of what he claims is the greatest curio shop in the United States. Drawing collectors from all over the world, the shop also supplied museums both in the United States and abroad with Native American artifacts.[5] Today this treasure trove continues to welcome people to the "world of the weird and wonderful," of the natural and the bizarre. It boasts among its rarities a motley collection of shrunken heads, Siamese twin calves, a pig with three tails, Native American artifacts, a ship made from Alaskan ivory, actual mummies (Sylvester the cowboy, coated in arsenic, and hence allegedly one of the best-preserved mummies in North America), and other unparalleled objects from around the world. One of the displays is a preserved mummy called "Sylvia" (the sign announces it is an early nineteenth-century dehydrated mummy from Central America). Framed in and by a case, it was not very clear to me, Silvia, whether they were really the remains of a human being or whether the entire display was a fake. In either case, the uncertainty was uncanny.

There is, however, perhaps no better example of the framing of Europe's others in order to promote a national agenda and commercial venture than that effected by Barnum's American Museum. Claiming to be America's first museum, it filled the vacuum left by the scientific backwardness of the United States and was a spectacular, gigantic, and exponentially growing Wunderkammer and natural history collection. Originally opening (appropriately) on New York City's lower Broadway in 1842, it absorbed the previous owner's collection of stuffed animals, exotic artifacts from overseas, and "pickled punks" (preserved specimens). More importantly, in 1845, when Charles Wilson Peale went bankrupt, Barnum also bought up the natural history museums Peale had established in New York City and Baltimore.[6] Shortly thereafter he also bought up

3.2. The Artist in His Museum
Charles Wilson Peale, 1822
Courtesy of the Pennsylvania Academy of Fine Arts, Philadelphia
Gift of Mrs. Sarah Harrison (The Joseph Harrison, Jr., Collection)

New York's Chinese collection and Peale's famous Philadelphia Museum.[7] By 1849 Barnum's American Museum claimed over 600,000 objects, and by 1864 the size of the collection had increased yet again, to 850,000. As with all collections, Barnum had to expand repeatedly and, predictably, his life was befallen by a series of bankruptcies. In order to stave off being ruined and in order to finance needed expansions, Barnum trafficked in not only exotic objects but also, increasingly, humans. He added an ever-growing menagerie of living human oddities (known as his "freaks"), creating shows with them that added sensationalist appeal to his natural history collections. Among them: small people such as the Thumbs, albinos such as the Lucasie family, the Siamese twins Chang and Eng, the bearded Madame Clofullia, Jo Jo the Russian Dog Face Boy, fat men and women, the Texas Giant Brothers, dwarfs, living skeletons, armless women such as Anna Leake Thomson, blanket tattooed men and women, and indigenous peoples from the United States and around the world, among many others. The shows involved the same juxtapositions of the Wunderkammern, but in a slapstick coupling of oddities: the giant with the dwarf, the fat man with the skeleton woman. In lieu of the recorded data that accompanied the gathering of specimens for natural history collections, Barnum supplemented the void of misplacing in which these "freaks" existed by inventing exotic and fabulous autobiographies for each one of them.[8] He amassed a fortune with them and they, in turn, became eccentric and interesting figures in their own right.[9]

3.3. *The Thumbs and a bearded friend*
Barnum's Human Menagerie
Credit: Picture History

3.4. *The Lucasie family*
Barnum's Human Menagerie
Credit: Picture History

Barnum not only framed human abnormalities in what was known as his "freak menagerie"; he also framed Native Americans as freaks. His biographers report several incidents in which he tricked non-English-speaking Native American chiefs to sit as exhibits in his museum.[10] One case that has been recorded is that

3.5. *Nine Native American Indians from the West*
Barnum's Indian Visitors
Photo Mathew Brady
Credit: Picture History

of Chief Yellow Bear. While he patted him on the back, smiling and seemingly complimenting him, Barnum introduced Chief Yellow Bear (who spoke no English) to the audience not only as a killer of whites but as a "lying, thieving, treacherous, murderous monster" (Kunhardt, 176). In London in 1844, Barnum met George Catlin—famous and financially successful as a painter of Native Americans (at that time having set up his studio in Egyptian Hall and exhibiting native artifacts, weapons, costumes, and even a huge wigwam)—and instantly talked him into a venture to bring a live troupe of American Indians to London. A telling letter shows his complete and utter disregard of their humanity: "I now have got the Indians under full blast, and what with them and Tom Thumb, my automaton writer exhibiting at the Adelaide Gallery, the Bell Ringers, Am. Museum and Peale's, giants, dwarf, etc., I guess I have enough on hand to keep one busy" (Kunhardt, 61).

In the spirit of the Wunderkammern, only trumping their theatricality, Barnum combined these "freak shows" with the public education of natural history. His collection soon expanded into seven huge rooms (evoking the seven wonders of the world, and including the first aquariums and giraffes, bears, and other wild animals, as well as other wonders of natural history and artificialia). The first room was called, true to the spirit of seeing/overseeing that I have been outlining, the "Cosmo-Panopticon Studio." The Wunderkammer here, however, has been transformed into a "kind of educational peep show," with 194 original scenes in "row upon row of face-sized windows, each opening onto an individual, lighted-up scene, perhaps of Italy or Egypt, Russia, or Jerusalem" (Figure 3.6). Other rooms contained haphazardly assembled collections of naturalia and artificialia, interspersed with his "freaks" as living exhibits (Kunhardt, 140). He also wrested the theater away from puritanical hands and entertained audiences with his ludicrous "morality" plays; on his payroll he had fortune-tellers, taxidermists, and phrenologists who read people's destiny from the bumps on their heads. Thus, while the European emphasis in the Wunderkammern lay on learning followed

by entertainment, Barnum inverted the equation, privileging entertainment over learning. Indeed, he redefined the Wunderkammern to appeal to a mass audience, going to any lengths—often unscientific, many times unethical, but always highly publicized—to create "wonders" (such as a monstrous mermaid still on display at the Barnum Museum in Connecticut) with which to advertise and attract increasingly large numbers to his museum.[11] His democratic embrace of the masses, however, had a positive side as well, for, in his intent to reach out to literally everyone, he came up with "most-beautiful baby shows" in order to attract a female audience. Thanks to these strategies, his museum became one of the first public spaces (along with department stores)[12] in the United States welcoming to unchaperoned women (Kunhardt, 105).

3.6. *Barnum's First Salon Cosmorama* *Courtesy of Bridgeport Public Library* *Historical Collections*

Perhaps most importantly, yet invariably overlooked, given the often negative publicity surrounding him, was Barnum's linking of science to spectacle. Like Jefferson, only more extreme and far less scrupulous, Barnum understood that the way to obtain continued funding for his growing natural history collections was by means of spectacular shows. Indeed, it is largely thanks to Barnum that to this day, scientific funding for the majority of projects, and the public's continued support of science, depends on the visibility of a few highly advertised projects (e.g., NASA's space project). As historians of the museum write: "Under the guise of entertainment and education the American Museum became the foremost house of spectacle of popular culture."[13] Going on to become instrumental in the creation of the American circus, Barnum was first and foremost a precursor of contemporary forms of advertising, promotional strategies, and crowd control (and manipulation). Although Barnum is known today mainly for his spectacular circuses, his museum had more visitors at any given time than the British Museum.[14]

Years after his second museum had burned down (and along with it not only his entire

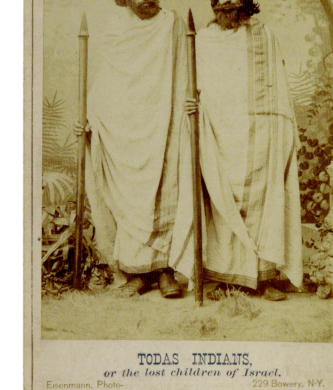

BAND OF NUBIANS,
from the Soudan.

Eisenmann, Photo-   229. Bowery, N·Y·

TODAS INDIANS,
or the lost children of Israel.

Eisenmann, Photo-   229. Bowery, N·Y·

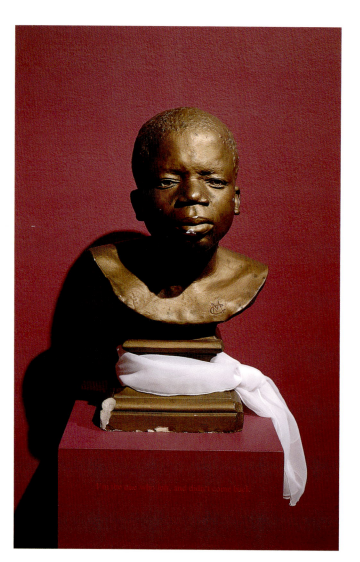

3.7a and b. *Barnum's Grand Collection of the World's "Uncivilized Races":*
   Band of Nubians and Todas Indians
McCaddon Collection of the Barnum and Bailey Circus, Manuscripts
   Division, Department of Rare Books and Special Collections
Photo Credit: Princeton University Library

3.8. *Bust of Ota Benga, a Bachichi man*
Caspar Mayer (1871–1931)
Plaster cast made from a life mask
Courtesy Hood Museum of Art
Dartmouth College, Hanover, New Hampshire. Gift of the American
   Museum of Natural History

collection, but also all the wild caged animals he kept there who were heard howling on Broadway throughout the night), he turned to the circus as a venue for continuing his "human freak" sideshows and took it by rail across the United States. Tellingly, his most important show was a grand collection of "uncivilized peoples," a human menagerie, a Noah's Ark of sorts, a performance of the casta paintings, for which consulates and U.S. officials all over the world were requested by the U.S. government to collect "specimens." Reportedly, the predominantly white audiences "howled with laughter at the 'inferior' beings on display" (Kunhardt, 296). "And yet," write his biographers, "introduced on the circus hippodrome track, and praised by New York's august Ethnological Society, Barnum's Grand Ethnological Congress became an eye-opening introduction for audiences all across America to the wondrous diversity of the human family" (Kunhardt, 296). While statements like these may make us cringe, the mindset driving them continues to underlie our cultural expectations about alterity. This is still evident in the showcasing of different cultures in schools and on college campuses across the United States and elsewhere, as well as other celebrations of human diversity such as Edward Steichen's 1955 famous photography exhibit at the Museum of Modern Art, *The Family of Man* (which included 503 photographs from 68 countries). While these practices may be rather benign (if at times rather boring), they signal a hierarchical, panoptical self-positioning vis-à-vis the cultural and racial other.

The less benign dimension of cultural showcasing was also apparent in 1904, when for the St. Louis World's Fair (Louisiana Purchase Exposition), the exhibit "University of Man" gathered cultural "representatives" from the Americas, Africa, and the Far East and grouped them into "living displays." Among these the fate of Ota Benga is particularly sorrowful. A twenty-three-year-old pygmy from the Congo, Ota Benga arrived in St. Louis having been purchased by collector, traveler, and anthropologist Samuel Verner. After the fair was over, he was given to the Bronx Zoo, where he was displayed with an orangutan in a cage. Thanks to the Colored Baptist Ministers' objections, Ota Benga was successively transferred to an orphanage in Brooklyn, then to a seminary in Virginia, and finally to work in a tobacco factory. Increasingly despondent, he shot himself through the heart in 1916.[15]

As we saw with the Real Gabinete and the development of natural history, science has developed increasingly sophisticated and powerful augmented vision technologies to scrutinize nature, showing us ever more marvelous manifestations of the universe as well as things at the subatomic level. Curious, we continue to move between two poles: we celebrate both natural and cultural diversity, but we also do violence to that diversity. The growing lists of both endangered species and dying languages are sad witnesses to our inability to couple our celebration of life's diversity with the protection and preservation of that diversity. Increasingly uncomfortable with this state of things, installation and performance artists as well as art critics and curators are becoming critical of the politics of display and what I have called the framing of the frame. Unpacking natural history museums, searching through dark and dusty object-laden deposits, and rearranging displays, they are attempting to complicate our relationship not only to the natural world but also to cultural and racial others. Interestingly, the most radical interventions are taking place through innovative re-creations of cabinets of wonders (that I call post-apocalyptic) and artistic interventions in natural history museums.

THE WUNDERKAMMERN TODAY: WRITING THE HISTORY OF OUR OWN EXTINCTION

. . . I called Rosamond Purcell, doyenne of decaying objects, photographer of taxidermo-logical specimens, memorist of Wunderkammern. Her studio in Cambridge is bedizened with objets trouvés in various stages of decomposition: rescued sheets of discarded metal and weather-beaten books that are transformed—by design, by vision, by respect—into objects of great beauty.

—Ricky Jay, *Dice: Deception, Fate & Rotten Luck*

I do not fully understand what it is about the visual effects of patina and decay that pushes the button for some of us, but I knew at first glance that the camera would treat each die as one piece of a cake after another: delectable abstractions of objects in transition.

—Rosamond Purcell, "Afterword," *Dice: Deception, Fate & Rotten Luck*

3.9. *Rotten Luck: The Decaying Dice of Ricky Jay" exhibition at the Museum of Jurassic Technology. Los Angeles.*
Photo Spitta.

While many cabinets of curiosities ultimately were broken up to serve as the foundation of Europe's first museums, some have been preserved (in rather rarified form) as museums in themselves. Among the most famous is Sir John Soane's Museum in London.[16] Other Wunderkammern were destroyed but have been recently reconstructed, including Tradescant Hall at Oxford University and the Anatomical Theatre of Leiden (1991). These spaces, museums of our early museums, in their all-too-orderly displays, somehow fail to communicate to the visitor the tension between order and disorder that must have been quite apparent, palpable even, in the early Wunderkammern. For this sensation we must visit the many natural history museums that have persisted unchanged, as if frozen in time. They are anachronistic yet marvelous spaces where the visitor enters a space from the past and is suddenly surrounded by musty, strange smells, and the even stranger displays of taxidermied animals and birds, preserved specimens, and odd scientific instruments. The space feels fragile, like moth's wings: you fear that if you touch anything, it will instantly become dust between your fingers. Impossible to decipher, the past confines us.

Many natural history museums, buckling under the weight of ideological critiques, have pulled most if not all of their holdings from the display cases. Today they feel like rudderless vessels. Unwary visitors wander about strangely empty rooms unsure as to why

3.10. *Display at the Fairbanks Museum of Natural History, St. Johnsbury, Vermont*
Courtesy of the Fairbanks Museum and Planetarium
Photo Spitta 2007
A wonderful example of an old natural history museum

3.11. *Chang and Eng*
Plaster cast
Mütter Museum, the College of Physicians of Philadelphia
Photo Brandon Zimmerman

they are there, or feeling as if they had somehow entered the wrong place, while masses of children suddenly freed from the constraints of school run about grand rooms while viewing some infantilized exhibit or other—the gradual emergence of *Homo sapiens* represented by plastic models seems to be a favorite. Largely unchanged by the passage of time, one museum that has both maintained the look and feel of early scientific museums and also succeeded in remaining a vital space is the College of Physicians of Philadelphia's Mütter Museum. Starting out in 1788 as a small library and cabinet of pathological specimens used as teaching tools, it was significantly expanded in 1849 with Thomas Dent Mütter's donation of a massive collection of specimens accumulated during his many years spent teaching while chief of surgery. The museum now has in its holdings over 20,000 items with which it documents the development of medicine. These include wax models of skin diseases, skulls and long bones showing the ravages of syphilis, the Soap Lady (the body of a woman that had turned to adipocere—a fatty wax similar to lye soap), a gangrenous hand, the skeleton of a woman's ribcage compressed by tight corseting, 139 skulls primarily from Eastern and Central Europe, microscopic analyses of hair and blood that show the development of forensic science in the nineteenth century, artifacts and images that explain how conjoined twins develop (showing the preserved livers of Barnum's Chang and Eng, autopsied at the museum in 1874), a huge human colon removed after death from a 29-year-old man, the bladder stones removed from Chief Justice John Marshall in 1831, giants and dwarfs that illustrate disorders of the skeletal system, a plaster cast of Laura Bridgman's brain and early teaching materials used to teach her sign language, as well as more than 2,000 objects accidentally swallowed by people and retrieved from their larynxes by pioneer branchoesophagologist Chevalier Jackson (all sorts of toys, dentures, enormous safety pins, etc.).[17]

The Mütter has been and continues to be successful in attracting a mass audience thanks largely to the vision, unflagging energy, flair for the spectacular, and constant public appearances (on NPR and *Late Night with David Letterman*) of the late Gretchen Worden, the museum's quirky and charismatic director. In the 1980s, when Worden became its director, the Mütter had at most a couple of hundred visitors a year and was well on its way to becoming aimless and obsolescent, like so many natural history museums today. Worden's creativity is seen at play in the gleeful juxtaposition of oddities in the collection. The results were interesting exhibits such as "When the President is the Patient," which featured displays on the subjects of displaying George Washington's carbuncle, Andrew Jackson's dueling wounds, Woodrow Wilson's disabling strokes, and Franklin Delano Roosevelt's fatal hypertension. Worden also asked renowned photographers to play with the exhibit and create interesting compositions such as Steven Katzman's flowering skull, or Max Aguilera-Hellweg's skin used as a bag, or having a plaster cast made of the conjoined twins Chang and Eng, who had enriched Barnum. Worden herself was a collector, and she created idiosyncratic Christmas crèches—lovingly photographed and posted in her memory on the Internet by her collaborators—with her own whimsical collection.[18] Worden first collected conjoined objects such as M&Ms, dolls, and oddly shaped foods as a child, and later, cow creamers, international toilet paper, and rubber and stuffed rats. Imitating the Mütter's collection, she even had a nineteenth-century photograph of a man with "enormously swol-

3.12. Demonstration of human skin Mütter Museum Exhibit

Max Aguilera-Hellweg explained that in this section of skin, "the cuts and numbers (angle in degrees) were made as part of a study of surgical incision and scarring. There are inherent lines in the skin, if you cut with the lines, there is less scarring, if you go against these lines, there is more scarring. Surgeons, especially plastic surgeons, would pay attention to this issue, and try to cut along the imbedded lines." (E-mail, June 11, 2007)

Photo © Max Aguilera-Hellweg 2000

len testicles."[19] Worden's flair for advertising, and her promotion of the work of artists and photographers, has resulted in the museum now attracting over 60,000 visitors annually. And while the Mütter's promotional materials mimic the rhetoric and self-understanding of the Wunderkammern ("A place like no other. Unique. Awe-inspiring"), Worden's insistence on making the strange and abnormal visible follows Buffon's injunction to make sight the preeminent tool of scientific inquiry and knowledge. A plaque soberly explains the reasons for exhibiting what to many visitors are shocking and upsetting abnormalities: "In clinical work, the eye is the main avenue for diagnostic information. . . . In medical education, again, the eye must take first place; it is from the wealth of material stored as visual impressions that the expert draws his comparisons and conclusions."[20] However, the exhibits are so shocking that the gaze is reversed: "In most museums you go to look at objects," writes Worden; however, "in the Mütter Museum, sometimes the objects seem to be looking at you."[21] The unsettling nature of the specimens destabilizes the equilibrium and the distance between subject and object, disallowing the visitor's detachment. Reminding us that wonder is a two-way street, the gaze of visitors of the Mütter can no longer merely take possession or take hold of the world; it is as if one is being taken hold of in an unusually poignant implosion on the borders between the subject and the object.[22]

A living diorama of preserved biological abnormalities, equally famous and notorious, the Mütter continues to both serve as a learning tool for future physicians and attract many curious visitors (like myself) with its simultaneously wonder—and horror—provoking exhibits. Perhaps more importantly, however, it has also served to inspire massive interest in other installations that break down the boundaries between subject and object and between what we consider beautiful and what we deem abject. Indeed, that we have come to expect this type of uncertainty to overcome us in natural history museums becomes clear by how different the public's response has been to the currently touring Bodyworlds exhibit. The promotional poster that I saw was of a plastinated donor's body stripped of skin, highlighting his musculature and reminiscent of Vesali's stripped body in the previous chapter. The donor is shown holding up his own skin as if it were a piece of cloth. This exhibit is "Barnumesque," in the words of a critic. The entire exhibit depends on spectacular, Ruysch-inspired, artfully shocking displays of absolutely lifelike, incorruptible, plastinated bodies that show one part of a body's function. Unlike Ruysch, whose innovative techniques of preserving body parts in the early part of the eighteenth century were used as allegorical ensembles reflecting on vice, the transitoriness of life, etc., it is unclear what the Bodyworlds plastinated bodies and body parts "lesson" is meant to do, other than to promote spectacular forms of voyeurism. Bodyworlds claims that its mission is "the anatomical exhibition of real human bodies" as well as the difference between healthy and unhealthy bodies (therefore, "clean" lungs are contrasted in a display to those of a smoker, etc.).[23] Initially circulating in art history museums, the exhibit created enormous controversy. However, highlighting the desensitizing effect of subject/object oppositions in natural history, once it was moved to natural history museums it gained immediate acceptance.

Like some natural history museums, the Mütter not only may have opened the gates to sensationalism-pandering exhibits such as Bodyworlds. Thanks to Worden's tireless efforts, it has also served as an invaluable source for photographers and installa-

tion artists, including Max Aguilera-Hellweg,[24] Rosamond Purcell, Richard Ross, and Harvey Stein, some
of whose photographs we saw above. Renowned among
them is Rosamond Purcell, important for my discussion
because of her collaboration with the late science writer,
evolutionary biologist, and friend Stephen Jay Gould.
Together they explored the interplay between art and
natural history and co-authored *Illuminations: A Bestiary* (1986); *Finders, Keepers: Eight Collectors* (1992); and
Crossing Over: Where Art and Science Meet (2000), while
Purcell is the author of *Special Cases: Natural Anomalies
and Historical Monsters* (1997) and *Owl's Head* (2003).[25]
This last book is her most recent reflection on the nature
of collecting; her fascination with decaying objects; and
her developing relationship with William Buckminster,
owner of Owl's Head junkyard in Maine.

I first encountered Purcell's stunning photographs of
natural history specimens and her playful installation/
exhibits re-creating the logic of the Wunderkammern
and examining the common border shared by science
and art in Madrid's natural history museum. The work
that I saw there, *Adam and Eve*, is largely responsible
for my own interest in the current transformation that
natural history museums are undergoing. Purcell had

3.13. Adam and Eve
Installation at the Museo de Ciencias Naturales, Madrid
Photo © Rosamond W. Purcell 2007
Courtesy of the artist

made a visually poetic exhibit/installation, perhaps unconsciously quoting Ruysch's
allegories—I realized only much later—that showed two proudly erect human skeletons in the middle of a large glass display case surrounded by natural history specimens. Greeting the visitor, the exhibit served as an index to the aesthetic dimension
of natural history. Purcell's other displays as well as her idiosyncratic photographs of
natural history specimens set the tone for the rest of my visit.[26]

Purcell's work frames the way in which we have come to see natural history museums: both as sites where art and science rub up against each other and commingle,
and as mute and dusty testimonies to the violence of colonizing forms of knowledge.
Instructive in this regard may be the words my then-thirteen-year-old son chose in
describing our visit to Harvard's Natural History Museum: "we went to a museum
where everything was dead: the birds, the fish." Purcell's own four-year-old asked her
in the same museum what would happen if all the animals suddenly came alive, to
which Purcell responded that there would be a lot of broken glass and straw. And yet,
Purcell's entire oeuvre is devoted to rescuing scientific and natural history specimens
from obsolescence. The "doyenne of decay," as she has been called, Purcell transforms
specimens either into art objects that reflect states of mind (see her collection of photographs *Half-Life*), or into aesthetically interesting juxtapositions that arouse curiosity and wonder.[27] Reminding us of Gretchen Worden's observation about the active
participation of the specimens in the Mütter, Purcell's installations and photographs
turn the gaze around, playing with the distortions of light filtering through aged glass

jars that hold specimens such as Ruysch's preserved babies ["El vidrio antiguo de los frascos de los siglos XVII y XIX tiende a estar hecho con menos perfección, y por lo tanto es el más perfecto para distorsionar y cambiar la luz"]. (See Purcell's photographs of Ruysch's preserved babies in Chapter One.)[28]

In addition to contributing to what seems to be a ghosting of her subjects, Purcell's photographs merge subject and object. One seamlessly blends into the other, because many of her compositions focus on different aspects and stages of decomposition and the myriad transformations that accompany processes of disintegration and preservation. Her work allows our interest in natural history museums to be sustained, equally, with her playful and artistic recombination and juxtaposition of "real" and "fake" specimens. These elicit a critical response to the "framing" of the museum even in the most disingenuous of visitors. As she states in *Naturalezas*, the volume reflecting on her installations at the Museo Nacional de Ciencias Naturales, natural history museums are receptacles of all that is strange and beautiful. Usually steeped in darkness, light filters in only here and there, randomly illuminating objects that have been lying around, gathering dust, sometimes for years. The fact that there is *so much* there that no one could ever possibly see it all or take it all in makes the collection appear endless, like Borges's labyrinths. In these spaces, "information, seemingly infinite, can never be recovered and is transformed into a monster" ["la información, inagotable, jamás puede recuperarse y se transforma en un monstruo"].[29]

3.14. Worm Museum
Installation Reproducing Ole Worm's famous cabinet of wonders
Photo © Rosamond W. Purcell 2007
Courtesy of the artist

True to her fascination with these marvelous, often whimsical, contingent, and overflowing collections, Purcell recently recreated (from the 1655 engraving) the no-longer-extant Danish physician and naturalist Ole Worm's famous seventeenth-century Wunderkammer at various universities across the United States

(Harvard; Mt. Holyoke College)³⁰ and put it in dialogue with her own collection of worn and weathered objects. These she had amassed by sifting over a twenty-year span through William Buckminster's increasingly dilapidated antiques shop and his eleven-acre junkyard in Owl's Head. While natural history museums depend on the massive collecting (and killing) of specimens, Purcell inverts the process. In her sifting through Buckminster's junkyard, she frees natural history from the shackles of museology by showing how natural history in turn works to reclaim consumer objects. The re-creation of Ole Worm's cabinet therefore includes real specimens of some of the more visible objects in the engraving representing the cabinet (a narwhal tooth, tortoise shells, and the branch of a tree growing around the jaw of a horse—now in a museum in Copenhagen—that has so fascinated Purcell). In addition to these items on loan from diverse museums, the "rusted, bent, chewed, twisted, oxidized, and worm-eaten objects" in Purcell's own collection were used and made to "look like" objects and specimens in Ole Worm's cabinet. In the second room, the contemporary cabinet is filled entirely with Purcell's own collection of junk from Owl's Head (piles of tattered books, discarded automobile parts, old clocks, and obsolete machinery). Purcell's re-creations of cabinets of wonders, from both the seventeenth and twenty-first centuries, in dialogue with each other, are a "contemporary homage," she explains, "to our all-American trash."³¹

Art made out of trash: a contradiction in terms, an oxymoron if ever there was one, trashart is generally discussed in the art world under the heading "recycled art." In Latin America, Africa, and other places where the incursion of capitalism is leaving trash on city streets and in growing heaps seemingly everywhere in the landscape, trash is most often recycled and reused out of necessity. Necessity here has quite literally been the mother of invention. While many western artists have been inspired by the myriad uses (recycling, reusing, transforming) to which trash is put in underdeveloped countries, the position of artists like Purcell vis-à-vis trash is very different. "I've never had to dig from necessity, only from curiosity," writes Purcell in Owl's Head (68). While artists like Purcell sift through junkyards, these artists' intervention within a western context makes visible precisely that which—like death—is banned from sight and sanitized (most often buried in "landfills" set under placid fields of grass and the insistent circling of seagulls, the idyll interrupted here and there only by vents). Indeed, Purcell makes of that which is discarded and that to which provenance is denied something not only visually but experientially central. Also, in her placing of trashart next to works traditionally considered "art," she calls into question the ways in which we create value and meaning, thus undermining the divide that separates "high" art from both artifacts (seen as use objects) and discarded consumer products. Purcell mines the Owl's Head junkyard in search of "specimens" just as natural historians formerly mined the world. Working at the limits of both art and natural history, she is fascinated by the many ways nature reclaims the discarded products of consumer culture in the junkyard. In what is probably the most vital passage in Owl's Head, she writes, "I spend most of my life surrounded by man-made objects. I am familiar with the surface of things. To find them embedded in the natural world was a newfound pleasure—still—I had never seen so much stuff to which so much had happened." Her list of what has happened is reminiscent of the many endless lists of specimens named and connected only by long series of "and" (the rhetorical figure of polysyndeton) that overtook so many natural histories—only, in this case, refuse refuses even that tenuous connection:

> Fraying, tattered, cracked, flattened, swollen, dried, scrawny, collapsed, shredded, peeling, torn, warped, weathered, faded, bristling, moldy, clenched, tangled, punctured, battered, bashed-in, scooped-up, withered, engorged, trampled, toppled, crushed, bald, listing, leaning, twisting, hanging, buried, wedged, jammed, impaled, straggling, stretched, disjointed, disemboweled, skinned, docked, gnawed, entrenched. Broken glass knotted to the earth by tenacious weeds, stinging burrs smothering the paths, scaffolding wrenched between boulders or gaping loose, leaving the framework to dangle from the sky (*Owl's Head,* 29).

Purcell reclaims these objects from the work of nature in her search for the impressionistic play of colors, shapes, textures, and patina that will allow her art to flourish. The pile of debris rising skyward in front of the transfixed eyes of Walter Benjamin's angel of history is transformed by the loving and laborious reconstruction of the installation artist. Books look like rocks, rusty nails and other metals look like animal specimens, old beat-up suitcases look like something else altogether. Set next to one another, like next to like, Purcell's junkyard objects are salvaged not only from the ravages of time but also from the forces of symbolization and commercialization to which they may have been subjected. She thus frees them and reclaims for them their original "objecthood" (*Owl's Head,* 19). The work of animals chewing and nesting through texts is crucial in this transformation. She photographs a beer can washed up by the ocean and found in Owl's Head, transformed into a marine specimen, and asks: "At what point does a manufactured object turn into an organism? Do objects *drown?* Do they ever possess a life—beyond batteries—that might be taken away? Is an object transmuted into another substance ever, like a fossil, turned from flesh and bone to stone? When does an inanimate object become worthy of a scientific name? I name the typewriter *Underwoodensis corrupta,* a close invertebrate cousin to an echinoid" (*Owl's Head,* 51).[32] As she explains, "a book that was just full of text" is usually disregarded as an object (one could add: much like a photograph) by readers who, intent on using it as a source of information, look through the object onto the text.

Her installation *Two Rooms* plays with this recycling of written texts by mice and mites. Indeed, Purcell's parallel "recontextualization" therefore works to bring to the fore the very "objecthood" of books. On Purcell's bookshelves they are read as a palette of weathered texture, color, and appearance—illuminated manuscripts of sorts.[33] Purcell's deep—visceral, if you will—obsession with books, however, is not limited to avidly reading or collecting them. Like many natural historians before her, in her own work she conjoins text and image, description and representation, thereby highlighting the ongoing and productive dialogue that has been taking place throughout the centuries between art and science. Perhaps more importantly, however, through the counterpoint between text and image in all her works, Purcell continues natural history's wresting of text and representation away from religion: illuminated manuscripts now no longer shed light on the immutable "word of God" but rather on the continually transformative work of nature.

The friendship between Purcell and Buckminster that developed over twenty years is

not devoid of tension. Purcell's desire for certain objects in his junk-yard, she writes, is usually thwarted whenever Buckminster can smell "provenance." The two therefore play a little game of cat and mouse: whenever Purcell intuits he will smell provenance—a genealogy of sorts—she shows no interest whatsoever in the objects she most covets. Lack of provenance is ultimately what lands objects in the trash heap; provenance in turn is what lifts them out of there. Provenance is also that which is so often misplaced when objects are taken away from their cultural contexts; the often-fictional account of an object's genealogy then replaces its biography. The need for provenance is what drove the insistence on tagging all the specimens arriving at the Real Gabinete, and it underlies archival museological practices.

3.15a. *Fred Wilson in Hood Museum storage*
Photo Barbara Thompson 2006
*Courtesy of the Hood Museum of Art,
    Dartmouth College*

3.15b. *Installation detail of Louisiana
    Exposition life-cast heads*
"Fred Wilson: So Much Trouble in the
    World—Believe It Or Not!"
*Photo Barbara Thompson 2006
Courtesy of the Hood Museum of Art,
    Dartmouth College*

In sifting through the debris left in the wake of cultures, archaeologists work not only to find objects but also to identify and create a narrative and a history or biography of sorts for the misplaced remains found. Objects with no tags, no provenance, no genealogies, and no biographies are set adrift; their fate is usually to gather dust in museums' basements. (Increasingly, however, as the recent lawsuit against the Getty Center and other museums shows, in the art world the lack of provenance generally indicates that a particular work of art was stolen. Conversely, as we will see in the Epilogue, provenance is sometimes invented in order to center-stage an object in a collection, such as the feather headdress from Mexico known until recently as "Montezuma's").[34]

Understanding that that which is not exhibited may in fact be equally important in shaping the meaning of a collection, installation artists like Fred Wilson look through entire collections, focusing particularly on what museums hold in their storage facilities and "mining" them in search of the hidden (or invisible because obvious) narrative of those museums. In the case of Dartmouth College's Hood Museum (one of the oldest and largest college museums in the country), Fred Wilson predictably unearthed hundreds of busts of Daniel Webster, but he also found that the museum had inherited part of Robert Ripley's *Odditorium*—a whimsical collection of the odd and marvelous first displayed at the Chicago World's Fair in 1933. Ripley, a high school dropout, received an honorary degree from Dartmouth College in 1939 with the help of a Dartmouth alum who was also the producer of Ripley's radio show. This collaboration opened the way for a large wooden plank labeled "Ripley's *Believe It or Not!*" and over one hundred items in Ripley's collection to find their way into the Hood Museum.[35] Among these "ethnographic" items were Native and African American busts that Fred Wilson displayed in rows with the title "Louisiana Purchase Exposition": life-cast heads referring to the 1904 Louisiana Purchase Exposition or St. Louis World's Fair centerpiece, the "University of Man" display, which assembled people from the Americas, Asia, and Africa in reconstructed villages as "living displays."[36] As Barbara Thompson puts it in the catalogue to the exhibition, early collections were amassed during a period "when 'religion,' 'science,' and 'technology' together became the foundation for colonialism and its conquering fulcrum" and thus, the Hood Museum's origins are no different.[37]

In the same way as Fred Wilson trawls through the bowels of museums in search of their apparently whimsical origins, Rosamond Purcell's fascination with discarded objects coincides with her and Stephen Jay Gould's search for those myriad specimens and objects collected but not displayed in natural history museums. Their sifting through these largely abandoned spaces is driven by the understanding that what the visitor sees at any given time is only the tip of the iceberg—what remains hidden from sight in a museum's bowels is what actually drives the narrative of who we are and what we know.[38] Indeed, the objects that remain jumbled, relegated to the basement, the ones that never see the light of day, are actually the ones that tell us most about "our intimate connections with all life" (*Illuminations*, 11). If classification is "truly the mirror of our thoughts [and] its changes through time the best guide to the history of human perception," then what remains unclassified, Purcell and Gould argue (much like Buffon before them), is therefore free of the constraints of order and hence provides the most artistic freedom. There is a very painful photograph in their postmodern bestiary (a bestiary that aims to detach the specimen from its use value for us) of a display by Harvard's curators of Goliath beetles. Instead of being placed in military rows, the beetles are randomly arranged; and instead of being pinned through the body with very thin, almost invisible steel wire, as is traditionally done, the beetles have very visible nails driven through them. In all their terrible beauty, as "shining points of metal in an organic matrix" (*Illuminations*, 29), they are mute testament to the accuracy of Nehemiah Grew's description of the collection at the Royal Society in London in 1681 as a most "noble a hecatomb."[39] Purcell also photographs two owls, their eyes stuffed with cotton balls. The caption underneath the picture reflects on the fact that the bird

3.16. *Owls*
Vertebrate collection
Museo Nacional de Ciencias Naturales, Madrid
In the publication reflecting on Purcell's work at the Museo de Ciencias Naturales in Madrid, where this photo appears, Purcell writes: "The Argentine writer Borges also was blind. He, and his blind father and another blind man before his father, were directors of Buenos Aires' National Library. Let us imagine a blind owl flying and a blind librarian."
(Naturalezas, 32)
Photo © Rosamond W. Purcell 2007

3.17a. *Stunning butterfly exhibit*
Harvard Museum of Natural History
Photo Spitta 2006

that is most farsighted at night is displayed as blind in the natural history museum. Poetically, blindness here is paralleled to that of Borges, who was renowned as a bibliophile and who made his living, ironically, as a blind librarian.

As a result of these reflections and their photography driven by such considerations, *Illuminations: A Bestiary* and *Swift as a Shadow* are probably two of the most terrifyingly beautiful and poetic books I have read, with the violence done by natural history to the environment apparent on every page. Each image a devastating memorial to loss, the reader's eyes try to avoid but are invariably drawn to the stunning photographs of stuffed flamingos, their hanging heads and beaks seen upside down and therefore as if smiling, bird skeletons, transparent frogs, rigid fish jaws, hare heads and bodies, elephant skin, fabulous quetzal feathers, etc. In all their splendor, the quetzal feathers almost seem to contradict "the general theme that death and procedures of collection and storage strip away information." It is art's role, as understood by Purcell and Gould, to undo the ravages of science, to "reanimate" the many millions

86

of specimens that have been left somehow stranded (*Illuminations,* 82). While the red quetzal feathers will indeed fade with time, the green, Gould explains, is not a pigment but iridescence consisting of microscopic granules that "break white light into brilliant greens, blues, and golds that shift and sparkle with intensity and angle of illumination." That which does not exist, then, is that which therefore cannot be killed to be preserved—the green color, an effect of refraction—the figment of our imagination, paradoxically, is what "will remain" (*Illuminations,* 82).

Of course, the uncanny logic that everything that exists can be killed and preserved drove natural history from its inception. The rows upon rows of mothball-smelling stuffed birds, insects, and animals in many museums are mute witness to this impossible logic and to the increasingly apparent paradox that those "preserved" specimens, given today's exponential rates of extinction, may end up being the only examples left of any particular species. Natural history museums that remain vital today do so paradoxically by warning visitors marching by collections of "preserved" animals about the dangers of global warming and of the imminent extinction facing millions of species, and indeed, our own. In *On the Natural History of Destruction* and *The Rings of Saturn,* W. G. Sebald takes these warnings one step further, writing from the perspective of a natural historian telling the story of the extinction of the human race. The visitor to these museums has somehow to reconcile simultaneously beautiful and gruesome exhibits with somber signs full of warnings. The illogic of preservation is maintained by the fiction of the museum, by particularly stunning exhibits where the underlying drive to find and display the rarest of all things shapes the exhibit and awes the visitor, and by the final mise en abîme that is the museum's shop. There, on your way out, the visitor is tempted by a beautiful Peruvian silver pin made from the wings of a butterfly like those in a glass case exhibit in the museum. Politically savvy, the shop sells butterfly wings harvested from butterflies that have lived out their natural lives on tropical farms. This activity, the museum claims, helps preserve wild butterfly populations and provides income for the local residents.[40]

3.17b. *Butterfly pin*
Museum shop, Harvard Museum of Natural History
Photo Spitta 2006

Like Purcell, another installation artist intrigued by the paradoxes of natural history is Mark Dion, whose work on the U.S. fascination with dinosaurs we encountered in the previous chapter. Dion, too, plays with natural history. His book *Polar Bear (Ursus maritimus)* is a collection of photographs taken of polar bear displays in natural history museums all over the world. A mute testament to captured and taxidermied polar bears, their white fur becomes a blank slate on which science has written its violence and—used as captions—on which museums display their poetics. Dion therefore includes no text in the book other than small labels that tell the reader only in what museum he photographed the display. Somewhat differently from Purcell but in the same spirit, he sifts through the trash heap of history, adopting the persona of the archaeologist to make his modern Wunderkammern. Wearing a hard hat, he dredges the bottom of the canals in Venice and looks through the muck in order to create his Wunderkammer *Raiding Neptune's Vault.* Elsewhere he recovers other trash and displays it in museums.

One of his more archaeological installations was a double-sided cabinet of wonders filled with the "treasures" or detritus (broken glass, nails, tin cans, and other unlabeled garbage) found in the dredging of the Thames (*Tate Thames Dig 1999*);[41] one consists of trash gathered on city streets, and yet another consists of cabinets filled with fragments, shards, and other garbage found at the construction site during the recent expansion of the Museum of Modern Art (exhibited in the basement of the MOMA when it reopened). In another installation Dion turns his critique toward universities and their collections.[42] In the same spirit and like Purcell, Dion is also fascinated with books. An installation at the Massachusetts Museum of Contemporary Art, *Library for the Birds of Massachusetts* (2005), consisted of a large cage and tree from which books and other reading materials hung. It was filled with African finches that flew about the branches and the books, perching, eating, nesting, etc. Visitors stood outside the cage watching the birds and the books, but in an interesting twist, they also watched visitors who had entered the cage wander about amid the birds perusing the books, and they, in turn, looked out at the visitors looking at them in the cage. Conflating three spaces traditionally kept apart (a library, a diorama, a zoo cage), the installation was part of a larger exhibit, Becoming Animal: Contemporary Art in the Animal Kingdom, to which Dion and other artists were invited to reflect on the implications of contemporary scientists' assertions that "they can no longer specify the exact difference between human and animal, living and dead."[43] Another installation entitled *An Account of Six Disastrous Years in the Library for Animals* sets taxidermied birds and other animals amid books, so as to signal the violence done nature by travelers and their accounts. Dion's libraries, of course, play with misplacement and the framing done by natural history museums, implicitly entering into a dialogue with Guillermo Gómez-Peña and Coco Fusco's celebrated performance *The Couple in the Cage* (1992), with which these performance artists reflected on the "encounter of two worlds" (as the quincentenary of the discovery was euphemistically referred to in Spain) by traveling throughout Europe, the United States, and Latin America in a cage as recently discovered "savages."

3.18. The Library for the Birds of New York
1996 Mark Dion

(opposite, top) 3.19. An Account of Six
    Disastrous Years in the Library for Animals
1992 Mark Dion

(opposite, bottom) 3.20. *Performance of*
    The Couple in the Cage
Coco Fusco and Guillermo Gómez-Peña
Madrid 1992
Photo Nancy Lytle
Courtesy of Guillermo Gómez-Peña

In the same vein but more tongue in cheek, the London Zoo reversed the gaze a few summers ago with its four-day exhibit of eight *Homo sapiens*.[44] The distinction between human/animal and living/dead depends—as with so many other distinctions and binaries that structure our certainties—on hierarchies of space and how objects are organized in space, all of which of course entail a prescribed relation between the object and the subject. As we saw in the Introduction, in 1913 Duchamp placed a urinal in a museum, leading the way. More than a thousand books or critiques, that simple act radically called into question the politics of display. Not much

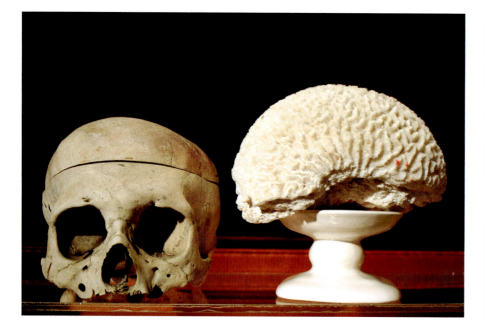

3.21a. *Skull and brains, detail*
Main Street Museum, White River Junction,
  Vermont
Courtesy of David Fairbanks and the Trustees
  of the Main Street Museum, 2008

3.21b. *Portrait of the museum director's great-*
  uncle, washer fluid, and dead cat
Main Street Museum, White River Junction,
  Vermont
Courtesy of David Fairbanks and the Trustees
  of the Main Street Museum, 2008

later, the surrealists and modern artists such as Picasso started to experiment with abstraction, inspired by exhibits of African and American indigenous "artifacts" in natural history museums (particularly the Musée de l'Homme and the Trocadero).[45] The surrealists re-created and reinvented the Wunderkammern with their famous 1936 display at the Charles Ratton Gallery (Paris) and in the Château d'Oiron.[46] They also inspired contemporary forms of collecting in the homes not only of the cosmopolitan rich, but of all classes in Europe. Indeed, it might not be altogether hyperbolic to affirm that, as in the period of the Wunderkammern, when collecting became a generalized craze across Europe, and much later thanks to the surrealists' fascination with and collections of African and Polynesian objects, probably few homes today do not boast of some Native American or African artifact. "The Turkmen saddlebag, Masai spear, Dinka basket," acquired because of the owner's "quest for novelty" and love of the rare, foreign, and beautiful, and arranged according to the logic of what Arjun Appadurai calls the "aesthetics of decontextualization," serve as *both* an index of world travel and thus cosmopolitanism, and also as anchors of personal memory.[47] In the end, tourism reproduces the violence of conquest simply on another level, when objects are radically misplaced to serve as proof of and anchors for the travelers' recollections of the trips they have taken.

The forms of misplacement that underlie the aesthetics of artists like Rosamond Purcell, Mark Dion, Fred Wilson, Guillermo Gómez-Peña, and Coco Fusco, and that of institutions such as the London Zoo (to mention only a few), and their interventions depend on inverting the gaze, putting people in place of the specimen, and generally messing with the order of things. In response to these emergent alternative ways of placing and positioning subjects and objects, two museums reposition both the subject and the object in such a way as to create an exhilarating and ultimately liberating epistemological crisis in the visitor. Famous in Los Angeles is the Museum of Jurassic Technology,[48] which is the topic of Lawrence Wechsler's *Mr. Wilson's Cabinet of Wonder: Pronged Ants, Horned Humans, Mice on Toast, and Other Marvels of Jurassic Technology* (1995). Closer to home, in the economically depressed town of White River Junction, the Main Street Museum, founded in 1992, organizes its motley assembly of junk and other objects according to the following rubrics: "Oxidation, Tangled Things," and, echoing Purcell and Dion's interest in decomposition and transformation, "Evidence of Deconstruction in the Construction and Carpentry Trades." An "experiment in material culture." The collection encompasses all sorts of things, including an exhibit framing a pair of shoes bought at K-Mart titled "Daniel Webster's Shoes (maybe)" and a huge papier-mâché "monster" displayed in a glass case.[49] (The sign explains that it was "dredged" out of the Connecticut River by the museum's founder, David Fairbanks Ford, and his mother.) It is clearly framed as a fake, thus serving as an ironic commentary on Barnum's practice of "inventing" monsters such as his famous "mermaid." The Main Street Museum's exhibit, however, clearly states that the difference between them lies in the framing, for, while Barnum would go to any lengths to attract an audience, the Main Street Museum attracts a devout following precisely because of its unpacking of the ethics and aesthetics of display and museology. The randomness of the objects collected serves as a reflection on how museums often depend on the whims of collectors and hence often refuse classification, instead serving as mere deposits of odd and quirky things. As the local newsletter, the *Vermont Standard,* explains, "Museums of the past were like antique shops of the present or any randomly selected day on e-Bay. Items as diverse and completely unrelated as a mink in a jar, the sword of Pilgrim John Standish, Elvis' gallstones, the toenail of a saint, and pieces of the downed *Challenger* might all show up in one place simply because of the whims of collectors."[50] In a similar vein, the Museum of Jurassic Technology in Los Angeles recently exhibited Jay's decaying dice photographed by Purcell. While Purcell, Dion, and others upset epistemological hierarchies and disciplinary boundaries by placing objects and subjects along different, hopefully more egalitarian planes and relationships, the Main Street Museum may go even farther in its manifesto, printed on flyers at the museum, which states that "there are no meaningless objects in the universe." Literally anything is worthy of telling a tale and serving as an exhibit. And because there are no meaningless objects, viewing subjects and viewed objects enter into a completely different relationship with each other.

Figures 3.22 a, b, c
Museum of Jurassic Technology
The miniature trailer and the pincushions are part of the exhibit "Garden of Eden on Wheels: Collections from Los Angeles Area Mobile Home and Trailer Parks."
Photos Joshua Polon

"Everything Matters" is a sticker on the purse of Nana Tchitchoua, whom I met on the roof of the museum where she was heating coals to make tea in a samovar. The sticker comes from a group of artists from northern Sweden who call themselves Raketa and who visited the museum in 2006 and befriended David Wilson, Alexis Hyman, and the other members of the Museum of Jurassic Technology.

Fairbanks asserts that items in the exhibits stay on display "based on the sustained interest that has been shown them and the attentiveness they demonstrate towards us." Perhaps articulating the unsettling Main Street Museum's agenda even more clearly is its manifesto: "If respect is the first criterion for the operation of the Museum, and love's ultimate derivation is respect, then we are a collection based on love. Hierarchies need not be oppressive" (museum flyer). Increasingly, then, critics, photographers, and installation artists are using the Wunderkammern as the frame with which to undo the frame. The Wunderkammern are reclaimed as whimsical, Baroque, magical, performative, post-apocalyptic yet pre-scientific spaces. These revisited spaces, where the gaze is reversed and objects either talk back or cannibalize the viewer, serve to formulate a critique of the hierarchies of natural history and its ethics and aesthetics.

Coming under more and more scrutiny is the distinction between high art and native art upon which the placing of art objects depends (high art in the art museum and indigenous art in natural history collections). Despite the radically different angles and positions from which all of the critiques outlined above are being leveled, however, they seem to have one thing in common: they are all *playful* and *sad*. And they all depend on playfully rearranging the order of the world by messing with and subverting the order of objects that we have come to depend on for our certainty. Moreover, by playfully throwing everything into disarray, these critiques refuse the subject/object opposition that underlies western epistemology. Purcell writes: "Anyone, I suppose, who contemplates dessicated animals and altered objects for a living is bound by one box or another: camera, cabinet, room, or institution within which floats the dark box that is the imagination. I am stuck with containment. And yet I am always trying to pick the lock" (*Owl's Head*, 175). The multiple destabilizations of these projects propose a mutually productive subject/object relationship. The choice of words used to signal this interrelationship is instructive: objects in museum's basements "scream out" at Fred Wilson (Hood pamphlet); Purcell

3.23a and b. Tudo continua sempre
   [Everything continues]
Farnese de Andrade
Belo Horizonte and Rio de Janeiro, Brazil
*This cabinet installation piece is made out of
   recycled materials found on city streets and
   while beachcombing. The child's head is reminiscent of Ruysch's preserved babies in jars
   and the photographs of them taken by Purcell
   that play with the light distortions.*

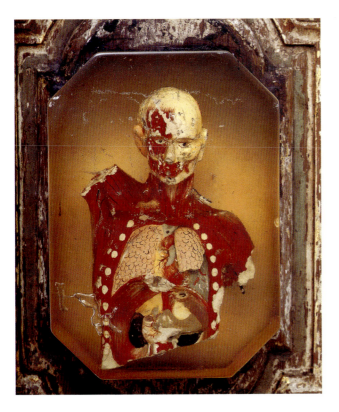

3.24. Untitled
Farnese de Andrade
Belo Horizonte and Rio de Janeiro, Brazil
This installation piece, again made out of trashed
objects, is untitled, but it is as if Farnese has
anticipated the Bodyworlds exhibits.

3.25. Hiroshima
Farnese de Andrade
Belo Horizonte and Rio de Janeiro, Brazil
This homage to the victims of Hiroshima is made
out of dozens of doll parts Farnese found
in the streets and in the trash. He further
mutilated them, meticulously burning and
otherwise doing violence to them.

"falls in love with the way things look" (*Owl's Head,* 19), or conversely, claims she spends a lot of time "impotent before the world of things" (*Owl's Head,* 219). Gretchen Worden asserts that objects seem to be, if not "looking at you," then sometimes even *being* you.[51] The divide between living organic beings and dead inorganic things shatters perhaps most visibly in Purcell's explanation of what happens when her teacher writes on the blackboard. Blackboards are made when sediments in salt and fresh water are put under metamorphic pressure and compacted into shale and slate. Chalk is made up of "millions of fossilized shells, algae, and single-celled animals called foraminifera" and lime made from "calcareous nano-fossils that died on shallow ocean floors, forming beds of chalk." Therefore, when, in order to explain the intricacies of the English language to her class, her English teacher takes up chalk to write on slate, she is "pressing creatures from an ocean against the bottom of a lake (*Owl's Head,* 79).

Purcell's implicit understanding that what at first looks "dead," such as chalk and slate, is in fact made up of organic matter, evidences a far richer way of viewing the world than that currently allowed by the operant science/humanities divide—insisting as it does on drawing a rather arbitrary line separating the subject from the object; the living, organic, from the dead, inorganic. Purcell's photographs and rescue of junkyard materials highlight moments of transition between subject and object: they play with ontological indeterminacy. A similar collapse of the person and the object, the subject and the object, drives the paintings of Spanish artist Cristóbal Toral, discussed in the Epilogue. Similarly, the Minas Gerais installation artist Farnese de Andrade (1926–96), adept at combing seashores and city streets in Belo Horizonte and Rio de Janeiro in search of trash and abandoned objects, represents Brazil as a land of immigrants by means of cabinets of wonders made up of driftwood and other found objects. Besides treating migration and poverty as so much driftwood, de Andrade is adept at critiqu-

ing natural history's framing of Latin America. Some of his "found" object compositions are multiply allegorical, and even seem to anticipate the current fascination of
exhibits of human plastination (and their spooky underlining of our bodies' objecthood in the displays). Reminding us of W. J. T. Mitchell's observation about our inability to distinguish between subject and object, and our continued "magical" relation to
images (and hence our inability to disfigure a photograph of our mother, for example),
de Andrade in his *Hiroshima* transmits the violence done to human beings by human
beings (embodied in the atom bomb) through a composition of myriad miniature doll
parts meticulously burned and disfigured.[52]

As if also reflecting on these artists' works, Steven Jay Gould insists that his collaboration with Purcell rescues that first moment when the Wunderkammern were
spaces of magical messiness, prior to the ordering of the world and the emergence of
science. "Intellectual life," he writes, "should not be construed as two cultures of science and humanities at war, or even at variance. Human culture arose from the material substrate of a complex brain; and science and art meld in continuity." The fossil
fish embedded in Solnhofen limestone, as discussed in the Introduction, is never just
simply that; it has been successively transformed over time and "overlayered" in multiple ways. There are cracks in the limestone showing the effects of time, a metal staple
where someone had tried to hold it together, various markings made by scientists; and
it was finally reinscripted as an art object when Purcell photographed it for the book
Crossing Over: Where Art and Science Meet (2000). Gould therefore advances the position that we need to understand things in their "complex totality." Only then do we
avoid the existential and theoretical aporias that stem from our systemic bypassing of
the "unbroken transition from things of nature to things of art, flesh to rock to paper
to ink," and the myriad ways in which mind is embedded in nature.[53] Taken as a whole,
the collaborative work between Gould and Purcell not only links scientific text to photograph in the tradition of natural science. What also emerges from their texts is the
utter indeterminacy of what constitutes matter and what constitutes mind, and their
highlighting of our inability to actually distinguish between them.

More importantly even, and going far beyond the questioning of the disciplinary
boundaries that shape our consciousness, Purcell's fascination—like that of many other
contemporary artists—with junk, trash, and the discarded and obsolescent points to a
fundamental shift at work in our culture. In his readings of Klee's "Angelus novus" as the
angel of history, Walter Benjamin seems to have intuited this shift. Transfixed by what
it is seeing, the angel is being propelled backward into the future by a storm blowing
from Paradise, as a mountain of debris rises skyward in front of him.[54] Perhaps explaining why Klee's angel looks like one of the pieces of twisted metal collected by Purcell in
Owl's Head, and as if to say that the angel has reached the outer limits of the possible,
contemporary artists see their work as that of sifting through the mountains of debris
that progress leaves in its wake. The gesture of reclaiming trash for art entails an important undoing of the binary subject/object relationship that underpins our epistemology
and that so depends on valuing certain objects over others (by their rarity, as was the
case in the early Wunderkammern, or by their investment value, as is the case today).
Art made from trash radically democratizes things and grants *all* objects not only the
same degree of interest but also the same potential for creating meaning.

PART II

MIGRATING ICONS AND SACRED GEOGRAPHIES IN THE AMERICAS

The trajectory of the conquistadores since their arrival in Mexico, that is, an authentic historical narrative, was wrought with the indigenous techniques of the marvelous Lienzo de Tlaxcala that allowed indigenous scribes to represent the conquistadores with their most significant elements: horses, guns, cannons and muskets, iron and armature, as well as those elements of the indigenous world such as temples, plumes, bows, and irons represented at the moment of their destruction by fire and brutal killing.

[El derrotero de los conquistadores desde su ingreso a México, esto es, una auténtica narración histórica, quedó plasmado con la técnica indígena en el maravilloso Lienzo de Tlaxcala, que permitió representar a los conquistadores con sus elementos más significativos: el caballo, las armas de fuego, los cañones y mosquetes, sus fierros y armaduras; y también los del mundo indígena: templos, penachos, lanzas, flechas, todo lo cual se destruía en medio del incendio y de la matanza aniquiladora.]

—Ernesto de la Torre Villar, *Breve historia del libro en México* (Translation mine)

CHAPTER FOUR

GUADALUPE NATION

Disappearing Objects, National Narratives

I F THE FIRST PART OF this study focused on the objects that arrived in Europe post-
1492 and their seismic effect on the epistemological table of the period and the role
they played in the inception of modernity, the objects the conquistadores brought with
them to the New World had an equally profound—if asymmetrical—effect. At the first
moment of contact, horses, guns, cannons, muskets, iron, armature, alphabetic writing, and religious images—the sword and the pen—faced off against native cultures
in the natural history of destruction as told by chroniclers and indigenous scribes in
post-Conquest histories (e.g., the *Lienzo de Tlaxcala* mentioned in the epigraph). The
Spanish and the Portuguese machinery of war were greeted with wonder by indigenous
peoples, but it was an altogether different form of wonder than that which had initially
greeted displaced objects in Europe. One could even say that it was a deadly form of
wonder; indeed, indigenous peoples had little time during which to process awe into
anything other than fear. Later, with the inception of colonial regimes, the initial violence of the first years of contact became codified as epistemic and legal violence by the
successive colonial administrations intent upon suppressing indigenous cosmologies
and epistemologies. In their lieu, racial and other classifications that had emerged in
Europe under the sign of Eurocentrism reorganized the hemisphere in the interest of
promoting unequal forms of exchange for centuries to come.

Much has been written about the effects of the Conquest and the transatlantic
exchange of diseases, agricultural products, and animals. And while much has also
been written about the syncretic religious symbols and practices that emerged as a consequence of the successive evangelization campaigns, less emphasis has been placed
on the highly performative cultural practices that arose in the New World. Indeed,
unlike in the early American English colonies, which were largely shaped by the Reformation and Puritanism, in Latin America the Counter-Reformation-inflected Baroque
aesthetics that arrived with Catholicism would allow for great creativity in how indigenous and Spanish cultures adapted to each other despite colonial violence. Given the
Baroque's aesthetics of inclusiveness and horror vacui, the decoration of thousands of
churches across the continent became the pretext for the training of indigenous artists,
many of whom of necessity, yet often inadvertently, went against Church dogma and
poured new wine into old vessels. Churches became rich and overflowing spaces that
encompassed western and indigenous conceptions of art and religiosity, sometimes
quite cozily. Imposed through sustained evangelization campaigns, Catholicism—as

critics working on syncretism have repeatedly pointed out—nevertheless therefore allowed transculturated indigenous forms of religiosity and performances to continue under the guise of Church ritual. Across the Americas, to give but one very visible example, indigenous altars that had formerly marked high mountains were destroyed and replaced by crosses. The result was that from as far north as Denver and extending across the U.S. Southwest and all the way down the continent as far south as Patagonia, space is marked as sacred. Indeed, this type of sacred space divides Anglo from Latin America much better and more effectively than the U.S.-Mexico border. This space and the syncretic religious performative tradition that arose in Latin America as it is embodied in the cult of the Virgin of Guadalupe in Mexico is the subject of the second part of this book.

Processes of transculturation were not set in motion immediately. Anthropologist James Lockhart points out that between 1519, when the Spaniards arrived in Mexico, and about 1540 or 1550 there was little productive contact between Nahuas and Spaniards. Náhuatl barely registered the presence of the Spaniards, other than bowing to evangelization in the adoption of Christian baptismal names. The presence of unknown objects brought by the conquistadores and the concomitant immense post-Conquest cultural and epistemological shift that would shape modern Latin America began to be massively registered in Náhuatl only after the Spaniards, with the establishment of towns between the 1540s and 1640s, gradually forced the reorganization of indigenous cultures. In this second stage, new terms entered the vocabulary, such as indigenized Spanish names for previously unknown objects, or outright adoptions of Spanish words. The names of new objects (such as *trigo*/wheat, *caballo*/horse, *vaca*/cow, *cochillo*/knife, *caxa*/box, *camixatli*/shirt) headed the list, entering the language along with the names for colonial posts that replaced indigenous forms of governance (*gobernador, regidor, alcalde*) and abstract legal and religious terms (*litigation, Mass*). The adoption of words designating different forms of measurement and value allowed Nahuas to function in a colonial context, which was of immense importance at this stage.[1]

The third stage that Lockhart outlines, the period from 1650 on, is crucial to this chapter. During this period indigenous forms of ethnic identification based on the notion of altepetl (locally based identification of a deity, a place, and a sense of ethnic belonging) began to expand beyond the local and regional to embrace what increasingly became a proto-nationalist understanding of place and identity. Toward the end of the seventeenth century, the local began to coexist with the proto-national, the radius of pilgrimages expanded, and the Virgin of Guadalupe became a centralizing cult that would unify people across ethnic and cultural divides. This period therefore saw the incorporation of Spanish verbs into Náhuatl (the Náhuatl ending *oa* was added to the infinitives, and the verbs were then conjugated like Náhuatl verbs), and it saw the increasing use of *calques*, whereby the meaning of native words expanded to accommodate foreign idioms and meanings (e.g., Náhuatl incorporated the verb *tener* and Spanish notions of possession).[2] Even more importantly, perhaps, it is during this stage that the first prominent written mention of the Virgin of Guadalupe appears. As a sign of the important social transformation that was taking place, the emergence of the Virgin in written accounts also points to the expansion of a highly syncretic and performative pilgrimage tradition.[3] This religious ritual was crucial in creating consensus and cohesion in the face of the threat and the potential for dispersion symptomatic of the third stage. Indeed, as Kertzer writes, basing himself on Durkheim's studies of rituals, "one of the crucial functions of ritual is to produce solidarity in the absence of any commonality of beliefs."[4] The spectacular space of religious performativity around the Virgin of Guadalupe worked both centrifugally to expand the cult far beyond its original site at Tepeyac and centripetally to embody the images of the Virgin, endowing them with magical power. Pilgrimages and other religious rituals therefore were instrumental in mitigating against the increased social stratification and marginalization of large numbers of people. These religious practices would therefore serve to somewhat soften the impact of the emergence of proto-nationalism in the seventeenth century. As was happening in the iconoclastic wars of Reformation and Counter-Reformation Europe, the real battle in the Americas was fought over the status of the image in general, and the religious image—demonic idol or Christian icon—in particular. Gruzinski's title for his history of Mexico during the post-Conquest period, *Images at War*, is notable in this regard;[5] instructive too is the history of the emergence that I will outline of the cult of the Virgin of Guadalupe, and how, most recently, the Virgin has become a runaway image (see Chapter Five). The focus here is on how the Church invented a corpus of narratives, myths, and legends not only to harness the rapidly spreading cult to the lettered city,[6] but also to create a new sense of place. The convoluted story that the priests developed with the intent of evangelizing actually resulted, then, in creating the script for the future nation and laying its foundation in a mestizo imaginary.

In the New World, the policies of the Council of Trent (in their three sessions between 1545 and 1563) regarding the insistence on religious images and on the visual as the privileged access to divinity[7] shaped the early evangelization campaigns and gave rise to the aesthetics of what we now call the New World Baroque. Sight was subjected to the spiritual as access to the divine and also as an instrument of power over idolatry.[8] An analysis of the methods used by the extirpators of idolatries shows that early on in the colonial period, priests learned that knowing is seeing.[9] In an anthropology avant la lettre, they realized that in order to detect idolatrous rites and objects (so as to eradicate them), priests had to be able to identify them, and in order to identify idolatrous practices, they had to obtain inside knowledge of indigenous cultures—otherwise these practices would remain invisible. Knowing is seeing. This became especially important after the initial period of conquest, when the Indians became savvy to the thinking of the Europeans and began to disguise their religious and cultural practices. As indigenous religious and cultural practices increasingly went underground, priests had to learn indigenous languages and learn about beliefs, rituals, sacred sites, and objects—and they could do this only by enlisting the help of native informants. Often, quite inadvertently, and even paradoxically, in their efforts to destroy idolatry, they ended up preserving and documenting native beliefs and sometimes even acting as ventriloquists for native discontent.[10] Sight therefore had a dual status in this context (as a way to God, and as a way of detecting idolatries and hence learning about the other), unlike in Europe, where the period post-Wunderkammern in Reformation-inflected areas increasingly harnessed sight to scientific knowledge, while in Counter-Reformation-dominated areas this emphasis was shared with and existed in tension with sight understood as the door to the divine.

The early Catholic tradition of sight as visualization of the divine was also complicated by the different relationship between images and written signs in Nahua culture, as well as by the fact that—given the incommensurability between languages and cultures—the Spaniards viewed the complexity of indigenous visual and representational practices as "illiteracy." The dismissal of Nahua forms of literacy erases an entire vital cultural register. Lois Parkinson Zamora, in her study of the New World Baroque, therefore argues instead for a concept of cultural *legibility* as opposed to narrow notions of literacy in areas where visual and verbal arts commingle in complex ways. She rescues the codices from the reification of the archive by highlighting the inextricable ties that—despite conquest and colonization—continue to bind the visual to the verbal in Latin America. Countering current theorizations of the "gaze," she shows that the New World Baroque, in its wild inclusivity, its irregular, decentered, asymmetrical, and non-normative perspectives, is the empire's response to colonialism. The Baroque therefore not only took root in Latin America but, outlasting the Baroque's demise in Europe, reached well into our time. Owing to its ability to incorporate and constitute itself out of the radically syncretic religiosity that was emerging from the incorporation of indigenous cosmologies and artistic practices, the Baroque continues its work to this day as a contestatory aesthetic.[11] The emergent artistic and religious syncretism undermined the Church's understanding of the religious icon as a mere index to the divine. Alejo Carpentier, as early as 1975 and paving the way for important current theorizations, pinned the New World Baroque's origins to the process of mestizaje. As he wrote, "all symbiosis, all mestizaje, engenders the baroque."[12] Viewed from this perspective, the Virgin of Guadalupe is not only Baroque, she is *the* mestizo form par excellence. Indeed, as I argued in the Introduction, mestizaje can *only* be "seen" through its manifestation in what, for lack of better words, are called "mestizo" forms and a mestizo aesthetic. The final shape that the Virgin's evolving iconicity (and with it her meaning) acquired was the result of the Church's emphasis on evangelization through images, the concomitant need to decorate thousands of churches and produce myriad religious images (given the economic and logistical impossibility of importing them all), and thus the dependence on the creation of schools of indigenous and mestizo painters and artisans who predictably transculturated Catholic rituals and dogma, creating new, blended, and syncretic forms.

Lack of certainty not only characterized that initial moment when rare and marvelous objects arriving from the Americas and elsewhere imploded Europe's self-understanding—much as grains of sand in a mechanism force it to grind to a halt—but also underlies this most visible of Latin America's national foundational hagiographies. The spectacular poetics and politics around Guadalupanism, which serve as a prime example, contrast with the increasing secularization of Europe. In the Americas the religious image became multiply polysemic and seemingly omnipresent—a runaway image of sorts—whose increasing power the Church invariably tried to control and, even more importantly, to harness through religious exegesis or intervening in the "creation" of national religious narratives. Indeed, unlike other colonial enterprises, and perhaps helping to explain the different outcomes today (e.g., why India and Africa in the postcolonial period are so different from Latin America), the Spanish colonial administration, together with Church exegetes, actively engaged in the creation of syncretic, polysemic symbols originally tied to religious rituals, mobilized as potent national symbols whose function was that of achieving "solidarity without consensus," much as political symbols do today in secular states.[13] No better example of the ambiguity of signs and fraught polysemy exists than that of the Virgin of Guadalupe: without achieving consensus, she unifies an entire nation under mestizaje, as Figure 4.1 shows, where she overlooks the different castes as well as the natural bounty of the Americas. The narrative development of the Guadalupan cult out of the miracles, miraculous paintings, and other religious objects clearly reproduces the way in which objects are central to our cultures and identities, yet are made to perpetually disappear from sight.

Her story is that of multiple appropriations, reappropriations, and migrations. From the town of Guadalupe in Extremadura, her influence spread across Spain as she united the Spanish, helping them finally fight off the Moors. As many of Cortés's men hailed from Extremadura, Guadalupe then became the banner under which they in turn conquered Mexico. In Mexico, she allegedly miraculously appeared to the recently Christianized Indian Juan Diego only ten years after the fall of Tenochtitlán. Not coincidentally, allowing the Spanish Virgin to be transformed into the "mother" and "protectress" of Indians, the shrine erected in honor of her miraculous appearance on Tepeyac hill subsumed an important indigenous cult. It was therefore not at all surprising that in the nineteenth century, when he issued his "Grito de Dolores," Father Hidalgo would choose her as the banner under which to unite Mexico's diverse population in the war of independence from the Spaniards. Today, the brilliant collapse of the Virgin with the nation continues to be celebrated in the annual commemorations of Father Hidalgo's rallying cry every September 16 when the President steps out onto the balcony of the National Palace, bearing the flag and shouting to the multitude thronging in Mexico City's central square, "Viva la Independencia! Viva Hidalgo! Viva Morelos! Viva Juárez! Viva México!"[14]

Rituals of cohesion such as these create consensus around fraught notions of nationality and belonging. The cult of the Virgin of Guadalupe is therefore crucial in underlining Mexican nationalism, since it served as the national hagiography of mestizaje. As many have repeatedly pointed out, "she" is the glue that holds the nation together.[15] Indeed, her dark color may also partly help explain why she would appear to an Indian, why her cult took root so readily in Mexico, and why she became patroness of Indians and poor people so soon after the Conquest. Mexico City was built on the ruins of Tenochtitlán, and many of the modern highways and thoroughfares follow the main routes of the former Aztec city. Perhaps more importantly still, the megalopolis is situated in the center of the country, at the crossroads between north and south, east and west. The Guadalupan Basilica at Tepeyac (once on the outskirts of the city) now is engulfed by the city and serves as the center both of the cult of the Virgin and of mestizaje as a foundational narrative. Moreover, in the immense main square (the symbolic center of the nation), dominated by an equally immense flag of Mexico, the cathedral stands next to the ruins of the former Aztec temple (Templo Mayor), making it necessary for the modern nation to establish its foundation on the basis of an idealized mestizaje even if in legal and political practice the nation has erased and/or marginalized living indigenous cultures. As the progression from Figure 4.2 to Figure 4.5 shows, the Virgin's representation has evolved parallel to her changing and ever expanding role: from the small, dark Virgin at Guadalupe in Extremadura, she has been successively whitened

4.1 *The Virgin of Guadalupe with mixed couples
and their mestizo children
Luis de Mena, eighteenth century
Museo de América, Madrid
Photo credit: Erich Lessing/Art Resource, NY*

and transformed into radiant GuadalupeNation. Indeed, there is no resemblance whatsoever between the Virgin that arrived in Mexico, brought by Cortés and his men, and the Virgin that dominates the national scene in Mexico. Today, that representation is again changing, as she is fast spreading her influence across the Americas (and particularly the U.S.) as a hemispheric symbol of Latin (and mestizo) unity beyond regional, religious affiliations.

The changes that took place in Europe and the Americas post-1492, when Europe discovered the Americas and the Americas discovered Europe, were not deeply asymmetrical only during the fifteenth century. Asymmetries continued to evolve along bifurcating paths, with the result that the difference between the continents today revolves around and is generally discussed in terms of different definitions and conceptions of modernity. If modernity, as is traditionally held, "is associated with the rise of a profane, rationalist culture in which explanations of the universe and human society in terms of a stable cosmic order give way to a scientific worldview which claims privileged access to truth,"[16] in peripheric modernities such as Mexico's, a pre-modern, indigenous worldview was allowed to persist, and indeed was fostered by the Baroque aesthetics of a Counter-Reformation-inflected Catholicism. Because of this, the crucial distinction between Europe and the United States and Latin America then (and particularly countries that to a great extent overlap with former indigenous empires) centers around the different status of the image and the very different visual and scientific economies that arise as a result. In the West, where the visual serves as an important tool of empiricism and scientific knowledge, the image is for the most part desacralized and subjected to writing. Images serve as an index of absence; that is, they re-present what is not there: flat and glamorous as photographic advertising, they are omnipresent in their attempt to fill the void that ensues when presence abandons images.

Despite this long secularizing trend, and despite images' long subjection to words, it is a fact nevertheless, as W. J. T. Mitchell argues, that we continue to hold "magical attitudes" toward images and hence a "double consciousness" in our response to different forms of representation. Images themselves seem to acquire a will of their own and subvert our intentions regarding them.[17] In contrast, in Latin America this double consciousness and images' refusal to be subjected to language is much more apparent.[18] Inflected by native visual traditions, the image-as-presence continues to coexist with the secular image-as-absence. As Parkinson Zamora explains: "Despite the diversity of indigenous groups in precontact America, then, a shared cultural substratum emerges that allows us to generalize an indigenous *image-as-presence*. Indigenous American cultures privileged the capacity of the visual image *to be*, or *become*, its object or figure. The image *contained* its referent, *embodied* it, made it present physically and experientially to the beholder. There was no dichotomy between presence and absence, no assumed

(opposite, top left) 4.2. *The Virgin of Guadalupe*
Guadalupe, Prov. Cáceres. Extremadura, Spain

(opposite, top right) 4.3. *Portrait of the Virgin of Guadalupe*
Basilica of Guadalupe
Tepeyac/La Villa, Mexico City
Photo Spitta 2004
According to Guadalupan tradition, this is Juan Diego's famous tilma (cloak) upon which the Virgin of Guadalupe imprinted her image in 1531. This miraculous image now hangs above the moving walkway in the new basilica.

(opposite, bottom left) 4.4. *The Virgin of Guadalupe*
Anonymous, nineteenth century
Restaurant in Malinalco, Mexico
Photo Spitta 2004
This is a typical nineteenth-century representation of the Virgin. Each individual ray is shown (versus the "mantle" shown today). The little angel at her feet cloaked in the colors of the Mexican flag connects this representation to Mexico's independence movement.

(opposite, bottom right) 4.5. *GuadalupeNation*
Sold at a stand in La Villa/Tepeyac, Mexico
Photo Spitta 2004

separation between image and object."[19] The Guadalupan cult is a prime example of this: the center of a massive pilgrimage tradition, the miraculous image mobilizes millions of people across Mexico. This pilgrimage tradition is largely driven by the pilgrim's desire to touch and, if that is not possible, then at least to be in the presence of the miraculous image. The result of this need for contagion with the sacred is a proliferation of embodied religious images and massive and spectacular forms of popular religiosity that contribute to subvert commonly held notions of what it means to be modern. Indeed, the relative centrality or marginality of science and scientific thinking as underpinning of national identities seems to be inversely proportional to conceptions of the image as either presence or absence. While in Anglo America science dominates national self-understanding, popular culture has become largely secularized, and the image has triumphed as photograph and as advertising, in Latin America, alongside these tendencies, we see the persistence of indigenous conceptions of the image-as-presence in the proliferation and sheer power of religious images.

It is therefore not surprising that popular memory in Latin America "has never been thoroughly secularized."[20] Indeed, suppressed native worldviews and conceptions of nature as a world of the spirit made manifest in religious images and icons insistently come to the fore. Images and religious icons do not stand in for something absent, or as an index to the divine, as the Counter-Reformation Church rather vehemently urged, but instead continually seem to revert back to native conceptions that view the image as presence, that is, as the *embodiment* of what they represent. There is, therefore, no absence to disavow, as in the West. The collapse of subject and object continues to be made patently manifest in ritual dances performed in festivals across the Andes and Mesoamerica, where "the spirit of the animal carved on a mask recognizes and inhabits its wearer: in what is called the wearer's *nagual*, the image and its meaning are one."[21] When I put on the jaguar's mask, I do so to let the spirit of the jaguar inhabit me. Jaguar and I are one. Likewise, as anthropologist Luis Millones has pointed out, formerly sacred images

4.6. *A very dark Virgin of Guadalupe, shown as protectress of Mexico's indigenous peoples*
La Villa/Tepeyac, Mexico
Photo Spitta 2004

that embodied the earth and the mountains and that acquired human (if divine) form after the Conquest have a life of their own. Echoing much more with the Greco-Roman world of gods and semi-gods than with Catholic dogma, in churches in Cuzco, late at night, saints and Virgins are said to come alive and flirt with one another, desire one another, and generally have a very active social life that they disguise during the day under a hieratic demeanor. "Saint Sebastian runs competing with St. Jerome during the Corpus Christi celebrations in Cuzco trying to get to the cathedral first. And he tries to make love to Santa Barbara behind the altar where the religious images get together on the nights free of processions." ["San Sebastián corre compitiendo con San Jerónimo durante las fiestas del Corpus Christi en el Cuzco, tratando de llegar primero a la

Catedral. Y enamora a Santa Bárbara detrás del altar, cuando las imágenes se reúnen durante las noches que descansan de las procesiones."][22] Within this lively and fluid relationship between humans and the divine, religious images partake of human desire and are anything but dead or hieratic.

Therefore, two systems come into tension across the Americas, and in particular in areas with a large indigenous presence: first, "the silent abstraction and discursive logic of European alphabetic form" that supplants native figural texts and communal performances[23] that one could also, with Angel Rama, subsume under the "lettered city," and second, the system of images-as-presence in a space that becomes performative because of these dynamics. Indeed, forms of syncretism studied by critics who traditionally focused on popular forms of religiosity are today increasingly being complicated by performance-centered theorists.[24] Opening up a third conception of the image that subverts the facile distinction we make between images and words is the Nahua conception of the image as ixiptla. Ixiptla is the image conceived and experienced as embodied and spectacular. "Native painting—on skin and agave codices, on the walls of sanctuaries," Gruzinski points out, "did not constitute, strictly speaking, an image. . . . When the Indians painted they designed shapes that were both illustration and writing, graphism and iconicity. The parallel nature of the 'image' that was emphasized in the West (or in China) was replaced here by a practice that melded the two."[25] The ixiptla was not, strictly speaking, representational. Fundamentally abstract, it was a *semblance* in the Spaniards' words, or it could be an idol in Christian terms: "a divinity that appeared in a vision, a priest 'representing' a deity by covering himself in adornments, or even a victim who turns into a god destined to be sacrificed. More than that, it was the container of a power; the localizable, epiphanic presence; the actualization of the power infused into an object; a 'being-here.'"[26] In this, it was miles apart from the Christian image that was, in concept at least, envisioned as a representation and an index of the divine (and this is problematic even in Europe, but for entirely different reasons). Over time, Catholic images in the New World began to lose their indexical function, and to inherit the fetish character of indigenous icons. Thus, contrary to the Church's teachings, they became holy in themselves.

Given the Church's understanding of ecclesiastical performance "as performance," the emphasis on dramatic re-presentations and visualizations, and the persistence of indigenous performances and pilgrimage traditions, spectacle, as Parkinson Zamora has pointed out, underlines and underlies every aspect of religious practice in the New World. Religious performativity and syncretic practices have therefore enacted[27] Latin American space in very specific ways: crosses and altars mark mountaintops; pilgrimages traverse national space and create cohesion and communitas across cultural and linguistic divides; church rituals embrace the senses; indeed, religious performance permeates all aspects of life regardless of personal belief. (In contrast, in the United States, the Puritans' Reformation-driven iconoclasm, print-oriented culture, emphasis on interior dialogue of the divine, and turning away from the body and the senses as conduits of divine apprehension shaped Anglo culture in ways that distinguish it quite radically from Latin America.) The difference between the conceptions of the Christian religious image and the ixiptla revolve, then, around two different forms of imagining visuality. For early modern Catholicism, sight was supposed to bounce off the image and onto the divine, rendering the material support simultaneously sensuous yet negligible. In contrast, with the Nahua conception of the ixiptla, sight got "stuck" (so to speak) on the material support: viewer and the viewed blend in a similar way to the nagual, where image and support become one.

I suspect that the notion of "getting stuck" on the ixiptla that I am elaborating on here (as opposed to a form of visuality conceived of in terms of sight bouncing off a religious image) emerged from the conquistadores' reaction to their first encounters with native idols. Given their evangelizing zeal, it is not surprising, as many have pointed out, that native religious objects were viewed as bad, unclean objects and framed as "idols." The unreadability and abstraction of native religious images, however, overwhelms the conquistadores and invariably elicits an additional aesthetic judgment: native religious icons are repeatedly described as *ugly*. From Bernal Diaz's description of the first native religious images that his party encountered in the Yucatan, to Alexander von Humboldt's descriptions of native religious art centuries later, *ugliness* emerges as a consistent criterion. This is in part because abstraction allows Bernal Díaz and his fellow soldiers to read into native religious icons their worst fears ("diabolic, badly represented, indulging in sodomy" ["tenían unos ídolos de barro, unos como caras de demonios y otros como de mujeres, altos de cuerpo, y otros de otras malas figures; de manera que al parecer estaban haciendo sodomías"]).[28] Upon reaching Cozumel in 1519, the conquistadores described native icons in a similar way, as misshapen ("disformes") and bad things ("cosas malas").[29] Their ugliness unleashes Cortés's iconoclastic fury; torn from their altars, native icons shatter as they roll down the stairs of the temple. He orders them to be replaced by a newly built, "clean, whitewashed altar" ("un altar muy limpio"), on which he puts an image of the Virgin of Guadalupe.[30]

This original scene in the Yucatan of simultaneously occurring violence, iconoclasm, and re-creation subsumes the productive tension between two very different systems of relationship between images and words that would shape the colonial period. Writing and the lettered city construct their lost object, and in so doing ghost the subject. The Virgin's status—embodying simultaneously the persistence of indigenous conceptions of images *and* their transculturation—is nowhere more apparent than in the way in which the origins of the cult of the Virgin of Guadalupe are historicized. In the narrative corpus revolving around the apparitions, we clearly encounter the attempt to contain the power of the image, or what I call in Chapter Five Guadalupe's "wheels." Following her gradual triumph in Mexico, and serving as the center of a massive pilgrimage tradition, a corpus of narratives arose that tried to contain the exponentially growing power of that image and harness it to a lettered proto-national agenda. In this tension between an image's runaway power and the lettered city's attempt to control that power, post-Conquest America echoes the West's early theologians' attempts to curb the power of images by trying to "explain" them. Hans Belting's description of this tension is instructive: "As soon as images became more popular than the church's institutions and began to act directly in God's name, they became undesirable. It was never easy to control images with words because, like saints, they engaged deeper levels of experience and fulfilled desires other than the ones living church authorities were able to address." Directly impacting my readings of how the narratives around the apparitions of the Virgin of Guadalupe evolved, Belting concludes that, "when theologians commented on some issue involving images, they invariably confirmed an already-existing practice."[31]

VANISHING OBJECTS/MIRACLE NARRATIVES

From the beginning, the Virgin of Guadalupe is a religious event and an aesthetic proposition. . . . In addition to eliciting massive outpourings of faith and allowing space for pain and existential homelessness, the Virgin is the foundational act of popular art in Mexico.

[Desde el principio, la Virgen de Guadalupe es un hecho religioso y una proposición estética. . . . Además de un acto de fe masiva y un espacio para el dolor y el desamparo, la Guadalupana es el acto de fundación del arte popular en México]

—Carlos Monsiváis, "La Virgen de Guadalupe y el arte
(necesariamente) popular" (Translation mine)

Miracles happen at points of intercultural stress and along cultural fault lines. Much like the electricity that Dr. Frankenstein applied to his creature to give it life, miracles are the spark that ensues when two cultures rub up against each other. Indeed, it is no accident that the "apparitions" of the Virgin of Guadalupe happened when and where they did.[32] Depending on the source, she is said to have appeared either three or four times in 1531, exactly ten years after the fall of Tenochtitlán, to Juan Diego, a poor, recently Christianized Indian. Connecting him to the Aztec foundational myth whereby the group wandering south from Aztlán was told by the gods to settle where they saw an eagle perched on a cactus holding a serpent in its beak, his name in Náhuatl was Cuauhtlatohucatzin or Cuauhtlatóhuac, which means "el que habla como un águila"/"he who talks like an eagle." As if this palimpsest between the myth of origins and the emergence of Mexico as a new nation were not enough, his wife's name was Malintzin—the same name as Cortés's Aztec "lover's" name (Malinche in Náhuatl and Doña Marina in its Christianized version) and, according to popular tradition, the mother of the first mestizo.[33]

Guadalupe appeared to Juan Diego as he was traversing Tepeyac Hill on his way to church. She assured him she was his compassionate mother and that her mission was to protect "all folk of every kind."[34] She asked him to go to the Archbishop to plead for the establishment of a shrine in her name on that hill. Juan Diego replied that he was only a poor, lowly Indian and that no one would listen to him, much less Archbishop Zumárraga. To prove her miraculous powers, she cured Juan Diego's dying uncle, Juan Bernardino. The last time she appeared to Juan Diego, she had him pick Castille roses, which had suddenly grown on the barren, formerly cactus-covered hillside, and fold them into his cloak made of maguey fiber—the now famous *tilma*. With these signs, Juan Diego went to see Archbishop Juan Zumárraga and, so goes the story: "As he unwrapped his tilma, the flowers tumbled at the churchman's feet, and suddenly, 'upon that Tilma, there flashed a Portrait, where sallied into view a Sacred Image of that Ever Virgin Holy Mary, Mother of God.'"[35] St. Michael is said to have carried the tilma from the Archbishop's palace back to Tepeyac, where the Basilica to the Virgin of Guadalupe was subsequently built (and where the miraculously imprinted tilma allegedly has hung for several centuries). If one adds to these fusions and confusions the "coincidence" that the Virgin appeared to three men called Juan and that the creole nation was imagined via St. John's (San Juan's) visions at Patmos and, moreover, that in 1531 another miracle is said to have occurred somewhere on the outskirts of Tlaxcala, where St. Michael appeared to another Indian, also called Juan Diego[36]—"coincidences" that Lafaye calls "onomastic esoterism"—the story of Guadalupanism and the foundational fictions of modern Mexico would seem to merit if not a novel by Umberto Eco, then at least a story by Borges.[37]

Indeed, the story of Guadalupanism, which initially seems quite straightforward, becomes a vertiginous mise en abîme when studied in depth. The central debate continues to rage and revolves around whether two texts invented the story of the apparitions outright. Moreover, the story itself changes radically depending on the (forever vanishing) objects that are privileged as a springboard for the highly divergent and often contradictory and impossible narratives. These objects are: Juan Diego's famous tilma; a wooden sculpture of the Spanish Virgin of Guadalupe, which may very well have been Zumárraga's own (and may have served as the original model for all subsequent reproductions; however, there is too little documentation to write anything further about it); an early miraculous painting of the Virgin of Guadalupe, made by the famous Indian painter Marcos Cipac de Aquino, hung in the shrine erected in her name on Tepeyac Hill shortly after 1531; and finally, two texts. The first is the 1648 published account of her apparitions by Bachiller Miguel Sánchez, entitled *Imagen de la Virgen Maria Madre de Dios de Guadalupe milagrosamente aparecida en la ciudad de México. Celebrada en su historia, con la profecía del capítulo doce del Apocalípsis.* This text is credited as the foundational narrative of an incipient creole nationalism that was to culminate in Mexico's war for independence. Around the second, the Náhuatl text now known as the *Nican mopohua,* there is fierce debate.[38] Originally published by Lasso de la Vega with the title *Huei tlamahuizoltica omoneixiti ilhuicac tlatoca ihwapilli Sancta,* some critics identify it as a translation into Náhuatl of Sánchez's text. It thus coexists alongside Sánchez's text as an after-the-fact, "fictional," "indigenous" national narrative. To others, its origin is much earlier (1556 or so) and the author indigenous.

As will become clear below, although each object and text gives rise to quite divergent interpretations of the miraculous (scholarly or otherwise), each invariably leads to a dead end—that is, each is constituted around a vanishing object—and cannot present a coherent or convincing interpretation of the events. Religious interpretations base their reasoning on the miraculous nature of the tilma and thus have faith as their starting point, while the scholarly works surrounding the two texts mentioned above—particularly the debates surrounding the authenticity of the *Nican mopohua*—depend on an "original," which asserts the miraculous nature of the tilma. Whether from a faith-based standpoint or from a secular scholarly position, then, the written tradition around Guadalupe is always already written after the "fact." It tries to reconstruct as seamless and to anchor to writing an oral, visual, spectacular, popular performative tradition that may or may not have been discontinuous. As if to prove Hans Belting's point, by means of these narratives (invented or not) of miracles (invented or not), the "lettered city" tries to harness to the letter and the letter of the law a massive popular and rapidly expanding religious cult.[39] In what becomes a dizzying closed circuit, the search for the "original" tilma parallels the search for the "original" text; both are elusive or vanishing, or ghosted objects that nevertheless, paradoxically, affirm the miraculous origin of Guadalupanism.

A brief analysis of how each of these four privileged Guadalupan and anti-Guadalupan objects and texts give rise to different interpretations regarding the foundation of modern Mexico should make clear the interconnectedness of the cult, nationalism, and mestizaje. I have placed objects (the tilma and Marcos's painting) alongside texts and given them the same status because of the deep and inextricable link between those objects and the narratives and paintings that arose around them. Just as the tilma and Marcos's painting anchor a popular tradition, the texts that arise from that popular tradition depend on those objects, in one way or another, for their existence.

Juan Diego's maguey fiber cloak or tilma on which the Virgin miraculously imprinted her image (one popularizer of the tradition goes as far as calling it the Virgin's "self portrait" [Benítez]) now hangs (allegedly) hermetically preserved in the new Basilica of the Virgin of Guadalupe. It is the object of much devotion; millions of pilgrims[40] pass before it on the moving walkway designed to keep viewers in motion. As fervent believers never tire of asserting, no object of Guadalupanism "commands this degree of respect; no hymn or ballad carries her symbolism with an equal impact; no oration or folk tale has the force of this visual image, its copies and applications."[41]

Given the tilma's fundamental role as the building block of Guadalupanism, it is not surprising that any questioning of its miraculous origins or existence puts the church in crisis. Indeed, efforts by the Guadalupans to confirm the original and miraculous nature of the tilma have been ongoing. In order to contest skeptics, the tilma has been studied and chemically analyzed over the years. A scientist using infrared technology concluded in 1979 that the image was "partially of inexplicable . . . manufacture," that the pigments used "puzzled" the researchers, and that the original pigments "defy analysis."[42] Likewise, in the preface to the 1990 translation and reprinting of the now-famous *Nican mopohua,* the editor affirms that the image of the Virgin inscribed on the tilma defies all natural laws and that it is a miracle in itself that the maguey-made cloak has been preserved over the centuries ["Es muy de tenerse en cuenta que la extraordinaria conservación del ayate y la técnica de estampación de la imagen, desafía todas las leyes naturales que conocemos"].[43] Studies such as these are endlessly reproduced in the argument made by the Guadalupans in the massive *Enciclopedia Guadalupana,* which was published in commemoration of the centenary of the October 12, 1895, papal crowning of the Virgin of Guadalupe. In the book's mission statement, the editors emphasize the miraculous origin of the tilma, an image that they argue is "única, axerotypa, no diseñada por manos ni técnicas humanas" ["unique, designed neither by human hands nor any known human technique"].[44] The tilma's uniqueness then lies in its paradoxical dual nature: as a Guadalupan icon of the utmost importance, it does not really exist as an object.

As is to be expected, the *Enciclopedia Guadalupana* backs its claims of the miraculous nature of the tilma by appealing to yet other scientific studies throughout the centuries. The authors point to numerous studies by different artists since the famous *Informaciones* of 1666 surrounding the nature and veracity of the miracles. All of these agree that the image was not painted either by human hands or with any known techniques. A study in 1787 showed that if the tilma were made of vegetable (maguey) fibers and not preserved in any special way, it would have naturally decomposed within at most twenty years. Not only had it not decomposed, but, hung completely unprotected and exposed during the first 116 years of the colony and in the different shrines and churches that replaced one another, and having had an extremely corrosive acid spilled on it in 1791, it had only a couple of marks to show for all the wear and tear of history. The writers of the encyclopedia also list a study undertaken by the 1938 Nobel Prize winner in Chemistry, Dr. Richard Kuhn, in which he allegedly asserts that the pigments used "belonged neither to the vegetable, mineral, nor animal world" (translation mine). The *Enciclopedia* also notes the fact that the reflection in the Virgin's eyes, recently studied by renowned ophthalmologists, clearly shows Juan Diego, although nothing much other than a blur can be seen. Having studied the stars of her mantle, they argue further that the forty-six stars that dot her cloak are not organized randomly but according to the Winter Solstice of 1531 ["las cuarenta y seis estrellas de su manto no están puestas al azar, sino que corresponden a la posición de las constelaciones en el cielo del solsticio de invierno de 1531"].[45] All of these Guadalupan-sponsored "scientific" analyses affirm the existence of an object that never existed as an object; indeed, it existed as a miraculous object only within the Guadalupan religious performance.

The second object around which Guadalupanism revolves is the Indian Marcos Cipac de Aquino's painting of Guadalupe. Not only does soldier/historian Bernal Díaz attribute this first American painting of the Virgin to the famous Indian, but the *Informaciones* of 1556 also mention him as the painter of the "miraculous" portrait.[46] This painting, so the informants tell us, soon acquired miraculous properties and became the origin of a dispute between Franciscans and Jesuits in the early colonial period. It acquired such magical properties and such widespread fame that Indians reportedly brought it alms and offerings, particularly food ["limosnas y ofrendas, sobre todo ofrendas de comida"], following age-old tradition.[47] Bishop Montúfar, the second bishop of Mexico and a Dominican, apparently promoted the cult of Guadalupe by means of this image, gathering funds with which to build the first shrine of Our Lady of Guadalupe at Tepeyac in 1555.[48] As the French historian Jacques Lafaye has pointed out, it was important for religious orders placed in Latin America to promote indigenous artists to paint in situ because all alms went to the source of the artwork, hence Spain, if it derived from there, or New Spain, if it had been created in Mexico. The gifts given Marcos Cipac de Aquino's painting in this proto-copyright spirit would therefore have gone to the coffers of Montúfar, enabling him to build the first shrine. Montúfar's exploitative economic practices (requests for alms and donations to the Virgin from impoverished Indians) so enraged Fray Francisco de Bustamante, a Franciscan, that he publicly attacked Montúfar in 1556 in a sermon delivered in front of members of the Inquisition.

Bustamante, in line with the Franciscan repudiation of the Jesuits' and other orders' syncretic religious practices and "flexibility," argued that Montúfar was promoting the cult of a painting that was leading to a dangerous collapse of the distinction the Church tried to maintain between representations of the Virgin and the Virgin herself ["que decirles (a los indios) que una imagen que pintó un indio hace milagros, seria gran confusión y deshacer lo bueno que estaba plantado porque les da a entender que hace milagros aquella imagen que pintó el indio Marcos"].[49] His attack was also driven by the fact that great amounts of money were flowing into Montúfar's coffers as a result of the establishment of the cult ["for the alms and legacies that the cult of Guadalupe must inevitably bring in"].[50] Bustamante's critique of the exploitative nature of the emergent Guadalupanism is still made today by many anti-Guadalupans. One of them, a very respected archaeologist and devout Catholic, told me that the Basilica does not have alms boxes as in normal churches; rather, the donations actually drop into immense rooms beneath the church. There, the priests dance in the mountains of coins much like Uncle Scrooge.

In all the sources I have studied, it is not clear whether the painting and the tilma are one and the same or whether they are different. The church affirms that the tilma is on display at the Basilica, and I just heard that it is actually touring, but as you pass underneath "it" on the moving walkway, it looks like a painting (Figure 4.3). Indeed, Bustamante and Montúfar's debates center around a "painting"—no mention is made of the tilma. Furthermore, some of the informants mention not only a painting, but also "palos de las ymágenes"—literally, "sticks of the Virgin"—so there may have been a painting by Marcos as well as one or several sculptures of the Virgin in Tepeyac at the time.[51] If Marcos Cipac did indeed paint the tilma, the lack of distinction between tilma and painting may be due to the Guadalupan church's desire to prove and maintain the myth of the miraculous origins of the tilma.[52]

The third object that serves as a building block of Guadalupanism is the 1648 text published by Miguel Sánchez, *Imagen de la Virgen Maria Madre de Dios de Guadalupe, milagrosamente aparecida en la ciudad de México. Celebrada en su historia, con la profecía del capítulo doce del Apocalípsis.* Sánchez was a creole born in Puebla in 1606. A student of theology, he frequented clerics well-versed in the apparitions, especially Bartolomé García, vicar of the shrine. Because it was written approximately one hundred years after the work of a Spanish friar, Father Diego de Ecija's *Libro de la invención de Santa María de Guadalupe* on the cult of the Virgin of Guadalupe in Spain, Lafaye asserts that Sánchez copied Ecija's text but Mexicanized it in order to invent a religious tradition on American soil for the creole population. The Mexicanization and creolization of the Virgin allowed creoles to voice their complaints against Spanish/gachupín[53] abuses and to promote an incipient Mexican nationalism, which was to culminate with Father Hidalgo's 1810 Grito de Dolores: "¡Señores, Vamos a coger gachupines!" [loosely translated, "Let's go screw/catch Spanish immigrant abusers"]. As Francisco de la Maza has argued, knowledge of Sánchez's hyperbolic proto-nationalist rhetoric may explain why Father Hidalgo picked the Virgin of Guadalupe as the standard under which he fought for Mexico's independence from Spain, picking her as the emblem for the nation, rather than choosing her due to the vagaries of an inconsequential conversation, as tradition has it.[54]

Several scholars (de la Maza, Lafaye, and others) credit Sánchez with having invented the whole story of Guadalupe's miracles outright. As Lafaye argues, following Francisco de la Maza's seminal earlier study and Sánchez's own assertions, "Before the bachiller Miguel Sánchez, no one had explicitly referred to an 'apparition' of the image of Tepeyac." (This would also explain why no mention is made of the miraculous tilma in the sixteenth-century debates.) In fact, Sánchez's work could be considered exegetic rather than documentary, given that he borrowed "his edifying account of the successive 'apparitions' of Mary from the depiction in the already numerous ex-votos in the basilica"[55] and, as I am becoming increasingly convinced, from popular oral tradition and pilgrimage rituals. Sánchez's work, then, erases the established and all-too-easily-taken-for-granted borders between oral, performative practices and written traditions, since it seems to invent a written tradition from popular practices. As Francisco de la Maza argues, Sánchez is the source of all Guadalupan apparition narratives ["de Sánchez parten, quieran o no, todos los demás relatos de las apariciones"].[56] Moreover, Sánchez's use of ex-votos and his striking visual narrative representation of the collapse between the Virgin and the nation, the woman and the city, the Aztec goddess Tonantzin and the Christian Mary all lead Lois Parkinson Zamora to argue that the distinction we make between oral and written verbal structures needs to be complicated to include visual literacy, which seems to have predominated in Latin America from the pre-Columbian world to the colony and up to this day (in her terms: literacy and legibility). What should stand out, then, is that Sánchez invents a written tradition for the lettered city, on the basis of a longstanding popular pilgrimage, charismatic, oral, and visual tradition. His genius consisted of mobilizing the palimpsest created between Tonantzin and Guadalupe, Tepeyac/Tenochtitlán, and Extremadura/Tepeyac in the interests of staking out what was to become an independent, lettered, geopolitical territory.

Sánchez's strategic ploy was to equate the Virgin of Guadalupe with the city of Mexico, and hence with the future nation, via a rereading of Revelations 12. The story he tells goes as follows: In the Apocalypse, St. John (the "eagle of Patmos")[57] has visions of a Woman dressed in the sun, with the moon at her feet and on her head a crown of stars. She is about to give birth while a dragon with seven heads waits for her son to be born, in order to eat him. However, when the son is born God takes him, the Woman flees to the desert, and the angels fight a great battle against the dragon and throw him down to earth. There he finds the Woman in the desert, but she is given great eagle wings with which she flees the serpent. Sánchez mostly makes this Apocalyptic vision resonate with the Aztec foundational myth (the eagle on the prickly pear eating a serpent on a promontory in the middle of a lake) and with Juan Diego's name, transforming them into the vision of an independent Mexico. Tonantzin, the venerated serpent mother ["nuestra venerada madre la mujer serpiente"], has become Guadalupe the killer of the serpent goddess. Place and nation coincide here. Tepeyac becomes the New Jerusalem seen in St. John's vision, the moon at the Woman's feet is the water of the lake on which the city of Tenochtitlán was built, and the dragon she fights off is Spain. As de la Maza concludes, a circle is closed between the Old and New Testaments, between the Old World and the New, and finally between one city and another. Mexico is suddenly placed as the second privileged nation of Universal History: Judea for Christ; Mexico for Mary ["De un salto queda México colocado como la segunda nación privilegiada y escogida de la Historia Universal; Judea para Cristo; México para Maria"].[58] Indeed, for de la Maza, Sánchez's whole text is really only an interpretation of the Virgin of Guadalupe as a national emblem.[59] As if corroborating Parkinson Zamora's argument about the centrality of visual culture to an understanding of the dynamics of the New World and the relationship between the visual and the written, Sánchez himself writes that he was the painter of that sacred image when he described her, and that he put much effort into copying her and showed much love of the motherland in painting her ["yo me constituí de pintor de aquesta Santa Imagen describiéndola; he puesto el desvelo posible copiándola; AMOR DE LA PATRIA DIBUJANDOLA . . ."].[60]

Miguel Sánchez's invention of a creole foundational narrative also became the eye of the anti-apparitionist storm. Anti-apparitionists see him as the creator of the whole series of fables ["de toda la quimera y fábulas de las Apariciones"].[61] This anti-miraculous tradition backs its skepticism with arguments referring back to Archbishop Zumárraga's own failure to mention any Guadalupan miracles despite the fact that, according to oral tradition, the Virgin of Guadalupe inscribed her image on Juan Diego's tilma in front of him. One explanation may be that Zumárraga, Mexico City's first Bishop, not only founded the renowned Colegio de Tlatelolco in 1536—the same year as the establishment of the Inquisition in New Spain, of which he reportedly was a zealous participant—but also promoted the construction of the first shrine in honor of Guadalupe in 1532.[62] His position was therefore deeply ambivalent, for he acted as an extirpator of idolatries (that is, destroying native idols and beliefs)—but was also involved in the production, preservation, and creation of códices and interviews with informants of the aristocratic Indian Colegio de Santa Cruz de Tlatelolco. However, in a text written at that time, Archbishop Zumárraga commented that God had no further need of miracles, since there were enough of them already in the Old and New Testaments ["Ya no quiere el Redentor del Mundo que se hagan milagros, porque no son menester, pues está nuestra Santa Fe tan fundada por millares de milagros como tenemos en el Testamento Viejo y Nuevo . . ."].[63] Zumárraga's failure to mention the miraculous apparitions has been taken by many critics and historians of religion as proof that they had not taken place. Serving as further proof that Sánchez invented the tradition of the apparitions outright to inspire and foment proto-nationalist sentiments is the fact that in Fray Bustamante's attack on him, only Marcos Cipac's painting is mentioned.

Unlike Sánchez's text, which culminated in independence, the last text that forms the basis of Guadalupanism set in motion, centuries ago, the drive toward the recent beatification of Juan Diego. On his fifth visit to Mexico City, on July 30, 2002, Pope John Paul II canonized Juan Diego and named him the protector and defender of indigenous Mexicans ["protector y abogado de los indígenas].[64] The text is written in Náhuatl and was originally published by Luis Lasso de la Vega (or Lazo, in some spellings) in 1649—one year after the publication of Sánchez's account. Its title is *Huei tlamahuizoltica omoneixiti ilhuicac tlatoca ihwapilli Sancta María,* or in Spanish, *El gran acontecimiento con que se apareció la Señora Reina del cielo Santa María.* It is now better known by the opening words of the text: *Nican mopohua,* which means "It is Narrated Herein" ["aqui se narra"]. Lasso had been the priest in charge of the church at Tepeyac since 1645 and was a friend of Sánchez's. Giving further ammunition to the anti-apparitionist camp, he writes in a letter to Sánchez that he had been a "sleeping Adam," having had no knowledge of Eve (read: Guadalupe) until he read his friend's work.[65]

The authenticity of the *Nican mopohua* has been hotly debated. Some scholars, beginning with Father Servando Teresa de Mier (1765–1827), have argued that it is an indigenous reclamation of the Virgin of Guadalupe-Tonantzin from the Virgin's appropriation by creoles such as Sánchez. For Mier, the *Nican mopohua* was to remind the

Indians that the Virgin of Guadalupe who appeared to Juan Diego was the same entity they worshipped under the name of Tonantzin ["el mismo numen que ellos reveren-ciaron bajo el nombre de Tonantzin"]. This interpretation led Mier to read the image of Guadalupe as a Mexican hieroglyph with a hermetic code intelligible only to wise and learned Aztecs ["jeroglífico mexicano con hermenéutica clave sólo inteligible para los indios sabios"].[66] In this manner he confirmed the fears of earlier extirpators' of idolatries, not only that a painting was being taken for the real thing, but that the cult of Guadalupe also served to continue the cult of Tonantzin in disguised form. Other scholars, such as Edmundo O'Gorman and León-Portilla, have questioned Lasso de la Vega's authorship and claim that he copied an earlier 1555 or 1556 Náhuatl account written by Antonio Valeriano, one of the first students (and later a teacher) at the Cole-gio de Santa Cruz de Tlatelolco. This "original" text is now said to be in the New York Public Library, although several scholars have questioned that it is actually there. The "fact," however, of an original sixteenth-century copy of the *Nican mopohua* appears in a work by an American Jesuit, Ernest J. Burrus, in his *The Oldest Copy of the Nican mopohua*, and this "fact" has been accepted and circulated unchallenged by O'Gorman and others, and has served to establish the centrality of the *Nican mopohua* to the whole Guadalupan tradition.

However, even as O'Gorman asserts the centrality of the *Nican mopohua*, he argues that Valeriano's text, which narrates the omnipresent popular story of Mary's appari-tion to the three Johns (Juan Diego, Juan Bernardino his uncle, and the Archbishop Juan Zumárraga, who witnessed the miraculous imprinting of the tilma)[67] in 1531, is actually an account of an apparition of the Virgin that took place sometime between 1555 and 1556 in Mexico City. Trying to explain this apparition and give it historical grounding, Valeriano, according to O'Gorman, then wrote up a "historical" account of the Guadalupan apparitions of 1531, basing his writings on the way the story was told in *autos sacramentales* of the period. Lasso/Valeriano, then, is credited with inventing— again—a written tradition based on oral and popular religiosity. O'Gorman concludes that in order to "lend an image which had appeared in 1555–1556 the backing of a mir-acle, Valeriano appealed to historical narratives loosely understood as stories or fables that gain their authentic meaning in the sphere of creative imagination" ["para lograr el objetivo de proporcionarle a la imagen 'aparecida' en 1555–1556 el formidable apoyo de un fundamento sobrenatural, Valeriano recurrió, así, al arbitrio de una narración histórica, pero no en el sentido propio de la palabra, sino en el de un cuento o fábula supuestamente acaecidos que sólo cobran su auténtico significado en la esfera de la imaginación creadora"].[68] In this manner, Valeriano's tactics mimic those of the most ardent Guadalupans: he creates an object that exists only within the realm of religious performance and harnesses it to the lettered city.

The creativity and fantasy that pervade the early texts and that surround and "cre-ate" the Guadalupan cult, the slippage of the time between history and story, also per-meate scholarly works today. In the introduction of the 1990 translation from Náhuatl into Spanish of the *Nican mopohua*, Guillermo Ortiz de Montellano hardly questions Valeriano's authorship of the text; instead, he derails his discussion by adding that the tilma has been inexplicably preserved and, moreover, that the way the image of Guada-lupe became inscribed upon the mantle defies all known physical laws ["desafía todas las leyes que conocemos"]. The authenticity and authority of the *Nican mopohua*, then, is anchored time and again on the miraculous nature and origin of the tilma—that simultaneously disappearing yet performative object.[69]

What seems clear from these vertiginously confusing accounts, arguments, and counterarguments, is that the very fact that the *Nican mopohua* was written in Náhuatl points to an important indigenous appropriation of the Virgin—who was said to have addressed Juan Diego in his language. By speaking Náhuatl, the Virgin's interlocutor not only becomes a human being with a soul (and not a soulless animal, as was hotly debated at the time), but she allows an indigenous redefinition of the nation that anchors its claims in a now-mestizo symbol/Virgin who appeared on Mexican soil. This indigenous reappropriation of the Virgin, the use of a composite name to refer to her—"Guadalupe-Tonantzin"—is upheld to this day, making Mexico a nation graced by God, second only to Jerusalem.[70] If the creole national imaginary was based on the erasure of living Indians in favor of the glorification of a past civilization, then living Indians, whether in 1556 or in 1649 (the date is irrelevant for these purposes), reclaimed her for themselves through the *Nican mopohua*. As León-Portilla underlines, the *Nican mopohua* is directed to all the Indians disenfranchised by the Conquest. It is addressed to those who, like Juan Diego, now viewed themselves as poor and abject "tails" of the world ["infeliz jornalero, como cuerda de los cargadores (mecapatl), cola y ala, cuyo destino es obedecer y servir, ser llevado y ser tenido como carga"].[71] As such, while transmitting a post-Conquest religious feeling, the *Nican mopohua* also revives a classical Náhuatl tradition, addressed as it is to a deeply traumatized and disenfranchised culture (as Nebel argues, this radical reappropriation of Catholicism predates modern liberation theology). These two merging traditions led to an intense polysemism that is further complicated by the cultural politics of creoles.[72]

Questions of authorship are never resolved and underline the intrinsically and apparently unidentifiable nature of transcultural productions. Was it the Indian Valeriano or the creole Lasso who "produced" an "indigenous" text in order to promote the cult of Guadalupe? To which culture does the *Nican mopohua* belong? Is it a post-Conquest Aztec text, or is it a creole appropriation of Náhuatl aesthetics in the interests both of evangelization and of establishing a parallel "indigenous" foundational narrative? As such, can it be considered a truly indigenous product? Or is it a copy or a parody or a recycling of an already recycled narrative? (Remember Lafaye's argument that Sánchez's text copies an earlier Spanish religious narrative of Guadalupe.) Authors and texts can be imbued in and mime the culture and context in which they exist, to the point of becoming indistinguishable from indigenously produced texts and art.[73] The history of the readings and misreadings surrounding the development of the cult of Guadalupe—indeed, the stake scholars and clerics alike have had in maintaining an indigenous production of the *Nican mopohua*, despite growing evidence to the contrary, and despite the recourse to increasingly convoluted narratives—problematizes notions of "cultural authenticity." The processes of transculturation that arise when two different cultures come into contact with each other produce a context in which each text, each work of art, each popular culture production can be read in very different ways. One reading affirms that all creation in the New World was merely a copy (usually a flawed one) of Europe. Another reads all post-Conquest New World texts as indigenously produced.

The last reads them in the light of the two original cultures and hence as a third, hybrid, and syncretic product. Guadalupanism is this whole series of readings and misreadings, the copying of copies, the parodying of originals, the invention of miracles, the production of a national script out of popular, oral, religious performative tradition. The new aesthetic sensibility that this history creates gives rise to an art and poetic sensibility that reconfigures a formerly Aztec landscape with a new meaning. Intrinsically migratory, and profoundly polysemous, when Guadalupe is "planted" on the ground where Tonantzin had thrived, a new culture and a new narrative of that culture arises. In the words of Pope Benedict XIV (1754), Guadalupe made of Mexico (like Israel before it) a nation singled out to be blessed by God: "He hath not dealt so with any other nation" ["Non fecit taliter omni nationi"].[74]

CHAPTER FIVE

GUADALUPE'S WHEELS

Runaway Image, Undocumented Border Crosser, Miracle Worker

Will the predatory Statue of Liberty devour the contemplative Virgin of Guadalupe or are they merely going to dance a sweaty quebradita?

—Guillermo Gómez-Peña, Enrique Chagoya, and Felicia Rice, *Codex Espangliensis*

During the fall of 1999, for the first time in over four hundred years, La Virgen de Guadalupe, patron saint of Mexico, crossed the border into the United States. Her Los Angeles Archdiocese Web page made it clear: "Tuesday, September 14, 1999, will be a historic occasion for the residents of Los Angeles. Arriving via train, a replica of Our Lady of Guadalupe, blessed by Pope John Paul II, will arrive in the City of Angels." "Her Arrival," or "Su Llegada," as the event was dubbed, promised to be a "multicultural" and "multilingual" affair. Appropriately, reenacting the journey taken by millions of Mexicans, the Virgin's first stop would be Plaza Olvera, site of La Placita Church, and Olvera Street—the historic Mexican downtown.

—Luis E. León, *La Llorona's Children: Religion, Life, and Death in the US-Mexican Borderlands*

In the little town of Santa Ana de Guadalupe, Jalisco, the street vendors sell "a pocket-size Migrants' Prayer Book," which opens with a bon voyage message from the local bishop and includes prayers for migrants to recite on their journey to the United States. Among them is the prayer for Crossing Without Documents. "I feel I am a citizen of the world," it says, "and of a church without borders."

—*New York Times*, August 14, 2002 (Quoted in *Puro Border: Dispatches, Snapshots, and Graffiti from La Frontera*)

T HE VERTIGINOUS RISE IN THE Virgin of Guadalupe's importance in the United States is an unprecedented phenomenon affected by bodies, beliefs, and objects displaced and in motion across borders and cultures. The profusion of names by which the Virgin of Guadalupe is known marks both her expanding and her changing role over the centuries. Documenting the rapid and centrifugal expansion of the Guadalupan cult and situating the Virgin at the vital center of conceptions of migration and mestizaje across the Americas, she began as the humble protectress of Indians during the early colonial period, only to see her ascendancy rise from the eighteenth century on, when she was successively named patroness of Mexico City and then patroness of all New

Spain. In the twentieth century she became patroness of Latin America (1910), and most recently Pope John Paul II named her patron saint of the entire hemisphere (1999). In Mexico she is referred to as "Our Lady of Guadalupe," "la Morena," "la Morenita," "the Brown Virgin," "the Dark Virgin," "la Virgen de Tepeyac," "la criolla," and "la pastora."[1] In New Mexico she is the "Protectress of New Mexico," and the "Madonna of the Barrios." Given the Hispanic colonial history of the U.S. Southwest, parishes to Guadalupe naturally dot the landscape everywhere. In New Mexico alone, churches in her honor include the earliest at Mission Church of Nuestra Señora de Guadalupe at Halona (now Zuni) Pueblo, founded in 1660;[2] settlements include Guadalupe (near Santa Rosa);[3] and landmarks are the Guadalupe Mountains (in Southeast New Mexico and West Texas), Guadalupe Peak, and Guadalupe National Park in Texas. In the Southwest, Guadalupe is considered predominantly protectress of Native Americans and Hispanic peoples, and she is the "fifth most frequent image in devotional art in New Mexico." Jemez, Pojoaque, Santa Clara, and Tesuque Pueblos all celebrate "her" day, December 12.[4]

The Virgin's "wheels," her polysemous plasticity, and the rapid expansion of her cult across borders are, oddly enough, already inscribed in the story of her origins. As with many religious icons, legend has it that the little dark sculpture of the Virgin was protected and hidden in a cave when the Moors invaded Spain. Misplaced for centuries, she was "found" by shepherds and commanded that a shrine be built in her name on the banks of the Guadalupe River (which in Arabic means "hidden river").[5] As in many origin legends of religious images, the images have a will of their own: when the humble shepherds tried to move her, she insistently returned to the site where she wanted her shrine built. And it is there that the famous monastery of Guadalupe was founded in the fourteenth century, as she went on to help the Spaniards fight off the Moors during the period known as the Reconquista (successful in 1492, with the fall of Granada). A favorite pilgrimage destination of Queen Isabella and King Ferdinand, it was there that Columbus first met the monarchs to discuss his voyages of discovery. This is the reason why Columbus, already in 1493, renamed the Caribbean island of Karukera in her name.[6] Given that many conquistadores hailed from Extremadura and Cortés himself was a devout Guadalupan, it is not surprising that he in turn undertook the Conquest of Mexico under her protection. As we saw in the previous chapter, having aided the Spaniards in their Conquest of Mexico, in the nineteenth century she was appropriated yet again, this time as the banner under which the creoles fought for Mexico's independence from Spain. Now equated with national freedom, the first president of Mexico, after winning a significant battle in Mexico's war of independence, changed his name to Guadalupe Victoria. In her honor, during the Mexican Revolution of 1910 Emiliano Zapata in turn fought under her protection.[7]

If we revisit the images representing the Virgin of Guadalupe in the previous chapter, the drastic changes in her iconography become immediately apparent. From the Virgin that the conquistadores brought with them to the New World (based on the dark sculpture that stands at the Monastery of Guadalupe in Spain), to the colonial sculptural representation of the Virgin highlighting her dark color in Mexico and showing individual rays of light emanating from her body (particularly in sculptures),[8] to the painting that currently hangs above the moving walkway at the basilica in La Villa/Tepeyac, to the most recent very unabashed collapse of the Virgin with the nation in popular contemporary representations, the image of the Virgin has changed so radically with each displacement that there is little resemblance between any of these representations. Indeed, the shifts in Guadalupe's significance have occurred simultaneously with her ever-expanding role. We have seen that, with her migration from Spain to the New World, she has been transformed from protectress of Spaniards during the Reconquest of the Peninsula to protectress of Indians shortly after the Conquest of Mexico, only to be appropriated as the banner under which creoles fought for independence from Spain. In the United States not only has she been the age-old protectress of Indians and Hispanics in the Southwest, but from there her cult spread to California, when it was adopted in the 1960s by the United Farm Workers as the banner under which they organized migrant labor. Indeed, December 18 is celebrated as the International Day of the Migrant, shortly after December 12 (Guadalupe's Day). Chicana feminists such as Norma Alarcón, Yvonne Yarbro-Bejarano, Maria Helena Viramontes, Gloria Anzaldúa, Cherríe Moraga, and Ana Castillo, and artists Ester Hernández, Alma López, Yolanda López, and many others, have either invoked her in the name of women's liberation, or have fought her off as an oppressive idealization of Woman.[9] In 1976 artist Ester Hernández started an iconoclastic feminist tradition when she represented the Virgin in a karate outfit, kicking out, entitled *The Virgin of Guadalupe Defending the Rights of Xicanos* [*Virgen de Guadalupe defendiendo los derechos de los Xicanos*].[10] Yolanda López soon followed in 1978, representing herself as the Virgin holding a serpent and running out of the frame in tennis shoes trampling the little angel usually at the Virgin's feet. These early feminist contestations of

5.1a. *Portrait of the Artist as the Virgin of Guadalupe*
© *1978 Yolanda M. López*
Courtesy of the artist and the Department of Special Collections, Davidson Library. University of California, Santa Barbara

5.1b. Josephina. Homage to the domestic worker, or the Virgin of Guadalupe as a cleaning woman.
Part of Judy Baca's mural for the Music Center of Los Angeles. Detail now at the entrance to SPARC (Social and Public Art Resource Center). Venice Beach. Photo Spitta 2007.

the passivity of the Virgin were followed by Alma López's controversial radical sexualization and queering. Her digital collage *Our Lady* (1999) shows the Virgin as a confident young Latina in a bikini of flowers staring at the audience defiantly, while the little angel at the Virgin's feet has been transformed into a mature woman, her breasts exposed. In the same iconoclastic vein, author Sandra Cisneros has called the Virgin of Guadalupe (or La Lupe) "a Goody Two-shoes meant to doom" her to a "life of unhappiness."[11] Presenting a challenge to the role of the Statue of Liberty in the American imaginary, it is no accident, then, that Guadalupe is being transformed yet again by the New York City-based Guadalupan Asociación Tepeyac into the Virgin of Undocumented Workers.[12] While for some, the question is still open as to whether these two national icons, the mother of exiles and the mother of migrants, will "dance a sweaty *quebradita*," as Guillermo Gómez-Peña has it in the epigraph, or whether the predatory Statue of Liberty will ultimately triumph, for others, it is clear that Guadalupe already has become the "major focus of pilgrimage devotion, and the dominant symbol of corporate identity, not only for all Mexico but for the entire Western Hemisphere."[13]

The ease with which the Virgin of Guadalupe has crossed continents and borders of all sorts (what I call her "wheels") was facilitated by the inner workings of Christianity itself, which depends on the proliferation of sacred images and their circulation and transplantation. Lee Nolan explains that what characterizes Western European Christianity is precisely "the separation of holy objects from holy places." Because a saint "was believed to be present in any place which had a small fragment of his or her body, or even a piece of cloth or other object that had touched that body," relics mark religious sites as sacred. For Christianity to spread, relics and images important at specific sites have to be sent away as gifts or set in motion by pilgrimages. This process began in the late fourth century "when pieces of saints' remains were sent as gifts from their shrine tombs to other parts of Christendom." According to Nolan, this mobility at the heart of Christianity is precisely that which allowed it to be so readily transplanted to the New World.[14] The circulation, displacement, and misplacement of religious objects and images is, then, also inseparable from their "power." All of the radical shifts in the Virgin of Guadalupe's significance—indeed, their very possibility—therefore depend on the circulation and displacement of the image itself. Her shrine in La Villa/Tepeyac is the radiating center from which all the Guadalupes of the Americas derive their religious power. Thus, parishioners hoping to establish new shrines in her honor travel to Tepeyac with newly made icons of Guadalupe to be blessed either by the Pope on his periodic visits to the site, or by the Archbishop of Mexico City, or simply to be imbued with religious significance by contagion with the sacred. The Virgin's radius of influence is therefore simultaneously centripetal and centrifugal, since with every expansion outward of the cult the Virgin herself gathers ever more presence, aura, and supernatural healing powers. Having been placed in the presence of "the" original Mexican Guadalupe at Tepeyac, all replicas (or third-degree signs)[15] accrue immense status as religious symbols. In what constitutes a multilayered process, the icon comes "alive" through this initial contagion. The rites, stories of miracles, pilgrimages, and other religious festivities that soon envelop the image serve as the performative space through which believers establish direct communication with the icon and through it with the divine. Unlike the image world that surrounds everyone in Europe and the United States as so much white noise, the image experience in this often-spectacular performative context is deeply sensual and viscerally present. Miracles are central to this process in that they allow for the transformation of the icon from its initial status as passive, universal, and merely representational "to an active, particular, mediating presence."[16] In what becomes an impossible search for an origin soon shrouded in the deepest of mysteries, believers commune directly with the embodied image, having had proof of its ability to perform miraculous cures.

In what must have been a grotesque practice of dismemberment, most Catholic churches' authority thus rests on possessing a saint's or church martyr's body part or piece of clothing (euphemistically called "relics"), usually embedded somewhere in the altar but sometimes gruesomely displayed. Even as public a figure as General Francisco Franco is known to have slept with the incorrupt arm of St. Theresa beneath his bed as an amulet for protection. That arm is now displayed at the Alba de Tormes convent in Salamanca, where she died. Whenever a saint's body part is unavailable, however, churches depend on the reproduction of religious icons that slowly, over time, accrue miraculous power. In Catholicism, seeing—literally—is believing. Therefore, the "main function of replication," writes Kay Turner, "is visibility." And she continues, "As long as iconic eye contact can be established, there follows the possibility of evocation. The more visible the Icon is, the more alive it is."[17] Important to this visibility, too, is what Victor and Edith Turner call the "innocence of the eye" or the "cleansing of the doors of perception" that occurs as a consequence of pilgrimage, which allows the pilgrim to see images viewed on a daily basis in a new, fresh fashion.[18] The need for visibility, then, drives the endless reproduction of religious images. (Recently, Mexico's leading newspapers bemoaned the fact that the market for Guadalupes was such that China was now producing and exporting them to Mexico.) Likewise, religious processions— or the annual and periodic dislocation of religious icons—heighten their visibility and are crucial to this process. Setting religions icons and national and transnational populations in motion, processions entail a double circulation: that of the religious object itself and that of pilgrims traveling from afar to see it. Carried on the shoulders of believers in often massively heavy and Baroque litters (much as royalty were transported in former times), icons in processions often travel by routes established long ago by agrarian societies' annual celebrations of the seasons and by the position of the sun in the heavens.[19] These ancient fertility rites relate contemporary pilgrimages to notions of community and hence, as we shall see below, are being mobilized today in the interests of promoting *latinidad* in the United States.

Reminding us that long before we became obsessed with the term "globalization," the Catholic Church functioned as both a globalized religion and a transnational corporation, the migration of Guadalupe as a religious and cultural symbol ironically foreshadows many of the same trajectories and ease with which globalization's time-space compression allows capital to cross borders. The vertiginous speed of her procession north—paradoxically facilitated by globalization—presents grassroots organizers with an efficient model for organizing across borders that could stem the current excesses of globalized capital. Indeed, while migrants cross the border into the United States carrying stamps, flags, T-shirts, magnets, images, and sculptures of the Virgin, the Virgin of Guadalupe herself, is touring the globe on the Internet, where there are seemingly infi-

nite sites built in her name: a cyberstamp promising good fortune to whoever forwards has been set into perpetual circulation, and a cyber-basilica is even announced. While globalization promotes the easy circulation of money across borders, the United States is militarizing its border with Mexico in order to stop what historically was the easy circulation of people across it. Despite this, Guadalupe marches back and forth with renewed vigor. Therefore, while in Mexico, as we have already seen, the Virgin of Guadalupe functions as the national symbol par excellence, in the United States her border-crossing capacity allows her to form alliances across many of the divides that separate different Latino communities in this country, in effect rendering her cult transgressive of the nation-state.

As anthropologists have pointed out, when religious shrines are identified with the nation-state, "they can play an important role as national symbols, linking the celestial and terrestrial power sources." Conversely, as in the case of the border-crossing Guadalupe, "When pilgrimage shrines are identified against the social order, gatherings and ritual practices can be subversive to state and power structures."[20] Not only is the Virgin of Guadalupe proving to be the "glue" that holds together a people divided by a border, but the quick spread of her cult could serve as an important model for the effective mobilization of workers and the building of what the Turners call "communitas" across the Americas. As they write, pilgrimage

5.2. *"Con la Virgen a cuestas" [Carrying the Virgin]*
Photo Pedro Meyer

5.3. Blessings for the Journey
© *2000 Fazal Sheikh*

with its deep nonrational fellowship before symbols of transmundane beings and powers, with its posing of unity and homogeneity (even among the most diverse cultural groups) against the disunity and heterogeneity of ethnicities, cultures, classes, and professions in the mundane sphere—serves not so much to maintain society's status quo as to recollect, and even presage, an alternative mode of social being, a world where communitas, rather than bureaucratic social structure, is preeminent.[21]

Paradoxically, the Virgin of Guadalupe's mobility is being effected in large measure by migrants crossing a border that has become, since the 1990s, a new version of the Berlin Wall and is the world's most militarized border that divides two countries not at war. Driven by economic necessity, fearing for their lives, and having to risk traversing through ever more arid and isolated areas, border crossers can rely only on the Virgin to help them arrive safely. Again overlaying past routes with new forms and necessities of migration, they often approach the United States along age-old border crossings. In El Paso del Norte, for example, there is a Mission to the Virgin of Guadalupe, founded in 1659. The streets are lined with restaurants with names such as Coyote Café and the like. Today, the mission serves as an important layover for migrants awaiting the right moment or the right coyote to help them across the border. Likewise, in Altar, Sonora, in the desert halfway between Mexicali and Nogales and 70 miles south of the border, the tiny desert town is dominated by the Nuestra Señora de Guadalupe Church, built in the early 1700s by Father Kino, which now serves as a gathering place for migrants and coyotes, pollos and pateros alike.[22] In areas where there are no such strategically located important trade and religious sites, migrants create them. Reports abound (Univisión, Galavisión) of new shrines to the Virgin all along the border, in caves and

other natural protective areas where border crossers can rest, get water, spend the night, and jettison garbage or excess belongings. Increasingly, with their litter, migrants also leave behind sculptures and other religious paraphernalia merely brought on the journey or taken along as promesas (votive offerings) in return for having made it that far, thus transforming layover sites into religious shrines and Guadalupe herself into the Virgin of migration.

Guadalupe's "wheels," her relatively fast migration and transformation across the Atlantic into New Spain, and shortly thereafter into New Mexico and other Southwest states, and most recently into the heartland of the United States,[23] emerge artistically in terms that echo the Virgin's mobility across borders. Her image is tattooed on bodies; it is spray painted on lowrider cars and their hubcaps; it appears as altars in taxicabs and taxi stands or *sitios* as well as private cars; it is imprinted on T-shirts sold to lowriders from the United States on pilgrimage to

5.4a and b. *Tattoos of the Virgin of Guadalupe*
Woman in a café in Santa Fe, New Mexico
Man on the street, Portland, Oregon
Photo Spitta 2004

5.5. *Guadalupe hubcap*
By artist Victor Martínez
Photo Charles Mann

Tepeyac; and it is even imprinted on a mouse pad. Other representations of Virgins made out of recycled computer parts serve as indices to the icon's cyber-mobility and the explosive growth of what Apolito has called a "postmodern Catholicism" that has found fertile soil and instant transmission on the Internet. As he explains, "While visionary culture first took root in the United States during the eighties, today the lion's share of the world's seers, messages, and visionary announcements come from the United States. America influences the rest of the world and, especially on the Internet, occupies many of the spaces that have been established for Marian visions . . . What has developed is an inextricable blend of archaic elements with elements of late moder-

5.6. *Guadalupe T-shirts for lowriders*
Tepeyac/La Villa stand, Mexico
Photo Spitta 2005

5.7. *Guadalupe and Frida mouse pads*
Shop in Chimayó, New Mexico
Photo Spitta 2004

5.8. La Virgencita
2000 Marion C. Martínez
Circuit boards, various computer components, wire
Courtesy of the artist

nity."[24] While never explicitly spelled out, and originating in the most widely divergent of cultural contexts, the coincidence of all these independently created representations of the Virgin's wheels reflects on and serves as an index to the Virgin's fluidity of meaning, ease of appropriation, and mobilization of Latino solidarity across borders, despite the lack of consensus.[25]

Even the tattoos of the Virgin inscribed on the bodies of Chicana/os held in prison (*pintos*) symbolize mobility and stand as an act of resistance against a vertiginously expanding incarceration system intent on criminalizing and arresting the free circulation of minority populations. For some, tattoos are "veritable 'billboards' proclaiming the virtues of collective 'criminality.'"[26]

Indeed, Chicano pintos in jails all over the nation have set up elaborate systems of counter-vigilance and solidarity in order to undermine and contest the constraining power of the panopticon.[27] Recycling staples from religious and other pamphlets distributed in prisons, and making the necessary india ink by burning plastic spoons and other prison objects to obtain charcoal, the Point Man stands guard while the tattoo artist inscribes the bodies of fellow prisoners with images that symbolize (within and without that system) their freedom from jailhouse constraints—all the while facing the prospect of months in solitary confinement if caught. Raúl Salinas, famous for his criminal record, is a tattoo artist, political activist, and poet particularly well known for his epic poem *A Trip Through the Mind Jail*. While incarcerated over a period of seventeen years in prisons all over the Southwest, and working by stealth, significantly, he had a tattoo of Christ (symbol of the social and economic victimization of Chicanos) inscribed on his back, and an image of a brown Virgin of Guadalupe (symbol of freedom and solidarity) inscribed on his chest. His body, in and out of prison, became a moving symbol of the often-tragic dialectic of Latino lives in the United States. These inscriptions, when read in conjunction with Salinas's poetry, with the gang graffiti (or *placas*) spray painted across barrios in the Southwest as a way of "marking" a territory, and with the aesthetics of *rasquachismo* (or lower-class and vernacular recycling and innovative creation) spelled out by Tomás Ybarra-Frausto in his groundbreaking essay "Rasquachismo: A Chicano Sensibility," become part of the much larger aesthetic and social phenomenon of Latinization of the contested space that is the Southwest.[28] If skin color is destiny and a tattoo of sorts, the tattoos "openly and defiantly record and give testimony to continued transgressions, especially among pintos for, 'like the mark of their skin color, the india-ink-colored marks under their skin are permanent.'"[29] Indeed, as Olguín argues, somewhat problematically, the tattoo as a "defacement" of prison property produces a transgressive body that "militates, almost essentially, against its own commodification, thus preserving the symbolic challenge to the overt and indirect forms of domination (i.e., peonage, proletarianization, and mass incarceration) of the Chicano people from their formal consolidation in 1848 to the present."[30]

Contributing toward the increasingly visible Latinization of the United States, Chicano pinto tattoos have had a large ripple effect in U.S. culture, fundamentally influencing the tattoo renaissance that began in the 1970s.[31] While former tattoo subcultures (to which mainly sailors, military, working-class people, social "deviants," and convicts belonged) relied on tattoo parlors and standard designs with thick lines, pinto tattoos, with their emphasis on fine-lined, intricate, single-needle, and individual designs (that allow for the creation of finely shaded "photo realistic" portraits on the skin), have become the rage of the moment, even among a middle class traditionally opposed to and critical of this practice.[32] Tattoos, along with piercing and scarification of the skin, formerly were decorative, or used as marks of affiliation to certain groups, as a mark of love for a special person, as a rite of passage (because of its association with pain and the ability to bear it), as a commemoration of an important event in one's life, as a mark of identity, or as a sign of rebellion against mainstream society. In addition to all of these, thanks to the pinto tattoos and the Modern Primitives'[33] new tribalism movement, the possibility of creating highly intricate tattoos is feeding into middle-class notions of individualism.[34] Particularly among New Agers, with their inward-looking focus on personal growth and self-help, the body is seen as a temple, and tattoos have become a way of decorating it or marking important resolutions or life transitions.[35] Imbedded in contemporary narratives of the self, having a tattoo enables middle-class wearers to distinguish themselves from the mainstream; it often serves as a reminder of a radical change in their approach to life, written on the body, and it is seen as having transformative power over their life, and even as a shield against bad influences.[36] Paradoxically, for women as for incarcerated Chicano pintos, for whom the body "is both the site for the inscription of power and the primary site of resistance to that power," the tattoo has become an important means of reclaiming their bodies from objectification and commercialization, since it enables them to "counterinscribe and self-mark their own bodies."[37]

5.9. Collectio navigationum in Indiam occidentalem
Theodor de Bry, 1528–1598
Francoforti ad Moenvm
Courtesy Rauner Special Collections Library, Dartmouth College

The Modern Primitives' new tribalism, interestingly, refers back to Europe's first encounter with the tattoo after 1492. The English word "tattoo" apparently derives from *tatu* or *tatau,* the word used by Polynesian tribes to describe body markings.[38] While it is well known that tattooed "savages" were regularly sent to Europe to be exhibited (and to be sold) as spectacular rarities, it is less known that European shipwreck survivors who had "gone native" and had themselves tattooed displayed themselves in fairs as freaks as well. As early as 1519, the chronicler Bernal Díaz del Castillo, in his *Verdadera historia de la conquista de México,* records one of the first encounters Europe had with native tattoos, when he reports that Spanish conquistadores had miraculously found alive a comrade shipwrecked off the coasts of the Yucatan several years earlier. Gonzalo Guerrero, however, had gone totally native: he had married a Maya woman, had children, was wearing traditional clothing, and even had pierced ears and an "embroidered" face.[39] More shockingly yet, perhaps, Guerrero refused to rejoin his rescuers, saying that he had found the paradise the Spaniards were searching for and that he preferred to remain there, since with his markings he could no longer rejoin Spanish society. Somewhat later, in the 1780s, Jean Baptiste Cabris was shipwrecked in the Marquesas Islands and assimilated into the local culture. He, however, was happy to be "saved" in 1804 and slowly made his way back to Europe via Russia (and a stint at teaching naval officers the art of swimming that he had learned in the Marquesas). Cabris proceeded to tour as a tattooed entertainer, imitating savages and exhibiting himself as a freak at fairgrounds and markets. Making his way back to France in 1817, he waited on Louis XVIII and Frederick William III, going on to become one of the stars of the "Cabinet des Illusions" of Paris.[40] Interestingly, having lived as an almost complete native in the Marquesas and having spent his life as a freak, he went to great pains to prevent his corpse from going to a museum as a scientific specimen.[41] In the 1820s and 1830s, John Rutherford's traveling caravan of wonders imitated Cabris in the display of almost entirely tattooed freaks. P. T. Barnum, who, as we saw, had displayed other freaks in his circus, was the first to include tattooed people as characters in a sideshow amid midgets, bearded ladies, giants, "waistless" women, and other such human rarities in his "Great Traveling World's Fair" in the 1870s.[42]

Adding yet another layer to the visibility of Latino culture in the United States, the Virgin of Guadalupe is spray-painted on Latino-customized (lowriding) cars. Embodying the paradoxical dynamics of the tattoo's mobility within immobility that I have been discussing, cars—which are the symbol par excellence of American identity and mobility—are transformed by Latino lowriders into moving altars that cruise a predetermined circuit in towns and cities across the Southwest. Lowriders (a term that refers to both the cars and the persons themselves) take great pride in transforming often-dilapidated cars into works of art, mobile altars, and spaces for self-expression and the affirmation of community. For lowriders, "joining the Sacred Heart Auto League is more important than a membership in AAA," writes Carmella Padilla.[43] Important as a lowriding capital is the city of Española in New Mexico, where lowriders from all over northern New Mexico have traditionally converged and participate in the annual Easter pilgrimage to the sanctuary of Chimayó (the Lourdes of lowriders). Lowriders are moving monuments to rasquachismo and Latinos' ability to recycle materials ready for the scrapheap. The impact of lowriding culture in the United States was registered by the Smithsonian Institution when, in 1992, it bought the lowrider "Dave's Dream" with the license plate "Chimayó" for its permanent exhibit at the National Museum of American History. "Dave's Dream," as the '69 Ford LTD was called, was blessed by the priest at Chimayó while hundreds of members of the surrounding communities gathered to wish the car well on its journey to Washington, D.C. Indeed, "Gallons of holy water were showered upon the acclaimed automobile."[44] Significantly, the racialized bodies of African Americans and darker Latinos (always socially inscribed as deviant) deny them complete access to the "freedom" of the open road because of constant police harassment and surveillance.[45] As a consequence, lowriders such as Dave's Dream are transformed into home altars on wheels. By means of a series of mechanical adjustments (such as the addition of different hydraulic systems) and rasquache spray-painted artwork on the chassis, the Virgin of Guadalupe rides low, while she inhabits a privileged place, amid other paraphernalia, on the dashboard. Like Raúl Salinas, who argues that the Virgin of Guadalupe is part of his "body altar,"[46] customized cars, like customized bodies,[47] inscribe motion-in-place and an aesthetics of transgressive im/mobility.

5.10. *"Dave's Dream"*
(Irene Maria and Dave Jaramillo, San Juan, New Mexico)
© 1980 Meridel Rubenstein

5.11. *"Los Unidos Car Club"*
Española, New Mexico
1980 Meridel Rubenstein

While New Mexicans claim they invented the lowrider, members of lowriding communities in East Los Angeles, Arizona, Texas, and Colorado claim its origins as well. Indeed, the origins of lowriders may go as far back in history as the first Spanish presence in the Southwest. As Benito Córdova, lowrider consultant to the Smithsonian and a professor of social sciences at the University of New Mexico, argues, the Spaniards who conquered and settled the Southwest had inherited from the Moors the tradition of decorating their horses with "elaborate silver saddles and other gear, sometimes draping their animals with roses."[48] Moreover, the current fashion of spray painting the Virgin on lowriders may also stem from this early period; many caballeros carried with them saddle Virgins (or *vírgenes arzoneras*), which were small images attached to the

high pommel of a rider's horse. First created in the 1940s when Hispanics put sandbags into the trunks of their cars in order to lower their rear ends, lowriders coincide, in their intentions, with those of tattoo culture as performative signs of community and rebellion against American middle-class culture.[49] This initial, relatively minor trans-formation, a Chicano adaptation of hot rods and customized cars,[50] was soon followed by radical alterations that included velvet interiors, dashboard altars, individualized hubcaps, chroming, exterior spray-painted images that ranged from decorative bor-ders to complex murals, and other mechanical improvisations. Hydraulic systems were altered in such a manner as to allow cars to "dance" while cruising. Important for the creators was the wresting away of the car as a symbol of American middle-class mobil-ity and individualism onto a community immobilized by colonization, second-class citizenship, and poverty. Cruising to show off these spectacular cars soon became an intrinsic part of lowriding. Likewise, "spectacle and communal specularity replaced speed and individualism." With the advent of lowrider culture, "the individualistic American dream of driving away to escape it all has been replaced with the notion of driving together. Lowriders organize in car clubs and go cruising on weekends on spe-cific boulevards, updating the old Mexican practice of walking around the town plaza on Sundays. . . ."[51]

As with most representations of Latinos in the mainstream media, however, low-riders soon came to be equated with gangs, drugs, and violence, despite the fact that most lowriders are generally "middle-aged, family-oriented, community-minded citi-zens who oppose negative social behavior."[52] Indeed, in the stories told around the creation of individual cars in *Low 'n Slow*, most of the lowriders created are long-range projects that include the entire family and the community. In these narratives of illumi-nation (often couched in religious terms), the process of transforming an old car into a lowrider becomes a process of self-transformation. The arduous and creative work involved in working over many years, and alongside friends and family, on cars once ready for the scrapheap reportedly heals wrecked middle-aged men (often struggling with alcoholism or some other problem). As an object is transformed, it in turn trans-forms the transformer.

Not only is the creation of a lowrider a life-changing process, then, lowriders also celebrate life-changing events in and with their cars: they marry in them or celebrate marriages with them; they paint the images of deceased family members on them and use them as moving altars; they affirm family ties when they spend hours cruising with their wives and children. The names "Los amigos" and "La familia" chosen for lowrider organizations signal this position vis-à-vis gang culture, and contrast as well with the emphasis on speed of hot-rodders who picked names such as "Road Runners," "Knight Riders," "Bungholers," and "Low Flyers" for their associations.[53] Indeed, "Unlike the hot-rodder, whose objective is to travel at breakneck speed, the objective here is to go as slow as possible; to be seen and (stereo blasting) heard. Destination: nowhere."[54] Lowriders are Baroque in their all-inclusive emphasis. "Cathedrals on wheels," as con-temporary artist Rubén Ortiz Torres calls them, they transform "American cars into sexualized moving altars of an American dream gone amok."[55]

While lowriders may be entirely a Southwestern phenomenon, the performativi-ty of cruising culture, the transformation of cars into cathedrals on wheels, and the use of lowriders for pilgrimage purposes and as cultural and social "glue" (as is seen annually at Chimayó during Easter, when lowriders descend on the site, and in La Villa/Tepeyac, where lowriders also go on pilgrimage) parallel the Virgin's "wheels" in Mexico. Throughout the year, large numbers of pilgrims from the provinces converge into the city (in buses, on bicycles, and on foot), wearing white and carrying flags and banners of the Virgin. Particularly on December 11 and 12 for "her" day, individual villages and towns from all over the country and beyond—in an Olympiad of sorts—send millions of pilgrims to La Villa carrying torches. Over and beyond the religious fervor that it gives rise to, this national tradition of pilgrimage to Guadalupe's shrine creates an interconnecting web whereby even the most remote (and often administratively "forgotten") places feel, establish, and reinforce their connection to a narrative of the national that is founded on the space of the Distrito Federal itself. If the centralization of Mexico in one city, and the collapse of the identity of that city with the idea of the nation, creates tension around questions of nationality and representation (legal and otherwise) for many Mexicans, the pilgrimage tradition helps to mitigate what could be seen as a centrifugal careening off the map. It would not be altogether hyperbolic to affirm that Mexico—despite its post-Cristero deep anticlericalism and radical separation of church and state—exists as a nation only through Guadalupe. The cult of Guadalupe "anchors" Mexican national identity more cohesively than any other narrative of the nation for, as Ignacio Manuel Altamirano had already observed in the nineteenth century, "The day in which the Virgin of Tepeyac is not adored in this land, it is certain that there shall have disappeared, not only Mexican nationality, but also the very memory of the dwellers of Mexico today. . . . In the last extreme, in the most desperate cases, the cult of the Mexican Virgin is the only bond that unites them."[56] Indeed, the Virgin serves as an umbrella symbol for the nation, under which all local cults and pilgrimages are subsumed.

Achieving solidarity but no consensus, this polysemous symbol is extending its radius not only in Mexico, but increasingly today across the U.S.-Mexico border and even well into Canada. Indeed, while Altamirano's statement remains relevant, what he could not have envisioned during a time when the United States was being perceived as a new empire (a monster, in Martí's words; a materialist Caliban for others) is the increasing presence of the Guadalupan cult north of the border and her enormous role in the Latinization of the United States. As a colonizer "from below," her increasing visibility in the United States is helping reinscribe a space Anglo-America has tried hard to shape exclusively in its name. Symptomatic of her "wheels" and paralleling the annual national pilgrimages to La Villa/Tepeyac, there is now a "Carrera Guadalupana," a relay race organized to connect Tepeyac to New York City. The trajectory of the runners is posted on the Internet, allowing Guadalupans everywhere to follow the progress of the torch as it makes its way north. Sponsored by the Asociación Tepeyac in New York City, Guadalupe's torch (both commemorating the Virgin's apparition to Juan Diego in 1531 and tracing the annual Aztec torch runs) is taken from La Villa; passing through many towns and Guadalupan parishes in Mexico, the U.S. Southwest, and the northern Atlantic seaboard, it makes its way to St. Patrick's Cathedral in New York City. With the theme "Messengers for the Dignity of a People Divided by a Border," the Tepeyac organization (established in 1997 with the support

of the New York Archdioceses) seeks legal status (amnesty) as well as better living conditions and wages for undocumented immigrants, besides promoting the Guadalupan cult throughout the United States and calling attention to the increasing violence at the border.

Symbolically trying to unite a people divided by a border, Cardinal Norberto Rivera of Mexico City and Bishop Josu Iriordo of New York City lit the torch at the Virgin's sanctuary in Tepeyac some years ago. While the relay reaches local media only as the torch passes through individual towns, the border crossing is a highly publicized event. In 2006 the crossing at the Matamoros International Bridge was used by Mexican congressmen to call for U.S. support for the Border Security and Immigration Improvement Act (HR 2899). Also publicized was the Carrera Guadalupana's runners' reception at Immaculate Conception Cathedral in downtown Brownsville, Texas, where the community organized a candlelight vigil in memory of all the undocumented workers who had died at the border. Besides carrying the torch to make the plight of immigrants visible across the nation, the relay runners act as ambassadors, stopping in Washington, D.C., with messages from the Mexican Congress to the U.S. government.[57] Having overturned a court order that would have prohibited the thousands of run-

5.12. *The Guadalupan relay race, starting on 110th Street in NYC at 8 a.m. on December 12, 2007. The runners with the torch run through Central Park and enter St. Patrick's Cathedral in time for the 11 a.m. mass.*

5.13. *Guadalupans exiting St. Patrick's Cathedral after mass, December 12, 2007*

ners in New York City, the torch reaches St. Patrick's amid cheers of "Viva Mexico!" and "Viva Guadalupe!"; from there runners fan out across the five boroughs to local parish churches. Brother Joel Magellan, director of Asociación Tepeyac, connects Guadalupe's role after the Conquest of Mexico directly with the plight of undocumented workers in the United States: "Her message," he argues, "was that she wanted a church with more compassion and help for indigenous people. . . . This is more or less the same situation. [Immigrants] need to have more support, compassion, and help and defense for their human rights and labor issues."[58]

Alongside this highly publicized race, the Asociación Tepeyac also stages an annual *via Crucis,* representing the twelve stages of Christ's journey to the cross. Starting in front of the INS building (now Homeland Security) in Manhattan, the procession ironically ends in front of the National Museum of the American Indian. As Ruiz-Navarro, an ethnographer who has studied this religious performance, observes, in this New York-Mexican staging of the *via Crucis,* the long-suffering Jesus is collapsed with the lonely, abused, illegal wetback crucified on his way north by his undocumented status. Individual parishioners dress themselves as Border Patrol guards who flagellate him along the way, all the while yelling, "Get up, you illegal alien!," "Work, you undocumented worker!" ["Levántate ilegal!," "Trabaja indocumentado!"]. Leaflets calling for amnesty, along with religious messages, are passed out to the crowd while members of the Asociación call out, "What do we want?," inciting the crowd to respond, "Amnesty for all immigrants now!" As with the Virgin of Guadalupe, the *via Crucis* staging conjoins the affirmation of Mexicans' deep religiosity with the vindication of undocumented workers' rights and the creation of a Latino identity in migration. The organizers' strategy, over and beyond their celebration of the Virgin and their fight for undocumented workers' rights, is the affirmation of Latino presence in the United States and the creation of Latino cultural celebrations—modeled on those of St. Patrick's and Columbus Day Parades, which have given Irish and Italian immigrants a sense of belonging and identity.[59] While these immensely popular New York City celebrations may have, at one time, included now forgotten and no longer current social vindications, the Carrera Guadalupana is an example of the strategic mobilization of culture and religion in favor of amnesty and the raising of consciousness in the U.S. mainstream of the desperate plight and substandard living and working conditions of the undocumented.

The feast of Guadalupe entails several simultaneous events: the Carrera Guadalupana, community candlelight vigils, the singing of "Las Mañanitas" on the morning of the twelfth, and the establishment of food stands, flower stands, and the general sense of community in festivity. Therefore, while individual parishes all across the Americas are lighting candles, singing and celebrating Guadalupe, they are being connected in space by the runners carrying the torch north from Mexico/Tepeyac. The Internet, where individual terminals are interconnected by high-speed conduits, mimics the simultaneous Guadalupan celebration-in-place and movement-through-space. This im/mobility is what provides both the Internet and the Virgin's celebration with such power. Because of the Tepeyac Association's strategic intervention, pilgrimages not only connect people and traditions across spaces and cultures, but also connect people normally divided by social and class differences. Moving both horizontally across borders and vertically across classes, then, the cult of the Virgin of Guadalupe functions increasingly as the "glue" that holds together a divided people and culture.

The annual pilgrimages from Mexico City to New York City, and other pilgrimages everywhere, as we saw earlier, also depend on the creation and circulation of specially endowed—and often miraculous—sculptures and paintings. Since every newly created parish needs a "specially" blessed or otherwise endowed image to serve as the focus of and conduit for religious life, as in colonial Mexico, so too today, all across the United States, religious images are being circulated in step with the rapid creation of local Guadalupan parishes. Like sculptures and images that gain their power from circulation, an accompanying corpus of miracle tales and myths and origin stories is arising that establishes important links "between the sacred center and its population."[60] As we saw in the previous chapter, stories of miracles, apparitions, and accidental findings of miraculous cult objects all underpin and anchor people's devotion to sacred sites and images. As Latinos become the largest minority, therefore, new shrines in Guadalupe's honor are accompanied by increasing reports of miraculous sightings of the Virgin, reminding us that miracles often happen during moments of great social and political upheaval, either as a means of forcing the transculturation of two different cultural icons or as a sign of hope. These occur almost daily, and ever more to the north of Mexico. The Virgin of Guadalupe's miraculous apparition in the migrant-dominated community of Watsonville, California, for example, is typical of this latter type of miraculous intervention. "Seemingly branded by divine hand into the bark of a tall maple in the hollow," she appeared in the mid-1980s at the height of a months-long strike of the predominantly female labor force at the Watsonville Canning and Frozen Food Company. The women went on to win the eighteen-month strike, aided by the renewed impetus they gained from the apparition of the Virgin, only to lose their jobs a few years later when the company was forced to close.

5.14a. *Logan Airport Newsstand*
Boston
Photo Spitta

Watsonville, however, remains at the center of migrant workers' political activism and is now the scene of the United Farm Workers' fight over workers' rights in the strawberry fields.[61] The maple tree with the Virgin still draws hundreds of pilgrims annually and has had to be protected by a fence.

Reminding us of Father Hidalgo's mobilization of the Virgin in order to fight off the Spaniards in the nineteenth century, in Mexico City, on June 22, 1997, a major apparition took place when the Virgin appeared (not altogether coincidentally!) at Metro Hidalgo.[62] Metro officials said the "apparition" was a mere water stain on the station floor, yet the site became an instant shrine. Thousands of people flocked to the site in order to touch the Virgin and leave candles, money, and flowers. The throngs stopped metro traffic, forcing the officials to lift the piece of cement and put it under glass and enclose it by a fenced shrine outside the metro station. Street vendors opened it for me and showed me where the tenuous imprint of the Virgin could be barely made out. While "events" of this sort are common in Latin America, they are beginning to be reported in the United States as well. Recently (June 27, 2003), my local newspaper (in rural New England) reported an apparition of the Virgin Mary in the windows of a nondescript medical building in Milton, Massachusetts. (When I mention this apparition to my classes, students from that state immediately know about it and report having either heard of it or actually seen it.) In the two weeks following the apparition, more than 40,000 people had traveled there, sometimes from hundreds of miles away, in a spontaneous Lourdes-style pilgrimage. Wanting to lay their eyes on the image and hopefully even press their palms against the red brick wall, the pilgrims had turned the site into an instant shrine. Some had even mobilized the image in an anti-abortion crusade against the hospital.[63] Further south, in Florida, another Virgin appeared on a tall glass building and overnight became a shrine attracting thousands. One of the pilgrims sent me photographs he had taken of the site. As is quite typical of these apparitions, for some they are truly miraculous, while for others they are "coincidence, the uncanny result of condensation."[64] More recently yet, on April 22, 2005, another apparition was reported under a Chicago freeway. What is a tenuous shape of a Virgin (inspectors said it was just a stain) instantly became known as "Our Lady of the Underpass." Pilgrims to the shrine infuriated Chicagoans because of the continually backed-up traffic.[65]

As if this were not enough, there is also now a Weeping Guadalupe in Las Vegas. The Covarrubias family brought the sculpture from Mexico to put in a shrine in their backyard. In their traumatic border crossing at Tijuana, they had saved her from being smashed by the Border Patrol in a routine search for drugs. In 1993, two years after their journey, their daughter first noticed the teardrops in the Virgin's eyes. A local CBS affiliate sent camera crews to film this miraculous event. In order to prove that there was no

5.14b. *Metro Hidalgo Virgin Apparition Shrine Mexico City*
Photo Spitta 2007
The piece of cement flooring in the metro station where the Virgin appeared instantly became a shrine. Authorities had the piece of cement lifted and put into this shrine outside the station to prevent congestion.

hidden water source, they ordered the sculpture removed from its pedestal, and "the statue began to weep again for the cameras, as if on cue." In what becomes a crescendo of religiosity, the "reporter" (all too clearly aligned with the Guadalupan cult) concludes by describing a kitschy religious event like those that can be found represented on religious cards everywhere in Latin America: "In October 1993 another miracle took place. On an unusually windy day in Las Vegas," he wrote, "thirty-two people were praying in front of the statue when suddenly the wind died down, the clouds broke, and the sunlit form of the Guadalupe Madonna appeared

5.15. *Virgin Apparition*
Clearwater, Florida
Photo Ken Horkavy

5.16. *Our Lady of the Underpass*
Chicago
Photo Spitta 2007
Notice the stain on the wall vaguely shaped
   like the Virgin.

in the sky. The glowing rays of the sun created the spiked, golden aura typical of representations of Our Lady of Guadalupe. Everyone in the prayer group witnessed the vision."[66] In a world divided by borders, where migrant workers who cross back and forth undergo often-traumatic crossings, it is no accident that miracles like this one would mark this trauma, and also that roadside altars all along the border mark the deaths of those who do not make it. Transforming the border into an almost uninterrupted series of shrines, the crosses that today mark the deaths of migrants have seen the addition of many more, placed by political activists and women's groups to memorialize and protest the horrifying murder of hundreds of women in Juárez and elsewhere. Under globalized transnational economic regimes, for migrants, crossing the border has quite literally come to mean "croXing" the border.

As we have seen previously, pilgrimage traditions layer the land and culture in many important ways. Pilgrimages depend on local parishes as stopover points; they rely on the creation and circulation of holy images or relics; they are accompanied by festivities that include the sale of food and religious paraphernalia; and stories are told about miracles that anchor a religious following to a place and a parish. Indeed, as anthropologists have shown, pilgrimages do not exist in isolation; they are "woven securely" into a "regional field."[67] "Because pilgrimage at its core is structured interaction of human belief and behavior with particular geographical locations," write Morinis and Crumrine, "it is also possible to trace the development of a pilgrimage in the changes wrought to landscape over time. Shrines are raised, steps are cut, topography is altered, and settlement patterns change, all as a result of the historical development of the pilgrimage."[68] Indeed, an altered and therefore "altared"—and thus sacred—landscape results from religiosity's impact on the landscape. Furthermore, given that the festivities surrounding pilgrimages (such as ritual dancing, singing, intoxication, etc.) entail the total immersion of the pilgrim in a space and logic radically othered, the act of going on a pilgrimage becomes a deeply "transformative process, from which the individual emerges altered from his or her previous situation."[69] As such, pilgrimages and migration to the United States not only follow many of the same routes/roots, they are also equally deeply transformative processes—both for the pilgrim/migrant and for the culture and space they traverse.

The Guadalupan cult, with its ever-widening centrifugal and centripetal pull, serves as the privileged icon of *latinidad* in the United States, despite the fact that not all Latinos believe in her.[70] It is not only a space-time (or Borgian aleph) that focuses all the different processes of transculturation that underpin mestizaje across the Americas, but also the privileged symbol under which myriad other practices are organized (such as the erecting of roadside shrines, altars in the home and in gardens, celebrations such as the posadas[71] and Day of the Dead, Cinco de Mayo, the creation of new border saints such as Juan Soldado, the pilgrimages to other shrines, etc.). Moreover, as Vasconcelos so aptly pointed out in his aberrant yet highly influential 1920s essay "La raza cósmica," mestizaje became the fundamental racial and cultural dynamic that underpins notions of identity in the Americas, following from the initial displacement of people (and, as I have been arguing throughout, objects) from Europe and Africa across the Atlantic to the Americas. Building a bridge (now the hyphen) across the continents, they set in motion a radical racial and cultural transformation.[72] The cult of Guadalupe performs the dynamics of mestizaje in its simultaneous and double articulation of the placement intrinsic to all displacements. Im/mobility spells the moment, and the multiple recyclings, inventions, and subversions of rasquachismo conform its aesthetics.

The years have gathered themselves in bags
under my eyes.
The young man that used to live here is gone.
Cold, the enemy of my bones, lying in constant
ambush.
Am I growing old or have I just changed?
I changed so easily,
Could I change back to the young man?
I don't think so; one time here was hard
enough.
I wonder what the years have gathered in the bags.
I bet it's like looking through old trunks,
old letters and photographs, an old shoe or two.

—Charles Lovato. Jeweler, painter, poet, potter from Santo Domingo,
New Mexico. This poem is displayed next to his work at the Taylor Museum
of Southwestern Study (Colorado Springs Museum of Fine Arts).

CHAPTER SIX

THE NEW MEXICO/ NEW MESTIZO EFFECT

Enchanted and Otherwise Enacted Spaces

When I think of death, I only regret that I will not be able to see this beautiful country any-more . . . unless the Indians are right and my spirit will walk here after I'm gone.

—Georgia O'Keeffe

THE SOUTHWEST HAS A MYSTIQUE that exceeds its reality. For the visitor imbued with its allure, expecting to find a place altogether magical, it is somewhat of a disappointment. The little towns that dot the landscape are often quite poor, and huge junkyards extend over the high desert into the horizon. One suddenly realizes how many hours Ansel Adams must have spent waiting to photograph the moon setting just right over Hernández. Many of the Pueblo Indian settlements on which the Southwest mystique is partly based seem today more like showcases for tourists than thriving centers (even Acoma Pueblo, spectacularly sitting atop a mesa, seems half-deserted). Indeed, while Anglo-Americans have appropriated adobe Pueblo-style houses (often quite grandly), many of the native inhabitants of the Southwest live in cement-tract housing or mobile homes. When visiting the Pueblos and Hispanic artists' shops, the tourist is struck by the contrast between the marketing that takes place here, in this seemingly poor and jumbled setting, in contrast to the glamorous packaging at the much-publicized Indian and Spanish Arts annual markets in Santa Fe and in the end-less rows of galleries in the commercial parts of Taos, Santa Fe, and elsewhere. While Arizona, Colorado, and California all partake of the allure of the Southwest, nowhere have elites worked so hard to market and promote it than in New Mexico, and par-ticularly Taos and Santa Fe. Indeed, the dynamics of "enchantment and exploitation,"[1] elucidated by deBuys, so associates New Mexico with Latin America and an "other" space within the United States that New Mexico's license plate reads "Land of Enchant-ment" and "New Mexico, USA." This state is the only one in the nation that has to clarify to which nation it belongs. The allure or "aura" of the Southwest (as a recent *New York Times* article called it)[2] is an Anglo-American creation that promotes an idiosyn-cratic version of New Mexico's colonial past that obfuscates and marginalizes native cultures while apparently center-staging them. These utopian-tinged visions neverthe-less coexist with the multiplicity of Indo-Hispanic cultural practices that inflect every aspect of the culture. Underpinning what became the marketing of the Southwest as an aesthetic to the rest of the United States is the obsessive collecting and preserving of

native Southwest arts by patrons from the East Coast, who settled in New Mexico and other areas from the 1920s on. They not only established many important museums that frame the Southwest as a faraway and exotic land of enchantment; they also created boards of venues such as the Indian and Spanish Markets, through which they attempted to control and even, it would seem, to freeze in time Native and Hispanic artists' works. With their often quite rigid guidelines, an emphasis on handmade objects, and a tendency to view art as folklore, these markets have interfered with traditional patterns of creation and innovation and have forced the endless reproduction of colonial (and anachronistic) forms. However, despite the preservation of what was understood as "traditional" folk art, East Coast art patrons and collectors nevertheless indirectly provided Hispanic and Pueblo artists access to a wider audience and to museum curators all over the United States, making way for today's Southwest arts renaissance. Indeed, I was inspired to research this period of American cultural history when I encountered contemporary southwestern figures of the Virgin of Guadalupe that resembled representations from Mexico's early colonial period that we have already seen. Why, I wondered, was the Virgin represented in the U.S. Southwest in the same way she was represented in Mexico in the seventeenth and eighteenth centuries, whereas in Mexico her representation had evolved and been radically and successively transformed?

Simultaneously, while many santeros continue representing the Virgin in this anachronistic manner, other artists, such as Marion Martínez, whose circuit board art we encountered in the previous chapter, experiment by recycling the image in quite radical ways. Indeed, artists such as Luis Tapia altogether circumvent the restrictions of New Mexico's official "markets" that force the reproduction of anachronistic "folk" art. His parodies of folk art collectors and his representations of the lowriders in Española as well as their dashboard altars have become signature pieces. The convergence of these trends (preservation/rarification and innovation), however, allows for a larger phenomenon to take place that could be termed the "profound New Mexico" or "New Mestizo" effect—an effect that resonates far beyond the Southwest. Contributing to the Latini-

6.1. *New Mexico's license plate*
Photo Jack Parsons

6.2. *Typical anachronistic representation of the
    Virgin of Guadalupe*
Taos santero shop, New Mexico
Photo Spitta 2002
*Notice the individual rays emanating from her
    body, as in typical Mexican colonial sculptures
    and paintings of the Virgin.*

zation of the rest of the United States, the Southwest's sacred landscape is exported to the rest of the country as an aesthetic, whether through the collections of objects in museums devoted to Southwestern arts, folklore, and modern art; or in the trinkets sold at art galleries seemingly everywhere, and particularly in Santa Fe and Taos; or as the presence-imbued bultos (sacred sculpted images) made by local saint-makers (santeros) seen in private workshops and churches.

THE CREATION OF A LAND OF ENCHANTMENT

The creation of the Land of Enchantment consists of several concurrent moves deeply reminiscent of the logic of the Wunderkammern: utopian projection by Anglo-Americans and foreign visitors, and the exploitation, preservation, and collection of the traditional arts of the region, all of which coexist in uneasy—and often creative—tension with the area's Indo-Hispanic culture and history. There is perhaps no better example of the dynamics and tension between destruction and preservation and between Anglo artists and native communities than the history embedded in the Mabel Dodge Luhan House. Overlooking Taos Pueblo and sited at the base of Taos's sacred mountain (significantly thought of by New Agers as directly across the world from Tibet), it was established

6.3. The Folk Art Collectors
Carved and painted wood
17¼ × 15⅛ × 8⅛ inches
1992 Luis Tapia
Courtesy of the artist and Owings-Dewey Fine
*   Art Gallery*

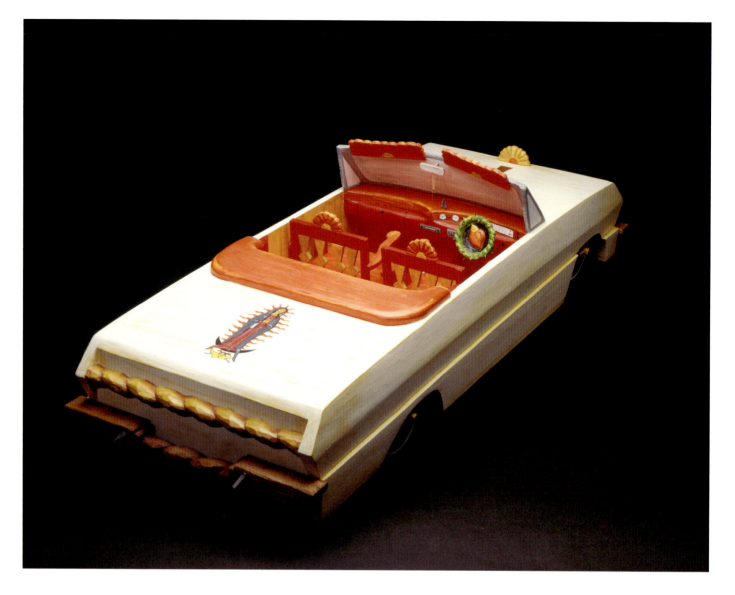

6.4. "Spanish Colonial" Carreta
Carved and painted wood
10¼ × 14 × 3 inches
1993 Luis Tapia
Courtesy of the artist and Owings-Dewey Fine Art Gallery
Luis Tapia's choice of title for his contemporary lowrider alludes to the colonial religious carretas, which were actually allegories for death.

6.5. Chima Altar II, Betram's Cruise
Carved and painted wood
34½ × 58 × 18¾ inches
1992 Luis Tapia
Courtesy of the artist and Owings-Dewey Fine Art Gallery

in 1916 by Mabel Dodge, a New York socialite. She remodeled the 160-year-old adobe house, symbol of the Eden and Shangri-La she had found in Taos, with her husband Antonio Luhan—a Taos Pueblo whom she married shortly after settling there.[3] The house, with its Spanish colonial flagstone placita with ceilings of viga [wooden beams], hand-carved doors, Pueblo fireplaces, and entries made of ancient altarpieces, is listed today on the National Register of Historic Places. An American Frida Kahlo and symbol of the 1920s counterculture movement, Mabel Dodge presided over a renowned salon at the house, attracting writers and artists, both housing them and using her great wealth to promote them. Writers D. H. Lawrence, Willa Cather, Mary Austin, Harvey Ferguson, Aldous Huxley, and Frank Waters; painters, sculptors, and photographers Georgia O'Keeffe, John Marin, Dorothy Brett, Nicolai Fechin, Laura Gilpin, Ida Rauh, Maurice Stern, Ansel Adams, Paul and Rebecca Strand, Cady Wells, and Edward Weston; activist John Collier; musicians Carlos Chávez, Dane Rudhyar, and Leopold Stokowski; designer Robert Edmond Jones, dance choreographer Martha Graham, and even psychologist Carl Jung were among the many notables who stayed there.[4] When Willa Cather (traveling with her lover, Edith Lewis) visited New Mexico in 1925, she was like so many others then, trying to escape industrialization, increasing urbanization, and a post-WWI world experienced as "broken." Housed by Mary Austin, they were persistently courted by Mabel Dodge until they moved into what is known as the Pink House (a small house set apart from the main building) and were left alone to write, undisturbed except for meals, and with Tony Luhan at their disposal as a silent yet very informed tour guide. As a result, he enters the pages of *Death Comes for the Archbishop* in the guise of the Indian.

If we expand from this one example to include the creation of the numerous star visitors of the Mabel Dodge Luhan House and the way their stay in New Mexico affected their art, it becomes clear that the Southwest is as much an artistic creation, and an aesthetic phenomenon in film, art, literature, music, painting, theater-set design, dance, and fashion, as it is a reality. More importantly even, American modernist art would be unthinkable without what I would call East Coast artists' "encounter with the totem" in the Southwest. As was the case with European modernism, indigenous art here, too, played a foundational role in its origins, development, and move toward abstraction. Unlike Picasso, Gauguin, and other modernist painters who had to go far afield, however, in the United States the "encounter with the totem" was possible within the confines of the country itself. And unlike European modernist art, which would learn about abstraction largely from African and indigenous art, and remain limited as an aesthetic phenomenon, the new art forms created in the United States and derived from this encounter would not only lead to a distinct Southwest artistic style, but also serve as an opening for Chicano artists to explore mestizo politics and aesthetics.

While Ansel Adams's and Georgia O'Keeffe's artworks are everywhere today, the indigenization of the Southwest now most apparent and popularly known in Juan O'Gorman's stylized paintings was begun in the 1920s by painters such as Maurice Stern, Andrew Dasburg, Marsden Hartley, Agnes Pelton, Dorothy Brett, and Arnold Rönnebeck, among many others. The most famous painter of the Southwest today, O'Keeffe began traveling to New Mexico in the late 1920s—leaving Alfred Stieglitz to enjoy the Lake George region where he was most at home. The trip to Taos by train that

she undertook with her friend Beck Strand changed her life. Very soon after her arrival in Taos, she visited D. H. Lawrence's utopian ranch and was invited to stay at the Mabel Dodge Luhan House, a visit that was commemorated by the bed-and-breakfast with its "Georgia O'Keeffe room." She painted the famous *The Lawrence Tree* and the *Fragment of the Rancho de Taos Church* in 1929, as well as many of the crosses that sacralize the landscape everywhere. The high desert, with its clear air, allowed her to see differently, she felt, and it changed her painting in fundamental ways.

Reminding us of W. G. Sebald's characterization in his novel *The Emigrants* of the "abysmal solitude brought upon us by the displacements of modernity" as a "mist that no eye can dispel,"[5] emigration to New Mexico was seen by O'Keeffe and many others as the possibility of acquiring clearer vision, artistically, politically, and emotionally granted by the special nature of that space. Even after she moved there permanently after Stieglitz's death, O'Keeffe would refer nostalgically to Northern New Mexico's vast and empty expanse as "the faraway place"—a space she explored alone in a Model A Ford, which she learned to drive after much anguish, converting it into a mobile painter's studio. Soon after settling in New Mexico, she started to collect the dry bones that have come to symbolize both her painting and the land that so inspired her to paint otherwise. *Ram's Head with Hollyhock* (1930), *Cow's Skull—Red, White, and Blue* (1930), and the bones that decorate her library at the house in Abiqiú (with the view of the flat-topped Jémez mesa range, which she also painted), now a museum, embody the feeling she had for that faraway place. The deadness and calcification of the bones nevertheless allow that "something that is keenly alive on the desert even tho' it is vast and empty and untouchable . . . and knows no kindness with all its beauty"[6] to show through.

6.6. *Setting by Robert Edmond Jones for Arthur Hopkins's production of* Macbeth.
The Pageant of America 1921
Anonymous
Photography Collection, Miriam and Ira D. Wallach Division of Art, Prints and Photographs
The New York Public Library, Astor, Lenox, and Tilden Foundations

(opposite, top) 6.7a. Rain over Desert Mesas
1931 Arnold Rönnebeck
Lithograph
Denver Art Museum Collection: Funds from The William D. Hewit Charitable Annuity Trust, 1985.304
© Denver Art Museum

(opposite, bottom) 6.7b. Taos Houses (New Mexican Village)
1926 Andrew Dasburg
Oil on canvas
24 × 30 inches
Collection of the New Mexico Museum of Art. Gift of Mrs. Cyrus McCormick, 1952.

6.8. Black Cross, New Mexico, 1929
Georgia O'Keeffe
Oil on canvas
Art Institute of Chicago

The high desert stretches inspired her and other visitors to feel as if they had entered a tabula rasa that they could inscribe at will. Yet at the same time, and as part of the same move, the vitality of indigenous cultures and the Hispanic and native colonial subtext of the region—unlike most other parts of the United States—served as a force that overwhelmed these artists and inscribed their work with its presence. In awe of and fascinated by the large wooden crosses of the *Penitentes* (a Hispanic religious sect discussed below) that dot the landscape and appear in the churches all over New Mexico, Georgia O'Keeffe famously and quite apodictically decreed: "Anyone who doesn't feel the crosses simply doesn't get that country."[7] Today one could add, for great parts of the United States and not altogether hyperbolically, that whoever does not feel the Guadalupes does not "get" the country.

As anyone who stays longer in New Mexico soon realizes, and as Lois Palken Rudnick writes in *Utopian Vistas*, her biography of the Mabel Dodge Luhan House in Taos, the dream of New Mexico as a modern-day Shangri-La actually commodifies New Mexicans' poverty and third-world reality. Overlooking both the Germanic settlement of the alpine valleys (marked by names such as Edelweiss and Der Markt [sic], all-pervasive in ski resorts, and the "oompah"-like quality of Rio Grande music) and the French evangelization attempts (best embodied in Santa Fe's Romanesque church), the Southwest is usually characterized as a "triethnic community marked by interethnic prejudice and conflict."[8] Palken Rudnick herself was made aware of the tragic contrasts that prevail in New Mexico. In the 1980s, on her first visit to Taos, a young boy was killed while urinating on someone else's property late at night. The next day, a fourteen-year-old runaway Anglo girl who worked at the Mabel Dodge Luhan House was chased through the kitchen with a knife by the Taos man with whom she lived while Rudnick was there giving her talk on the relationship between D. H. Lawrence and Mabel Dodge. The same history of violence is readily apparent when the visitor stops to read the memorials at roadside shrines. Expecting to read about deaths due to automobile accidents, we stopped at two roadside crosses that denounced the unsolved murders of two young men. While these observations may be anecdotal, the disjunction between the myth and allure of the Southwest and the underlying poverty and violence that they mask overwhelms the visitor and serves as an index of the fraught relationship between colonialism and commercialization that I have been outlining. "Enchantment and exploitation," as historian William deBuys has termed it, inhabit the same space.[9] Indigenous cultures serve as the gathering grounds for the objects coveted by collectors yet remain invisible. It is impossible not to draw a parallel between the situation in the Southwest and New Mexico in particular and Latin American forms of indigenismo and the politics of mestizaje as state ideology.

When Palken Rudnick writes, "Those who lived and worked in the Luhan house have had much to do with constructing the image of Taos as a multicultural Eden, whose indigenous people live in peace and harmony with the land,"[10] the parallels with Latin America become even more apparent. Arnold Rönnebeck, a painter and visitor at the Mabel Dodge Luhan House, immediately saw the process as one where Americans turned to the "indigenous traditions of Native Americans in order to create an original national culture."[11] Equally true, however, is the fact that what I would call the "New Mexico/New Mestizo effect" permeates artistic sensibilities all over the United States—

from dance, to literature, to photography, to music, to home-decorating fashion—to an unaccounted-for extent. Indeed, it is in the Southwest, from the 1898 creation of the Taos Artists Colony, to the successive waves of immigrants to the region in the 1920s, 1960s, and most recently in the 1990s that mestizaje as a reality and as an aesthetic agenda begins to be formulated (if not explicitly, at least implicitly) and to create a ripple effect across U.S. culture. I write "implicitly" because so many important institutions, such as the Harwood Museum, explain their mission not in terms of mestizaje but of "convergence" of Anglo artists, the New Mexican landscape, and traditional Native American and Hispanic cultures of the region. That ripple effect situates the Southwest in dynamic tension with the Northeast and contests the official version of U.S. history, which has its origins in the thirteen colonies, thus effectively erasing the Spanish colonial period. As many foreign visitors to the Mabel Dodge Luhan House immediately recognized, New Mexico was a special place in the United States because of its Spanish colonial history and its multicultural and multiracial underpinnings. What seems clear in particular is that today's rewriting of U.S. race relations, in terms of both whiteness and mestizaje (most apparent in the recent, highly publicized Jefferson family history), can be traced back to the dynamics established in Taos in the 1920s and would be unthinkable without them.

As with Latin American ideologies of mestizaje, multicultural thinking here too depends on the establishment of a past native Eden at the expense of contemporary reality and contemporary natives. To a great extent—and this is true for both Latin America and U.S. indigenism—the positing of an Edenic past (a land so remote) rests on the creation of great collections of Native and Hispanic artifacts that served as the building blocks of most of the Southwest's most important museums. Mabel Dodge Luhan herself was not only a renowned patron, she was also a collector of native and colonial Hispanic arts. Her great collection served as the founding block of the famous Harwood Museum and is but one example among many others of the collectors' zeal that beset Anglo-American settlers in the Southwest. Mary Austin, too, aside from her novels *The Land of Little Rain* (1903), *Starry Adventure: The Book of New Mexico* (1931), and others, founded the Spanish Colonial Arts Society in 1925 with artist and writer Frank Applegate. The Spanish Colonial Arts Society's mission is that of preserving and perpetuating Hispanic art forms produced in New Mexico and southern Colorado since Spain's colonization in 1598. It has sponsored the semi-annual Spanish Market, become a leader in educating the public about traditional Hispanic art and culture, and recently founded the Spanish Colonial Arts Museum atop Museum Hill in Santa Fe.[12] Paralleling the establishment of Spanish Market, Native Americans called for the founding of Indian Market in the 1920s. Earlier still, at the turn of the twentieth century, the founding of the Taos Artists Colony, and later the creation of the Taos Artists Society, brought important sponsors (individual, corporate, and museums) in touch with artists.[13]

The Millicent Rogers Museum is another case in point. With its collections of Pueblo pottery (particularly the family collection of Santa Clara potter Maria Martínez), photography, textiles (Navajo "psychedelic" textiles), Hispanic historic and contemporary santos, Hopi and Zuni kachina dolls, Navajo and Pueblo jewelry, Río Grande Pueblo paintings, and Southwestern basketry, the stellar collection was created by Millicent Rogers (1902–1953), the granddaughter of one of the founders of Standard Oil, Henry Huttleston

Rogers. A sickly child beset by rheumatic fever, Millicent Rogers had spent much of her life living in New York City and traveling in Europe. She settled in Taos, drawn there by the landscape and the healthier climate, where she, like Mabel Dodge Luhan, lived in a remodeled adobe house. Her museum was first housed in Taos's artists' lane—located originally on the famous Ledoux Street and then moved outside town to a site built and donated by Claude and Elizabeth Anderson and renovated and expanded by renowned architect Nathaniel Owings in the 1980s.[14] Today, the collection is continually expanding, thanks to donations by numerous patrons and collectors. Millicent Rogers was also known for her work with famous clothing designers of her time, and while the museum in Taos contains one room with some of these, the greater part of her fashion collection is housed in the Brooklyn Museum in New York City. The separation between both collections, locating fashion in New York whereas native and Hispanic folk and religious art is collected in the Southwest, is a distinction that underlies the creation of wonder.

A crucial example of these dynamics is the large collection in the Museum of International Folk Art, now sited on "museum hill" on the outskirts of Santa Fe. Its showcase is the Girard Foundation Collection, consisting of the 106,000 pieces of folk art assembled throughout a lifetime by architect and designer Alexander Girard and his wife, Susan, and donated to the museum in the 1980s. With offices in New York, Detroit, and finally in Santa Fe, Girard was renowned in his time for his revolutionary and wide-ranging Santa Fe–inflected designs (furniture, textiles, buildings such as the famous Hotel Fonda del Sol, the L'Etoile restaurant in New York City, Braniff International Airlines' revolutionary "look" in the 1960s, etc.). An American of Italian descent, Girard was well connected, and he and his wife traveled extensively, building up their collection in order to save different cultures' valuable folk art from disappearance—in what could serve as a prime example of what James Clifford has called "salvage ethnology."[15] Girard reflected that "we should preserve evidence of the past, not as a pattern for sentimental imitation, but as nourishment for the creative spirit of the present."[16] Consisting mainly of miniatures from over one hundred different cultures, the wing that houses the collection was arranged into a multiplicity of "scenes"—reminding us of Barnum's cultural panopticon—representing typical moments in the life of different cultures. The objects assembled range from toys, puppets, tapestries, masks, sculptures, and toy theaters to religious and devotional art. The displays of hundreds if not thousands of figures (e.g., a Peruvian Andean fiesta, a Spanish bullfight, a Mexican baptism, an Indonesian wedding, etc.) all mimic the arrangement of figures in traditional nativity scenes. The Girards were different than most collectors in that they did not collect "one of a kind" art; rather, they bought hundreds of pieces from the same artisans and soon needed several large barns built on their property to store a collection that was growing incrementally. Sheer numbers of objects were needed to replicate the nativity scenes that fascinated Girard in the Florentine churches he visited as a young child. His insistence on the handmade nature of folk art mirrored the Indian and Spanish Markets' emphasis and guidelines. Yet despite Girard's belief in the need to preserve traditional folk art, he himself was inspired by it to revolutionize the world of design. He managed to personalize and instill life into what he perceived was increasingly an aseptic, mechanized, and "auraless" modernity in large measure responsible for the fast disappearance of the folk art he was bent on salvaging.

The Girard wing of the museum seems like a massive, multifaceted diorama of world folk art and is very similar to the extensive miniature display "Market at Tenochtitlán" in Mexico City's Archaeology Museum. As in natural history museums, the diversity of the world is both celebrated and displayed, and lies at arm's reach much as the village of the famous humanist saying that characterized the Girards' worldview: "Tutto il mondo e paese"/"the whole world is hometown," and which serves as the title to a short catalogue of the exhibition (*Folk Art from the Global Village*).[17] However, unlike the usually fairly discrete dioramas of natural history museums, the objects in Girard's exhibition, appropriately entitled "Multiple Visions: A Common Bond," do not stand alone but are arranged in what seem like huge orchestras of feeling, reflecting his belief that things alone and out of context lose their meaning. "Part of my passion," he writes, "has always been to see objects in context. As a collector who was often able to visit the workshop of the artist and see the actual environment in which a piece was made, I've often felt that objects lose half their lives when they are taken out of their natural settings. . . . I believe that if you put objects into a world which is ostensibly their own, the whole thing begins to breathe."[18] Because of their collection's location atop "museum hill" in Santa Fe, because of its inclusion of a massive Southwestern folk art collection, with Navajo geometric tapestries, Córdova woodcarvings, Cochiti ceramics, etc., and because of their renown in and around Santa Fe, the Girards, like the other collectors I have mentioned, were instrumental in creating what I have been calling the "allure" of the Southwest and imposing the Southwest as a "look" and an aesthetic across the rest of the United States. As the mission of the New Mexico Arts Society puts it: "From prehistoric basket weavers to Spanish santeros to members of the Taos Society of Artists, the people of New Mexico have long recognized and cherished their diverse artistic expressions. This ongoing commitment to cultural integrity has blossomed into a well-recognized profile for New Mexico . . . one which equates arts and culture with the identity of the state itself."[19] In turn, the Gene Autry Western Heritage Museum in Los Angeles, named after one of the creators of the "Southwest" in film and a great collector of Southwestern art, describes its mission as that of offering "an entertaining and educational opportunity to discover the legacy of the American West [since to] *a great degree the story of the West is a contrast of the historical and the mythological*" (Emphasis mine).[20]

These words reflect the enormous contribution and "marketing" of the Southwest effected by the eastern elite that had moved to Taos and Santa Fe since the 1920s. These artists and arbiters of culture made it possible for the Spanish borderlands to be imagined as a cultural composite or mestizaje of Native American, Hispanic, and Anglo-American contributions (the Taos Society of Artists). Indeed, like mestizaje promoted through muralism as state ideology in Mexico by Minister of Culture José Vasconcelos after the Mexican Revolution, here, too, the ability to think a mestizo space (or "cultural composite," as the wording usually goes) depends on a double move reminiscent of Latin American forms of indigenismo: with a negation of live indigenous peoples, the past is affirmed through collections dependent on the reproduction of colonial forms. The successive waves of socialites, writers, philosophers, painters, photographers, musicians, and filmmakers who arrived in the Southwest were drawn there for its wildness, its desertedness, and the view they had of it as a new frontier (particularly for women in the 1920s) that could be inscribed by their vision and desire. They ended up as avid collectors, subjected to their amassing of native objects. Paradoxically, seeing native culture and traditions as a potent antidote against the urban materialism that they were escaping, they were able to establish their immense collections thanks to great fortunes—like oil—that were in part responsible for the destruction of the world from which its heirs were seeking refuge in the Southwest. Reminding us that processes of transculturation always involve a give and take, the desire to see the Southwest as a frontier, a desert, a land faraway, was constantly corrected, perhaps even frustrated, and always enriched and informed by the pervasive native and Hispanic presence and culture. The *Penitentes'* crosses that so overwhelmed Georgia O'Keeffe serve as a symbol of the two-way exchange that was taking place beneath all the rhetorical noise made about the desert and the huge emptiness of the land.

Making the great American Southwest a multiply-mythologized space, these Anglo-American indigenizing narratives exist in counterpoint to the whole complex of thinking around a mythic region (called "Aztlán" by Chicano activists in the 1960s) that grafts that space onto a larger Mesoamerican geography and culture. Beginning with its inscription in the códices—particularly that of the little feet walking south, represented in the "Tira de la peregrinación" of the *Codex Boturini*—the land of herons and of the seven caves, the great Mexican Northwest, mythic point of origin and return of the Mexicas, the land to which Moctezuma I is said to have sent an expedition, has become a new focus of study for archaelogists and ethnologists. Miguel León-Portilla points out that scientific findings confirm a cultural continuum that ranges from the U.S. Southwest or Mexican Northwest—depending on the point of view—that passes through Mexico-Tenochtitlán, all the way south to Central America. Archaeologists and ethnologists both in Mexico and the United States concur that "from the time of Teotihuacán (from the third to the eighth century A.D.) and even before, beyond the vast cultural region of

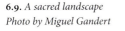

6.9. *A sacred landscape*
Photo by Miguel Gandert

Mesoamerica, situated in the center and south of Mexico, many inhabitants of those northern lands participated in the cultural achievements of the Mesoamericans."[21] León-Portilla finds evidence of Náhuatl words in existence even today in the Southwest. "Analco," meaning "on the other side of the water or the river," for example, is still the name of one of the oldest quarters of Santa Fe.[22] "Aztlán" was already known and named in the sixteenth-century writings of Aztec historians Alvarado Tezozomoc and Alva Ixtlilxochitl. This land, continually traveled and traversed in two directions throughout the centuries, the U.S. Southwest and Mexico's Northwest, is inscribed in competing narratives that both overlap and are incommensurate with each other. The recent magnificent exhibition of the Los Angeles County Museum, "The Road to Aztlán: Art from a Mythic Homeland," as well as CARA's (*Chicano Art: Resistance and Affirmation: An Interpretive Exhibition of the Chicano Art Movement, 1965–1985*)[23] critical response to this exhibition, "Other Roads to Aztlán," document the new geography of this land in-between, or nepantla.[24] The exhibitions trace the native Hispanic culture of the Southwest from its origins in the 1500s and the search for El Dorado and the Seven Cities of Cíbola to its reconfiguration by the Chicano movement and contemporary Mexican and Mexican-American artists.

SACRED GEOGRAPHIES AND PILGRIMAGES

A few years ago, when I was in New Mexico researching this chapter, the *Santa Fe El Norte* reported on the arrival of a group of pilgrims from Michigan traveling with a statue of the Virgin of Guadalupe. They had started out from Mexico City, had visited seven other Mexican cities, and were headed home to Grand Rapids. On their way, they were stopping in five U.S. cities, including Albuquerque and Santa Fe. The pilgrims (a dozen or so) would be housed in the hall of the Our Lady of Guadalupe parish, and special masses were being planned in honor of the statue and the pilgrimage. Commissioned by Reverend José Quintana, pastor of St. Francis Xavier parish in Grand Rapids—and one of the pilgrims himself—the statue was the work of Mexican sculptor José Antonio Silva. It was made of gold leaf and Central and South American wood and was nine feet tall. It had been blessed in Mexico City during Pope John Paul II's highly publicized canonization of the Indian Juan Diego and would be housed permanently in Rev. Quintana's parish in Grand Rapids. "It is really big," parishioner Estrella Ortiz is quoted as saying.[25] While it is not quite clear what is big (the event? the statue? the pilgrimage?), the *Santa Fe El Norte*'s front-page coverage of what some would consider a minor event is significant for the sacred geography that it assumes so matter-of-factly.

This sacred landscape starts in the vicinity of Denver and spreads south, reminding us that during the Spanish colonial period of U.S. history, New Spain comprised the greater part of what is today the West and Southwest United States. Significantly, a 22-foot-high hilltop statue of Jesus overlooks the city of Denver. Discovered in 1912, the spring with the healing powers was discovered by Mother Frances Cabrini (1850–1917), an Italian famous for having founded many schools, hospitals, and orphanages across the United States, Latin America, and Europe.[26] Considered "America's first saint," she was at a picnic when she touched a stone with her cane and asked someone to lift it, thus miraculously uncovering the spring. Today, the Mother Cabrini Shrine attracts over 150,000 pilgrims a year from around the world.[27] Farther south, in northern New Mexico, in the foothills of the Sangre de Cristo Mountains, the sanctuary at Chimayó is the central convergence point of the most popular pilgrimage site in the United States. During Holy Week, thousands of pilgrims arrive from all over the Southwest and beyond, and can be seen on the roads leading to Chimayó bearing crosses, walking on their knees, and otherwise fulfilling "promises" made to the Señor de Esquípulas in exchange for his intervention on their behalf. Chimayó boasts a seemingly endless supply, not of water but of miraculous red earth. In fact, indexing the Southwest's Indo-Hispanic cultural and geographic continuum, earth connects Guatemala with Chimayó, since in the shrine to the Christ at Esquípulas in Guatemala the white earth of the site is said to have acquired healing properties when a dark cross was taken there.

Chimayó, like Esquípulas, figures prominently in Indo-Hispanic foundational myths and has been a pilgrimage site since ancient times. For the Tewa-speaking people of nearby pueblos, "Chimayó is one of the cardinal cosmological sites," as it was the scene of a heavenly battle that helped prepare the world for human habitation in the regional traditional Creation story." Fire, smoke, and scalding water spewed forth from the earth in the place named Tsimayopokwi ("tsimayo" for "where the big stones stand," and pokwi for "pool"). The Tewa ancestors began visiting the sandy spring at Chimayó for the healing properties of the earth to be found there.[28] True to most of the myths surrounding holy icons and sites, and as with the original Spanish Guadalupe story, they have a mind of their own and insist on a specific place where they want shrines in their honor erected. A more recent tradition therefore has it that Shamnoag, a Picurís Pueblo Indian, found a cross buried in the ground. After Shamnoag removed it, the cross returned to its original site twice. Yet another version of this myth that circulates among the Tewa pueblo of Isleta has it that another shepherd found "Escápula," a little carved head in the ground. Fearful, his wife told him to burn it, whereupon she became paralyzed. And like in the Picurís version, when the priest told him to take the head to Santa Fe, it too disappeared and returned to its original site. The wife was cured when she and her husband realized its holy powers and prayed to it. Because of these miraculous powers, to this day, writes Lamadrid, the Tewa consider San Escápula "one of the most powerful saints."[29] In Spanish-Mexican versions of this same legend, Bernardo Abeyta began to negotiate the building of the Sanctuary of Chimayó in honor of the Christ of Esquípulas (to whom he was already devoted) in 1813, when the Christ miraculously appeared to him and healed him. In another version, Abeyta is said to have found the miraculous image of the Christ of Esquípulas, and when he tried to take it away, it returned time and again to its original site, thereby signaling where the sanctuary was to be built. Reminding us in some ways of Mother Francis Cabrini, Abeyta, too, was not only a religious man but also a leading citizen and Chimayó's most successful merchant. He realized the powerful appeal religious sites have at the crossroads of commercial routes and that a "shrine in Northern New Mexico would be sure to attract the faithful and enhance commerce based on local industry as well as hospitality for the pilgrims."[30]

Chimayó was completed in 1816, thanks to the overlaying of these foundational myths. As with so many of these stories, the building of the shrine depended on the discovery of a series of miraculous objects that insistently mark a particular space as holy. The sanctuary is a massively walled fortress church literally built on and around

the site of the original spring, where fire, smoke, and scalding water had spewed forth from the earth in humanity's battle against the titan. Unusual is Chimayó's dual appeal. Another shrine on the same site is dedicated to the Santo Niño de Atocha, whose symbols coincide with those of the pilgrim: the shell, the staff, the water of salvation, the road, and the cloak. Patron of travelers, captives, and children, his *bulto* receives all the *promesas* carried by the pilgrims. This site, too, has its own foundational myths that resemble those of the Christ of Esquípulas. Today, pilgrims enter the church and face the altar that bears the cross Abeyta found, which is framed by five *reredos*, or wooden altar screens, made by famous colonial *santeros* José Aragón and Miguel Aragón. Pilgrims exit to a small room adjacent to the altar, where they can gather some of the miraculous red earth from a hole in the ground—refilled daily by the sanctuary's priest with earth from the Sangre de Cristo Mountains. They exit the church through a larger room in which they can leave their promesas. This room is filled with paintings, ex-votos, crutches, and all sorts of bric-à-brac hung on or put around a statue of the Santo Niño de Atocha and which the priest empties when overflowing.[31] While this room is the depository of objects carried from afar, the pilgrims engage in an exchange with Chimayó's deities: in return for their visit and the objects (milagros, ex-votos) they leave behind, they carry away with them some of Chimayó's red earth, metonymically charged with the power of the Santo Niño de Atocha and the Lord of Esquípulas, whose authority rests on that earth. Seamlessly merging religion with commerce, in the stores around the sanctuary, pilgrims can conveniently buy attractive vials in which to hold the miraculous earth.

As we saw in the previous chapters, the belief that Christians could establish intimate communication with saints of their devotion through saints' representation in paintings or through objects associated or touched by them underlies all pilgrimage traditions. Union with the saint of one's devotion, then, takes place either by direct contact, by having been blessed in the presence of the venerated icon, or by touching the sacred image or painting. But nothing is more concrete, according to Teresa Gisbert, than "when one can possess a part of the desired object," particularly since relics were thought to be the repositories of the saint's transferred power.[32] This belief would, of course, foster

(**opposite**) **6.10.** *Room next to where pilgrims get a sample of red earth. In exchange, they leave their "promesas" in this room.*
Chimayó, New Mexico
Photo Sam Howarth

6.11. *Pilgrim on his way to Chimayó, New Mexico*
Photo Sam Howarth

6.12. *Arriving at Chimayó for Easter*
Chimayó, New Mexico
Photo Sam Howarth
Notice the Penitente with his cross.

the creation and multiplication of religious icons most visible in massively popular pilgrimage traditions and the myriad splendid Latin American churches. These expressions of the Baroque, however, are almost entirely absent in New Mexico, because most churches doubled as fortresses during the colonial period. Also to blame are the Pueblo Revolts, which caused much lasting destruction of religious art and architecture. Unlike in Latin America, therefore, and somewhat oddly, in the U.S. Southwest the Baroque persists in religious practices, despite its absence as an artistic aesthetic.

As the *Santa Fe El Norte*'s report on the pilgrimage from Grand Rapids shows, with migration to the United States the sacred landscape that starts in Denver and extends south to the tip of South America is now fast expanding north and including more and more cities. Anthropologists who have studied Latin American pilgrimage traditions have concluded that pilgrimages not only are sites of negotiation between the sacred and the profane, but that, given the intricate sociocultural web that sustains them, they are over and beyond anything else a "celebration of the social identity of a people, or *nation*."[33] The pilgrimage from Grand Rapids can be read as an incipient attempt at establishing a link between Grand Rapids and other pilgrimage sites in the Americas, and thus as a process of transformation of an American city into the immigrants' city. By means of the pilgrimage, the Mexican pilgrims are actually wresting an Anglo-American space away from itself and grafting it onto and into an earlier, colonial, Hispanic/Catholic context. This is particularly interesting since Grand Rapids' original white settlers were primarily Dutch Calvinists. Furthermore, because pilgrimages, with the penance and festivities that they entail, are "meant to be transformative processes, from which the individual emerges altered from his or her previous situation," the pilgrimage from Grand Rapids can also be seen as the process of the creation of a new identity.[34] In this case,

6.13. *Las Trampas church*
Photo Spitta 2004
Notice the fortress-like structure, which would explain the lack of the Baroque in the U.S. Southwest.

because the Virgin of Guadalupe to be housed in Grand Rapids was blessed by the Pope in Mexico City, the pilgrims are clearly establishing a Mexican identity-in-migration. The identity that is being affirmed is not only subversive of the nation-state; it is also subversive of the Anglocentric national imaginary constructed by a historiography that elides the Spanish colonial period from U.S. history. While not overtly subversive, then, the Grand Rapids pilgrimage nevertheless has to be contextualized within a subtle yet persistent chipping away at the image of "America" by Latinos.

In addition to pilgrimage centers themselves, there is also a large infrastructure that nurtures and sustains them. Crumrine and Morinis point out that pilgrimage does not "exist in real isolation. As a popular institution and an institution of popular culture, the pilgrimage is woven securely into its regional cultural field." Thus, Bernardo Abeyta negotiated the building of Chimayó between 1800 and 1850, an era that paradoxically coincides with Mexico's "secular interlude" and the expulsion of priests from the public sphere.[35] Catholicism went underground during this time. The scarcity of priests, particularly in the outlying areas, has led many historians who depend exclusively on written records to assert the collapse of the Mexican mission system and dominion over its borderlands. Yet, as the example at Chimayó shows, religious sentiment not only survived—it flourished in the Southwest during this period. The renewed impulse can be attributed to the creation of informal, local sui generis infrastructures that were quite creative in filling the vacuum left after Mexico's expulsion of clerics in 1828 and before the inception of missionary efforts by U.S. clergy. The most important of these "Do-It-Yourself" types of "folk Catholicism," and others Nuevo Mexico profundo, is the still-extant brotherhood of the *Hermanos Penitentes*.[36]

The *Penitentes'* origins are still a mystery and a matter of debate among historians: some, seeing resemblances between native kivas and the moradas or houses of worship, argue that they had a Native American origin, while others detect vestiges of medieval flagellanti, and still others claim that they were an outgrowth of the Third Order of St. Francis. What is known is that they were organized by groups of Catholic Hispanic men in New Mexico and southern Colorado between 1776 and 1833 as secret societies in order to fill the vacuum left by expelled priests, and to do pious works as a way of affirming their Catholicism.[37] Focused around celebrations of Holy Week and the Passion of Christ, the *Penitentes* provided economic support and religious solace to members of their communities. They constructed hundreds of *moradas*, or religious meetinghouses—built to be as inconspicuous as possible. These dot the landscape in the Southwest.[38] Even as late as 1960, and despite the return of the Catholic Church, they numbered between two and three thousand, which leads critics to suspect that there may have been many more between the late eighteenth and mid-nineteenth century at the height of Mexico's anticlericalism. The *Penitentes'* pilgrimages, focusing as they do on the Passion of Christ, involve doing penance, carrying large crosses, and even being symbolically crucified—a practice that has led to inflammatory stories about them that are often fueled by religious institutions whose authority they parallel in an unorthodox manner. The exaggerated accounts of the *Penitentes'* extreme practices mask the fact that, aside from these public ritual displays of religiosity, they actually served as an important community-based social agency. They raised money to help bury impoverished members of their communities, to pay for and help in the celebration of ritual passages such as baptisms, weddings, and death rites, and otherwise to help needy members. In fact, despite numerous prohibitions against their practices and concomitant deepening secrecy, "it remains clear that neither Church representatives nor local Brothers were diametrically opposed. Not all moradas espoused the more zealous rites, and not all parish priests considered themselves above compromise," writes Marta Weigle.[39] Furthermore, the *Penitentes* were involved in local governments, often being prominent players in local elections. Many suspect they were behind the Taos Rebellion of 1847, rallying behind the schismatic Father José Martínez—a figure who is revered even today (Weigle, 16), and who appears as the looming shadow protagonist in Willa Cather's *Death Comes for the Archbishop*. Later, with the annexation of New Mexico into the United States and the separation of church and state, the *Penitentes* had to reorganize as benevolent societies, thus acquiring "political and judicial expertise."[40] Of a significance that went well beyond the upholding of Catholic rituals and the help extended to the needy, the *Penitentes* were largely responsible for the maintenance of Hispanic New Mexican culture, traditions, and language.

The moradas the *Penitentes* built were adobe structures marked by a cross, with a very simple fortress-like interior. They did, however, contain altars on which santos or bultos (sculptures of different religious figures, usually made of wood and sometimes painted and made by local santeros) and *retablos* (two-dimensional images) were displayed. Given that there were hundreds of churches and moradas in the Southwest (even the smallest of towns often boast relatively large churches), given the tradition of homes having both indoor and outdoor altars and private shrines, given the revival in Hispanic and native arts spearheaded by the Spanish Colonial Arts Society and others, and furthermore, given the increasing impact of tourism, it is not surprising that the demand for religious folk art both was and remains great. In northern New Mexico, roads are dotted by signs to the *talleres* (or workshops) of local santeros (makers of religious sculpture); the centerpieces of most museums consist of retablos, bultos, and reredos made by colonial and contemporary Hispanic artists.[41] The Taylor Museum of Southwestern Study, the most important wing of the Colorado Springs Museum of Fine Arts, boasts of having in its possession the *entire* chapel at Talpa, New Mexico—a chapel built by Nicolás Sandoval on his land in 1838 in honor of the Our Lady of the Rosary of Talpa and painted by the famous santero José Rafael Aragón (ca. 1797–1862). Incidentally, due to the Pueblo Revolts of 1680 and 1696, when the Pueblo Indians rose up against the Spanish encomiendas and the Church and pushed the Spaniards all the way back to El Paso, most churches and religious artworks were destroyed. Most collections, therefore, date roughly from the mid-eighteenth century on. Thus, the history of Hispanic arts is discontinuous and marked by a tremendous gap. Indeed, the Pueblo Revolts may go a long way in explaining the relatively sparse church decorations and aesthetic that prevails in New Mexico to this day, as well as what I have called the "bypassing of the New World Baroque" in the Southwest.

Echoing Guillermo Bonfil Batalla's seminal study of the indigenous invisible underside of Mexico, *México profundo: Una civilización negada* (1990) [*México profundo: Reclaiming a Civilization* (1996)], photographer Miguel Gandert and critics Enrique Lamadrid, Ramón Gutiérrez, Lucy Lippard, and Chris Wilson recently compiled a book of essays and photographs documenting the deeper, profound, Hispanic culture

6.14. *Penitentes*
Chimayó, New Mexico
Photo Sam Howarth

of New Mexico. Entitled *Nuevo México Profundo: Rituals of an Indo-Hispano Homeland,* this visually spectacular book focuses on the dance of the matachines (dancers popular around the Rio Grande who perform a drama based on the story of Montezuma, Cortés, and Malinche during Lent). As Lamadrid writes, echoing Bonfil Batalla's agenda: "For half of Mexico to become a region of the United States, it had to be naturalized, its history erased, its people obscured. These are the shadows Gandert's camera has illuminated, setting the scene for remembrance to replace oblivion and for a new vision of history and identity to be realized and reinscribed."[42] However, in contrast to what happened in Mexico, where live Indians were sacrificed to the indigenismo idealization of a heroic and very past Aztec culture in order to create a myth of origins for a mestizo nation, in New Mexico, indigenismo (Indianism, in Lamadrid's terms) created a cultural dichotomy between Indians and Hispanos whereby Indians were valorized and Hispanos denigrated, despite the fact that these two groups had formed a lasting alliance since the Pueblo Revolt of 1680. Hispanos and Indians were "literally indistinguishable" ("casi no se distinguen de nosotros"), wealthy rancher Pedro Pino wrote to the Cortes de Cádiz in 1812.[43] For a Latin American visiting New Mexico today, accustomed to colonial divisions between Hispanics and natives, the lack of distinction between Pueblo Indians and Hispanos is quite confusing and even disorienting. At the Millicent Rogers Museum, for example, one reads that María Martínez is the most famous of the Santa Clara Pueblo potters. With a name like María Martínez, she is classified as Pueblo Indian—is she then Indian or Hispanic? As Colin Calloway, director of the Native American Studies Program at Dartmouth College, answered when I asked him about this lack of distinction: "That is completely irrelevant to them." Indeed, the term "Pueblo Indian" is symptomatic of the merging between two cultures.

It is precisely this irrelevance that is stressed in *Nuevo México Profundo.* More importantly, irrelevance to racial mixing is used as an antidote to U.S. fears of racial mixing, which view miscegenation as debasement. Hence in the Southwest, Indians (allegedly because of their purity of blood) are placed higher on the racial scale, while Nuevo Mexicanos (Indian-Hispanic mestizos), *because* they are more mixed, have a lower status, reflected in different life standards. If indeed there is no distinction between Nuevo Mexicanos and Pueblo Indians, the only difference between them would be *where* each group makes its home (whether on a reservation or Pueblo or not) and what objects mark that identity. In linguistic terms, however, there is a difference in that Spanish enters novelistic language while native languages do not. Like the *Penitentes'* crosses, Spanish pervades Mary Austin's writings. More than a token used for local color, as with so many regionalist writers, Spanish permeates every sentence as if the toponyms (Sangre de Cristo, Río Arriba, la Atalaya) and geographical terms (*acequia, ciénaga, cañon, placita, hondo, barranca, mesa, acequia madre, monte, piedra, rito*), as well as the folk Catholicism underlying it (its myriad *santos, bultos, nichos, indios,* and *Penitentes*), which situate the narrative in New Mexico, overwhelmed it as such. Austin's use of Spanish is not limited only to the many Spanish words systematically inserted throughout her novels. What is more important is that these are only randomly translated or italicized, as if to signal that one could only write about the land inflected by Spanish, and with only an unsystematic nod to English monolingual speakers.[44] While native languages do not enter texts, and while Indians are negatively stereotyped, they are revered in the popular imaginary for possessing an organic form of wisdom—as psychic warriors of sorts—for which the West is nostalgic. It is almost as if the exaltation of the great Indian resistance to Anglo domination in the past ghosted the present, hiding under the mantle of greater wisdom. New Mexican indigenism is very apparent in the many photographs of Antonio Luhan and Mabel Dodge that show Luhan in proud Indian attire, Mabel Dodge having "gone native" at his side with her shoulders covered by an Indian blanket. However, unlike Latin American forms of indigenismo that focus on the past, New Mexican indigenism transforms Native Americans into spiritual guides of Anglo-Americans.[45] In Latin America, none of the glorious past seems to have reached into the present, as if the colony had successfully abjected the whole indigenous population, and as if the hundreds of violent Indian uprisings that characterized the colonial period and that continue well into the present did not happen.

In the face of this dichotomy, works such as *Nuevo México Profundo* and the important exhibition *The Road to Aztlán: Art From the Mythic Homeland,* as well as many of the books being published today in the Southwest, stress the continuity between indigenous and Hispanic cultures. Those works inscribe that space-culture onto a geographic continuum that exceeds the boundaries of several nations and begins north of what used to be the borderlands of New Spain. Central to this reinscription of space are the pre-Columbian-Catholic traditions of annual pilgrimages, which mobilize hundreds of thousands, if not millions, of people in both Americas around privileged religious sites, creating loops of sacred space and the identities on the move that we saw at work in the cult of the Virgin of Guadalupe. With increasing Hispanic migration to the north, these circuits are expanding gradually to encompass ever more northern cities, as if to prove Vasconcelos right when he asserted that mestizaje was a phenomenon set in motion when Europeans formed a bridge to the New World—only this time the bridge is being spanned from the south to the north.

PART III

FOUND OBJECTS
AND RE-COLLECTING
SUBJECTS

THE SHIPS

From Imagination to the Blank Page. A difficult crossing, the waters dangerous. At first sight the distance seems small, yet what a long voyage it is, and how injurious sometimes for the ships that undertake it.

The first injury derives from the highly fragile nature of the merchandise that the ships transport. In the marketplaces of Imagination, most of the best things are made of fine glass and diaphanous tiles, and despite all the care in the world, many break on the way, and many break when unloaded on the shore. Moreover, any such injury is irreversible, because it is out of the question for the ship to turn back and take delivery of things equal in quality. There is no chance of finding the same shop that sold them. In the marketplaces of Imagination, the shops are large and luxurious but not long-lasting. Their transactions are short-lived, they dispose of their merchandise quickly and immediately liquidate. It is very rare for a returning ship to find the same exporters with the same goods.

Another injury derives from the capacity of the ships. They leave the harbors of the opulent continents fully loaded, and then, when they reach the open sea, they are forced to throw out a part of the load in order to save the whole. Thus, almost no ship manages to carry intact as many treasures as it took on. The discarded goods are of course those of the least value, but it happens sometimes that the sailors, in their great haste, make mistakes and throw precious things overboard.

And upon reaching the white paper port, additional sacrifices are necessary. The customs officials arrive and inspect a product and consider whether they should allow it to be unloaded; some other product is not permitted ashore; and some goods they admit only in small quantities. A country has its laws. Not all merchandise has free entry, and contraband is strictly forbidden. The importation of wine is restricted, because the continents from which the ships come produce wines and spirits from grapes that grow and mature in more generous temperatures. The customs officials do not want these alcoholic products in the least. They are highly intoxicating. They are not appropriate for all palates. Besides, there is a local company that has the monopoly in wine. It produces a beverage that has the color of wine and the taste of water, and this you can drink the day long without being affected at all. It is an old company. It is held in great esteem, and its stock is always overpriced.

Still, let us be pleased when the ships enter the harbor, even with all these sacrifices. Because, after all, with vigilance and great care, the number of broken or discarded goods can be reduced during the course of the voyage. Also, the laws of the country and the customs regulations, though oppressive in large measure, are not entirely prohibitive, and a good part of the cargo gets unloaded. Furthermore, the customs officials are not infallible: some of the merchandise gets through in mislabeled boxes that say one thing on the outside and contain something else; and, after all, some choice wines are imported for select symposia.

Something else is sad, very sad. That is when certain huge ships go by with coral decorations and ebony masts, with great white and red flags unfurled, full of treasures, ships that do not even approach the harbor either because all of their cargo is forbidden or because the harbor is not deep enough to receive them. So they continue on their way. A favorable wind fills their silk sails, the sun burnishes the glory of their golden prows, and they sail out of sight calmly, majestically, distancing themselves forever from us and our cramped harbor.

Fortunately these ships are very scarce. During our lifetime we see two or three of them at most. And we forget them quickly. Equal to the radiance of the vision is the swiftness of its passing. And after a few years have gone by, if—as we sit passively gazing at the light or listening to the silence—if someday certain inspiring verses return by chance to our mind's hearing, we do not recognize them at first and we torment our memory trying to recollect where we heard them before. With great effort the old remembrance is awakened, and we recall that those verses are from the song chanted by the sailors, handsome as the heroes of the Iliad, when the great, the exquisite ships would go by on their way—who knows where.

—C. P. Cavafy, translated from the Greek by Edmund Keeley and Dimitri Gondicas

CHAPTER SEVEN

RE-COLLECTING THE PAST

Latinidad's *Found Objects, Photographs, and Home Altars*

I remembered the way I had caressed my mother's diamond brooches, her ruby and sapphire rings, her engraved sterling bracelets, how it felt to hold things so dear.

—Kaye Gibbons, *On the Occasion of My Last Afternoon*

. . . my attention is distracted from her by accessories which have perished: for clothing is perishable, it makes a second grave for the loved being. In order to "find" my mother, fugitively, alas, and without being able to hold on to this resurrection for long, I must, much later, discover in several photographs the objects she kept on her dressing table, an ivory powder box (I loved the sound of its lid), a cut crystal flagon, or else a low chair, which is now near my own bed, or again the raffia panels she arranged above the divan, the large bag she loved . . .

—Roland Barthes, *Camera Lucida: Reflections on Photography*

My grandparents turned their house, an architectural oddity that mixed Deco, Mission, and even a bit of Western rustic, into a shrine to Mexican memory. When they talked of Mexico in their later years, they spoke bitterly of the chaos and poverty and corruption, but it was nonetheless in their blood, and so a grand framed Virgin of Guadalupe dominated the living room and votives flickered in the bedrooms.

—Rubén Martínez, *Crossing Over: A Mexican Family on the Migrant Trail*

WHILE THE FIRST TWO PARTS of *Misplaced Objects* focused on the parallel, if asymmetrical, changes that the massive post-1492 transatlantic displacement of objects brought with them, this last section of the book returns to the more personal, autobiographical, bracket opened in the Introduction. The grand narratives of wonder, taxonomy, science, and modernity (whether alternate or not) have dominated the discussion until now. Underlying and indeed enabling these grand narratives, as we saw, was the laborious, ant-like, and often obsessive (if not outright compulsive) personal energies devoted to collecting and placing the misplaced. While collecting became a royal obsession in the early days of the Wunderkammern—even a necessity, insofar as royal collections became equated with power and reach—the drive to collect that spread across Europe to all levels of society did not end with the creation of modern taxonomies and scientific centers. Collecting and collections of objects continue to inflect both national and individual identities. Indeed, the continued importance of museums in our day would be inexplicable if it were not mirrored by private practice. The myriad collections in individual homes, the need to showcase identity through the possession of prized objects, the appropriation of commodities for a personal, ethnic display of difference that constitute our "identity kit" (the objects we possess, the ones we lovingly bring back from our place of origin, and the ones we buy as tourists to signal how far and wide we travel), indeed, the objects with which we surround ourselves and which we cherish, serve to anchor the self to the place we call home. In this last section, the focus is on the more intimate, less shared—even though quite public—modes of recuperating and re-collecting the past.

These last two chapters turn first to the family autobiography of two sisters (Sheila and Sandra Ortiz Taylor), through which they establish the continuity of a Mexican-American presence in the United States, despite official historiography's insistent ideological misplacement of the Hispanic colonial legacy of this country.[1] This is the narrative, as many Mexican-Americans like to assert, of the people whom the border crossed in 1848—not those who crossed and continue to cross the border. In counterpoint to the Ortiz Taylors' narrative, the installations of Cuban artist Sandra Ramos, discussed in the last chapter, are a mournful reflection of the waves of exiles leaving Cuba (as a consumer wasteland) lured by the United States (as a consumer paradise) and the irreversible losses they suffer. Here, too, the emphasis shifts away from the standard critical frame: no longer focusing on the Cuban exile community of Miami, Sandra Ramos instead views exile as it is experienced by those who remain on the island, losing many loved ones, year after year. I have chosen the Ortiz Taylors' experiment in autobiography and Ramos's installations because of their central preoccupation with objects as anchors of memory and identity. However, while in practice these artists' works depend on objects to tell a story, as with most narratives (recalling the sleight of hand by means of which the Guadalupans harness the cult of Guadalupe to the nation), here, too, the objects that serve as pretexts tend to recede, if not disappear altogether.

As the epigraphs to this chapter all illustrate, the loving and laborious art of recollection of the past entailed by the work of memory invariably involves re-collecting, cherishing, and remembering objects inscripted by the care and attention of loved ones in the past. The salvaging of a misplaced ethnic identity and the concomitant intimate coupling of recollection with re-collection runs through Sheila and Sandra Ortiz Taylor's *Imaginary Parents: A Family Autobiography* (1996).[2] "A childhood memory made present by the concrete objects" that made up and filled the past, *Imaginary Parents* is the result of the collaboration of two sisters who decide to tackle the past.[3] Together, the older one an artist, the younger a writer, the sisters reconstruct their childhoods and the life of their family in the Silver Lake district of Los Angeles from the 1930s to the 1950s. Reminding us that representation quite often depends on remembering and re-collecting, and that etymologically to "represent" is to make present once again, the narratives of Sheila use photographs from the family album as pre-texts that evoke the narrative, sharing textual space with photographs of Sandra's miniature installations ("so small most could fit into a pocket"),[4] composed of "found objects" and photo-collages and photo-sculptures reproduced in a central photo "Gallery." Unlike the space of the Wunderkammern that could be characterized as a kind of studied incoherence, here the incoherence imposed on the sisters by an Anglocentric national and popular imaginary is countered by the loving re-collection of fragments and dispersed, random objects often found at flea markets.

Sheila and Sandra Ortiz Taylor have followed similar trajectories: both teach or have taught at universities, and both have engaged in artistic work throughout their lives. While Sheila is a well-known writer, author of *Faultline* (1982), *Spring Forward/ Fall Back* (1985), *Southbound: The Sequel to Faultline* (1990), *Coachella* (1998), and the poetry collection *Slow Dancing at Miss Polly's* (1989), and most recently *OutRageous* (2006), a novel unveiling intrigues in academia, her sister Sandra has exhibited her miniature installations in various galleries and museums in the United States. While the book and the installations created for the book have never been displayed together, the miniature installations have been exhibited in different configurations in art galleries and exhibitions. To my knowledge, their visit to Dartmouth College provided the sisters the first public venue in which they reflected on their collaboration together. Here, Sandra showed some of her work while Sheila read from the autobiography. What emerged from their reading and subsequent conversations was that their close, intense re-collection process (through frequent coast-to-coast phone conversations) resulted in a text that underlines not only the contrapuntal and intimate relationship between memory, identity, and objects, but also a text that highlights the ensuing unsettling and uncanny revelation that a shared common past can give rise to often quite divergent recollections of that past.[5]

Daughters of an Anglo father in love with all things Mexican (including the language) and a Mexican mother who not only refuses to speak Spanish but who also refuses the label "Mexican-American," indeed, members of a family that insist they are "Californios," by which they signal their continuity with a Hispanic tradition in California before 1848 and even before the founding of the United States, Sheila and Sandra Ortiz Taylor have refused all the easy stereotypes that frame Mexican-American identities here.[6] As a consequence, both have been marginalized by the academic canon because they have neither underlined the "Latino" elements in their behavior, in their way of speaking and inflecting English, or in their art. That is, they have not allowed themselves to be determined by a certain type of ethnicity that depends on stereotypical elements in great demand today—a constrained notion of *latinidad* promoted in great measure by some of the major editorial houses, artistic centers, and Hollywood. Indeed, up until *Imaginary Parents*, Sheila Ortiz Taylor had situated her protagonists in an Anglo, lesbian world. Tortillas are eaten only now and then, the Virgin of Guadalupe is all but absent, and "*lo mexicano*" assumes only one place amid a series of other, equally important and valid characterizations. As she assumes an identity that is more complicated than that generally associated with the world of *latinidad*, few critics and readers have known how to situate her work, since it exceeds the parameters established for Latinos by the popular imagination and the media.[7] Because of this, Sheila Ortiz Taylor's work has merited the sustained rescue mission of critic Juan Bruce-Novoa— who has dedicated much of his career to promoting Latino writers like the Ortiz Taylors—and others such as Cecile Pineda, Laurence González, Ernest Brawley, and John Rechy, who do not "mark" their works ethnically. They are therefore marginalized from a canon erected by mainstream critics on the one hand and a dream machine that continues reproducing the early essentialism of the Chicano movement on the other.[8]

Imaginary Parents is the first work in which Sheila Ortiz Taylor reflects on her childhood in Los Angeles. Written in the 1990s, years of renewed right-wing political attacks on Mexicans in the United States and the Clinton-propelled militarization of the border, *Imaginary Parents* "anchors" Mexicans in California before the United States imagined and constituted itself as a nation. This historically accurate affirmation of Hispanic continuity on land now claimed as Anglo-American allows the sisters to critique the historical amnesia of the United States as a strategy used by conservative politicians and the media to represent Mexican-Americans as eternal wetbacks, aliens and, even as Chicano 1960s activist and lawyer Zeta Acosta would have it in his famously titled autobiography, cockroaches. Indeed, the continual and pervasive erasure of the Hispanic colonial past in official historiography (which begins with the founding of Jamestown in 1607—that is, one hundred years after Spain had colonized much of the West and Southwest) allows nativists to question the presence of *all* Mexicans in the United States, regardless of their genealogy and regardless of the fact that their presence preceded that of Anglo-Americans. The writer and the artist then narrate the genealogy of a family of Californios, and through them, the biography of a whole people. The family album, the home altar, and the collection of objects that anchor the memory of the girls function in the book much in the same way as the shards of household objects in museum exhibits serve as the basis for reconstructions of entire past cultures. In contrast to these anthropological narratives, which often posit an alterity through which we imagine ourselves as a community, *Imaginary Parents* recuperates and rearticulates a history strategically silenced by the U.S. national imaginary.

The narratives in *Imaginary Parents* use the pretense of the author leafing through the family album as a point of departure and often begin with descriptions of specific snapshots (some of them real, some of them recollected). The narratives around these real or imagined photographs are often quite short, and in their brevity parallel the snapshots that compose family albums. Hence, there is no linear or "coherent" family autobiography; instead, as in family albums, there are only snapshots of memory. The different typefaces used throughout the book reflect the divergent memories each sister has of specific events; they also reflect different interpretations of past events that arose in the intense conversations between them. In this unusual text, the photographs of Sandra's miniatures interspersed in "la Galería" refract the written narratives.[9] While some of the photographs seem only to illustrate the written text, others remain incomprehensible for a viewer relying solely on the visual, and still others diverge from the interpretation given by the text, thus pointing to the fact that, as the sisters insist, they often remembered things completely differently. When I asked them whether this was uncanny or unsettling, they said they actually felt a great sense of relief at being liberated from each other's versions of the past. Thus, they insist, the photographs of the miniatures do not reflect, they *refract* the written text.

The contrapuntal relationship between these miniatures (of the mother's Singer sewing machine, the father's saxophone, the girls' Robin Hood outfit, etc.) and the narrative text reinforces the intimate connection the book as a whole establishes between memory, objects (photographs-as-objects), and narrative. The insertion of photographs into both the text and the miniatures circumvents our culture's all-too-ready divorce between the materiality of the photographic image and the image itself.[10] *Imaginary Parents* refuses to treat photographs as mere conduits or "support" for images. As Edwards, writing about photographs as physical objects, argues, "it is not merely the image *qua* image that is the focus of contemplation, evocation, and memory," but its "material forms . . . [that] are central to its function as a socially salient object. These material forms exist in dialogue with the image itself to make meaning and to create the focus for memory and evocation."[11] Sandra's use of tiny boxes in which to "insert" and display her childhood memories also underlines the common practice of putting family photographs in shoe boxes or other containers, with the result that many people feel that those receptacles "hold" their entire collection of memories and, indeed, their very lives.[12]

MEMORY, YOU OLD COYOTE!

Snapshots are part of the material with which we make sense of our wider world. They are objects which take their place amongst the other objects which are part of our personal and collective past, part of the detailed and concrete existence with which we gain some control over our surroundings and negotiate with the particularity of our circumstances.

—Patricia Holland, "Introduction: History, Memory, and the Family Album," *Family Snaps: The Meaning of Domestic Photography*

We know that our childhood memories are not really "ours." We depend on the family album and the stories our parents, families, and friends tell us to "remember" our childhoods.[13] As Lorie Novak has shown with her installation *Collected Visions*,[14] the family album, on the other hand, follows quite rigid generic conventions that make all family albums somewhat interchangeable and lacking in individuality. Watching the installation *Collected Visions* (Monterrey, 2001), in which photographs from family albums were projected on two screens, I came away with the uncanny yet simultaneously wonderful sense that I too could be "that" girl shown swinging in the yard in the photograph exhibited, that her happy childhood could have been mine. Indeed, the photographs in family albums consist of fairly stereotypical and staged poses that reflect commonly held middle-class assumptions about "happy families." Susan Stewart has argued that the snapshots in the family album display "a moment or instance of the typical [and] articulate the individual . . . according to a well-defined set of generic conventions . . . [and] in such a conventionalized way that all family albums are alike."[15] There is no better illustration of this principle than the omnipresent "Kodak moment"—as constructed in advertisements created by Kodak, a company that was instrumental in the creation and promotion of the technology that made the snapshot possible and, at the same time, established the limits and conventions of the genre. Indeed, Jeremy Seabrook goes so far as to write that the photographs everyone collects (and the boxes full of photographs that accumulate and are often discarded) preclude the possibility of forming collections of meaning. Photographs today "are accumulations. . . . It is harder to discern their meaning. People say, 'You need something to look back on. These are my memories.' Memory itself, it seems, has been expropriated, commodified, and sold back to us."[16] *Family Snaps: The Meaning of Domestic Photography* unveils the extent to which domestic photography is intertwined with white middle-class consciousness and consumerism. Indeed, the essays included in the collection all show how working-class people and minorities are underrepresented on film and how photography colludes with contemporary forms of colonialism that I showed at work in the first part of this book.

Despite the fact that snapshots in family albums are all more or less generic, they still serve as anchors of memory for the individual perusing the album; indeed, a single photo may recall either the same or a different event in the family's life for the two sisters viewing it. The objects in the installations are also common, everyday things that most often do not even belong to the family. They are "found objects" that Sandra collected in flea markets and antique malls. Perfectly common consumer objects, they fascinate the girls in very much the same way described by Kaye Gibbons and Roland Barthes in the epigraphs to this chapter. And like those writers, the girls go stealthily through their parents' closets and things—and touch them with wonder, awe, and a certain sense of familial, sweet transgression. Sandra and Sheila Ortiz Taylor reproduce none of the photographs described in *Imaginary Parents* except in some of the miniature installations that include photo-object collages. Here again, the effect is of the typical. Figure 7.1, *Catch the Wave*, shows the sailboat dreamed of and then finally built by the father, an ocean wave, a miniature of the father's saxophone, and a cutout picture of the girls standing in front of the boat. Even the objects described as having been collected in the grandmother's (Mymamá's) personal Wunderkammer are perfectly typical things: miniature cups and teakettles, a tiny glass dog bought on Olvera Street, a ceramic ashtray made by one of the sisters in school, a tiny elephant tusk, a German medal that the uncle sent from Guam while in the military, tiny Mexican perfume bottles that the grandfather sent Mymamá, etc. Unlike in the Wunderkammern, however, where wonder was initially produced by the juxtaposition of truly one-of-a-kind, rare, and marvelous things, here, wonder is produced by the work of memory, imagination, and narrative distance from or, perhaps better yet, nostalgia for the past.[17]

7.1. Catch the Wave
Photo Philip Cohen
Courtesy of Sandra Ortiz Taylor

Imaginary Parents depends on a double move: remembering the lost objects with which the girls grew up (lost, since the house was sold after the father's death and most of its contents were lost), and re-collecting them as metonymic miniatures. I asked Sheila Ortiz Taylor what happens to memories when the objects that anchored them disappear; her reply echoes the classical art of memory I discussed in the Introduction:

> I think we never quite discard objects. That is, the objects are linked to the recollection, but
> when we no longer have them around literally and physically, we still have them around

in memory. To me this is linked to the ways metaphors work. You have the object and the inexplicable. You point to the object to indicate what the inexplicable contains. In Frost's metaphor, "you are a rose," *you* is explained by pointing to the rose. And yet the rose doesn't exist either. I do not have a rose next to my computer. And yet I carry in my mind or memory or imagination a concept of roseness. I could think of it so intensely that I could bring on a fit of hay fever. In "Pocadillas" [one of the snapshots around the memorabilia of her grandmother] I do not have any of the objects mentioned, and yet they are absolutely real to me, palpable even. To me, having this faculty—one which anyone may have but must cultivate—constitutes richness in life: the creative power of memory and imagination. *Perhaps I am saying it's not possible for me to distinguish between memory and imagination,* or perhaps I am saying I'm not interested in doing so.[18]

She could be echoing the eloquent words of Toni Morrison, reflecting on the act of memory entailed in all her work: "Memory weighs heavily in what I write, in how I begin and in what I find to be significant. Zora Neale Hurston said, 'Like the dead-seeming cold rocks, I have memories within that came out of the material that went to make me.' These 'memories within' are the subsoil of my work. But memories and recollections won't give me total access to the unwritten interior life of these people. Only the act of *imagination* can help me."[19] Like Morrison, Sheila Ortiz Taylor underlines the fact that memory has to be cultivated, that it is a double process consisting of transferring one thing from one place to another (from the Greek *metapherein*) and also substituting an idea for an object. In this symbolic transfer and substitution, imagination plays a central role; it is what keeps the forces of dispersal at bay.

As we already saw in the Introduction, there is a big difference between the intellectual art of memorizing, what is termed "artificial memory" in the art of memory, and the personal experience of remembering one's life in all its sociality and everydayness. We know that personal memory is quite selective—we are confronted with this discomfiting fact almost daily, when we talk with friends and family and they remind us of things we have utterly forgotten or, conversely, when their memories are diametrically opposed to ours. I believe that our ambivalence toward objects and our lack of will to concede them the place they deserve in our lives follows from the fact that we know that objects contain our memories, but in the noise of daily life, we lack the attention necessary to make this concerted effort. We know that even though we might lose everything we own, we will not forget everything, but at the same time we worry that if we lose things we will also forget things. We know that we associate memories with objects sometimes quite accidentally and often much against our will. And that we also forget much. Moreover, we know that the reconstruction of our past is very much like the narratives reconstructing past cultures in museums, narratives that periodically change even if the fragments themselves remain the same. The expression "shards of memory" says it all: even though the object and one's memory can be reconstituted from fragments, imagination is the "glue" that holds shards together in an often precarious balance. In sum, we know that what connects an object to another and to our memory is the narrative we construct around them. This narrative places both them and us, signifying who we are.

We never quite manage to reconstitute a totality of the past, either personally or culturally. In fact, the reconstitution of a totality through fragments is a wonderful illusion. As Salman Rushdie points out when he describes the process of writing his memoir of the India of his childhood, no one has the capacity to remember everything. Indeed, the notion of "total recall" belongs to science fiction and to Borges's fabulous memory master Funes, who is handicapped by his inability to forget. He is therefore unable to generalize and abstract. In Rushdie's case, the partial nature of memory is highlighted in *Midnight's Children*. While writing, Rushdie found that his memory distorted things and held on to the most insignificant objects of his childhood. "The shards of memory," he writes, "acquired greater status, greater resonance, because they were remains; fragmentation made trivial things seem like symbols, and the mundane acquired numinous qualities. There is an obvious parallel here with archaeology. The broken pots of antiquity, from which the past can sometimes, but always provisionally, be reconstructed, are exciting to discover, even if they are pieces of the most quotidian objects" (*Imaginary Homelands*, 12). It is interesting to note that Rushdie starts out by writing about the fragmented nature of our memory and ends up writing about everyday household objects, which provide him with access to that partial memory, but which also unexpectedly acquire a symbolic importance that they lacked previously. There is of course no better example of the mnemonic transformation of the quotidian into the symbolic than Proust's famous madeleine. Like the madeleine, the household objects exhibited in museums create our sense of the past and ground national imaginaries. The illusion of totality, hence, is based on that leap of the imagination, that transference, that shift from one thing to another, that dis-location, that is, that process of misplacement, transformation, and continual recycling of the past in and into the present.

Imagination, narrative, and memory are inseparable, and much that we remember is therefore a construct—hence one of the possible meanings of "Imaginary" in the title of the Ortiz Taylors' book. Much, too, consists of fragments or shards of memory that do not add up to a whole totality but rather accumulate somewhere. Highlighting the cumulative nature of memory, Sheila Ortiz Taylor reflects that she cannot construct a totality; indeed, she can only "heap up evidence" (*Imaginary Parents*, xiii). The possibility of duplication is implicit in this "heaping up" as in any process of metaphorization (whereby one miniature gun found in a flea market stands in for another "real" gun in the past). Yet the imaginary totality composed of shards consists equally of the shards themselves as well as the gaps and cracks that accompany any reconstruction of the past. Some of these "gaps" are described in *Imaginary Parents* as memories that belong to the lore of each individual family. For, just as these memories are created for us by tales told in the family and by the photo album, so, too, some things are repressed and excised from that narrative. Aunt Winifred's story is one such example: the parents cut her out of the album after she committed suicide, and talk about her only in hushed voices out of the girls' earshot. In return, the girls reinvent what happened to their aunt, and while doing so add a feminist perspective that implicitly blames her suicide on an abusive husband. There are also events the children remember but which the parents question, as when the girls mention having seen homeless people living in the park in their neighborhood after the war but the parents say this is not possible, arguing that the girls "remember" this only because they must have seen a documentary on TV

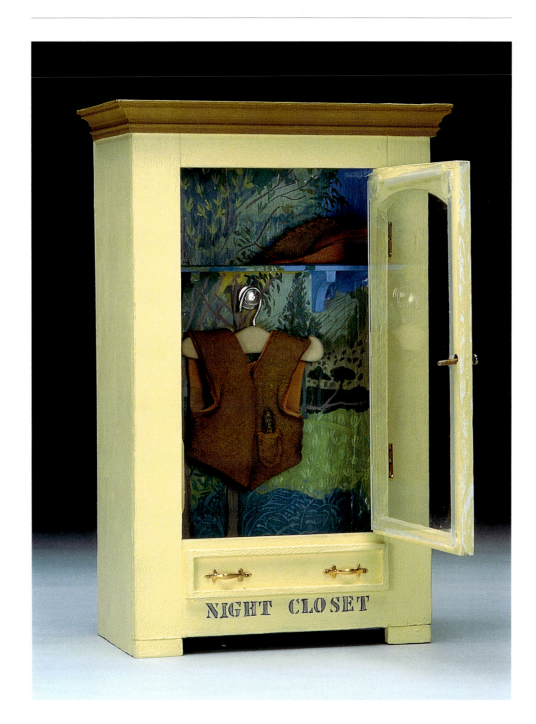

7.2. Night Closet
Photo Philip Cohen
Courtesy of Sandra Ortiz Taylor

(*Imaginary Parents*, 86). Also significant are objects Sandra buys in flea markets to which she is unconsciously drawn. When she buys a miniature Robin Hood outfit, her sister reminds her that their mother had sewn a very similar one for them. The Robin Hood attire comes to symbolize the generation gap between the parents and the 1940s ideal of womanhood they tried to impose on the girls—an ideal the girls resisted by being tomboys and exploring their attraction to women. Figure 7.2 is significantly titled *Night Closet* ("it is Hazel Medina, with her dark, dark eyes smoldering like extinguished candles, Hazel I love," writes Sheila) (104). Or, after the father's death, while driving together and wondering what happens to the dead, one sister remembers that while their father did not believe in God, he did believe in some sort of afterlife where he would return as a "sylph, a gnome, or a fairy." The passage that follows could stand for the complicated and unstable way in which memory operates in the whole text: "The elder daughter, a Taurus, neither believes in such creatures nor that her father believed in them, though she does remember, will always remember in sharpest detail, a flea circus she and her sister saw when they were nine and six that featured a formal wedding between two fleas, one in a white gown, the other in a pearl gray tuxedo, an event her parents deny ever occurred" (*Imaginary Parents*, 235).

Memories crisscross and cancel each other out, both in this passage and throughout the whole text. The reader wonders what remains but also realizes that what makes the sisters different are their distinct—and individual—ways of reading past events. This patchwork of remembering and forgetting, of narrative weave and narrative gaps, creates a highly individualized memory web. The age-old wisdom embedded in etymologies becomes apparent when we recall that the name given such narratives is autobiography. When Sheila and Sandra were working on the book and comparing notes, they realized that this was happening. Sheila wrote to me that "we both became aware that our versions of our shared childhood were quite different. Or both the same AND different. We tried to allow each other the freedom of creation and were interested in rendering these differences within the book itself." While this difference is inscribed and marked in the text through the use of two different typefaces, the book as a whole is held together by the sisters' creative imagination. For, in the end, as Sheila wrote to me, "We wanted to say something about the power and even the validity of imagination."[20]

The movement back and forth between remembering and forgetting in the autobiographical process parallels the movement back and forth of those who live "on the hyphen" between Mexico and the United States. This go-between-ing is significantly described as the work of the coyote. "Call me coyote too, driving my Selves too fast in weather too hot, through ambiguous zones of time, gender, and race with all the windows down. When you ask for my papers I hand you this book," reads the Preface (*Imaginary Parents*, xiv). The coyote, that legendary Aztec trickster figure, today also names the people who serve as go-betweens not only between individuals and Mexico's labyrinthine bureaucracy but also between the two sides of the U.S.-Mexico border. Mostly recognized as shadowy figures that do not respect borders, they help people negotiate the dangerous crossing. Like tricksters, they can be good or evil; they can save you or abandon you to a certain death. The careful memory-work of re-collection (object and memory) of which *Imaginary Parents* is composed likewise parallels the movement back and forth of the coyote across the border and the deep unsettling of all certainties encompassed by this real and mythical figure. Like the act of recollection, the coyote, too, negotiates between life and death, one side of the border and another, memory and forgetting. In the passage between the past and its re-collection, just as in the passage between the Mexican and the American that constitutes any transculturation, many things are gained but just as many things are lost. Indeed, the "voyage" to the past entailed in all memory-work resembles voyages to a premodern era (which is how tourism to Mexico is marketed in the United States). It is through the figure of the coyote that the book establishes the parallel between crossing the border and crossing back into the past. Moreover, assuming the coyote as trickster allows the sisters to effect yet another important border crossing: namely, that between the forever disappearing, Mexican legacy of this country—generally bypassed and sometimes altogether denied in its historiography in the all-too-real disappearance of pre-1848 colonial Mexico's inhabitants—and their transformation into illegal aliens despite the fact that they are Californios.

Indeed, *Imaginary Parents* tells the story of how the girls' Anglo father carefully constructed a Latino "identity kit" for himself and his family, countering the erasure of *latinidad* by the culture at large. The house he built in Silver Lake is an exact replica of a Mexican house, with a patio, tiles, bright colors, and authentic iron rejas made on Olvera Street. That it is described as a replica signals an unorthodox meaning for the hyphen in Mexican-American in this text and for these sisters. Indeed, the hyphen is inscribed by them as the father's attempt to "colonize" their mother and her "exotic"[21] identity, even going so far as to adopt a typical form of Mexican machismo: he does not allow his wife either to drive or to work outside the home, and yet, like a Mexican, he literally works himself to death (holding two jobs throughout most of his life) in order to obtain an "American" standard of living for his family. It is significant that the family never goes to Mexico until after his death, as if he preferred the simulacrum to the real thing. While the family lives "as if" in Mexico, stereotypical Hollywood ideals of beauty tailor in with the father's upwardly mobile aspirations. The collages in Sandra's installations all show the parents as Fred Astaire and Ginger Rogers—though the mother is sometimes said to resemble Dolores del Rio, star of classical Mexican cinema. As the authors reminisced while at Dartmouth, the mother swept the sidewalk in a slinky dress and a hibiscus tucked behind her ear, cutting such a glamorous figure that all their friends envied them for their stunning parents.

7.3. El músico y la dama *[The Musician and the Lady]*
Photo Philip Cohen
Courtesy of Sandra Ortiz Taylor

Unlike the daughters, who, because of their light skin color and their training, seem more Anglo-American than Mexican-American (thereby misplacing their Latino identity), the mother never could circumvent being racially stereotyped—indeed, she seems to have purposefully provoked being exoticized, although she refused to speak Spanish while her husband was alive. In *Ofrenda for a maja*, an installation in the form of a retablo (an altar to their deceased mother), Sandra Ortiz Taylor dramatizes how dominant images of women intercept their Latino identity, by including a photo of the mother with the girls in which all three wear the clothes sewn by her and which represents their parents' dream of having the girls look like Shirley Temple and Elizabeth Taylor. Instead, just as the mother refuses to be exoticized linguistically by the father, the girls refuse their parents' imposition of a glamorous, Hollywood-shaped identity. The installation *Night Closet*, with the Robin Hood vest and hat pointing to their childhood "tomboyishness," also inscribes their adult desire and aesthetics as queer. With great pride, Sandra reflects that she came upon the title for the book as a way of reflecting on a double process: while the parents imagine and shape themselves according to Hollywood codes, the sisters' access to their parents through memory is also imaginary. Queer, they refuse mainstream notions of femininity, yet through the aesthetics of queerness, later in life they reclaim the Latino identity they misplaced in childhood.

The form of *Imaginary Parents* challenges Hollywood's slick renderings of exotic others by emphasizing the artisanal nature of the miniatures and by giving the text itself an altar-like structure.[22] If "glamour" is the word that best sums up how the girls recall their parents, "aura" is the word that best describes the miniature installations. Indeed, the tiny miniature cases have all been lovingly painted and feel as though they had been carefully handled over many years. Holding them allowed me to experience firsthand what Walter Benjamin might have intended with his notion of aura. Having these miniatures in my hands also made the book much more present to me

7.4. Ofrenda for a Maja *[Offering for a diva]*
Photo Philip Cohen
Courtesy of Sandra Ortiz Taylor

7.5. Recuerdo para los abuelitos *[In Memory of Our Grandparents]*
Photo Philip Cohen
Courtesy of Sandra Ortiz Taylor

in a way I would not otherwise have experienced. Embodying the knowledge that touching photographs relates "directly to visualizing," the miniatures witness how many times these tiny objects have been fondled in the process of evoking memories.[23] Unfortunately, the work, constant touching, and loving care that has shaped them is lost for readers who only see them as photographs in the "Gallery" at the center of the book.

Finally, given the fact that the pictures in the family album and the objects that trigger childhood recollections are common and quite conventional objects, how does *Imaginary Parents* nevertheless articulate a personal and individualized family?

In three ways. The first is quite obvious: with every use, even the most quotidian objects get imprinted with our history. Thus, Stallybrass wears his friend's jacket with the creases and spots that the deceased imprinted on it (see Introduction). These creases individualize and personalize a fairly common consumer object and turn a simple garment into "Aldon White's jacket." Or the way in which a certain mug or jacket or thing becomes associated with a certain person, or a ring, always worn, does with another. The second way is by anchoring the memory-objects through a narrative that inserts them within the family history. Thus, for example, the tiny play perfume bottles in Mymamá's Wunderkammer sent to her by the grandfather reveal the tragedy that she had to marry him at such a young age, when all she wanted to do was play with dolls. It is the narrative woven around these objects slowly over time, then, that gives them meaning within the greater context of the family's history and dynamics. Or the miniature rifles and pistols in the installations become meaningful when the narrative tells the story of how (and sometimes why) various members of the family committed suicide: the grandfather after the grandmother's death; the aunt married to an abusive man. In a sense, then, the narrative reveals the life that has left its imprint on the object, much like a photographic negative.

As *Imaginary Parents* shows, the objects and the photographs acquire their full potential meaning only when embedded within a contextualizing narrative. Only then do we come to understand fully what the objects mean to the family, what they themselves mean, and what the Ortiz Taylors want them to mean to us. In her latest reflection on photography, Susan Sontag critiqued the position she had upheld in *On Photography* (1977), arguing that the photographs of horrors that fill our visual landscape only acquire meaning and have an emotional impact on us when they are contextualized. Shock value alone will not bring about significant change in the viewer. She concludes *Regarding the Pain of Others* almost telegraphically: "Can't understand, can't imagine" (126). Likewise, when Fazal Sheikh presented his work (collected in *A Sense of Common Ground*) on the situation of African refugees to my undergraduates, we were all deeply moved by his photographs because, unlike most photographers, he personally and quite intimately knew each of his subjects' names and circumstances. His personal, ethical, and political stance thus radically refuses the more common attitude of most photographers-as-scavengers who, like crows, grow fat on lots of roadkill.[24]

The third way that *Imaginary Parents* articulates family autobiography is more symbolic, and parallels the construction of a national imaginary under the flag, or the iconographic representation of the Virgin Mary upon which all variants depend, or the Virgin of Guadalupe as a border-crossing American symbol: it orders all the objects in the family household under the sign of a one-of-a-kind, privileged symbolic object. In *Imaginary Parents,* that ordering object-symbol is a whip that was, according to family lore, given to them by Pancho Villa. While that whip no longer exists, and in fact may never have existed, Sheila Ortiz Taylor reflects that it assumes such a central position because the Pancho Villa story "was always presented as absolute truth. Beyond that, I'm afraid I can't shed light. The family might well have been living in Imperial Valley on land given to their grandfather Miguel Ortiz by the Mexican government. There—at least according to lore—'they had a cattle ranch.'"[25] Because the whip and its owner connect the family to the land and to a history of dispossession, Pancho Villa serves as a leitmotif of the family's specific situation as a generations-old Mexican family in Los Angeles. Even though neither Pancho Villa nor his whip appear in the miniatures, the narrative tells us that it had hung in the dining room, displayed in a prominent position right behind where the father always sat. The girls grew up hearing their mother tell what is probably a very romantic version of how the whip came into their possession:

> Pancho Villa and his men riding up to the family's ranch house. My mother scooped up in his right arm and held inside the sweet odor of sweat and trail. Pancho Villa arriving or leaving, she is not sure which. But amidst embracing and shouted greetings. And when Pancho Villa sets down my mother he lifts a long coiled whip of braided leather from his saddle horn and hands it to my grandfather, who accepts it in all honor. There it hangs on the wall just to the side of my father's left ear (*Imaginary Parents*, 91).

Indeed, this object-symbol is so fraught that when the girls go to Mexico after the father's death, the first thing they buy is a huge piñata of the revolutionary.

The whip not only subsumes the genealogy of this family as Mexican, but also points to the loss of lands granted them by the Mexican government before 1848. If the border has today become increasingly militarized and viewed as a site of Mexican violence and lawlessness, this was not always so. Before 1848 and leading up to it, the aggression and violence characterizing the border and border states were directed by Anglos against the area's Mexican inhabitants. Promoted at both an individual and an institutional level, and replayed in the press and publications of the era—particularly in their creation of the "greaser" stereotype[26]—this aggression was a way of justifying the takeover of Mexican-owned lands. The post-1848 border, at least until well into the twentieth century, was a space characterized by fluidity: Pancho Villa and many others naturally rode back and forth across it. Villa even rode into Los Angeles, trying to raise funds for his participation in the Mexican Revolution. The film *Como agua para chocolate* [*Like Water for Chocolate*] thematizes this continuous back and forth, showing one family coexisting on both sides of the border. Unlike other Chicano narratives, in *Imaginary Parents*, the family's post-1848 loss of lands is attributed to a "certain characteristic vagueness about property and ownership." Most likely, this loss occurred despite the fact that the Treaty of Guadalupe-Hidalgo guaranteed Mexican-Americans their lands, customs, and language (*Imaginary Parents*, 52). The fact that the mother does not speak Spanish and that the girls do so only insecurely is an eloquent sign of the effectiveness of that Anglo aggression. Significantly, Pancho Villa's whip is taken down from its privileged place on the wall and used by the grandmother to attack the principal of her son's school in return for the principal's punishment of the boy (again, we are left to presume for speaking Spanish at school) (*Imaginary Parents*, 92). The reiteration of the terms "whip" and "whipping" in the autobiography serves to merge the family's history with the greater history of the discrimination and escalating violence against Mexican-Americans. The whip therefore connects them to a history of revolt against Anglo abuses and inserts the autobiography within the greater narrative of the Chicano movement. This movement of cultural vindication started in the 1960s by questioning what Tomás Ybarra-Frausto calls the historical "amnesia" of the United States—an amnesia which functions to continually disavow the cultural contribution of Latinos to the United States.[27]

It comes as no surprise, then, that when the girls go to Mexico with their mother for the first time—and where the mother suddenly begins to speak Spanish fluently—they buy a huge piñata of Pancho Villa. Here again, though, we are confronted with the issue of how consumer objects are transformed into individualized family history. In the case of the "magnificent" Pancho Villa, a thoroughly conventionalized and iconic figure in Mexico (like the Virgin of Guadalupe) is transformed into something else altogether when the girls bring him back to the United States, where the icon first and foremost a "bandido" points to and serves as a symbol of the family's "Mexicanness." This transformation parallels the trajectories and (il)logic of misplacement that I have been tracing throughout this book. Serving as an index of the power of misplaced objects and their ability to destabilize certainties, Pancho Villa's transference from one cultural context to another also changes the lived environment, just as the Mexican-style house built by the father in Los Angeles, along with all the other ersatz Mexican houses in Los Angeles, changes the lived environment and people's experience of the city itself.

Likewise, in its structure, *Imaginary Parents* fits in with a longstanding artistic tradition of combining photographs with sculptures that emerged in Mexico in the 1920s, called foto-esculturas, or photo-sculptures. Sandra Ortiz Taylor's miniatures, in their altar-like quality, parallel the development of this art form by contemporary artists Felipe Ehrenberg, Richard Anguía, and Carlos Jaurena and master carver Bruno Eslava.[28] Initially constructed when artists enlarged black-and-white photographs, added color to them, and glued them on to cutouts of cedar or mahogany carved in low relief in order to simulate clothing, photo-sculptures were highly valued as art objects. They were sold door-to-door, appealing to an emergent middle class and especially to recent immigrants from the provinces. Foto-esculturas had their heyday in Mexico City in the 1940s and 1950s, a period of rapid modernization and the beginning of mass migration to the city, when families used the medium to represent themselves as adhering to normative notions of "decency." The manipulability of the photographs allowed families to "whiten" themselves, to improve their attire, and even to represent unwed couples as married. To this day, many Mexican households prominently display foto-esculturas of their families in their living rooms, and there is a Spain-based online business that caters to the continuing demand for such photos. Given the surreal, kitschy, and often altar-like quality of this artistic tradition, contemporary artists have revived and reinvented the medium.[29] Sandra Ortiz Taylor's work coheres with this tendency, and her photographic sculptures in their retablo-like frames or tiny suitcases and boxes have been exhibited alongside those of Mexican artists. Her particular reinvention of the tradition is the use of the foto-escultura to evoke the altar as the form and frame for Latino memory. Indeed, the retablo as a religious (private and public) form determines the form and genre of *Imaginary Parents,* transforming it into an altar-book.[30] "I say it is an altar, an ofrenda," they write. And as with all home altars, the book is composed of "small objects with big meaning set out in order. Food, photographs, flowers, toys, recuerdos, candles . . ." (*Imaginary Parents*, xiii). The book, like all home altars, not only memorializes the patron saints (in this secular-minded family, Pancho Villa comes closest to that role), but also commemorates cycles of birth and death as well as large and small events in the family's genealogy—the sum of its parts constituting an altar to memory.

Death is doubly present in these miniatures, for, while altars are traditionally associated with death, photography, as Roland Barthes reminds us, is also intimately linked to death. Photography reproduces interminably an instant that will never be repeated again. The person photographed, the referent of the photograph, becomes, as Barthes theorizes, "a kind of little simulacrum, any eidolon emitted by the object, which I should like to call the Spectrum of the Photograph, because the word retains, through its root, a relation to 'spectacle' and adds to it that rather terrible thing which is there in every photograph: the return of the dead."[31] In these home altars/miniature installations, this double dimension is conjugated: mementoes to death, they are at the same time spectacles/performances of Latino identity in the United States. It is no accident, then, that Sandra Ortiz Taylor's little installations also reproduce photography's function of "holding" death, in the same way that coffins "hold" the dead. Like photography, they, too, endlessly re-present that which becomes spectral at the very moment of its creation. In the same manner that photography's capacity for infinite reproduction (always, by definition, of the past) implies an accumulative process, all the home altars, as well as the altar-book of the sisters, are constituted by "small objects with big meaning . . . Food, photographs, flowers, toys, recuerdos, candles . . ." (*Imaginary Parents,* xiii). Reminding us of the sudden prominence of the quotidian, "Artifacts," writes Edwards, "are often at their most powerful and effective as social forces when they appear to be most trivial."[32] In the same manner as in my friend Veronika's "Memory Box," which contains all the magical knickknacks collected by a young adolescent, the altar-book and home altars can only "heap up evidence" (*Imaginary Parents,* xiii). As we have seen, this "accumulative" process—all the while reproducing the cumulative effect of photography—counters the specter of individual and collective cultural death. The accumulation of things, therefore, is at once a sort of simulacrum and a spectacle.

Indeed, as I argued in the previous chapters, beyond individual memory-work, *latinidad* is constructed largely through the objects and symbols (both in the broadest sense and including foods, choice of home decorating, markings on bodies such as tattoos, etc.) that Latinos privilege and surround themselves with to conform to what is becoming increasingly identified as a sort of Latino "identity kit."[33] The current ubiquity of the Virgin of Guadalupe as both a cultural and a religious symbol (flag, tattoo, mouse pad, wall hanging, magnet, devotional painting, kitsch decoration, etc.) elaborated upon in earlier chapters is but the most spectacular example of this otherwise personal and laborious construction of Latinization. Within this context, *Imaginary Parents* is a fraught, interesting intervention in that process, given that the sisters are re-collecting an identity from a multiply purloined base.

Its attempt to "deborderize" Latinos and to give Latino cultural production a central space in U.S. culture and history relies on the misplacement of icons from one side of the border to another, as well as the creation of a new aesthetic composed of collages, palimpsests, and the secularization of religious and political symbols. Tomás Ybarra-Frausto, arguably one of the most important critics who have moved Latino cultural production to center stage, describes the way Latinos recycle things with the eloquent Spanish expression "hacer de tripas corazón," roughly translated, to transform guts into heart. According to Ybarra-Frausto, Chicanos in the 1960s used amalgamation and transculturation as a sort of voluntary and willful postmodernism to establish three bases for the affirmation of Latino cultural production: the archive, embodied knowledge systems, and a bank of images.[34] Whereas most Latino artists adhere to one or another of these modalities, *Imaginary Parents* refracts text and image, installation and photograph, personal experience and collective memory—thus simultaneously conjugating the archive, embodied knowledge systems, and the image bank.

VUELTA A DEYÁ SIN TI
A BUD

. . .

Subo los pasos lentos
la escalera
saludo al árbol que sólo a mí
me pertenece
y sabe que soy otra
pero aún soy la misma.
La luz está cambiando
Se ha vuelto rosa el Teix
contemplo tu silla
en la terraza
y levanto mi copa.
Estás conmigo, amor
Pero tampoco estás.

RETURN TO DEYÁ WITHOUT YOU
FOR BUD

. . .

With halting steps I climb
the stairs
I greet the tree that belongs
to me alone
that knows I am a different woman
yet also the same.
The light is changing
the Teix is bathed in pink
I stare at your chair
on the terrace
and lift a glass.
You are with me, my love
and yet you are not here.

—Claribel Alegría, *Soltando amarras/Casting Off*

CHAPTER EIGHT

SANDRA RAMOS

AND THE

CUBAN DIASPORA

La vida no cabe en una maleta

We associate nostalgia with the Cuban-American exile sensibility of Miami.

—Ruth Behar, *Bridges to Cuba/Puentes a Cuba*

Objects keep death away by helping us to remember.

—Carol Mavor, "Collecting Loss"

Emma Lazarus's 1883 poem "The New Colossus," written to raise funds for the pedestal on which the Statue of Liberty now stands, proclaims the United States as the "Mother of Exiles"— a mother who calls out to the entire world the oft-quoted words of promise and hope:

> *Give me your tired, your poor,*
> *Your huddled masses yearning to breathe free,*
> *The wretched refuse of your teeming shore,*
> *Send these, the homeless, tempest-tost to me,*
> *I lift my lamp beside the golden door!*[1]

GIVEN THAT THE UNITED STATES is the only country in the world to be and to conceive of itself as a nation of immigrants, one would expect the national discourse surrounding immigration to be layered, multifaceted, and richly diverse. That is not the case. In fact, occluding all the rest, the mass media privilege the narrative of the Cuban exile community over that of other immigrants and always at the expense of Latin American (particularly Mexican) immigrants. I am being hyperbolic, perhaps, but in the everyday noise of the world, the right-wing stridency of the Cuban community, and of the politicians who back it, tends to drown out all the other voices engaged in creating a nuanced and measured discussion of migration. Louis DeSipio, in his *LARR* review of seven publications on the Cuban-American community, corroborates this when he writes: "The adaptation of post-1959 Cuban migrants in the United States has been a uniquely public affair. From this migration stream's earliest days with the failure of the Bay of Pigs operation to the more recent controversy over the immigration status of Elián González, the nation has watched, and analyzed, the adaptation of Cuban emigrés more closely than it has that of other recent migration streams."[2] He also finds that the publications he reviews are extremely politicized and slanted toward the position of the most conservative elements of the Cuban-American community. Indeed, the same stridency that characterized U.S. anti-communism during the Cold War anachronistically persists in the national obsession with the experiences of this particular group of exiles, as if by doing so, Cuba—the last vestige of the Cold War (and only 90 miles away)—could be erased as it is erased from maps on TV news and weather channels.

There is no better illustration of what I am alluding to, of course, than the national commotion following the near-miraculous "saving out of the waters" of Elián González in spring 2000. Because he was a Cuban child who saw his mother drown (and because he was taken in by a seriously disturbed Cuban family in Miami), the story of his journey became a soap opera (a veritable *culebrón*) that lasted for months on end. In what became an increasing crescendo that reached near-mythical proportions, motherless Elián was forcefully embraced in the hysterical arms of the "Mother of Exiles." "Why," asks DeSipio, "do the most conservative elements of the Cuban-American community drive its political culture?"[3] It is as if the "Mother of Exiles" named as a promise to all peoples by Lazarus has become, unbeknownst to most of us, the mother of all exiles fleeing from communism, regardless of where they are from. Beyond this painful co-option of a highly charged symbol of American identity, the obsession with Elián was startling when compared with the public's utter lack of interest in other migration tragedies (shipwrecks and border incidents) that occur almost daily off the coasts and/or along the U.S.-Mexico border, but which, because they involve Haitian, Dominican, Mexican, or other migrants, are systematically underreported, and thus lack the power to move people. The contrast between what I am calling "too much" attention turned on the Cuban exile community, and the relative uninterest in the fates of other Latin American migrant tragedies, is reflected in the stridency and stereotypes, fear-mongering, and utter misinformation that have driven recent national debates and have ultimately derailed the possibility of drafting a reasonable policy regarding immigration.

There have been innumerable narratives by Cuban exiles since 1959[4] that follow a by-now-familiar pattern. Perhaps because this narrative is so seductive, they all more or less tell of the "salvation" of the prodigal son who flees from communism into the ever-open arms of the United States-as-consumer-paradise. Again, in contrast, there is no such narrative of salvation for Mexican and other migrants (despite the fact that for many of them, the United States *is* the promised land). In the popular imaginary and in the mass media, these migrants are viewed as parasites who come to suck the wealth and the social services (as if there were any left) of this country dry, and what is worse, as mere border-crossing cockroaches who multiply too fast. Aliens forever, they are doomed to be treated as the wretched refuse of teeming shores alluded to in the poem by Lazarus. Their lack of legitimacy in terms of citizenship rights is mirrored by the lack of a redeeming narrative that might envelop them in the cloak of the real. When compared to the cultural cachet of the Cuban diasporic story (and its power to eclipse all the other migration narratives through its cold embrace), the contrast is startling. It is even more startling given the fact that there are other exile narratives that complicate this unnuanced and dominant popular version. Prime examples of these are collected in Ruth Behar's *Bridges to Cuba/Puentes a Cuba* (1995), the culmination of a sustained effort made jointly by more progressive academics and activists as well as second-generation Cuban-Americans (or Cuban exiles who assumed *latinidad* as their identity) to reconnect Cuba to the United States.[5] Unfortunately, given the belligerency of the Bush administration, this project was submerged once again, and the trajectory and future of the Bridges Project is now up in the air, while the triumphal return of the prodigal son into the arms of the "Mother of Exiles," awaited with impatience, is also being increasingly jeopardized by the recent shift left across Latin America.[6]

In this chapter, I will focus on a narrative that complicates this scenario in interesting ways, because it presents an alternative to the "Colossus" story by coupling the exile to the non-exile. Largely unknown in this country, Sandra Ramos's entire artistic production has been obsessed with rewriting the Cuban diasporic community's narrative and representing exile from the reverse angle of those left behind. Ramos's intellectual, personal, political, and artistic project is that of expressing—in multiple forms and media—what exile has meant for the Cubans staying behind on the island. The exile of so many (her first husband and many friends) has meant experiencing exile as a personal, tragic, continuous, and anticipatory state of abandonment. Indeed, the numbers alone (for once) tell it all: in the 1990s alone, DeSipio reports, more than 180,000 people migrated from Cuba to the United States.[7] Those are exorbitant numbers, considering the population of the island. Beyond the feeling of existential crisis and the anguish of abandonment, exile is critiqued by this artist (and others of her generation) as the process that produces the shipwreck of Cuba's socialist project. Figures 8.1 and 8.2 neatly sum up her position: the choice between the weight of the dollar and that of the Cuban peso is a choice between two systems that drives many into exile, leaving Cuba behind as yet another raft shipwrecked in the ocean.

8.1. Los problemas del peso *[Weight Problems]*
1996 Sandra Ramos
Courtesy of the artist

los   problemas del   peso

la balsa

Exile, and the dreams of exile of so many, is the symptom of the impossibility of compromise or change from *within* Cuba itself. Figure 8.3, "The Silence of the Lambs," shows Ramos's stinging critique of those who do not dare speak up. The idea of staying behind, then, is presented as the radical option that opens the only door to political action within the island itself.

An artist residing in Havana, Ramos belongs to the young "generation of the '90s," which rapidly filled the vacuum left by the mass exodus of previous generations of artists in the 1980s who had suffered under the repression and increasing censure of the Cuban government after the fall of the Berlin Wall, the interruption in the flow of aid from the Soviets, and the concomitant tightening of the U.S. embargo. As a Spanish NGO official who had traveled to Cuba with aid for the last 30 years told me in Havana, in those days the crisis was so great that people walking down the street "looked like skeletons."[8] The generation of the 1990s benefited from the political aperture and cultural transformation—the result of the so-called "Special Period" that followed, during which Castro started to promote a free-market economy in some sectors in order to ease the situation. Artists were allowed to live and work and sell their works both in Cuba and abroad, thus bringing in much-needed dollars. For the first time since 1959, they could earn in dollars and live very cheaply on the island. As a consequence, not only did artists no longer feel the need to go into exile like former generations, but the improved conditions created for cultural work in Cuba attracted artists from everywhere else in Latin America. The problematic "double economy" (under which a Cuban doctor earned in a month what a taxi driver earned in a day) allowed artists to become independent of state subsidies for the first time since the Revolution, and to live relatively comfortable lives on the island. During this "Special Period," censure still existed, but artists now established the limits of the possible in consultation with the censors. "The generation of the 90s constitutes an evolution of new Cuban art in post-utopian times," writes Gerardo Mosquera. "Its cynicism has been pointed out, its greater interest in formal aspects, and its veiled discourse to avoid censorship. All this must be taken in relative terms, because the artists remain non-conformist and interested in free artistic investigation. Some of the critical works of greatest impact have been made in the past decade."[9] Sandra Ramos's work is a perfect example of this fragile negotiation and equilibrium between censorship and critique.

In 1994, two great cultural events transformed the artistic scene in Havana: the foundation of an extra-official artistic space known as Espacio Aglutinador, by artists Sandra Ceballos and Ezequiel Suárez, and the Fifth Havana Biennial. Espacio Aglutinador was founded as a reaction to the state's abrupt closing of Suárez's exhibition "El frente Bauhaus," due to the fact that he had written the sentence "all institutions are shit" on some of his paintings. This seemed to remind the censors too much of the controversial exhibition "El objeto esculturado" (1990), in which the artist Angel Delgado created an uproar when he shat upon the official newspaper *Granma* in a sort of "spontaneous performance." Delgado's actions came at the end of a long period of censorship and increasing rigidity of the state apparatus, and led to the immediate closing of Suárez's exhibition, which then moved to Espacio Aglutinador. This space quickly

8.2. La balsa *[The raft]*
1994 Sandra Ramos
Courtesy of the artist

8.3. El silencio de los corderos *[The Silence of the Lambs]*
2005 Sandra Ramos
Courtesy of the artist

became an extra-official venue and a center of artistic experimentation and innovation. A few months later, the official Fifth Havana Biennial opened its doors with a large collection of Latin American and Cuban artworks. The two spaces, however, were ruled by different principles: while Espacio Aglutinador resisted integration and the easy appropriation of artistic work, the works displayed in the Fifth Biennial "feigned integration, disguising suspicion with transparency."[10] Cuban art in the 1990s can be situated along these two poles.

Sandra Ramos is an integral member of and participant in the achievements of this generation. Born in 1969, she won the Premio Nacional de Arte Cubano in 1997. She also followed a trajectory similar to those of her generation: she has studied and lived outside Cuba (England, Italy, Japan) and, although she lives in Havana, she exhibits her works both there and in New York, San Francisco, Mexico City, and Tokyo. Her position toward the Revolution is ambiguous, like that of her whole generation: in her installations *Máquina para ahogar las penas* [Machine to Drown Sorrows] and the series *Inmersiones y enterramientos* [Immersions and Burials] (1999), she critiques the political situation in Cuba that still leads people into exile or into alcoholism—as a form of interior exile—while simultaneously problematizing exile as the lack of faith in the Revolution and a refusal to engage in political change. In her representational shorthand, people leave the island and risk drowning and death for a simple mirage of things symbolic of the United States. She repeatedly emphasizes this material covetousness and significantly downplays questions of "political freedom."

This artist's obsession with the loss incurred by exile is so deep and so personal (having been abandoned by her first husband, who left for the United States, and also by many friends and relatives)

8.4a. *The artist Sandra Ramos in her home in Havana*
Photo Spitta 2000
Notice the two engravings at her feet. The first shows Sandra Ramos's 1993 engraving of herself as the island of Cuba and is entitled La maldita circunstancia del agua por todas partes *[The Damned Circumstance of Being Surrounded by Water]. The second,* El bote *[The Boat], shows her rowing alone in the ocean in a makeshift raft under the stars.*

8.4b. Los ojos de Dios *[God's Eyes]*
Installation in the artist's home
Sandra Ramos
Photo Spitta 2000

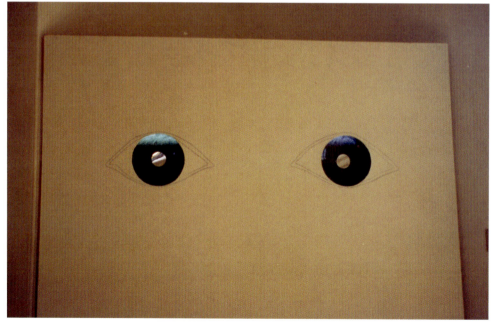

8.5. Espejismos *[Mirages]*
Installation suitcase
Sandra Ramos
Courtesy of the artist

that when I visited her in her apartment in Havana, one whole corner of the living room was dominated by an installation called *Los ojos de Dios*—a wall with a TV screen in the middle, playing and replaying ocean waves. Cassandra-like, she said it represented the last thing drowning exiles saw: "es lo último que ve una persona al tratar de salir de Cuba."[11] Ramos's compromise with Cuba is so fraught that she repeatedly—obsessively, almost—imbricates both the exiles and the non-exiles in the same narrative and the same trauma. Her insular existence as a woman/island/Cuba fills her with desperation; exile is seen as the exterior and interior shipwreck of the ideals of the Revolution. Nobody is safe from this catastrophe.

The installation *Migrations II* (1994), exhibited in 2001 at the Modern Latin American Art Museum, where I first saw Ramos's works, consists of a series of open suitcases and trunks of different shapes and sizes. On the surfaces and interiors of these objects, the artist represents her version of the "exile complex" that involves both the exiled and those left behind in a narrative of trauma and displacement. These suitcases mounted on the walls show various scenes: Ramos herself, seen from the back, standing under the stars with one bag in each hand, or Ramos as an Alice in Wonderland in the shape of the island, lying in the bottom of a suitcase with planes taking off and landing on her body. The upper lid of the case represents a U.S. city full of neon signs at night. A huge Coca-Cola sign dominates the scene. Other installations show a couple swimming in the darkness under the stars toward the U.S. flag (she holding on to him as if in an embrace); a boy lying in the bottom of a boat, dreaming of a paradise of consumer goods (radios, cars, TVs, etc.) among which a Cuban flag also floats. Another installation is of a suitcase painted as a plane, from an airline company called "Espejimos" [Mirages]. Significantly, reminding us of the use of the Virgin of Guadalupe as the umbrella symbol that subsumes myriad local religious practices in the Americas into one overarching symbolic mestizaje, Ramos always includes the Cuban flag amid the island of things that represent the United States in her works. While floating amid many

other consumer goods, the Cuban flag naturally forces a reordering of all those things under the mantle of "cubanidad," as it has
indeed done in Little Havana and other Cuban-American enclaves
in the United States. The Cuban flag, too, functions as the only
"thing" exiles take with them, whether they reject what it stands
for today or not, as if Ramos were saying that they would unconsciously and inevitably reconfigure their whole lives under that
symbol. While these works represent her somewhat simplistic critique of the dreams (of freedom and things) that lead people into
exile, other installations in the series represent exile as trauma and
death. One suitcase entitled *The Song of the Siren* has the skeleton of a drowned woman
also at the bottom of the ocean. It is not clear whether the tires are lifesavers or simply
trash at the bottom of the ocean. In another, several drowned people hold on to a smiling skeleton, all floating at the bottom of the sea amid other rubbish. And in another
series of installations, *Criaturas de isla* [Island creatures], made a year later, these same
themes are repeated: in a suitcase, two people swim in opposite directions: the one who
appears to be swimming toward the United States is surrounded by sharks. In another
one, there is a male doll enveloped by the Cuban flag lying in the bottom of the suitcase
as if thrown there like discarded rubbish.

The hyphen so flaunted as the grand connector of American identities, then, is for
Ramos the boat, the narrative void, the shipwreck, and trauma. While it connects the
Cuban to the American, it also serves as the symbol for all that has been lost. Indeed,
Ramos's empty suitcases and empty trunks all convey her sense that obtaining things
(which she sees as a crude form of soulless materialism) is not worth exile and the
accompanying personal and social losses. Cuba may be devoid of things, but it is full
of the people, spaces, family, and life lived that exiles leave behind. In her installations,
everyone drowns in ninety miles of water, and all that is left is death—or the mirage of
things—forlornness, and a heap of garbage at the bottom of the ocean.

8.6. El canto de la sirena *[The Siren's Song]*
1994 Installation suitcase
Sandra Ramos
Courtesy of the artist

8.7. Brazos *[Arms]*
1995 Installation suitcase
Sandra Ramos
Courtesy of the artist

Ramos's obsession with the significance of the exile of so many people, and the internal exile of so many on the island whose plans and endless dreams of going into exile sustain them, is repeated also in her engravings and paintings. Two that are very representative of her posture are *Y cuando todos se han ido llega la soledad* [Solitude Arrives When Everyone Has Gone] (1993), in which the artist again is an Alice in Wonderland waving good-bye to people on a plane about to take off. In another one, made a couple of years later, she ironically represents the last person left alone on the island, and in *Ahogarse en lágrimas* [To Drown in Tears], the exile is joined to those left behind by different kinds of water: while many drown in the passage to Miami, the persons on the island drown in tears. And her engraving *Rostros que desaparecen para siempre* [Faces That Disappear for Good] joins the exile to the non-exile in a continuum of feeling and loss. Her 1997 installation *Autorreconocimiento del pez* [Self-Knowledge of Fish] again shows her as an Alice in Wonderland, surrounded by tear-shaped glass water containers.

The exiles represented in Ramos's work not only drown repeatedly, but obsessively. Indeed, such is the obsession of this artist with the loss (of a place, people, objects, memory, identity) entailed by exile that another of her installations is tellingly entitled *La vida no cabe en una maleta* [Life Does Not Fit into a Suitcase] (1995), in which the trunk has the shape of a coffin in which a dead pregnant woman lies. As the title already announces, the artist tries to show that with exile, all is lost, not only for the person leaving, but also for the person left behind, and even for the baby whose future will be uncertain. More importantly, the unborn fetus is also the stillborn potential of socialism in Cuba. Even though we know that Cuban exiles in the United States have re-created vibrant communities (the "Little Havanas" that now dot U.S. cities), the focus of the artist is on the initial trauma of exile, on the loss of everything, and on the literal and metaphoric fact that life does not fit into a suitcase. When balseros leave Cuba on fragile, makeshift rafts with the shirts on their backs and their empty suitcases, they not only lose everything, but they also, often, lose their lives. Indeed, Ramos's

8.8. Y cuando todos se han ido llega la
soledad . . . *[And when everyone has left
comes loneliness . . .]*
1993 engraving
Sandra Ramos
Courtesy of the artist

8.9. Aurorreconocimiento del pez
[Self-Knowledge of Fish]
1997 installation
Sandra Ramos
Courtesy of the artist

Y cuando todos se han ido, llega la soledad

"empty" suitcases stand in stark contrast to Sheila and Sandra Ortiz Taylor's "full" version of the past and the family's history discussed in the previous chapter. Driven as they are by different historical circumstances, the trauma of exile versus the difficulty of being Latino in the United States, the one-way ticket of exile versus the history of continuity of an early Mexican-American family, and other divergences, these different artists' works clearly make for contrasting understandings of how family memories get constructed (or not). Yet, despite these differences, both the "full" and the "empty" versions of the past concur in the focus on objects and narrative as the crucial "web" of signification that holds a self in place.

LA VIDA NO CABE EN UNA MALETA

While *Imaginary Parents* underlines the importance of memory-objects in the construction of a past and an identity—particularly in relation to the inscription of those Mexican families who did not cross the border but whom the border crossed—the empty suitcases and trunks of Ramos's installations underline the radical difference between migration, hyphenated American identities, and the transcendental rootlessness of exiles. In contrast to the migrants' routes/roots, the exile follows a one-directional trajectory; indeed, exile is a one-way ticket, much like death. While with migration, people experience leaving as an act of their own free will (even if forced to leave their communities by poverty or political circumstances), they nevertheless frame their departure as the search for a better life and the arrival in a promised land; they "know" they can return (even if they are poor and cannot). Indeed, as Saskia Sassen, Roger Rouse, and others have shown, migrants usually follow well-established migratory routes and a circular pattern of departure and return.[12] Given this fact, it is not surprising that narratives enveloping migration and exile differ in both content and tone. While narratives of exile are characterized by the pathos of nostalgia, political stridency, sentimental melodrama, and other symptoms of traumatic displacement, narratives of migration often adopt the form of the Bildungsroman: they tell the story of the migrant who reaches the promised land after much trial and travail, finding him- or herself marginalized and exploited there, but with hope for the future of his/her children. In narratives of exile, the sea that separates Cuba from Miami becomes a terrible circumstance, whereas the border that separates the United States from the rest of the Americas is seen as a porous—if increasingly militarized—zone of possibility. As if to illustrate this porosity, one has only to recall the miles and miles of tunnels (built by drug lords) discovered under Tijuana a few years ago and along other parts of the border. Thanks largely to the efforts and political savvy of the Chicano movement in the 1960s, proponents of which recuperated the notion of Aztlán as the place of origin of the Aztecs, as we saw in Chapter Six, Mexican-American migration today is viewed as the continuation of a millenary cycle of migration from Aztlán to Tenochtitlán/Mexico and back. Likewise, thanks to the daily flights of the "guagua aérea," or flying bus, which connects San Juan to New York City,[13] the idea of a migratory "identity in the air" can be imagined for the Nuyorican experience.[14]

With exile, however, this knowledge is not there: exiles feel violently forced out of their countries and "know" that their journey is a one-way trip, much like death itself.

Along with her representation of the danger entailed in crossing 90 miles of treacherous waters in unseaworthy, fragile, homemade, improvised contraptions of an often surreal appearance, Ramos simultaneously criticizes the exponentially growing rate of migration worldwide, which is destabilizing the role of the citizen in national cultures. Increasingly, fewer and fewer people participate in the democratic processes of either their home countries or the countries to which they have emigrated. This destabilization of citizenship rights and duties is compounded today by the ease afforded by the Internet for corporations to "export" or "offshore" work to countries like India and China in search of very qualified and very cheap computer programmers and workers. The dissociation of these corporations from any sense of commitment, to either the places or the communities where they are located, thus contributes to creating communities devoid both of a tax base and of citizens who assume any citizenship rights or duties. Compounding this problem, many people across the United States today work from their homes for corporations situated elsewhere. Rendering them virtual for all practical purposes, they inhabit places much as tourists inhabit tourist resorts. These dissociations from both place and community are creating the crisis of representation that we are currently experiencing at the local political level and national level. Transforming nationality into yet another consumer fetish, national character and identity have either been Botoxed off the map altogether or have been relegated to the infinite non-spaces of suburbia and devoured by cheap forms of big-box consumerism. In contrast, as we saw above, while Ramos critiques the United States as a mere consumer paradise that attracts people off the island, she always represents Cuban exiles accompanied by a Cuban flag floating amid a sea of products, as if to say that despite crass forms of consumerism, Cuban exile will nevertheless manage to organize all those objects according to an idiosyncratic Cuban sensibility, thus Latinizing them. And indeed, as we see in the Little Havanas, Chinatowns, and barrios across the United States, "identity" has been relegated to immigrant communities and the vital spaces they create.

On the other hand, leaving only with the shirts on their backs and undergoing a dangerous ocean crossing in shark-infested waters, exiles (like migrant workers crossing the increasingly dangerous U.S.-Mexico border) experience their journeys as trauma. While both experience traumatic journeys, for the exiled, as New York City–based poet Lourdes Casal poignantly describes it in "La Habana 1968," there is no arrival and no return, since the poet has spent her past ten years without tasting Havana or speaking about her except as a hole ["hablarla excepto en hueco"]. Exile in New York City has transformed the city of her childhood into sheer loss and absence, a fragment without context.[15]

All that anchors one to a place, the memories successively inscribed to those spaces and places, to one's home, the relations between family and friends, and the objects that one held dear, are all lost, and with them one's memory of who one is. And there is no return—not even the promise of a return. One becomes a stranger to oneself. A pioneer of the notion of a "bridge" to Cuba in the 1970s, when she established the Antonio Maceo Brigade (by means of which 55 exiles returned to the island and were warmly received as the prodigal children of the Revolution, in a specular counterpart to the U.S. treatment of Cuban exiles), Casal argues that exile marks a person forever. She describes in many of her poems the violence of the rupture of the connection between one's self in the past and one's self elsewhere. In "Para Ana Veldford," she writes:

> Pero Nueva York no fue la ciudad de mi infancia,
> no fue aquí que adquirí las primeras certidumbres,
> no está aquí el rincón de mi primera caída,
> ni el silbido lacerante que marcaba las noches.
> Por eso siempre permaneceré al margen,
> una extraña entre las piedras,
> aún bajo el sol amable de este día de verano,
> como ya para siempre permaneceré extranjera,
> aún cuando regrese a la ciudad de mi infancia,
> cargo esta marginalidad inmune a todos los retornos,
> demasiado habanera para ser newyorkina,
> demasiado newyorkina para ser,
> —aún volver a ser—
> cualquier otra cosa.[16]

> [But New York wasn't the city of my childhood,
> it was not here that I acquired my first convictions,
> not here the spot where I took my first fall,
> nor the piercing whistle that marked the night.
> This is why I will always remain on the margins,
> a stranger among the stones,
> even beneath the friendly sun of this summer's day,
> just as I will remain forever a foreigner,
> even when I return to the city of my childhood
> I carry this marginality, immune to all turning back,
> too *habanera* to be *newyorkina*,
> too *newyorkina* to be
> —even to become again—
> anything else.]

> Translated by David Frye, in Ruth Behar, *Bridges to Cuba*, 22

And in "Exilio," she describes this same rupture in the following way:

> Exilio
> es vivir donde no existe casa alguna
> en la que hayamos sido niños;
> donde no hay ratas en los patios
> ni almidonadas solteronas
> tejiendo tras las celosías.

Estar

quizás ya sin remedio

en donde no es posible

que al cruzar la calle nos asalte

el recuerdo de cómo, exactamente,

en una tarde de patines y escapadas

aquel auto se abalanzó sobre la tienda

dejando su perfil en la columna,

en que todavía permanece

a pesar de innumerables lechadas

y demasiados años.[17]

[Exile

is living where no home exists

where we have been children;

where there are no rats in the patios

nor starched spinsters

knitting behind the blinds.

To be

maybe already without help

where it is not possible

that while crossing the street

a memory overcomes us of how, exactly

on an afternoon on skates and escapades

that car rammed into a store

imprinting its profile on the column,

on which it still remains

in spite of a lot of whitewash

and too many years.]

Similar to Casal, Ramos expresses the same rupture between one's self in the past, in a place of the past, and one's self in the present, in another place, in the title of one of her engravings: *Quizás hasta deba partirme en dos* [Maybe I should even split myself in two].

Playwright Eduardo Machado also significantly deploys the language of trauma (of the loss of identity and the narrative of self) to talk of his experience as a member of the Peter Pan generation: "I think giving up your culture is a big deal. The alienation we experienced when we got here was so extreme and colored so much of the rest of my life. Caribbean people are Caribbean people and it's a whole other way of life. You have to become someone else to navigate life here. It's a big price to pay."[18] In fact, the Peter Pan generation was one of those most traumatized by exile. Called "Peter Pan" because of the young age of the exiles, it was an "air bridge" created by the U.S. government that allowed Cuban parents to send their children to the United States to "save" them from Marxist indoctrination in Cuba's schools—a notion disseminated by the CIA. Machado, who always resented this separation from his family, comments with great irony: "They were teaching us Marxism in school. . . . But my parents treated it like they were gassing us."[19] Unfortunately, in many cases these children suffered the double trauma not only of being forcefully separated from their families, but also of mistreatment at the hands of the American families that housed them. The heart-wrenching rupestrian sculptures and installations of famous Cuban-American artist Ana Mendieta also eloquently speak for this entire generation.

Echoing these sentiments, in a philosophical-testimonial essay reflecting on her own traumatic rape and near-murder, Susan Brison writes that survivors of trauma "frequently remark that they are not the same people they were before they were traumatized."[20] It is significant that different trauma victims (be they Holocaust survivors, Vietnam veterans, or sexual abuse survivors) describe this loss of self in the same way: a survivor of the Nazi death camps observes, "One can be alive after Sobibor without having survived Sobibor," and many Vietnam veterans say, "I died in Vietnam." Migael Scherer expresses a loss commonly experienced by rape survivors when she writes, "I will always miss myself as I was."[21] Brison theorizes this loss of self as a breakdown of narrative about the self: "Locke famously identified the self with a set of continuous memories, a kind of ongoing narrative of one's past that is extended with each new experience," she writes. As she continues, "In this view, person A (at time 1) is identical with person B (at time 2) if B remembers having the experiences of A. This view of the self as narrative, modified to account for relational aspects of the self, is the one I invoke here in discussing the undoing of the self by trauma and its remaking through acts of memory."[22]

Brison emphasizes the need of so many trauma victims to give testimony of what they experienced as a way of healing themselves. Indeed, the parallels between narratives of trauma and the narratives of the Cuban Diaspora are telling. Lourdes Casal's collection of poems *Palabras juntan revolución* is yet another modality of the same need for articulation. As Casal writes/unwrites in her poem "De la escritura como tabla de salvación,"

> he naufragado en un universo de palabras,
> pero sólo la palabra salva;
> arma única que he aprendido a empuñar
> contra la soledad.[23]

> [I have drowned in a universe of words,
> but one word only saves;
> a unique weapon I have learned to carry
> against solitude.]

And Octavio Armand writes: "Ya no fui lo que soy" [I no longer was who I am].[24]

Typical of this narrative vacuum that is trauma is the obsessive attempt to fill the void of exile with a profound nostalgia. As Behar expresses in the epigraph to this chapter, nostalgia characterizes the emphasis on return, the inability to be "here," the often strident rhetorical and political projections, the sense of shame at being inauthentic, having lost one's language (and luggage), and/or having learned to function in another one. Ana Mendieta too embodied that nostalgia in her desperate attempts to merge with the earth and her final success when she was invited to return to Cuba and create her famous "Rupestrian sculptures" in "a series of haunting, semiabstract figures carved into the soft rock of caves in Jaruco Park, on the outskirts of Havana." Significantly, she gave them the name of Taino goddesses worshipped by a people that had disappeared with the arrival of the Spaniards.[25] In contrast to Mendieta's tragic nostalgia, Gustavo Pérez Firmat writes flippantly, and making translation impossible (choteando): "Después de cuarenta años de exilio, durante los cuales se ha desvanecido poco a poco la esperanza del regreso, he aprendido a saber no-estar, y a estar sin saber."[26] The difficulty for exiles to imagine themselves in and finally belonging to the space they have inhabited for over half their lives, therefore, coexists uneasily with the fact that Cubans have created successful communities all over the United States. In contrast to a migrant who would have adapted readily, the exile does not, even though s/he might have arrived here as a young child. Indeed, many Cubans still remain reluctant to consider themselves immigrants. And again, Gustavo Pérez Firmat writes:

> En mis libros y mis poemas nombro a Cuba obsesivamente. . . . Cuba se ha convertido en otra cosa: un espacio sin dimensiones, un lugar sin lindes que pueblo con imágenes, obsesiones, fantasmas, mentiras. Los cubanos de verdad también mienten, pero sus falsedades se revisten de geografía—de calles y lomas y árboles y adoquines y fachadas y lentas tardes de sol.[27]

> [In my books and in my poems I name Cuba obsessively. . . . Cuba has become something else: a space without dimensions, a space with no limits that I people with images, obsessions, ghosts, lies. Real Cubans also lie, but their lies are clothed by geography—of streets, mountains, trees, cobblestones, façades, and slow sunny afternoons.]

As if the obsessive writing and rewriting and the incantatory naming of Cuba would or could bring back the past, the exile realizes that s/he invokes the name of Cuba in vain, indeed, that his or her past and present are spent in a phantasmagoria of shadow images and mirages. Significant in Machado's trajectory is the fact that, of 27 plays, "all but 7 deal with his family or Cuba in some way." Only during the period when travel restrictions between Cuba and the United States were eased and he was able to return to the island periodically, was he finally, like so many other Cuban-Americans, considering becoming a U.S. citizen—as if the ability to return had shifted his position from that of eternal exile to the more flexible psychic position of the migrant, who can adapt and adopt another country as a home.

If, for Machado and many others, exile meant never arriving at the promised land, but rather transforming the past and childhood into a lost paradise (that characteristic of what is now labeled as the 1.5 generation), Sandra Ramos's entire oeuvre in contrast is dedicated to those who stay behind and who need to be considered too, since they have to confront the transformation of loved ones into persons who have suddenly, irrevocably been rendered inaccessible.

Ramos's self-representation as Alice in Wonderland situates her, like Cuban exiles in the United States, within the space of the mirage and the mirror, where all experience is rendered surreal. As she looks somewhat like Alice, I asked her about the genesis and significance of this self-representation. She explained that "Alice" symbolized how she feels her position in Cuba reproduces that of the girl in Lewis Carroll's text as embodying the simultaneous feelings of alienation from and wonder at the situation in Cuba. Fascinated with Lewis Carroll's novel, which she had read and reread numerous times, she had seen Tenniel's illustrations and also a wooden sculpture of a nineteenth-century Dutch queen that had moved her, and so had conflated all three into her "Alice-Sandra-Princess" image in order to represent both the innocent dreams of childhood and the split between the real person and the surreal context that Cuba's political situation forces her to inhabit. Moreover, people who believe in queens and kings remain irremediably childish.[28] As is evident from this explanation, Ramos's position toward the Cuban Revolution, like so many other artists of her generation, is ambiguous. While she criticizes the current political and economic situation as "surreal," she also envisions Cuba as a land of wonder in need of citizens willing to stay and commit to life there and change from within. Exile, both interior and exterior, is producing the instability of the system. This is reminiscent of the argument that, were it not for the fact that the United States serves as the escape valve for the disgruntled and the landless and poor, Mexico would have had another Revolution shortly after that of 1910. Thus, Ramos's stance both envelops and conjoins exile and non-exile.

Unlike Mexican-American and other narratives of migration, all sorts of liquids (seawater, tears, beer) underlie many of Ramos's representations and installations. Her installation *Máquina para ahogar las penas* [Machine for Drowning Your Sorrows] (1999) includes a beer dispenser, a TV, and a barrel in which a video is projected. The viewers become performers who repeat what is happening today in Cuba when they drink the beer-that-is-the-sea. "This installation," she writes, "reflects another phenomenon characteristic of contemporary Cuban culture: alcohol and music as elements of evasion of the difficulties of contemporary life in Cuba. In this case alcohol and the ocean function in a similar way . . ." ["Esta instalación reflejará otro fenómeno característico de la vida cotidiana contemporánea cubana: el alcohol y la música como elementos de evasión del pueblo ante las dificultades de la vida cotidiana. En este caso la cerveza y el mar se igualan . . .]. Another installation, *Buzos* [Scuba Divers] (1999), consists of a garbage container, a video, and a TV, and represents

a common practice in the life of the city: the return of the "scuba diver," that is, people who are forced to make a living "diving" into garbage containers in search of something useful or food. . . . Scuba divers are marginalized individuals. Most of them are children or old people who live in a precarious economic situation. They reflect the inherent contradictions of our society that pretends to self-define itself as egalitarian.

[un hecho común en la vida contemporánea de nuestra ciudad: la reaparición del 'buzo', individuos que se dedican a 'bucear', a buscar cosas útiles, o comida en los latones de basura. . . . Los llamados 'buzos' son individuos marginados. La mayoría son niños o viejos que viven en una precaria situación económica. Ellos son reflejos de las contradicciones inherentes a nuestra sociedad, que pretende autodefinirse como una ciudad igualitaria.]

8.10. Mi diaria vocación de suicida *[My daily vocation as a suicide]*
1993 engraving
Sandra Ramos
Courtesy of the artist

The video installation *Promesas* alludes to the persistence of ways of life and cultural forms that are primitive and marginal, such as that of the "paying for promises" to St. Lazarus—a religious practice that has been maintained as a living tradition despite socialist state ideology.[29] Besides lamenting the return of marginal means of subsistence on the island, and the aberrant double economy of the Special Period, the artist represents herself as the Alice in the land of mirrors, the Alice who believes in salvation, and the Alice who commits suicide every day in her commitment to an often indefensible political project. A Cuban Cassandra, she is also the visionary who admonishes those who lack faith in socialism and who abandon everything because they believe in nothing. A single wooden shoe, reflected in a mirror and with a miniature lamb on top, is called *Camina sobre el agua hombre de poca fe* [Walk on Water Man of Little Faith].

As we have seen, Ramos's feeling that she has to walk on water, and live surrounded by water, shapes many of her engravings, which show her in the shape of the island surrounded by water and are tellingly entitled *La maldita circunstancia del agua por todas partes* [The Damned Circumstance of Water Everywhere]. Other engravings, like the one in her home, show her in a raft, surrounded by bottles of liquor floating about, adrift all alone under the stars, just as Cuba. Her obsession with the sea, mirrors, and mirages (real and imaginary), and psychic and social postures as shipwrecks, stands in

197

"La maldita circunstancia del agua por todas partes"

stark contrast and serves as an important corrective to Cuban exile narratives in the United States. Ramos's position and her critique complicate the nostalgic mythmaking and the often sentimentalizing tone of many of these narratives, which, until the Bridges to Cuba project, served to foster dreams of yet another U.S. intervention in Latin America. Like Lourdes Casal, Ruth Behar, Dolores Prida, and many others, Ramos offers us a key to understanding

8.11. La maldita cirunstancia del agua por todas partes *[The damned circumstance of being surrounded by water]*
1993 engraving
Sandra Ramos
Courtesy of the artist

exile and trauma, unlike Cuban-Americans of the first generation of exiles, who transform trauma into a symptom that is expressed stridently but that remains unnamed. Moreover, if in the contemporary world migration and exile have become escape valves that function to maintain obsolete, corrupt, and repressive regimes, for Ramos the impulse to stay and fight for change is a radical alternative. To be surrounded by water is a damned circumstance; simultaneously, it is a great possibility.

EPILOGUE

A fetish, so the dictionaries tell us, is a spirit attached to a material object.
　　　　　　　—Charles Simic, *Dime-Store Alchemy: The Art of Joseph Cornell*

IN THE MUSEUM OF ETHNOLOGY in Vienna, under inventory number 10,402, is a fabulous, ancient, Mexican feather headdress made of over 450 brilliant quetzal tail feathers. It dates from the early sixteenth century and was, according to the museum's pamphlet, "undoubtedly part of the garments of a deity impersonated in rituals by Aztec priests."[1] The object (Figure 0.1 in the Introduction) has been known for centuries as the "feather crown of Montezuma," but the museum now argues that it really could not have been Montezuma's crown, because according to Aztec pictorial manuscripts and Spanish accounts of the sixteenth century, "Aztec rulers were wearing turquoise diadems (symbolizing their domination of time) rather than feather headdresses as part of their insignia of office." Indeed, as the account in the museum's pamphlet continues, Aztec accounts do not include this object in the list of things that Montezuma sent Cortés upon his arrival in Mexico, and it is also not on the list of things Cortés relates having gotten. Indeed, what Cortés does write is that he received "four garments of deities, including appropriate feather headdresses." Thus, if anything, and circumventing questions of ownership, what came to be known as Montezuma's headdress may have really been the headdress of an Aztec deity. Playing with the indeterminacy of the possessive, what the museum does not say, however, is that the headdress might have belonged to Montezuma but not been worn by him. Grammatical quibblings aside, I wonder how the story that the feather headdress was Montezuma's got started, how it spread, who spread it, why it persisted over the centuries, and why now, suddenly, the museum is intent on contesting a story that they in all likelihood had a hand (and probable stake) in creating? Indeed, I seem to remember that the first time I consulted the museum's website, a few years ago, they proudly announced possession of this item as the centerpiece of their ethnographic collection.

The museum's account of the trajectory of the object might help clear up some of the mystery, since recent research, again according to their pamphlet, states that the Vienna feather headdress "can be traced back to 1575, when it was listed together with other pieces of featherwork in the inventory of the Kunstkammer of Count Ulrich of Montfort in Tettnang (Upper Suebia) under the title 'all kinds of Moorish garments of featherwork.'" The Museum of Ethnology surmises that the Count could have gotten the piece while serving as ambassador to Spain in the 1560s, which would explain why he might have mistaken it for a Moorish featherwork. The museum's claim that this is a period when Spain's connection to Mexico had already been lost, and moreover that at that time Spain was intent on removing "heathen" artifacts from its collections, seems highly implausible. But going on with the story, the Tettnang Kunstkammer in Upper

Suebia was bought up by Archduke Ferdinand to expand his own famous collection at Ambras Castle. From there, the feather headdress made its way to Vienna in the early nineteenth century, where it was rediscovered at Lower Belevedere castle in 1877. Following the increasing fine-tuning in classificatory mechanisms, in 1880 it became part of the collection of the Anthropological-Ethnographic Department of the Museum of Natural History, and finally entered the collection of the Museum of Ethnology when it was founded in 1928. One very plausible explanation, then, for the loss of the object's provenance was simply a matter of its having been relocated repeatedly, and thus it is highly likely that the accompanying tag (if there ever was one) could have been misplaced, and the object's provenance misplaced along with it.

The museum actually ends up blaming the misattribution of the object as "Montezuma's headdress" to the Mexican Revolution of 1910, "when the government in search for symbols of its legitimation and claim of identity with its pre-Spanish roots had a copy made of the Vienna headdress" (pamphlet). A replica is presently exhibited at the Museo Nacional de Antropología in Mexico. Failing to mention that the kopillu ketzalli, a Mexican indigenous group, is fighting for the repatriation of the object, and that the Mexican parliament backed their demands in 2006, the museum's explanation of Montezuma's headdress ends rather cryptically with the following statement: "Questions relating to the history and meaning of this cultural document are being discussed since 2002 by an Austrian-Mexican expert commission. Since June 2005 these discussions are supplemented by discussions of [sic] a political level." If the feather headdress is really not Montezuma's (and indeed, even if it were), it is unclear to me why the Austrian government does not simply return the headdress and exchange it for the replica in Mexico City's Museo Nacional de Antropología, as the kopillu ketzalli are asking—unless, of course, they are afraid that that would open the floodgates to an emptying of Vienna's incredible museums. Or that it is better to have an original of dubious provenance than a duplicate of known manufacture.

What is clear in the labyrinthine account accompanying Montezuma's headdress, and the reason why I go over it in such detail, is that misplacement involves not only the real loss of objects, but also, and perhaps more importantly, the loss of the object's provenance (or biography), and its misattribution (in this case as Moorish). What is gained is a *mise en abîme* that for all practical purposes makes it impossible for indigenous groups to reclaim objects. The gathering storm regarding repatriation worldwide is also bringing to the fore the extent to which what has constituted national culture to date is created largely by sanctioned forms of theft. Cultures are therefore cultures of theft. Europeans have long been aware of this, since in the many wars that have shaped the continent, the first places to be plundered would inevitably be museums or royal collections. The French and the Germans have famously plundered each other for centuries, and Hitler plundered all of Europe in the interests of building an enormous museum to be hidden in the caves in the mountains of Linz. When Germany began to lose the war, Stalin in turn ransacked numerous German art collections. More recently, we all awoke to the horrifying news that Iraq's National Museum, holding artifacts dating back 7,000 years, had been plundered. Some news reporters claim that American soldiers instigated Iraqis to go in, calling out "Ali Baba, it is yours, go get it," and the like. However, amid all the mourning regarding the loss of our heritage, there are websites claiming that Iraq's National Museum's curators allegedly had, in anticipation of probable loot-ing, hidden the most precious items in the collection and that, as a consequence, what was lost was of little significance.[2]

While European countries have negotiated the return of plundered objects over the centuries, why is a native group's call, such as that of the kopillu ketzalli in Mexico for the repatriation of Montezuma's headdress, so threatening? Why is it *not like* that of one European country's negotiation with another? I can only surmise that that call symbol-izes, better than anything else, the threat that anticolonial movements pose to western hegemony, and that hence threatens to destabilize the entire order of things. It fits in with the repatriation of the body of the "Negro de Banyoles," the Southern African tribal leader who had been taxidermied and displayed in a Catalan museum until 2000, and that of Saarjite Baartmann, referred to as the Hottentot Venus (discussed in Chap-ter Three). Increasingly, calls for repatriation from native peoples worldwide under-mine the very opposition that structures western epistemology: between the West as producer of knowledge and the rest as producers of raw materials. Within this scheme of things, possessing Montezuma's headdress is of paramount importance in keeping in place all the unequal forms of exchange that structure our world system. And what could be more telling than the fact that Vienna's Museum of Ethnology claims copy-right of any and all photographs taken of the headdress?

If the misplacing of Montezuma's headdress is an example of how colonial inequal-ity underpins western modernity, the displacement of people that is currently under-way on a global scale should not be overlooked. As if only to provide a frame for what I am arguing, in painting after painting, contemporary Spanish artist Cristóbal Toral shows people, usually women, in transit from nowhere to an even more uncertain nowhere, abandoned, if not outright despondent. They sit in no-places, such as train and bus stations, amid battered suitcases that oddly seem to resemble them. As if to echo a friend's words who, a few days before traveling (and in anticipation of the rough handling we currently experience in airports), begins to turn himself "into a package," in one of Toral's paintings, a woman is treated as if she were one more piece of luggage on a conveyor belt. Even more pointed is Toral's version of Velázquez's "Las meninas" (1656), which inspired Foucault's reflections on representation with which I began. In "D'après las meninas" (1974–75), three hundred years later, Toral has faithfully copied yet radically transformed this famous painting, replacing the infanta and her entou-rage of servants and dwarfs in the foreground with a jumble of old suitcases and boxes typical of the ones carried by poorer migrants. Filling the room and threatening to rise skyward, they seem to have displaced the artist, who is tellingly absent, as if Toral were unsure as to the status of representation. These oddly inert yet threatening piles of boxes and luggage simultaneously put into question the space of royalty, that of the royal painter, and the privileged position of the viewer of the painting, already pointed at by Velázquez. Toral's insistent use of suitcases as a synecdoche for migration and migrants signals current unease with the paradigm shift that is underway when global mass migration (often theorized as a counter-Conquest) threatens to displace the cen-trality of Enlightened individuality. Even more, in Marchán Fiz's words, Toral's entire oeuvre is "a metaphor for dispossession, hopelessness, and the decline of a certain kind of humanity" ["una metáfora del desahucio y, todavía más, del ocaso de una

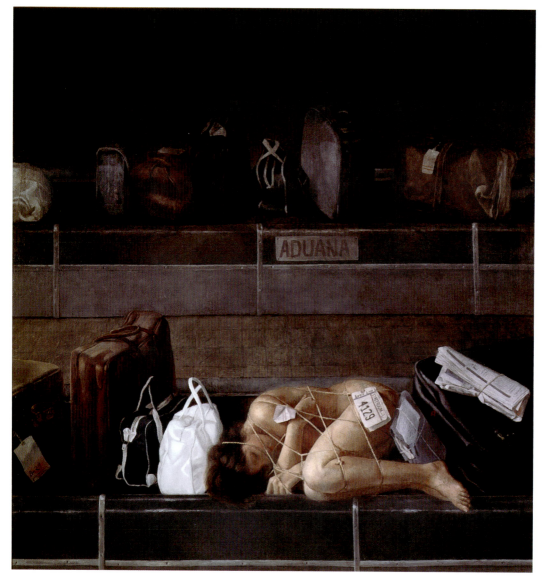

9.1. Mujer mirando una
    fotografía *[Woman Looking
    at a Photograph]*
1982 Cristóbal Toral
Oil on canvas
Courtesy of the artist

9.2. La aduana *[Customs]*
1972 Cristóbal Toral
Oil on canvas
Private Collection, New York
Courtesy of the artist

9.3a. Las meninas
Diego Velázquez (1599–1660)
Museo del Prado, Madrid
Photo credit: Scala/Art Resource, NY

9.3b. D'après las meninas
1974–1975 Cristóbal Toral
Oil on canvas
Courtesy of the artist

determinada humanidad"].[3] In a similar vein, in La Gran Avenida (The Great Avenue), to date an unfinished painting, what once was a major boulevard (presumably in Madrid) is now too overcome by trash, battered suitcases, and people lying about, indistinguishable from society's refuse. Benjamin's idea of progress as a pile of debris rising skyward seems strangely premonitory of the juncture at which we find ourselves.

9.4. La gran avenida *[The Great Avenue]*
Unfinished
1994 Cristóbal Toral
Oil on canvas
Courtesy of the artist

And while migration, as I showed in the last two chapters, may result in terrible forms of uprooting and loss, followed by forms of resistance and great creativity, the millions of people on the move, displaced, and unaccounted for often run the danger of being misplaced, much as the objects that are the focus of this book. (Think of Ramos's skeletons of would-be exiles, lying at the bottom of the ocean amid other trash.) It would seem that, like objects that are misplaced, humans too stand to lose their place in the world. Slavery, sexual trafficking, the traffic in children, forced labor and forced marriages, torture, and other such manifestations of human bondage are on the rise again, despite successively drafted and approved international conventions.[4] Forms of violence in and of themselves, the dis- and misplacement of people can result in gruesome forms of violence such as that against women in Ciudad

Juárez, Mexico (now spreading to other cities along the border). Indeed, since 1993, only two years before the signing of NAFTA, hundreds of young girls, many of them maquiladora workers, have been raped, tortured, and dismembered. In testimonies the mothers report searching for whatever is left of the bodies and clothes of their daughters in the trash heaps in and around Ciudad Juárez.[5] As if only to highlight the relation between these apparently completely dispensable and disposable bodies, the image used by women's activist groups is that of a white high heel thrown in the desert amid other litter.[6] Equally horrific, yet less in the news, is the femicide of over 2,500 young, poor, indigenous-looking women in Guatemala, according to the Washington Office on Latin America (WOLA). Indeed, "police data show a continuous increase in the murders of women, from 313 in 2002 to 351 in 2003, 531 in 2004, 580 in 2005, and close to 600 in 2006. Most of the victims were young and poor, and in many cases, the victims were raped, strangled, decapitated, or otherwise mutilated." As with Ciudad Juárez, "[P]rogress in the investigation of the murders of women has been fraught with numerous shortcomings, including a lack of technical capacity to preserve crime scenes, interrogate witnesses, and collect and preserve evidence, as well as a lack of political will to resolve the murders."[7]

On the other side of the spectrum, some of the richest women in Mexico posed for photographer Daniela Rossell. While the photographer played with the light and camera angles, the women (all in Rossell's circle of acquaintances) were at complete liberty to choose the poses and the backdrop in which they would be photographed in the heart of their homes. *Ricas y famosas* (*Rich and Famous*) documents these sessions and the interior life of Mexico's ruling elite—many of them from the PRI, and many of them the beneficiaries of the policies instituted by NAFTA. The only statement made by Rossell collapses fiction and the real at the beginning of the book: "The following images depict actual settings. The photographic subjects are representing themselves. Any resemblance with real events is not coincidental."[8] The exhibition of these photographs as well as the publication of *Ricas y famosas* reverberated as shock waves across Mexico, for how could people collect precious rarities so obsessively, and what is worse, how could they so tastelessly flaunt their wealth in a nation with such terrible degrees of poverty? The woman on the cover lounges on a brocade couch, in a gold lamé dress, under a massive crystal chandelier, with an oil painting of little angels and a sheep in the background (representing, some critics have asserted, the PRI's self-representation as the guardians of the flock). Other images show women surrounded by their collections of teddy bears and in their children's playpens. They seem happy returning to the magical realm of childhood and at ease with their social infantilization. Yet another sits on a riding seat, with a cowboy hat, a fabulous painting of revolutionary Emiliano Zapata on the wall behind her, and one foot in a red high heel resting on a taxidermied crocodile. Throughout, the performances of obscene wealth, the home as the exhibition space of that wealth, and the self-representation of the woman as trophy wife predominate. While many of the houses display stuffed animals hunted by the women's husbands in Africa, in one photo in particular a woman chose to have herself photographed dressed in a white fur jacket, white pants, her hair bleached blonde, and surrounded by two taxidermied bears, a lion, a gazelle, and a mountain goat. The space seems to be an office (where her husband works?), and one wonders at her identification with the hunted animals and her desire to be photographed as in a diorama, thus giving renewed vigor to the expression "trophy wife."

Sadly enough, these two frames (the high heel lying in the desert and the woman in the diorama) constitute the two poles that frame the misplacement of people and objects today. While on one side, migrants are equated with trash, on the other side, the globalized fabulously wealthy do not know where to turn in their search for rare and marvelous objects with which to show off their wealth and power. Increasingly, as Patricia McLaughlin has shown, the luxury trade "is booming" and rose 27.7 percent in the first five months of 2007 alone. In a country where today 1 percent of the population owns 30 percent of the wealth, the efforts of the mega-rich try to distinguish themselves from the rich and think nothing of buying a $10,200 Asprey alligator handbag,[9] a $1.2 million Bugatti EB 16.4 Veyron sports car, a "cute" $47,400 Rolex "with a leopard-spotted band to match its leopard-spotted face," a "cool" $19,450 Vertu cell phone, and luxury apartments that range from half a million dollars to the $26 million penthouse being built by architect Cesar Pelli in New York City's uptown.[10] Despite their prices, these are still commodity items. Disguising the scarcity of marvelous objects and most people's inability to ever possess them, therefore, is the constant news regarding the continued illegal sale of antiquities (both from the East and from the Americas) and the astronomical prices that artworks are fetching. The rest of us still collect, playing the edge with kitsch, and our homes are cozy or artistic as the case might be.[11] It would seem, then, that along with the shift from a society of producers to a society of consumers, we are mourning the waning of the object's aura by the exponentially increasing proliferation of mass-produced things and images. More has become better, or "Quantity," in Benjamin's words, "has been transmuted into quality."[12] Contemporary artists who work to reclaim refused objects, like Purcell, Dion, and others, do so to reclaim the aura they acquire with the slow working of time, weather, and thus multiple processes of decay. The weathered books, burnt dice, corroded metals, etc., that is, the refused, discarded objects that land in the trash, are somehow precious—precisely because the action of decay and time has transformed them into more than they ever were as commodities.

But for the majority of us, there are no marvelous objects within reach. We may thus intuit, and even re-create, some of the sense of awe that was experienced across the continent post-1492 when we pick up a beautiful rock at the beach and think that nature is wonderful, as almost everyone came to feel around 1500, or when we visit the museums of our time. I am thinking in particular of recent visits to the Treasury of the Hapsburgs in Vienna—a truly astonishing collection of the rare and priceless objects with which the Hapsburgs legitimated their power. The Green Vault in Dresden, painted in Saxony's green, built in the mid-sixteenth century as a concealed treasury in Dresden, thanks largely to Augustus the Strong, elector of Saxony and King of Poland, allied to the Hapsburgs as a member of the Order of the Golden Fleece, had by 1723 grown to seven more rooms, constituting it as the world's first treasury museum and first specialized museum of decorative arts. When viewing some of the marvels crafted by master artists in these collections, we may fully understand the hold that marvelous objects have over us. In Cortázar's famous story "Axolótl," the visitor is so entranced by the Mexican salamander in the aquarium in the Jardin des Plantes that, following some ancient Aztec ritual, he is cannibalized by it and in the end *becomes* it.[13] But the status of the marvelous object has changed, and Cortázar's story may be read as a nostalgic reflection of that passing. Reflecting on this change, Walter Benjamin wrote that formerly, a man concentrating before a work of art, like the protagonist in Cortázar's story, was "absorbed by it," whereas today, the "distracted mass absorbs the work of art."[14]

Unlike in the early Wunderkammern, where the privileged visitor had the marvels of the world within arm's reach, and the world (as encyclopedia) entered the home, today, when we visit museums, we are unable to touch objects, much less dream of possessing them. As we have repeatedly seen in the first chapters of this book, the unbridled urge to possess—as well as the means to do so—underpinned the genesis of most of the great collections that were broken up into today's museums, yet today, the few who *can* have it all at their fingertips do not leave anything that elicits awe, other than awe at their wastefulness. In Vienna's treasury, we may stand transfixed by a particularly stunning example of Artificialia or Naturficialia (skillfully blending coral; gold with superb feats of craftsmanship), yet the heavy glass protection serves to forever remove that object in time from us. Or we may admire a painting in a museum, only to be distracted by the people milling about. Wonder-arousing objects therefore come to us shimmering from afar and mediated by an enormous distance in experience. Even all the taxidermied animals that formerly had such cultural cachet, now in natural history museums (somewhat more accessible than the precious objects made by master craftsmen), have become musty, and we wander about great halls in awe of what we did to the natural world, and oddly sad. Exhibits today are dominated by the extinction of the dinosaurs, and as we pass under these huge creatures and wonder how they could have disappeared, we are invariably led to exhibits warning of impending global warming, accelerated desertification and the future lack of water, impending massive migrations of people, and exponential rates of extinction of all animals. Signs that read EXTINCTION dominate the space, as if to connect the dinosaurs' passing with the natural history of our own destruction.

Other spaces that were created when the Wunderkammern were created, and that coexisted alongside them, however, continue to tell a different story and hold a promise of salvation. Profoundly democratic spaces and always open to the public, and where every plant could be "touched, smelled, and sketched from the gravel or grass walks,"[15] botanical gardens have existed for centuries as living encyclopedias and Gardens of Eden. Replicating the accounts in the chronicles of the New World, where conquistadores from Columbus on reported searching for or even having reached paradise (nevertheless destroying it), botanical gardens imported plants from the Americas and the rest of the globe. From the famous Botanical Gardens at Padua, Leyden, and Montpellier, founded in the sixteenth century, and those at Oxford, Uppsala, and the famous Jardin du Roi in Paris, founded in the seventeenth century, where Buffon studied natural history, to Bartram's Garden in Philadelphia, founded in the late eighteenth century, botanical gardens everywhere have survived, unlike the Wunderkammern. Attempts to re-create the Garden of Eden, they were deeply religious in their view of plants as "restful things, free from motion, and, so it was generally imagined, from the perturbations of sex," and thus "could offer a complete guide to the many faces of the Creator." As John Prest concludes, however, after the relatively bleak medieval outlook and division of

Christendom with the Reformation, "these attempts to re-create the Garden of Eden, backward looking as they were, came as a sensitive, and immensely optimistic interlude in Western European history, before the march of modern science and the industrial revolution began."[16]

9.5. Sign in the desert
Paracas National Reserve, Perú
Photo Spitta 2006

While visitors today throng to botanical gardens to escape the city, often without having to leave the city, the notion of gardens of Eden has reverberated provocatively across cultures and led to the creation of national parks and bio-reserves worldwide.[17] At Paracas National Reserve, one of Perú's richest archaeological and animal sanctuaries, in the middle of the desert, a sign greets the visitor. It reads: "When human beings understand that they are an integral part of nature they will learn to benefit from it without engaging in activities that will result in our destruction." I do not know who wrote this, and no one seemed to know who put that sign there. Misplaced, it nevertheless articulates better than anything I have written here the challenge we are facing.

NOTES

INTRODUCTION

1. George Kubler argues that this "shape in time" is a "visible portrait" of collective identities in the past and becomes the "portrait given to posterity." *The Shape of Time: Remarks on the History of Things* (New Haven: Yale University Press, 1962), 9.

2. Stephen Greenblatt, *Marvelous Possessions: The Wonder of the New World* (Chicago: University of Chicago Press, 1991), 19.

3. Ibid.

4. Lorraine Daston, "Neugierde als Empfindung und Epistemologie in der frühmodernen Wissenschaft," in *Macrocosmos in Microcosmo: Die Welt in der Stube. Zur Geschichte des Sammelns 1450–1800*, edited by Andreas Grote (Berlin: Leske and Budrich, Opladen, 1994), 59.

5. See Mary Louise Pratt's important observations regarding the genesis of natural history and the "seeing man" positionality of travelers, explorers, and scientists in the Americas. *Imperial Eyes: Travel Writing and Transculturation* (London; New York: Routledge, 1992). For an important history of wonder, see also Lorraine Daston and Katharine Park, *Wonders and the Order of Nature 1150–1750* (New York: Zone Books, 2001).

6. Michel Foucault, *The Order of Things* (New York: Vintage, 1973), xv.

7. The Philadelphia Museum of Art sent this much more artistic rendering of Duchamp's urinal and did not give me permission to use the photograph I had taken, which showed its profound misplacement in the museum among "high art."

8. Foucault, *The Order of Things*, xv.

9. Lautréamont, in *Les Chants de Maldoror* (Chant VI; 1868–1869), had written "comme la recontre fortuite sur une table de dissection d'une machine à coudre et d'un parapluie." This description of surreal encounters was taken by André Breton as the symbol for surrealism. See http://www.gutenberg.org/etext/12005 for text. In turn, Alejo Carpentier's reflections on the marvelous in Latin America, in his well-known preface to *El reino de este mundo*, critiqued the surrealists' all-too-contrived juxtapositions of things: "Lo maravilloso, obtenido con trucos de prestidigitación, reuniéndose objetos que para nada suelen encontrarse: la vieja y embustera historia del encuentro fortuito del paraguas y de la máquina de coser sobre una mesa de disección . . ." In contrast, he argued, in Latin America, wonderful and incongruous juxtapositions emerge naturally. Alejo Carpentier, *El reino de este mundo* (Mexico: E.D.I.A.P.S.A., 1949), 8.

10. To quote Kubler again, a shape in time emerges because "[T]he cultural clock . . . runs mainly upon ruined fragments of matter recovered from refuse heaps and graveyards, from abandoned cities and buried villages" (*The Shape of Time*, 14).

11. See Enrique Dussel, *El encubrimiento del Otro: Hacia el origen del mito de la modernidad* (Madrid: Ediciones Abya-yala, 1994), translated by Michael D. Barber as *The Invention of the Americas: Eclipse of "the Other" and the Myth of Modernity* (New York: Continuum, 1995).

12. Jared M. Diamond, *Guns, Germs, and Steel: The Fates of Human Societies* (New York: Norton, 2005).

13. See the Smithsonian's fabulous study *Seeds of Change: Five Hundred Years Since Columbus. A Quincentennial Celebration*, edited by Herman J. Viola and Carolyn Margolis (Washington: Smithsonian Institution Press, 1991).

14. For some important examples of critiques of colonialism and Eurocentrism, see Edmundo O'Gorman, *La invención de América: El universalismo de la cultura de Occidente* (México: Fondo de Cultura Económica, 1958); Edmundo Desnoes, *Memorias del subdesarrollo* (México: J. Mortiz, 1980); all of Eduardo Galeano's works, including *Memoria del fuego* (Madrid: Siglo Veintiuno de España Editores, 1982–1986); Johannes Fabian, *Time and the Other: How Anthropology Makes Its Object* (New York: Columbia University Press, 1983); Peter Hulme, *Colonial Encounters: Europe and the Native Caribbean,*

1492–1797 (London; New York: Methuen, 1986); Iris Zavala, *Colonialism and Culture: Hispanic Modernisms and the Social Imaginary* (Bloomington: Indiana University Press, 1992); José Rabasa, *Inventing America: Spanish Historiography and the Formation of Eurocentrism* (Norman: University of Oklahoma Press, 1993); Margarita Zamora, *Reading Columbus* (Berkeley: University of California Press, 1993); Enrique Dussel, *The Invention of the Americas: Eclipse of "the Other" and the Myth of Modernity*, translated by Michael D. Barber (New York: Continuum, 1995); Walter Mignolo, *The Darker Side of the Renaissance: Literacy, Territoriality, and Colonization* (Ann Arbor: University of Michigan Press, 1995); and Alberto Moreiras, *The Exhaustion of Difference: The Politics of Latin American Cultural Studies* (Durham, NC: Duke University Press, 2001) among others.

15. See her essay "Las tretas del débil," in *La sartén por el mango: Encuentro de escritoras latinoamericanas*, edited by Patricia Elena González and Eliana Ortega (Río Piedras, PR: Ediciones Huracán, 1985).

16. See *Mestizajes tecnológicos y cambios culturales en México*, edited by Enrique Floriscano and Virginia García Acosta (México: Centro de Investigaciones y Estudios Superiores en Antropología Social, 2004).

17. Mary Douglas, *Purity and Danger* (New York: Routledge, 2003), 44.

18. See the important catalogue to the exhibition of casta paintings that was instrumental in bringing attention to this genre: María Concepción García Sáiz, *Las castas mexicanas: Un género pictórico americano* (Mexico: Olivetti, 1989); and Ilona Katzew, *Casta Painting: Images of Race in Eighteenth-Century Mexico* (New Haven: Yale University Press, 2004), and her "Casta Painting: Identity and Social Stratification in Colonial Mexico," http://www.gc.maricopa.edu/laberinto/fall1997/casta1997.htm. See also the exhibition *New World Orders: Casta Painting and Colonial Latin America*, organized by the Americas Society Art Gallery, September 26–December 22, 1996.

19. Nazi concentration camps, of course, top this list of "total" institutions. Jean Améry, a Holocaust survivor, writes that not only is everything taken from you upon entrance, but everything is taken from you to allow "the robber to deride you because you owned nothing." *At the Mind's Limits: Contemplations by a Survivor on Auschwitz and Its Realities*, translated by Sidney Rosenfeld and Stella P. Rosenfeld (Bloomington and Indianapolis: Indiana University Press, 1980), 10.

20. The military's need to erase signs of individuation and to construct a collective body is due, of course, to the need of relieving individual soldiers of the blame for the excesses and violence committed by the army.

21. See, for example, Octavio Paz's seminal essay *El laberinto de la soledad* (Madrid: Cátedra, 1993), translated by Lysander Kemp as *The Labyrinth of Solitude: Life and Thought in Mexico* (New York, Grove Press, 1962).

22. See Alberto Flores Galindo's seminal *Buscando un Inca: identidad y utopia en los Andes* (Lima, Perú: Editorial Horizonte, 1988).

23. José Vasconcelos, *La raza cósmica: Misión de la raza iberoamericana* (Paris: Agencia Mundial de Librería, s192–).

24. In particular, see Richard Rodríguez's formulation in *Brown: The Last Discovery of America* (New York: Viking, 2002).

25. For an insightful discussion of the terms "Latino" and "*latinidad*" and their trajectory, see Alberto Sandoval-Sánchez's personal statement in the Introduction to *José, Can You See? Latinos On and Off Broadway* (Madison: University of Wisconsin Press, 1999). As he writes, "Latin" and "Latino" are denominations imposed on Hispanic residents of the United States and hence are deeply symptomatic of the ways race is read in this country. Being "Latin" means "to come from a Spanish-speaking country, to be an immigrant whose identity as 'Latin foreign other' is marked by, and anchored in, a Spanish accent and exotic looks. Such conceptions of the 'foreign other' are perpetuated by ready-made stereotypes: the Latin bombshell, the Latin lover, Latin music, Latin rhythm, Latin dance, Latin type, Latin temper, Latin time. These ideological constructs confine Spanish-speaking immigrants to a politics of representation that often racializes them and perpetuates racist practices" (14). These highly charged terms are contested by Latinos in the United States—hence "*latinidad*" results, as he adds, "from Latino/a agency and intervention when U.S. Latinos/as articulate and construct cultural expressions and identity formations that come from a conscious political act of self-affirmation. Hence, any Latino cultural performance and ritualistic enactment constitutes an affirmation of 'Latinidad.' From this perspective, all kinds of activities—exhibits of ethnocultural symbols and icons, celebrations, parades, street fairs, festivals, *fiestas patrias* (national holidays), religious ceremonies, literary readings, political manifestations and activism,

college courses and student organizations, and the broadcasting of Spanish television shows—constantly reactivate and mobilize 'Latinidad.' In these activities, mainly through music, dance, theatre, literature, and food, 'Latinidad' is circulated in an evolving process that facilitates the invention of U.S. Latino/a identities, Latino local and national imagined communities, and 'Latinidad' itself" (15). For other important elaborations on *latinidad*, see also Frances R. Aparicio and Susana Chávez-Silverman's Introduction to their edition *Tropicalizations: Transcultural Representations of Latinidad* (Hanover, NH: Dartmouth College Press, 1997); and the essay by Juan Flores, "The Latino Imaginary: Dimensions of Community and Identity," in that edition (183–193). See also Laurie Kay Sommers, "Latinismo and Ethnic Nationalism in Cultural Performance," *Studies in Latin American Popular Culture* 10 (1991): 75–86; "Inventing Latinismo: The Creation of 'Hispanic' Panethnicity in the United States," *Journal of American Folklore* 104, no. 411 (1991): 32–53; and "Symbol and Style in *Cinco de Mayo*," *Journal of American Folklore* 98, no. 390 (1985): 476–482.

26. Kupferminc's work is viewable on her website, http://www.mirtakupferminc.net/nuevo2/index .htm.

27. Peter Stallybrass, "Worn Worlds: Clothes, Mourning, and the Life of Things," *Yale Review* 81, no. 2 (April 1993), 39.

28. See Kay Turner, *Beautiful Necessity: The Art and Meaning of Women's Altars* (New York: Thames & Hudson, 1999); Dana Salvo, *Home Altars of Mexico* (Albuquerque: University of New Mexico Press, 1997); Martha Egan, *Milagros: Votive Offerings from the Americas* (Albuquerque: University of New Mexico Press, 1991); José Juárez, *Ofrenda* (Mexico: Dolores Olmedo, 1983); Marie Romero Cash, *Living Shrines: Home Altars of New Mexico*, photographs by Siegfried Halus (Santa Fe: Museum of New Mexico Press, 1998); Jorge Durand and Douglas S. Massey, *Miracles on the Border: Retablos of Mexican Migrants to the United States* (Tucson and London: University of Arizona Press, 1995); and Margarita de Orellana, ed., *Retablos y exvotos* (Mexico: Museo Franz Mayer and Artes de Mexico, 2000).

29. Ibid., 50.

30. Joan Didion, *The Year of Magical Thinking* (New York: Alfred A. Knopf, 2005), 164–165.

31. This event was recorded in Cicero's *De Oratore* and the anonymously written *Ad Herennium* (ca. 86–82 B.C.). See Frances A. Yates, *The Art of Memory* (Chicago: University of Chicago Press, 1984).

32. Yates, *The Art of Memory*, 2.

33. James Clifford, *The Predicament of Culture: Twentieth-Century Ethnography, Literature, and Art* (Cambridge: Harvard University Press, 1988), 230.

34. See Diana Taylor, *The Archive and the Repertoire: Performing Cultural Memory in the Americas* (Durham, NC: Duke University Press, 2003).

35. Stephen Jay Gould, *The Mismeasure of Man* (New York: W. W. Norton, 1981), 82.

36. Henri Bergson, *Matter and Memory*, translated by Nancy Margaret Paul and W. Scott Palmer (New York: Zone, 1988), 25.

37. They seem to disappear from sight no sooner than we have focused on them, leading W. J. T. Mitchell recently to argue that objects tend to become images. See Part Two, "Objects," in W. J. T. Mitchell, *What Do Pictures Want? The Lives and Loves of Images* (Chicago and London: University of Chicago Press, 2005).

38. Arjun Appadurai writes that the "diversion of commodities from specified paths is always a sign of creativity or crisis, whether aesthetic or economic." Appadurai, "Introduction," in *The Social Life of Things* (Cambridge: Cambridge University Press, 1986), 26. See also Valerie Martin's novel *Property* (New York: Nan A. Talese, 2003).

39. For important work on memory, exile, and trauma, see Marianne Hirsch and Leo Spitzer's forthcoming *Ghosts of Home: The Afterlife of Czernowitz in Jewish Memory*; Hirsch's *Family Frames: Photography, Narrative, and Postmemory* (Cambridge, MA: Harvard University Press, 1997); Hirsch's "Projected Memory," in *Acts of Memory: Cultural Recall in the Present*, edited by Mieke Bal, Jonathan Crewe, and Leo Spitzer (Hanover, NH: University Press of New England, 1999); and Leo Spitzer's *Hotel Bolivia: The Culture of Memory in a Refuge from Nazism* (New York: Hill and Wang, 1998). See also the website http://www.columbia.edu/cu/irwag/events/main/memory/index.html for the conference "Objects and Memory: Engendering Private and Public Archives" at Columbia University (March 23, 2007).

40. See Marcus G. Raskin, "Reconstruction and Its Knowledge Method," in *New Ways of Knowing: The Sciences, Society, and Reconstructive Knowledge*, edited by Marcus G. Raskin and Herbert J. Bernstein (New Jersey: Rowman and Littlefield, 1987), 9.

41. Today, this principle unfortunately seems more exclusionary than inclusionary, despite the continual mention in the news of "sitting" different parties down "at the table" to negotiate.

42. Susan Stewart, *On Longing: Narratives of the Miniature, the Gigantic, the Souvenir, the Collection* (Durham, NC: Duke University Press, 1993).

43. *Things*, edited by Bill Brown (Chicago: University of Chicago Press, 2004), 16.

CHAPTER 1

1. For an interesting discussion of the role of things in the history of European ideas, see Germán Arciniegas, *Cuando América completó la tierra* (Bogotá: Villegas Editores, 2001).

2. P. Findlen adds the necessary corrective to Foucault, noting that the history of museums (that is, modern forms of ordering) can be traced back to the curiosity cabinets of the Renaissance, those Wunderkammern that were early attempts at collecting as a way of managing "the empirical explosion of materials that wider dissemination of ancient texts, increased travel, voyages of discovery, and more systematic forms of communication and exchange had produced." Cf. P. Findlen, quoted by Sharon Mac-Donald, "Exhibitions of Power and Powers of Exhibition: An Introduction to the Politics of Display," in *The Politics of Display: Museums, Science, Culture*, ed. Sharon MacDonald (New York: Routledge, 1998), 6. As MacDonald corroborates, "Such an empirical profusion posed problems for ways of knowing that had centered upon the inscribed wisdom of the Bible and of the ancients: here was material that was neither contained within nor immediately accountable by them" (6).

3. As José Ramón López points out, dioramas allow urban dwellers (whose only encounters with nature otherwise are the occasional dove or mosquito) to adopt a comfortable, privileged, and voyeuristic position vis-à-vis nature: dioramas allow the visitor to enter the lair of a beaver and to see through the eyes of a caterpillar ["por los ojos de una oruga"], to walk on the depths of the ocean ["se pasea por el fondo del mar"], or to run as fast as and alongside a lion and to be present at the instant when it slays a zebra ["o corre a la par de un león en el momento que abate una cebra"]. José Ramón López, "La fábula del tiempo," in *Richard Ross: Historia natural* (Madrid: Museo de Ciencias Naturales, 1994), 10. (This is the pamphlet that accompanied Madrid's Museo de Ciencias Naturales's exhibit of the dioramas of Richard Ross.)

4. Indeed as Arjun Appadurai argues, studies of the genesis of capitalism, such as C. Mukerji's *From Graven Images: Patterns of Modern Materialism* (New York: Columbia University Press, 1983), which posits that the West changed because of a rise in demand for goods, provide "fresh evidence and arguments for placing taste, demand, and fashion at the heart of a cultural account of the origins of occidental capitalism, and for the centrality of 'things' to this ideology in Renaissance Europe." "Introduction: Commodities and the Politics of Value," in *The Social Life of Things: Commodities in Cultural Perspective*, edited by Arjun Appadurai (Cambridge: Cambridge University Press, 1986), 3–63.

5. Writing from the perspective of Madrid's Museum of Natural Sciences, López explains the emergence of modern museums in the following way: "Geographic discoveries were therefore accelerating a process that would otherwise not have been produced since a large number of unknown things—especially flora and fauna—became available. The need to integrate this whole unknown world into the mental operant epistemological paradigm of the times caused a much greater fissure in European consciousness than is apparent at first sight. . . . The value of objects was changing, as was the way of conceiving the world. . . . In the second half of the XVI century the cumulative effect of novelties is such that it becomes impossible to evade the problem any longer and science steps in to help account for this new state of affairs. Collections now center around everything and anything that could count as unknown, or curious, regardless of whether it has magical properties or not and the cabinets of wonders start being filled with turtles, armadillos, serpents, snail shells, and minerals. Museums arise only when these collections become classified with the aim of integrating the unknown into the known. Only when objects are ordered in the cabinets do museums arise as collections that posit a scientific thesis about reality" (translation mine). ["Los descubrimientos geográficos por tanto estaban acelerando un proceso que de otra forma quizás no se hubiera producido, ya que se aportó en muy poco tiempo gran cantidad de objetos desconocidos, especialmente en cuanto a fauna y flora se refiere. La necesidad de integrar todo este mundo desconocido dentro de los esquemas mentales operantes acerca de la realidad provocó una fisura en la conciencia europea mayor de lo que a primera vista se puede sospechar. . . . En definitiva el valor del objeto estaba cambiando, al igual que la forma de concebir el mundo. . . . En la segunda mitad

del siglo XVI el cúmulo de novedades es tal que se hace irrenunciable abordar el problema, lo cual se va a hacer desde una faceta científica. Las colecciones se centran ahora en todo lo que llama la atención por desconocido, todo lo 'curioso,' tenga valor mágico o no, y comienzan los gabinetes a llenarse de tortugas, armadillos, serpientes, conchas de caracoles y minerales. Solamente cuando estas colecciones se comiencen a clasificar con el fin ya expresado de integrar lo desconocido dentro de lo conocido y los objetos se ordenen en el espacio del gabinete, surgirá el museo, en el cual siempre hemos de pensar como una colección que plantea una tésis científica sobre la realidad"], López, "La fábula del tiempo," 9.

6. See James Clifford, *The Predicament of Culture* (Cambridge: Harvard University Press, 1988), 220.

7. See Barbara Maria Stafford, "Revealing Technologies/Magical Domains," in *Devices of Wonder: From the World in a Box to Images on a Screen*, edited by Barbara Maria Stafford and Frances Terpak (Los Angeles: Getty Research Institute, 2001), 7. For an informative discussion regarding cabinets and famous cabinetmakers, see Reinier Baarsen, *17th-Century Cabinets*, translated by John Rudge (Amsterdam: Waanders Publishers, Rijksmuseum, 2000).

8. For a helpful history of Ole Worm's famous cabinet, see Torben Wolff, "The History of the Zoological Museum, University of Copenhagen," http://zoologi.snm.ku.dk/English/om_zoologisk_museum/history/museets_historie.

9. *Enciclopedia Universal Ilustrada Europeo Americana* (Barcelona: Espasa, 1924).

10. Barbara M. Benedict, *Curiosity: A Cultural History of Early Modern Inquiry* (Chicago: University of Chicago Press, 2001), 4.

11. Ibid., 2.

12. "Curious in Our Way: The Culture of Nature in Philadelphia, 1740–1840" (November 18–21, 2004), focused on the visual culture of natural history in the United States. The title of the conference and many of the papers delivered there foregrounded the importance of curiosity in the development of science. In turn, the accompanying exhibit, "Stuffing Birds, Pressing Plants, Shaping Knowledge: Natural History in North America, 1730–1860," at the American Philosophical Society played with the importance of sight ("Learning to Look . . . Looking to Learn . . .," read some of the captions) and conjoined natural history collections to epistemological shifts. Together, the conference and the exhibit focused on the different artistic techniques used in the representation of natural history and hence on the interplay between science and visual representation.

13. The curators of the 1994–1995 exhibition *Wunderkammer des Abendlandes* explain that "they were the expression of a humanist, encyclopedic education and witnesses of material ownership and wide-reaching commercial endeavors" ["Sie waren Ausdruck einer enzyklopaedischen humanistischen Bildung und Zeugen von materiellem Besitz und weitreichenden Handelsverbindungen"] (translation mine). *Wunderkammer des Abendlandes: Museum und Sammlung im Spiegel der Zeit*, catalogue of the exhibition at the Kunst- und Ausstellungshalle der Bundesrepublik Deutschland in Bonn, edited by Annesofie Becker and Arno Victor Nielsen (Bonn: Kunst- und Ausstellungshalle der Bundesrepublik Deutschland und Autoren, 1994), 32.

14. Barbara Stafford sees in the box mirror, which appeared toward the fifth century B.C., a forerunner of the Wunderkammern's desire to make everything visible: "The concept of revelation or epiphany (from epiphainein, 'to show forth') lies at the heart of three principal Greek words for 'mirror.'" Stafford, *Devices of Wonder*, 24. See also David Freedberg, *The Eye of the Lynx: Galileo, His Friends, and the Beginnings of Natural History* (Chicago and London: University of Chicago Press, 2002); Rosalind Krauss, *The Optical Unconscious* (Boston, Cambridge: MIT Press, 1993); and Jonathan Crary, *Techniques of the Observer: On Vision and Modernity in the Nineteenth Century* (Boston, Cambridge: MIT Press, 1992).

15. In aesthetic terms, the Wunderkammern exemplify the Baroque horror vacui, the horror of empty spaces that characterizes the art of the seventeenth century, an aesthetic that in turn reflects the cumulative, inclusive, non-differentiating, theatrical spectacle that underlies Baroque representation. In Latin America, of course, the Baroque would be mobilized differently, and it becomes particularly apparent in the decentered, inordinate, and multiple points of view seen in art and architecture, as well as the counterpoint between verbal and visual modes of representation theorized by Lois Parkinson Zamora in *The Inordinate Eye: New World Baroque and Latin American Fiction* (Chicago: University of Chicago Press, 2006). Mabel Moraña has called the emergent colonial Latin American forms of the Baroque, and Baroque intersections of the verbal and visual, "barroco de Indias." See her edition *Relecturas del barroco de Indias* (Hanover, NH: Ediciones del Norte, 1994); and also *Viaje al silencio: exploraciones del discurso barroco* (México, DF: Facultad de Filosofía y Letras, UNAM, 1998).

16. Many of these magnificent objects were displayed in the Wunderkammern, but many more were hidden away in courtly treasure collections that served as depositories and guarantors of royal power. A truly fabulous collection of these treasures, the Imperial and Ecclesiastical Treasury, is now on view at the Kunsthistorisches Museum in Vienna. Since many of these royal collections of treasures were either plundered during the many centuries of European wars or broken up and housed in different museums, the Viennese collection is one of the few extant. See *The Kunsthistorisches Museum Vienna: The Imperial and Ecclesiastical Treasury*, edited by Manfred Leithe-Jasper and Rudolf Distelberger (London and Munich: Scala Books, 2003). In celebration of the quincentenary of the discovery of the New World, the Portuguese royal collection was reassembled for a one-time exhibition at the Palácio Nacional da Ajuda. See the catalogue, *Royal Treasures* (Lisbon: Palácio Nacional da Ajuda, Instituto Portugués do Patrimonio Cultural, 1992).

17. Ruysch's famous cabinet—containing 2,000 specimens—was bought up by Peter the Great and is displayed to this day in St. Petersburg's Kunstkammer. See F. González-Crussi (with photographs by Rosamond Purcell), *Suspended Animation: Six Essays on the Preservation of Bodily Parts* (San Diego: Harvest, Harcourt Brace, 1995), 78–83.

18. At Bologna, which boasts the oldest European university (ca. 1088), there were dissections of male and female corpses performed as early as 1405, and by the mid-seventeenth century a famous anatomical cabinet had been built by Antonio Levanti. Shortly thereafter, entire amphitheaters devoted to anatomy were built in order to satisfy the public's growing demand for these spectacles. González-Crussi describes these spaces as spaces of spectacle as much as of learning. The Bolognese anatomy amphitheater "was magnificently decorated for the occasion: the walls were hung with damask, and two large torches, placed respectively at the head and feet of the cadaver, illuminated the working area. . . . The audience consisted of successful physicians, prominent members of the community, intellectuals, and the inevitable idle and rich snobs, apart from medical students. . . . Liveried lackeys appeared who circulated amidst the attendees distributing bouquets and oranges to the ladies, that 'the perfume of the ones and the aromas of the others' assist them in brooking the unpleasantness of the emanations wafting to their noses" (González-Crussi, *Suspended Animation,* 50–51).

19. See, for example, the stunning Mütter Museum in Philadelphia. I thank Rauner Special Collections librarian Jay Satterfield for bringing Vesali's fabulous book to my attention and for his annual public presentations unearthing the rarities of the collection.

20. See Frances A. Yates, *The Art of Memory* (Chicago: University of Chicago Press, 1984), especially Chapters Six ("Renaissance Memory: The Memory Theatre of Giulio Camillo") and Fifteen ("The Theatre Memory System of Robert Fludd"). As Jonathan Spence writes of Ricci's memory theater in China, "all through the sixteenth century 'astrologically centered mnemonic systems' were being constructed with extraordinary care in such cities as Venice and Naples and not only used at home but also exported by their eager creators to France and England, among many countries. These systems organized the forces of the universe into 'memory theatres,' concentric diagrams, or imaginary cities in such a way that those forces could be consulted directly and drawn upon, making the practitioner of the art a 'solar magus' of potentially great power. The theatre created by the remarkable Italian scholar Camillo in the 1540s suggests the range: in the foreground were piles of little boxes, intricately arranged and jammed with all the works of Cicero; rising away into the distance were arrays of cosmic images designed to show the 'universe expanding from First Causes through the stages of creation,' so that the theatre master would be like a man gazing down upon a forest from a high hill, able at last to understand both the individual trees and the shape of the whole. As Camillo explained: 'This high and incomparable placing not only performs the office of conserving for us the things, words and acts which we confide to it, so that we may find them at once whenever we need them, but also gives us true wisdom.'" Jonathan D. Spence, *The Memory Palace of Mateo Ricci* (New York: Penguin, 1985), 20. For a definition of theater or "Schauplatz" as a "showplace," designed for seeing and for laying bare or revealing the marvels of the world, the workings of nature, and the secrets of the body in anatomy theaters, see Pontus Hulten's introductory remarks to the 1994–1995 Bonn exhibition "Wunderkammer des Abendlandes," in *Wunderkammer des Abendlandes: Museum und Sammlung im Spiegel der Zeit* (Bonn: Kunst- und Ausstellungshalle der Bundesrepublik Deutschland und Autoren, 1994), 24.

21. Giulio Camillo called these memory spaces "theatres" because he conceived of the theaters as a space for "corporeal looking." This observation is derived from Erasmus's report of his visit to Camillo's theater. See Yates, *The Art of Memory*, 132.

22. As Jochen Brüning writes, zoological and botanical collections served both the "lay person and the scientist as archive, living memory, and theatre of nature" ["Die selbstständingen botanischen und zoologischen Sammlungen waren bis dahin Archive und Schauräume der Schöpfung für den Laien, für den Naturforscher 'sein lebendiges Gedächtnis, darin lieget ihm zu jeder Zeit die Natur zur Ansicht, zur Vergleichung, zur Untersuchung vor!'"], Jochen Brüning, "Der Teil und das Ganze—Motive einer Austellung," in *Theater der Natur und Kunst: Theatrum Naturae et Artis* (Berlin: Humboldt-Universität, 2000) 20–30.

23. Susan Stewart, *On Longing: Narratives of the Miniature, the Gigantic, the Souvenir, the Collection* (Durham, NC: Duke University Press, 1993), 44.

24. Interestingly, Hartmann Schedel's *Nuremberg Chronicle*, published in 1493 (one year after Columbus's first voyage), still based itself largely on a map of Ptolemy. The known world therefore included Europe and large parts of Asia, and even the Portuguese discovery of the Gulf of Guinea, but excluded the discovery of the New World. Cf. Hartmann Schedel, *Liber cronicarum* (Nuremberg: Anton Koberger, 1493).

25. That Mercator knew his Greek etymologies is made clear by his having the Titan Atlas holding up the world on the frontispiece. I thank Mikel Valladares for showing my class these books in the Rauner Collection at Dartmouth.

26. Reinier Baarsen, "The Cabinet as Gesamtkunstwerk: Philipp Hainhofer and His Followers," in *17th-Century Cabinets*, translated by John Rudge (Amsterdam: Waanders Publishers, Rijksmuseum, 2000), 11–21.

27. The title of Andreas Grote's volume of essays on the history of collecting of the period epitomizes this phenomenon: *Macrocosmos in Microcosmo: Die Welt in der Stube. Zur Geschichte des Sammelns 1450–1800* (Berlin: Leske and Budrich, Opladen, 1994).

28. Ulloa, quoted in *Las minas hispanoamericanas a mediados del siglo XVIII: Informes enviados al Real Gabinete de Historia Natural de Madrid*, edited by Isabel Galaor et al. (Frankfurt am Main: Vervuert-Iberoamericana, 1998), 19.

29. The X-ray was discovered in 1895 by the German physicist Wilhelm Roentgen.

30. Collecting was not limited to the wealthy, however. It became a craze across Europe. Driving a massive market for exotic goods, objects from far and wide were displayed sometimes even in the most humble of homes. See Philipp Blom, *To Have and to Hold: An Intimate History of Collectors and Collecting* (Woodstock and New York: Overlook Press, 2004).

31. C. B. Macpherson has called this drive to define the self by owning things "possessive individualism." See James Clifford's illuminating chapter on collecting culture in the West in *The Predicament of Culture: Twentieth-Century Ethnography, Literature, and Art* (Cambridge: Harvard University Press, 1988), 217. After Walter Benjamin's meditation on collecting books in "Unpacking My Library," I would caution that "possessive individualism" and the drive to collect are quite different things. As Benjamin observes, the collector is not only precariously poised between order and disorder, but his existence is also tied "to a very mysterious relationship to ownership . . . also to a relationship to objects which does not emphasize their functional, utilitarian value—that is, their usefulness—but studies and loves them as the scene, the stage, of their fate." What is more, for Benjamin, "collectors are the physiognomists of the world of objects." See Walter Benjamin, *Illuminations*, translated by Harry Zohn (New York: Schocken Books, 1969), 59–67, 60.

32. Rembrandt's collection was astonishing (and outlandish by today's standards)—both in terms of content and value—as becomes evident from the inventory made of his house during his bankruptcy proceedings in 1656. He owned paintings by Raphael, van Eyck, Michelangelo, Holbein, Titian, and Breughel the Elder, among many others, as well as rare manuscripts, prints, antique textiles, numerous busts and sculptures, and anatomical, botanical, and zoological specimens. Cf. Walter L. Strauss and Marjon van der Meulen, *The Rembrandt Documents* (New York: Abaris, 1979), 349–387.

33. As George Foster, a scientist who accompanied Cook's second expedition, wrote in 1777: "Facts were collected . . . and yet knowledge was not increased. [The learned] received a confused heap of disjointed limbs, which no art could reunite; and the rage of hunting after facts, soon rendered them incapable of forming and resolving a single proposition." Foster, quoted in Jonathan Lamb, *Preserving the Self in the South Seas, 1680–1840* (Chicago: University of Chicago Press, 2001), 61.

34. See Hazel Gold, "A Tomb With a View: The Museum in Galdós' *Novelas contemporáneas*," MLN 103, no. 2 (March 1988): 312–334, 320–321.

35. The impulse of accumulation therefore overcame not only many collections, but also many famous accounts of the period.

36. See Oliver Impey and Arthur MacGregor, *The Origins of Museums: The Cabinets of Curiosities in Sixteenth- and Seventeenth-Century Europe* (Oxford: Clarendon Press, 1985).

37. See "The King's Kunstkammer: Presenting Systems of Knowledge" on the Internet. Bente Gundestrup and Tine Wanning, National Museum of Denmark, http://www.archimuse.com/mw2004/papers/gundestrup/gundestrup.html.

38. As Linnaeus recognized, "The Ariadne thread in botany is classification, without which there is chaos." Quoted in Pratt, *Imperial Eyes*, 25.

39. M. de Buffon, *Histoire naturelle générale et particulière avec la description du cabinet du Roy* (Paris: De l'imprimerie royale, MDCCL: 1750 Seconde Edition), 18.

40. Ibid., 6.

41. Buffon privileged the visual over and beyond anything else. In his narrative dioramas he follows Spanish chroniclers like Acosta and Oviedo in emphasizing time and again the crucial role that careful observation plays in scientific endeavors ["Rien n' est plus capable de contribuer à l'avancement de l'Histoire Naturelle, que la vûe continuelle des objets qu'elle comprend, ils nous frappent avec bien plus de force et de verité, que les descriptions les plus exactes et les figures les plus parfaites"] (Ibid., 2). Buffon's desire is to render everything instantly and visually comprehensible. Only after having overcome the initial astonishment and wonder at the things displayed and having observed them with great care should the scientist proceed to let others' discoveries and opinions "illuminate" him ["empruntes des lumières de tous côtés"] (Ibid., 11). Only then will he be able to distinguish useful and accurate scientific "frames" from useless ones; only then will he be able to distinguish true and natural combinations from false ones (Ibid., 7). In this way, he will proceed from a particular to a general history.

42. Ibid., 6.

43. Ibid., 3.

44. Ibid., 7.

45. Indeed, the shift between the Middle Ages and the Renaissance can be better understood as the process whereby wonder and curiosity were wrested away from religious belief, and instead both religion and early science were increasingly yoked to and dependent on the power of observation of the natural world. Count Buffon never tired of insisting that a good scientist is first and foremost a good observer. Moreover, as Pratt writes of natural history specimens: "The eighteenth-century classificatory systems created the task of locating every species on the planet, extracting it from its particular, arbitrary surroundings (the chaos), and placing it in its appropriate spot in the system (the order—book, collection, or garden) with its new written, secular European name." Pratt, *Imperial Eyes*, 31.

46. W. J. Rathje, in his March 22, 2001, CNN report "Why the Taliban are destroying Buddhas," www.usatoday.com/news/science/archaeology/2001-03-22-afghan-buddhas.htm.

47. *Encyclopedia Britannica*, "Telescopes," 505; "Galileo," 639.

48. Cf. *Encyclopedia Britannica* and *Encyclopedia Americana*. While the *Encyclopedia Britannica* credits Hans Lippershey, Hans Jansen, and Jansen's son Zacharias with the invention of the first compound microscope in 1608 and the Dutch Antonie van Leeuwenhoek with the seventeenth-century invention of the first simple microscope, and ignores the creation of the first telescope, the *Encyclopedia Americana* attributes the creation of the telescope to Hans Lippershey. It becomes clear that both the microscope and the telescope were invented more or less at the same time. Although Galileo adapted his telescopes to study miniscule objects, he did not know of the compound microscope until 1624.

49. Stewart, *On Longing*, 54.

50. Ingrid D. Rowland, "Through a Glass, Darkly." *New York Review of Books* 49, no. 2 (February 28, 2002): 10. The panoptical perspective of the owner/visitor of the Wunderkammern was paralleled by the sixteenth-century discovery of perspective in western art that depended on everything being seen from a specific, privileged angle. The distancing of the subject from the object that both these moves embody coincides with the creation of a subject that sees and therefore knows, and a continent (the Americas) that are the object of that subject's knowledge.

51. Stafford, *Devices of Wonder*, 5.

52. The legacy of the Wunderkammern, according to Stafford, "extends into cyberspace. Consider the universal flea market of eBay, an Internet swap meet hosting two million-plus online auctions per day,

listing some four million items organized into over three thousand categories of mostly nonstandardized goods. Today, the collectible is everywhere." Stafford, *Devices of Wonder*, 3, 20.

53. As the curators recall, the idea for the exhibit was born when they visited a collector of mechanical and optical treasures of the Wunderkammern in his Los Angeles home. Mr. Ricky Jay, a Hollywood actor and sleight-of-hand wizard, pulled out, sometimes from under his bed, eighteenth-century magic props, shadow-show posters, leaflets from diorama shows, and a rare 1713 print called "O Rare Show." This drawing displayed an English peddler singing stories to a "curious group of schoolchildren about the fantastic and exotic objects tucked inside his portable wooden cabinet." Executed well before the dawn of television, photography, and film, this drawing "captured a change in the way media were being disseminated," a change that the exhibit aimed to trace from the Renaissance until today. David Hochman, "Cabinets, Ancient and New, Full of Wonder for the Eyes," *New York Times* (Sunday, December 30, 2001): 35, 37.

54. As his latest biographer has written, not only did "he [aim] at something beyond the reach of human art and industry," but "alchemy and physics and theology were parts of a . . . single search for knowledge that God had placed within his grasp." James Gleick, "A New Newton," *New York Review* (July 3, 2003): 4–6.

55. While Johannes Kepler was the first to coin the term in the early seventeenth century, the camera obscura had already been mentioned in the fifth century B.C. by the Chinese philosopher Mo-Ti, who called such a room "a collecting place" or a "locked treasure room." From the East, this discovery very soon headed West: the Arabian scholar Alhazen of Basra is known to have had a portable tent room for astronomical observations; Aristotle (384–322 B.C.) used it to observe a partial eclipse of the sun. See Jack and Beverley Wilgus's wonder-full website (an Internet Wunderkammer), devoted to their growing collection of such devices. Wilgus and Wilgus, http://brightbytes.com/cosite/collection.html.

56. Ibid. The drive to visibility and panoptical logic evident in this spoof was already contested by the New World Baroque, in Lois Parkinson Zamora's argument in *The Inordinate Eye*, and it continues to be contested as the native resistance to anthropology's interpolation. See also Doris Sommer, *Proceed with Caution, When Engaged by Minority Writing in the Americas* (Cambridge: Harvard University Press, 1999).

57. Jonathan Lamb, *Preserving the Self in the South Seas, 1680–1840* (Chicago: University of Chicago Press, 2001), 77.

58. Isabel Galaor, et al., eds., *Las minas hispanoamericanas a mediados del siglo XVIII: Informes enviados al Real Gabinete de Historia Natural de Madrid* (Frankfurt am Main: Vervuert-Iberoamericana, 1998), 17.

59. There were also miniature pocket world globes. Katherine R. Goodwin, announcing the acquisition of a prized three-inch pocket globe by the Compass Rose of the Special Collections Division at the University of Texas at Arlington Libraries, tellingly titles her essay "The World in Your Hands: Recent Cartographic Acquisitions." Pocket globes were generally encased in a fitter papier-mâché case lined with zodiac charts and allowed the entire world in miniature form to be revealed. They therefore very quickly acquired great symbolic value and were prized possessions. Joseph Maxon, for example, made a luxury globe for Queen Anne to offer as a gift to the King of Prussia. Cf. Katherine R. Goodwin, "The World in Your Hands: Recent Cartographic Acquisitions," http://libraries.uta.edu/SpecColl/croseoo/cartacq.htm.

60. She based this observation on a study of miniatures and time undertaken by the School of Architecture at the University of Tennessee, where researchers had volunteer subjects look at models 1/6, 1/12, and 1/24 of full size and imagine living and traversing that space as if they had shrunk to fit it. As they were doing this exercise, they were asked to tell the researchers when they felt 30 minutes had elapsed. Oddly enough, what they found was that the smaller the scale, the faster people felt 30 minutes had passed. As Stewart explains: "30 minutes would be experienced in 5 minutes at 1/12 scale and in 2.5 minutes at 1/24 scale." She concludes that this "compressed time of interiority tends to hypostatize the interiority of the subject that consumes it in that it marks the invention of 'private time.' In other words, miniature time transcends the duration of everyday life in such a way as to create an interior temporality of the subject." *On Longing*, 66.

61. *Stuffing Birds, Pressing Plants, Shaping Knowledge*, the publication of the American Philosophical Society of the exhibit accompanying the conference "Curious," quotes Benjamin Franklin's justification of the American Philosophical Society's foundation in 1743 (a national library, museum, and academy of

science) as there to "promote useful knowledge." As the heading of one of the exhibits made clear: "The history of science in America starts here."

62. European history became all too easily conflated with universal history and, as J. H. Elliott underlines, "The impact of Europe on the world (which was regarded as a transforming, and ultimately beneficial impact) seemed a subject of greater interest and concern than the impact of the world on Europe." J. H. Elliott, *The Old World and the New: 1492–1650* (London: Cambridge University Press, 1970), 3; Edmundo O'Gorman famously stated that America was "invented." Edmundo O'Gorman, *La invención de América: El universalismo de la cultura de Occidente* (México: Fondo de Cultura Económica, 1958); and Enrique Dussel argues that modernity was "born" in 1492 in Europe's "confrontation with the Other" and that "By controlling, conquering, and violating the Other, Europe defined itself as discoverer, conquistador, and colonizer of an alterity likewise constitutive of modernity" ["La Modernidad . . . nació cuando Europa pudo confrontarse con 'el Otro' de Europa y controlarlo, vencerlo, violentarlo; cuando pudo definirse como un 'ego' descubridor, conquistador, colonizador de la Alteridad constitutiva de la misma Modernidad"]. Given this constitutive confrontation between I/Other, it is clear why Columbus is the first "modern" for Dussel. Enrique Dussel, *El encubrimiento del Otro: Hacia el origen del mito de la modernidad* (Madrid: Ediciones Abya-yala, 1994), 10. Translated by Michael D. Barber as *The Invention of the Americas: Eclipse of "the Other" and the Myth of Modernity* (New York: Continuum, 1995), 12. Johannes Fabian argues that the physical distance separating the anthropological other from Europe was translated into a distance in time. Thus the Americas, in contrast to Europe, are always already situated in what we could call archaeological time. See Johannes Fabian, *Time and the Other: How Anthropology Makes Its Object* (New York: Columbia University Press, 1983). Eric Wolf, thinking along the same lines, tellingly titles one of his books *Europe and the People Without History* (Berkeley: University of California Press, 1982); and Walter Mignolo expands upon this denial of coevalness in *The Darker Side of the Renaissance: Literacy, Territoriality, and Colonization* (Ann Arbor: University of Michigan Press, 1995). Feminist scholars like Iris Zavala have outlined how natives and the continent itself were feminized and rendered passive and exploitable. See *Colonialism and Culture: Hispanic Modernisms and the Social Imaginary* (1992). See also Peter Hulme's *Colonial Encounters: Europe and the Native Caribbean, 1492–1797* (London; New York: Methuen, 1986), and the early manifesto by Eduardo Galeano, *Open Veins of Latin America: Five Centuries of the Pillage of a Continent*, translated by Cedric Beltrage (New York: Monthly Review Press, 1973).

63. Octavio Ianni refers to modern Brazil as a "kaleidoscope of many epochs, ways of life, of being, working and thinking, marked above all by the legacy of slavery." "A ideia de Brasil moderno," in *Through the Kaleidoscope: The Experience of Modernity in Latin America*, edited by Vivian Schelling (London: Verso, 2000), 9.

64. Galeano, *Open Veins*, 267.

65. See "*America* by Johannes Stradanus (1523–1605)," by Edward J. Gallagher. Department of English, Lehigh University, http://www.lehigh.edu/~ejg1/ed/strad1.html.

66. Pratt writes that Alexander von Humboldt overcame Spain's secretiveness in the New World and convinced Charles IV to sponsor his scientific voyage to Venezuela in 1799 (aboard the vessel appropriately called *Pizarro*). Pratt, *Imperial Eyes*, 116.

CHAPTER 2

1. See Enrique Dussel, *The Invention of the Americas: Eclipse of "the Other" and the Myth of Modernity*, translated by Michael D. Barber (New York: Continuum, 1995). For a skewed account of the scientific discovery of the Americas that does not center-stage Spain's accomplishments, see Henry Lowood, "The New World and the European Catalog of Nature," in *America in European Consciousness, 1493–1750*, edited by Karen Ordahl Kupperman (Chapel Hill, NC; London: North Carolina Press, 1995), 295–323.

2. María de los Ángeles Calatayud, ed. and compiler, *Catálogo de documentos del Real Gabinete de Historia Natural (1752–1786)* (Madrid: Consejo Superior de Investigaciones Científicas, Museo Nacional de Ciencias Naturales, 1987), x.

3. Another very famous and all-encompassing seventeenth-century cabinet of wonders that inexplicably disappeared with the death of its owner was that of Vicencio Juan Lastanosa in Huesca. A patron of Golden Age Jesuit writer Baltasar Gracián (author of the lengthy allegorical novel *El criticón*), Lastanosa published two books on numismatics; he was also interested in alchemy, medicine, history, languages,

poetry, and gardens. In his palace he had a labyrinthine garden that was to be "a prodigy of calligraphy and geometry" ["un jardín que era un prodigio de caligrafía y geometría"]. He collected everything, including books, sculptures, coins, arms, maps, scientific instruments (among them two newly invented and much-coveted instruments of augmented vision, that is, telescopes), and paintings by Titian, Dürer, Caravaggio, Tintoretto, and others. As Anton Castro writes, it must have been strange "to imagine messengers and muleteers arriving in Huesca with elephant tusks, Indian idols . . . rolled-up paintings, and even heavy sculptures as readily likenesses of Laocoön as of the equestrian figure of Marcus Aurelius" ["Resulta curioso imaginarse a los mensajeros o arrieros llegando a Huesca con colmillos de elefante, ídolos indios . . . lienzos enrollados e incluso pesadas esculturas que igual imitaban a Laocoonte que a la figura ecuestre de Marco Aurelio"]. See Anton Castro, "2007: El año de Vicencio Juan de Lastanosa," at http://antoncastro.blogia.com/2006/120901-2007-el-ano-de-vicencio-juan-de-lastanosa.php (accessed October 10, 2007).

4. Chiyo Ishikawa, ed., *1492–1819: Spain in the Age of Exploration* (Seattle: Seattle Art Museum, University of Nebraska Press, 2004), 83. This expedition may be the one mentioned repeatedly by Lewis and Clark (1804–1806).

5. See María de los Ángeles Calatayud Arinero, ed., *Catálogo de las expediciones y viajes científicos españoles a América y Filipinas (Siglos XVIII y XIX)* (Madrid: Museo Nacional de Ciencias Naturales, 1984), 16.

6. Earlier still, Spain's "reach" in not only scientific but also political matters is evidenced by the little-known fact that Charles III assisted George Washington's army during the Revolutionary War: "Among the fascinating vignettes brought to light [is] the fact that the uniforms U.S. soldiers wore in Yorktown, as well as their rifles and ammunition, were Spanish" (Ishikawa, *1492–1819*, 26).

7. Ibid., 29.

8. Calatayud, *Catálogo de documentos*, x.

9. See Miguel Angel Puig-Samper and Sandra Rebok, "*Virtuti et merito*. El reconocimiento official de Alexander von Humboldt en España."_HiN: Alexander von Humboldt im Netz_V, no. 8 (2004), www.uni-potsdam.de/u/romanistik/humboldt/hin/hin8/rebok-ps.htm (accessed June 25, 2007).

10. Alexander von Humboldt, *Essai politique sur le royaume de la Nouvelle Espagne* (Paris, 1811), 164. Translation mine. See also Alexander von Humboldt, *Political Essay on the Kingdom of New Spain*, translated by John Black (London: Longman, Hurst, Rees, et al., 1811), xvi.

11. "The library of El Escorial was likewise designed to celebrate Philip's intellectual range. Organized around the theme of the seven liberal arts, it included rare manuscripts in Greek, Latin, Hebrew, and Chaldean, published books in a variety of languages, and maps and engravings gathered from across Europe. It housed an invaluable collection of items reflecting Philip's curiosity about the Americas, among them a magnificent series (now lost) of botanical drawings by Francisco Hernández, a physician sent by Philip to Mexico in the 1570s on what was arguably the first scientific expedition to the New World" (Ishikawa, *1492–1819*, 62).

12. See J. Miguel Morán and Fernando Checa, *El coleccionismo en España: De la cámara de maravillas a la galería de pinturas* (Madrid: Cátedra, 1985). Having depended on shipments of gold and silver from the New World since 1492, and financing three war fronts simultaneously (against England, Holland, and France), Spain found itself in a deep financial crisis when the production of silver (particularly at Potosí) declined steeply after 1600.

13. The expedition's aim was to establish the shape of the world once and for all and thus lay to rest the debate whether the earth was a sphere, as asserted by the French (Cartesian geography), or a spheroid, flat at the poles, as asserted by the English (Newton). Mary Louise Pratt, *Imperial Eyes* (New York: Routledge, 1992), 16.

14. Hence already in 1752, alongside his promotion of the foundation of the Real Gabinete, Ulloa also started up his own metallurgical laboratory, informally known as "Casa del Platino." In turn, the Real Gabinete initially primarily included minerals in its collection. See the excellent study of this period, Isabel Galaor, et al., eds., *Las minas hispanoamericanas a mediados del siglo XVIII: Informes enviados al Real Gabinete de Historia Natural de Madrid* (Frankfurt am Main: Vervuert-Iberoamericana, 1998), and Antonio de Ulloa, *Noticias americanas: Entretenimientos phísicos-históricos, sobre la América Meridional, y la Septentrional Oriental. Comparación general de los territorios, climas, y producciones en las tres especies, vegetales, animales, y minerales: Con relación particular de las petrificaciones de cuerpos marinos de los indios naturales de aquellos países, sus costumbres, y usos: De las Antigüedades: Discurso sobre la len-*

gua, y sobre el modo en que pasaron los primeros pobladores (Madrid: Imprenta de Don Francisco Manuel de Mena, 1772), 218.

15. Perhaps not inappropriately, Ulloa, finding himself out of favor at court, resigned as the Gabinete's director and was sent to the New World as a Spanish functionary in charge of the famous mercury mine in Huancavelica (Perú).

16. María de los Ángeles Calatayud Arinero, ed., *Pedro Franco Dávila: Primer Director del Real Gabinete de Historia Natural Fundado por Carlos III* (Madrid: Consejo Superior de Investigaciones Científicas, Museo Nacional de Ciencias Naturales, 1988), 57.

17. Ibid., 59.

18. Relatively little is known about Pedro Franco Dávila's private life. It seems that he was the son of a well-to-do merchant based in Guayaquil, and that he had had a peripatetic, adventure-filled life before his arrival in Paris. His private life in particular is of interest to historians, since it seems that on his way to Spain with a shipment of cacao he survived a shipwreck and had to wait quite a long time in the small town of Iscuandé (700 kilometers from Bogotá) to resume his travels. There he married Doña Manuela Reina y Medina, with whom he never lived, yet to whom he sent a miserly allowance from Europe. Bafflingly, little more is known about him through his extensive extant correspondence other than that he was an obsessive collector and avid possessor of things, and that he repeatedly went bankrupt.

19. For a study of cabinets of wonders across Spain, and particularly Philip II's at El Escorial, see J. Miguel Morán and Fernando Checa, *El coleccionismo en España: De la cámara de maravillas a la galería de pinturas* (Madrid: Cátedra, 1985).

20. Calatayud, *Pedro Franco Dávila*, 113.

21. Galdós, arguably the most famous Spanish novelist of the nineteenth century, repeatedly thematized the growing importance of the museum as a structuring device, not only in the cultural life of Madrid but also in his characters' lives. In his early novels he sets his characters in museums—there to learn the lesson of democracy but also to understand taste and aesthetics as they pertained to class status. In the later novels of that cycle, Galdós has his characters erect their own "museums," sometimes indulging in spending sprees in order to fill emotional loss with objects. Hazel Gold argues that "These characters' exaggerated predilection for collecting provides not only insight into their dominant psychological traits (avarice, vanity compulsion, and fetishism), but also specific information regarding the esthetic and moral values they hold, values which are in great part determined by the ideological forces governing their membership in Spanish middle-class society." Hazel Gold, "A Tomb with a View: The Museum in Galdós' *Novelas contemporáneas*," MLN 103, no. 2 (March 1988), 312–334, 320. Galdós himself reflects that it is hard to understand the use of people spending their lives at flea markets rummaging in search of book covers, buttons, horse shoes, soles of shoes, and other such junk ["No resulta tan clara la utilidad de los que pasan la vida revolviendo los puestos del Rastro para coleccionar tapas de libros, botones, herraduras, suelas de zapatos y otras chucherías"]. Benito Pérez Galdós, *Obras inéditas*, edited by Alberto Ghiraldo (Madrid: Renacimiento, 1923), 199. In contrast, in *Lo prohibido* (1884–1885), he critiques the generalized urge to collect that overtook Europe from rich patrons' collections of the rare and marvelous to poor people's collections of kitsch and junk. Eloísa's "pathological drive to collect, one of her many psychological aberrations, finally destroys" her "criterion of selectivity. When she cannot afford real antiques she buys fakes, and her house begins to resemble some baroquely overstuffed warehouse." As Gold points out, the narrative itself reflects this unsystematic jumble of kitsch by linking objects one to another with "and . . . and . . . and" (the polysyndeton discussed in the Introduction) (320–321). No one in Galdós collects seashells or rocks—only cheap mass consumer trinkets that mark a person's status; his characters begin to refer to their loved ones as objects and possessions. Gold argues that in Galdós' novels, "this same system of industrial capitalism and mass production which so radically affects the tastes of nineteenth-century consumer society can also be seen to affect interpersonal relationships. Individuals, too, become objects, to be collected by those with more money and power than their hapless victims: witness the life stories of Fortunata and Tristana, or the prostitution of Isidora Rufete. . . . Given the familial relationships that obtain psychologically among the miser, the collector and the fetishist (the urge to hoard; the compulsion to view furtively and/or exhibit publicly; the sexual preference for the disembodied part over the whole body)," Gold concludes by asking, "what better object to enlist for one's own than woman, viewed by nineteenth-century society as a source of property, value, cipher of artistic beauty and trigger of erotic stimulation?" (326, 327–328).

22. Calatayud, *Pedro Franco Dávila*, 126.

23. The fast transition from cabinet of curiosity to museum signals not only how quickly curios as objects of wonder and curiosity were transformed into objects of scientific knowledge and economic interest, but also the shift that occurred between the "collector" and the "scientist." A letter by one of Dávila's contacts reveals the development of this new type of person, the "Académico" or savant associated with a particular institution devoted to the study of science, such as the diverse academies of science that were arising all over Europe. In 1755, D. Manuel Joseph de la Viya writes Dávila from Madrid that he recommends he cultivate the friendship of D. Miguel Gijón, who is very well connected and can do much for the Cabinet; being one of the first Academics, he could be lobbied to help move Dávila's cabinet to Madrid ["Le recomienda que cultive la amistad de [D. Miguel Gijón que] está muy bien relacionado y podrá hacer mucho por su Gabinete . . . uno de los primeros Académicos . . . podrá proponerle para que se traslade con su Gabinete a Madrid"]. Quoted in Calatayud, *Pedro Franco Dávila*, 22.

24. Typical of the traces left by an imperial organization of knowledge, the 1924 Spanish *Enciclopedia Universal Ilustrada Europeo Americana* (Barcelona: Espasa, 1924) claims Pedro Franco Dávila as a Spaniard born in Guayaquil, whereas Calatayud's recently published *Catálogo de documentos del Real Gabinete de Historia Natural*, following contemporary notions of nationality as based on birthplace, simply states he is an Ecuadoran. According to Abel Romeo Castillo, Dávila seems to have been an Ecuadoran born of a Spanish father and an Ecuadoran mother, although, as Castillo argues, he was so prominent that other countries have repeatedly tried to appropriate him as one of their own ("que otros países, intencionada o inintencionadamente, han querido arrebatárnoslo . . ."). Abel Romeo Castillo, *Don Pedro Franco Dávila (1711–1786)* (Guayaquil: Editorial Casa de la Cultura Ecuatoriana, 1966), 6.

25. J. Miguel Morán and Fernando Checa, *El coleccionismo en España: De la cámara de maravillas a la galería de pinturas* (Madrid: Cátedra, 1985).

26. Calatayud, *Catálogo de documentos*, 49.

27. William Wood, ed., *Natural History. General and Particular by the Count de Buffon* (London, 1812), xxviii. The fact that pirates knew of the importance of these collections may not be altogether accidental. While serving as a physician in Jamaica, Sir Hans Sloane (1660–1753) started the largest cabinet of wonders in the world. Significantly, it served as the cornerstone of the British Museum. Sloane was a professor of medicine, President of the Royal Scientific Society of London, and extremely rich (after inheriting 100,000 pounds sterling from his deceased wife). His cabinet was so enormous it was known in Spain as Almacén de Londres (Calatayud, *Pedro Franco Dávila*, 72). Ships laden with objects destined for London must have continually traversed the Atlantic, since the collection consisted of 50,000 volumes of books; 32,000 coins and medals; 1,125 antiques; 268 seals; 700 cameos; 2,256 precious stones and agates; 1,275 fossils, flints, and stones; 5,843 shells; 1,421 corals and sponges; 659 starfish; 1,555 fish; 1,886 insects; 756 human anatomical preparations; 12,506 parts of plants; and thousands of other items. As the makeup of this collection shows, the Americas—in this case Jamaica—while being the initial gathering ground for Sloane, figure only as natural history. See Calatayud, *Catálogo de documentos*, 59.

28. Designed by Neoclassical architect Juan de Villanueva in 1785, the Prado was originally destined to serve as the Royal Laboratory of the Natural Sciences. "With a botanical school, chemistry laboratory, library and science museum, the Laboratory would have been a pedagogical complement to the neighboring Botanical Garden." Due to the French invasion, however, the building remained incomplete and served as a barracks for a number of years. When the French were expelled and the building was finally completed, it opened its doors in 1819 as the Royal Museum. See Leticia Ruiz Gómez, "The Prado Museum: A Spanish Perspective," in *The Majesty of Spain: Royal Collections from the Museo del Prado and the Patrimonio Nacional* (Jackson, MS: Mississippi Commission for International Cultural Exchange, 2001), 20.

29. Despite the fact that we fail to fully interiorize this knowledge, we are all aware of the fundamental changes (in the landscape, agriculture, nutrition, and cultural habits) brought about in different cultures because of the worldwide displacement (and misplacement) of plants. Indeed, suffice it to say that sweet potatoes, potatoes, cacao, coffee, and tobacco arrived in Europe from the Americas, and wheat, rice, garbanzo beans, sugarcane, oranges, bananas, and grapevines from Europe (sometimes via Africa and Asia). See Herman J. Viola and Carolyn Margolis, eds., *Seeds of Change: Five Hundred Years Since Columbus. A Quincentennial Celebration* (Washington, D.C.: Smithsonian, 1991).

30. Calatayud, *Pedro Franco Dávila*, 129.

31. See, for example, the 1777 questionnaire titled "Cuestionario para la formación del completo conocimiento de la geografía, física, antigüedades, mineralogía y metalurgia de este reino de Nueva España e

instrucción sobre el modo de formarlas" [Questionnaire for the formation of the complete knowledge of the geography, physical characteristics, antiquities, mineralogy, and metallurgy of this kingdom of New Spain and instruction on how to make them]. Francisco de Solano, *Antonio de Ulloa y la Nueva España* (México: Universidad Nacional Autónoma de México, 1987), cxliv–cl.

32. This process could be described in terms of "scientific mestizaje." The attempt to account for all the different American indigenous species so overwhelmed court doctor and historian Francisco Hernández, who worked in Mexico collecting specimens in the seventeenth century, that he attempted to arrive at a new linguistic classification that systematically incorporated Náhuatl terminology. In his seminal multivolume *Historia Natural de Nueva España,* for example, one entry reads: "Of the YOHUALA-HUACHXIHOITL or evening dew herb" ["Del YOHUALAHUACHXIHOITL o hierba del rocío nocturno"], which is described as a little herb with small and soft leaves the shape of hearts . . . being of a cold and damp nature . . . administered against fevers, and which to a certain degree resembles scorpion grass in our country ["es una hierbecilla con hojas de figura de corazón, pequeñas y blandas . . . es de naturaleza fría y húmeda . . . se parece hasta cierto punto a los géneros de alsine de nuestra tierra, y se administra tomado contra las fiebres"]. Francisco Hernández, *Historia natural de la Nueva España* (México, DF: Universidad Nacional de México, 1959), 1.

33. María del Carmen González Muñoz, "Estudio preliminar," in Juan López de Velasco, *Geografía y descripción universal de las Indias* (Madrid: Biblioteca de Autores españoles, 1971), xiii.

34. Ibid., xiii.

35. For examples of intrusive religious questionnaires, see Chapter Three: "'Dagon Is Their Ark, and Christ Their Baal': Christianization, Transculturation as 'Contamination,' and the Extirpation of Idolatries," in my *Between Two Waters: Narratives of Transculturation in Latin America* (Houston: Rice University Press, 1995, Texas A&M Press, 2006).

36. See María del Carmen Velázquez and Joseph Antonio de Villaseñor y Sánchez, "Prólogo," in *Theatro Americano,* edited by María del Carmen Velázquez (México: Editorial Trillas, 1992), 5.

37. Fray Ramón Pané, *Relación acerca de las antigüedades de los indios (el primer tratado escrito en América),* edited by José Juan Arrom (México: Siglo Veintiuno, 1988).

38. See Bernard Cohen, *The New World as a Source of Science for Europe. Actes du IXème Congrès International d'Histoire des Sciences* (Barcelona-Madrid: Asociación para la historia de ciencia española, 1959), 103. Signaling its importance, the *Historia natural* was immediately translated into Italian (1596), Dutch (1598), German (1601), Latin (1602), and English (1604) (Ishikawa, *1492–1819,* 156).

39. Ishikawa, *1492–1819,* 149.

40. Ibid.

41. Francisco Hernández, *Antigüedades de la Nueva España,* edited by Ascención H. de León-Portilla (Madrid: Historia 16, 1986), 152. Important too were the natural histories written by exiled Jesuits from Spanish America: Molina, Velasco, and particularly Francisco Clavigero's *Historia antigua de México.*

42. The first instruction of the 1752 questionnaire is a good example of this. It states: "The Viceroys should give orders and circulate widely to all the owners of mines be they of gold, silver, or cinnabar, as well as those of copper, lead, zinc or any other metals or precious transparent stones such as emeralds, rubies, garnets, topazes, etc., so that from all of these species of more or less rich minerals they send a sample according to the directions below and that each one be accompanied by a description in which the site of the mine from which the sample is taken be specified as well as the province or jurisdiction, the day in which it was taken and the name of the miner to whom they belong" ["Los virreyes habrán de expedir órdenes circulares a todos los dueños de minas sean de oro, plata o cinabrio, como a las de cobre, plomo, estaño, u otros cualesquier metales o piedras preciosas transparentes, como las esmeraldas, rubíes, granates, topacios, etc., para que de todas las especies de minerales más o menos ricos les envíen una porción de piedras según abajo se explicará, y con cada una de las especies, acompañen una relación en que especifiquen la mina y sitio o paraje de ésta, de donde se hubieren sacado las piedras, la provincia en donde estuviere, la jurisdicción o corregimiento adonde pertenece, el día en que las tales piedras se hubieren sacado y el nombre del minero a quien pertenece"]. Quoted in Galaor, et al., *Las minas hispanoamericanas a mediados del siglo XVIII,* 26.

43. See Abel Romeo Castillo, *Pedro Franco Dávila: El sabio guayaquileño olvidado* (Guayaquil: Ediciones Casa de la Cultura, 1952), 7.

44. Quoted in Calatayud, *Pedro Franco Dávila,* 51.

45. See Wordsworth's poem "The Tables Turned."

46. These accounts, as we have already seen, often end up as an accounting: that is, as endless (and tedious) lists of the objects and specimens collected, and descriptions of the circumstances under which they were found. Alexander von Humboldt, funded by the Gabinete, was adept at papering over the world with his lengthy descriptions and multivolume productions reflecting on the findings of his numerous expeditions (see Mary Louise Pratt's discussion of this famous traveler and scientist in *Imperial Eyes*).

47. Calatayud, *Catálogo de documentos*, 60.

48. One interesting example is the production of the trope of what Peter Hulme calls "magic technology." That is, navigational objects such as the astrolabe and European technologies used in warfare were used to impress (and subject) native populations and would contribute to the division of the world into the West (producer of knowledge and technology) and the rest (producer of raw materials and labor power), which is still largely operative. Perhaps no image better represents this dynamic than Stradanus's representation of America as a female figure lying naked in a hammock facing Vespucci, who is dressed and holding the astrolabe, as I discussed in the Introduction. See Hulme, *Colonial Encounters: Europe and the Native Caribbean, 1492–1797* (London; New York: Methuen, 1986).

49. I had access to a very useful transcription of the text (which is illegible in reproductions of the painting), thanks to Francisco de las Barras y Aragón, "Una historia del Perú contenida en un cuadro al óleo de 1799," *Boletín de la Real Sociedad Española* 12 (1912), 224. References hereafter in text.

50. While some animals and plants that do not belong are included (showing that neither Thiebaut nor Lequanda were botanists or zoologists), other details such as the location of certain cities are quite exact. The city of Tarma, for example, is precisely situated on the map at "11 degrees 33 minutes, 12 seconds of latitude and 69 and 29 of longitude: it is inhabited by 5,538 people" ["11 grados 33 minutos, 12 segundos de latitud y 69 grados y 29 de longitud: está poblada de 5,538 personas"] (Barras y Aragón, 242).

51. The text written by Lequanda that accompanied and elaborated upon the paintings shows the persistence of the sixteenth-century notion of natural history. As Foucault points out in *The Order of Things*, the "historia" of a plant or an animal not only includes a description of the parts and elements but, as is clearly evident in Buffon's writings in natural history, it is also an account of the "resemblances that could be found in it, the virtues that it was thought to possess, the legends with which it had been involved, its place in heraldry, the medicaments that were concocted from its substance, the foods it provided, what the ancients recorded of it, and what travelers might have said." The shift in the seventeenth century was away from this universe of similitudes and resemblances "to an episteme based on notions of order and discrimination (and hence identity and difference)," on which our modern rationality is based. Foucault concludes that from then on, "The activity of the mind . . . will therefore no longer consist in drawing things together, in setting out on a quest for everything that might reveal some sort of kinship, attraction, or secretly shared nature within them, but, on the contrary, in discriminating, that is, in establishing their identities, then the inevitability of the connections with all the successive degrees of a series. In this sense, discrimination imposes upon comparison the primary and fundamental investigation of difference. . . ." (*The Order of Things*, 54–55). Lequanda's text, written in the eighteenth century, is an odd mixture of these notions of how natural history is written and of the later emphasis on use and economic exploitability.

52. Barras y Aragón, 259.

53. He bemoans the fact that "Al reverso de este Quadro Histórico se había propuesto su Autor colocar unas tablas de resortes, en las que se manifestasen ya Aritmetica y ya en relación, los valores universales de aquella Real Hazienda y Patrimonio, las Rentas Eclesiásticas sus gastos; los de la Magistratura y Guerra, con su compendio de su método de gobierno en aquellos Dominios, etc." Barras y Aragón, 250.

54. Ibid., 235.

55. Ibid., 226.

56. Ibid., 234.

57. Ibid., 246.

58. See Jane Jacobs, *Cities and the Wealth of Nations: Principles of Economic Life* (New York: Random House, 1984).

59. Only as if to illustrate that we breathe hierarchies much as we breathe air, and that like air, hierarchies so pervade our lives that they remain invisible to us, had the museum guard at the American Philosophical Society's exhibit "Stuffing Birds, Pressing Plants, Shaping Knowledge: Natural History in America, 1730–1860" (Philosophical Hall, June 20–December 31, 2004) not pointed out this ascending order to me in Charles Wilson Peale's 1822 self-portrait "The Artist and His Museum," I would never have paid attention to it.

60. As Yasmin Ramírez concludes about our recent rediscovery of the caste paintings, "Multicultural advocacy has liberated casta paintings from the curio cabinet. . . ." Yasmin Ramírez, "New World Orders: Casta Paintings and Colonial Latin America at the Americas Society," *ArtNet,* December 2, 1996, http://www.artnet.com/magazine_pre2000/features/ramirez/ramirez12-02-96.asp.

61. He argues that this is a mestizaje largely of convenience, sought out intentionally by Indians in their attempt to have mestizo children. Exempt from taxes, unlike Indians, mestizos had a chance at social mobility ["procuran tener hijos mestisos, para verlos libres de Tributo y acercarse á la gerarquía española"].

62. Barras y Aragón, 250.

63. Lima's aristocracy therefore has been intent on "purity of blood" and on whitening its lineage from the early days. Indeed, sociologist Alberto Flores Galindo most recently highlighted this same black/white mestizaje in his seminal *Aristocracia y plebe en Lima,* only to have this aspect of his work completely marginalized, while his work on Indian uprisings, *Buscando un Inca,* has become very influential. See my Preface to *Más allá de la ciudad Letrada; Crónicas y espacios urbanos,* co-edited with Boris Muñoz (Pittsburgh: Biblioteca de América, Instituto Internacional de Literatura Iberoamericana, 2003), 7–23.

64. Fred Wilson's installations also upset these hierarchies. See the catalogue of the exhibition at Dartmouth College's Hood Museum in 2006, edited by Barbara Thompson, *Fred Wilson: So Much Trouble in the World*—Believe It or Not!

65. Cohen, *The New World,* 113.

66. Indeed, the scientific backwardness of the Americas and the United States was such in the nineteenth century that "no European scientist of any stature whatever would have dreamed of coming to America for training or study. Those Europeans who did come to the New World did so to make money, as by giving lectures, or to study man and nature in the Americas" (Ibid., 96).

67. Francisco Pelayo, *Del diluvio al megaterio; Los orígenes de la paleontología en España* (Madrid: Consejo Superior de Investigaciones Científicas, 1996), 295. Pelayo writes that Bru immediately wrote Thomas Jefferson about the finding of the megaterio but is unaware of their ensuing correspondence. See José María López Pinero, *El megaterio de bru y el presidente Jefferson: Relación insospechada en los albores de la paleontología* (Valencia: Universidad de Valencia, 1957).

68. On its website, the Academy of Natural Sciences, founded in 1812, claims it is the oldest natural history museum in the western hemisphere and boasts a "Dinosaur Hall." The website describes the history of the discoveries of "big bones" but fails to mention the role Madrid's Real Gabinete played. They write that "Although the Comte de Buffon had been dead for almost a decade, Jefferson was apparently still bothered by his theory of American Degeneracy. The possibility of a giant cat that dwarfed the Old World lion combined with a Mammoth (American mastodon) that dwarfed the Old World elephant may have proved irresistible in his longstanding effort to discredit the theory." Of Buffon's theory of degeneracy, they write that "Comte de Buffon was the most influential naturalist of the 18th century. In 1766, he published his *Theory of American Degeneracy,* which stated that an adverse climate in the New World inhibited the development of native quadrupeds (an archaic classification that includes most mammals) and resulted in the degeneration of those transplanted from the Old World. Buffon extended this effect to Native Americans and some of his disciples extended it to include transplanted Europeans as well. Naturally, these transplants took offense and challenged the theory. Thomas Jefferson was the most prominent of these critics." See "Welcome to the Thomas Jefferson Fossil Collection," http://www.ansp.org/museum/jefferson/index.php (accessed November 4, 2007).

69. W. J. T. Mitchell, *The Last Dinosaur Book: The Life and Times of a Cultural Icon* (Chicago: University of Chicago Press, 1998), 156.

70. Ibid., 112.

71. Indeed, his collection of animal specimens and gigantic skeletons was finally housed in a cabinet on his estate in Virginia.

72. María de los Ángeles Calatayud, so instrumental in bringing the fundamental role of Pedro Franco Dávila and the Real Gabinete to light, also invokes this trope. Her own lament echoes through the words of Don José Celestino Mutis who, in 1760, traveled to the New Kingdom of Granada as the Viceroy's physician. He spent much of his time gathering specimens to send to Spain, but despite the immensity of his dedication and his travails, his findings were met with utter indifference. In a letter to the Crown quoted entirely, Mutis describes page after page and in great detail the vicissitudes and travails of the naturalist in the field, contrasting his experiences with the relative ease under which European armchair naturalists

worked. Gathering specimens during the day, he works surrounded by angry swarms of nasty bugs, frightened by wild animals, in danger of being poisoned by venomous snakes, his body tortured and subjected to the elements. As if this were not enough, at nightfall his labors do not end, since he has to work labeling and preserving what he had gathered during the day. His fate, Calatayud argues, "serves to illustrate the degree to which Spanish monarchs disregarded the information and studies done by many in their travels across the Americas. As if this were not enough, they also failed in offering to help others, such as Mutis, who were willing to give glory to the nation with their discoveries in the sciences as well the arts and commerce" ["nos va a ilustrar hasta qué punto nuestros monarcas descuidaron, primero, aprovechar los estudios que muchos viajeros habían ya recogido en sus viajes por América; Segundo, el no haber ayudado, a tiempo, a otros que, como Mutis, estaban dispuestos a dar, con sus descubrimientos, gloria a la nación, tanto en las Ciencias y Artes como en el comercio"] (Calatayud, *Pedro Franco Dávila*, 43, 49).

73. María de los Ángeles Calatayud Arinero, ed., *Diario de Don Francisco de Paula Martínez y Sáez. Miembro de la Comisión Científica del Pacífico (1862–1865)* (Madrid: Consejo Superior de Investigaciones Científicas, 1994), 246.

74. Mitchell, *Last Dinosaur*, 117.

CHAPTER 3

1. As Pratt elaborates: "As Christianity had set in motion a global labor of religious conversion that asserted itself at every point of contact with other societies, so natural history set in motion a secular, global labor that, among other things, made contact zones a site of intellectual as well as manual labor, and installed there the distinction between the two." Mary Louise Pratt, *Imperial Eyes: Travel Writing and Transculturation* (New York: Routledge, 1992), 27.

2. Steve Russell, in an interview commemorating the passing of Maria Pearson, tells of her reasons for championing NAGPRA. The crew her husband was working on as an engineer in the Iowa Department of Transportation had, one day, uncovered a cemetery containing white and Indian remains. Shocking to Pearson was the different treatment these received: while the crew immediately reburied the white remains, they boxed up the Native American remains and sent them to the Office of the State Archaeologist. See K. Kris Hirst, "The Roots of NAGPRA," About.com Archaeology, http://www.archaeology.about.com/cs/ethicsandlaw/a/russell.html.

3. See Susan Martin-Márquez, "Anatomy of a Black Legend: Bodies of Cultural Discourse and Madrid's National Museum of Anthropology," *Journal of Spanish Cultural Studies* 4, no. 2 (2003), 205; and for a journalist's novelized account of this tragic episode, see Frank Westerman, *El Negro: Eine verstörende Begegnung*, translated into German from the Dutch by Stefan Häring and Verena Kiefer (Berlin: Ch. Links Verlag, 2005).

4. See Krista A. Thompson, "Exhibiting 'Others' in the West," Emory University Department of English, http://www.english.emory.edu/Bahri/Exhibition.html; and Zola Maseko's film *The Life and Times of Sara Baartman: "The Hottentot Venus"* (First Run/Icarus Films, 1998). I thank Alberto Sandoval for bringing this case to my attention.

5. See "Ye Olde Curiosity Shop" (pamphlet) and Kate C. Duncan, *1001 Curious Things: Ye Olde Curiosity Shop and Native American Art* (Seattle: University of Washington Press, 2000).

6. In the United States as in Europe, the first museums were also natural history collections. The Charleston Museum (1773) and the 1788 collection of Charles Wilson Peale (famous for his portraits of George Washington and Benjamin Franklin) of taxidermied animals in New York City and Baltimore are among the better known. The Peabody Essex Museum in Salem, Massachusetts, began as a Wunderkammer for the sea captains of Salem, who founded the East India Marine Society and built a hall (still extant) for their curios. Founded in 1799, it is the oldest continually operating public collection in the country. See http://www.pem.org. The United States' oldest public art museum—the Wadsworth Atheneum in Hartford, Connecticut—was founded as late as 1842, followed shortly thereafter by the Smithsonian Institution (1846).

7. Philip Kunhardt, et al., *P. T. Barnum: America's Greatest Showman* (New York: Alfred A. Knopf, 1995), 71. Further references appear in text.

8. See Michael Mitchell, ed., *Monsters: Human Freaks in America's Gilded Age* (Toronto: ECW Press, 2002).

9. Of interest is the controversial 1932 movie *Freaks*, directed by Tod Browning. Filmed exclusively

with "abnormal" traveling circus sideshow performers, the film's plot revolves around the question of whether a full-grown woman can be in love with a midget. Classified as both horror and drama, the film was so controversial in its time that it ruined Browning's career. It is of interest today as a document of how abnormalities were viewed in the early twentieth century, as well as for its cast of characters and its sympathetic look at those performers' lives. Important in bringing to the table such questions, this film may have influenced the making of the 1995 Argentinean film *I Don't Want to Talk About It* [*De eso no se habla*], directed by Maria Luisa Bemberg, featuring Marcelo Mastroianni in love with a female small person.

10. Another famous episode is his display of "the Aztec children," Maximo and Bartola, described as "two active, sprightly, intelligent little beings" who were also hosted at the New York Society Library in 1852. For an interesting account of the history of this episode and Barnum's fascination with John Lloyd Stephens's travels in Central America and his proposed Museum of American Antiquities, see R. Tripp Evans, *Romancing the Maya: Mexican Antiquity in the American Imaginary, 1820–1915* (Austin: University of Texas Press, 2004), and in particular his chapter "Incidents of Transcription: 'American' Antiquity in the Work of Stephens and Catherwood" (44–87).

11. This kind of manipulation of science and scientific evidence continues unabated today. See Richard Lewontin, "Dishonesty in Science," for a discussion of the Bush administration's misuse of science and different cases of scientific fraud. *New York Review of Books* 51, no. 18 (November 18, 2004): 38–40.

12. See Mona Domosh, *Invented Cities: The Creation of Landscape in Nineteenth-Century New York & Boston* (New Haven: Yale University Press, 1996).

13. Robin Freed, "'In Business for Myself': P. T. Barnum and the Museum of Spectacle," University of Virginia, http://xroads.virginia.edu/~MA02/freed/Barnum/museumessay.html.

14. John D. McEachran, Syllabus for "Museums and Their Functions," Texas A & M University, http://wfscnet.tamu.edu/COURSES/wfsc421.htm (accessed November 4, 2007).

15. I found out about Ota Benga at Dartmouth's Hood Museum's exhibit of Fred Wilson's 2005 installation, "So Much Trouble in the World—*Believe It or Not!*" I am quoting curator Barbara Thompson's "Making *So Much Trouble in the World*," published in the Hood Museum pamphlet that accompanied the exhibit. The problematic subject/object relation that I have been alluding to, and the abuses to which it can lead and which Fred Wilson unpacks, has become apparent again recently in the shocking photographs of Iraqi prisoners arranged as "quasi-pornographic" tableaux at Abu Ghraib.

16. While valuable for the study of early modern Europe's Wunderkammern, these contemporary spaces with their all-too-orderly displays belie the terror of chaos and the threat of imploding posed by the sheer volume of objects, which must have been quite evident in the early Wunderkammern.

17. See the virtual tour of the Mütter Museum at its website: http://www.collphyphil.org/virt_tour/museum_5.htm; see also Gretchen Worden, *Mütter Museum of the College of Physicians of Philadelphia* (New York: Blast Books, 2002).

18. Photographs of some of the idiosyncratic Christmas crèches that she made with her collections were posted by a photographer at the request of Worden's colleagues and in her memory. See Laura Blanchard, "Remembering Gretchen Worden," Northwest South Philly, http://www.southphillyblocks.org/photos_essays/gretchens_creche/

19. John Strausbaugh, "A Curator's Tastes Were All Too Human," *New York Times* (Tuesday, October 11, 2005): B1.

20. Plaque at the Mütter Museum in Philadelphia, quoting from S. H. Daukes's 1929 *The Medical Museum*.

21. Worden quoted by Marc Abrahams, "In Memorium [sic]: Gretchen Worden." Improbable Research blog upon Worden's passing.

22. In the exhibit of Dresden's famous cabinet of wonders (the so-called Green Vault or Grünes Gewölbe, for the color of its ceiling), some of the objects crafted by artisans of the eighteenth century were so detailed, so laborious, so immensely rich on every level, that it seemed as if the object had taken hold of me, much as the axolótl in Cortázar's famous story cannibalized the disingenuous visitor to the Jardin des Plantes. Significantly, in Cortázar's story the object's swallowing up of the visitor was not merely described as cannibalism, but in Cortázar's words, it was a cannibalism "of gold" ["de oro"]. It was here that I understood the power of awe and the desire of artisans to create objects of such beauty that they would literally make the visitor awestruck. Julio Cortázar, *Final del juego*, ed. Jaime Alazraki (Madrid: Anaya & Mario Muchnik, 1995).

23. As Strausbaugh concludes in his piece on Worden and the Mütter in the *New York Times*, the Mütter under Worden "probably cleared a path for the smash success of the touring 'Bodyworlds' exhibition by the artist Günther von Hagens, a kind of Barnumesque road show version of the Mütter featuring preserved human corpses in artistically arranged poses." *New York Times* (Tuesday, October 11, 2005): B7. The technique invented by von Hagens allowed him to preserve hundreds of bodies donated by friends and anonymous donors. An heir to Ruysch, von Hagens invented plastination to preserve bodies perfectly and thus to allow them to be used in the teaching of anatomy as well as to "enlighten" the public at large about the fragility of the body in a mechanized world and as an aid in helping them "envision" the ravages of diseases (e.g., the dangers of smoking). See the exhibit's website, *Bodyworlds: The Anatomical Exhibition of Real Human Bodies,* at http://www.bodyworlds.com/en/pages/home.asp; and also the German site *Günther von Hagens' Körperwelten: Die Faszination des Echten,* http://www.bodyworlds.com/index.html (accessed November 4, 2007).

Even more extreme is the grotesque so-called "Visible Human Project," which consists of myriad digital images taken of the thinly sliced and frozen body of a killer who donated his body to science while on death row. These now circulate on the Internet, allegedly as a visual teaching aid and anatomical theater. The website that serves as the site from which to order the images announces: "The image database contains 1,878 CT scans, obtained by sectioning the body into 1mm thick fillets and capturing a digital colour image at every level. This is intended to be used for teaching applications such as identifying anatomical structures on the cross-sections and visualising the motion of the human form using supercomputer modeling. It's gruesome, but all in the name of science. E-mail Dr. Michael Ackerman at the National Library of Medicine for a 'free license' to access the imagery via the Internet. http://neuro-www.mgh.harvard.edu/creepy.html." See also David Rothman, "The Murderer's Gift: The Life and Eternal Cyberlife of Paul Jernigan." *NetWorld*. Reprinted at http://www.davidrothman.com/murderer.html.

24. Max Aguilera-Hellweg started out as a photographer and was inspired to study medicine when he was asked by a woman's magazine in 1989 to photograph a female neurosurgeon at work. He was fascinated, and he went on to photograph over one hundred surgeries over an eight-year span. In an interview with Terry Gross on NPR, he tells of one particular surgery that stunned him: the procedure consisted of a surgeon's removing the entire skin off a patient's face—it brought him to reflect on where identity is located. That interview and that question led me in turn to question where mestizaje is identified. The operations Max Aguilera-Hellweg photographed inspired him to change careers and study medicine. As he recalls, "As I watched the spinal cord surgery, I saw the painting above my grandmother's fireplace. The one of Jesus, his heart bleeding, wrapped in thorns, engulfed in flames. I realized I was in the presence of something so precious, so powerful, so pure, I couldn't bear the intensity. Yet I did. And yearned to experience it again and again." As he reflects on the publication of his book *The Sacred Heart,* reminding us of the conflation of awe and visibility that I have been outlining with respect to the Wunderkammern, "With the completion of this project, I have come full circle to what originally captivated me about photography—the power to reveal the unknown. These operations piqued in me a curiosity that could only be satisfied by enrolling in medical school." Max Aguilera-Hellweg, "Authors: Max Aguilera-Hellweg," Time Warner Bookmark, http://www.twbookmark.com/authors/6/600/ (link no longer works).

25. See also F. González-Crussi, with photographs by Rosamond Purcell, *Suspended Animation: Six Essays on the Preservation of Bodily Parts* (San Diego: Harvest, Harcourt Brace, 1995).

26. See Rosamond Purcell, *Naturalezas* (with texts and photographs by Rosamond Purcell), the catalogue of the exhibit at Madrid's Museo Nacional de Ciencias Naturales (Madrid, 1991). To understand Rosamond Purcell's willingness to document the decay of Ricky Jay's dice, see the recent compilation of this sleight-of-hand artist, actor, and scholar of the unusual in his quarterly *Jay's Journal of Anomalies* published in the 1990s. This quirky series made to look like a nineteenth-century publication has been compiled as Ricky Jay, *Jay's Journal of Anomalies: Conjurers, Cheats, Hustlers, Hoaxsters, Pranksters, Impostors, Pretenders, Sideshow Showmen, Armless Calligraphers, Mechanical Marvels, Popular Entertainments* (New York: Farrar, Straus, Giroux, 2001).

27. See also Terry Gross's interview with Rosamond Purcell on the radio program *Fresh Air*, February 2, 2004, http://www.npr.org/templates/story/story.php?storyId=1628953.

28. Purcell, *Naturalezas*, 17.

29. Ibid., 8.

30. http://www.hno.harvard.edu/gazette/2004/11.04/27-worm.html.

31. See the excellent virtual tour of this exhibit and the artist's explanation on the website that accom-

panied the 2003 installation at Tufts University, "Rosamond Purcell: Two Rooms" (http://ase.tufts.edu/gallery/shows/purcell.html). "On one afternoon during installation, the students placed an assortment of corroded metal fragments—a rusted lock, buckles, half a faucet—on a work table covered with brown craft paper. These were destined for a glass case titled 'Recent Archaeology from Maine.'" Purcell picked up a piece of twisted wire, noting its resemblance to a question mark. "Objects like this," she said, "remind me of parts of a sentence, and once they're lined up look like the shapes of letters." Elsewhere in the gallery, a 12-foot-high temporary wall was in the process of being covered with plates of scrap metal; a heap of turquoise-colored toilet bowl floats filled an old bin; and a jumble of rusty household gadgets—ladles, eggbeaters, and the like—sprang upward from an ancient-looking trunk, as if clamoring to tell their stories. They recall a touching passage in *Owl's Head* in which Purcell imagines the dead rising from the grave and coming back for their discarded things: "'That's my puck . . .' 'and raincoat . . .' 'I've come for the goal post'" (New York: Quantuck Lane Press, 2003). Further references appear in the text.

"Two Rooms" is a fascinating primer on impermanence. Books that were once the newly published apples of their authors' eyes have been ravaged by termites or turned into stones, their pages fused and unreadable. No doubt someone made fabulous meringues with those rusty eggbeaters—but where is the pie maker now? "I have chipped these things from the matrix of the almighty thingness of our all-American world," Purcell wrote in *Owl's Head*, "and, as I did not stop to mourn their demise, why not revel now in the stages of their inevitable disintegration?" "The Collector: MHC Museum Hosts Rosamond Purcell Exhibition," *College Street Journal*, January 30, 2004, http://www.mtholyoke.edu/offices/comm/csj/013004/purcell.shtml (accessed November 4, 2007).

32. To view some images of this book on the Internet, see "Photographer and Writer Rosamond Purcell," http://www.npr.org/templates/story/story.php?storyId=1628953 (accessed November 4, 2007).

33. As she notes, for her father, despite his irritation at their condition, they continue to serve exclusively as a source of information. Chewed-up books also serve to mirror the fragmentary and partial nature of re-collecting, and in particular Purcell's own frustration with how much she reads yet how little she remembers of what she, an avid reader, reads. She therefore also keeps these objects on bookshelves, allowing them to be eaten away at by mites and silverfish. The work of nature here provides her constantly with a different reading and the emergence of "alternative meanings" as the letters fall to the floor as dust.

34. In these cases lack of provenance may diminish an art object's display value for a museum, but it may also, in fact, increase its desirability to unscrupulous collectors.

35. Barbara Thompson, *Fred Wilson: So Much Trouble in the World*—Believe It or Not! (Hanover, NH; London: Hood Museum of Art, Dartmouth College, distributed by University Press of New England, 2006), 14.

36. Ibid., 18.

37. Ibid., 13.

38. One immediately thinks of Freud's definition of the unconscious; Purcell and Gould, however, never refer to psychoanalysis. It would be interesting to pursue why the focus on objects seemingly disallows a Freudian reading.

39. Nehemiah Grew, *Catalogue and description of the natural and artificial rarities belonging to the Royal Society* (1681), quoted in Purcell and Gould, *Illuminations*, 17. Further references appear in text.

40. See http://www.butterflyartworks.us.

41. Mark Dion, "Tate Thames Dig 1999," Tate Museum, http://www.tate.org.uk/servlet/ViewWork?cgroupid=999999961&workid=27353.

42. See *Cabinet of Curiosities: Mark Dion and the University as Installation*, edited by Colleen J. Sheehy (Minneapolis and London: University of Minnesota Press in Cooperation with the Weisman Art Museum, 2006).

43. See the catalogue to the exhibition, *Becoming Animal: Contemporary Art in the Animal Kingdom*, edited by Nato Thompson (Boston: MIT Press, 2005).

44. Cassandra Vinograd, "Beastly Exhibit at London Zoo," *Valley News* (Saturday, August 27, 2005): A11.

45. See James Clifford's excellent chapter on this period in *The Predicament of Culture: Twentieth-Century Ethnography, Literature, and Art* (Cambridge: Harvard University Press, 1988).

46. See Patrick Mauries, *Cabinets of Curiosities* (London: Thames and Hudson, 2002).

47. Arjun Appadurai, "Introduction," in *The Social Life of Things* (Cambridge: Cambridge University Press, 1986), 28.

48. You enter this dark, meandering, and quirky museum off bright and billboard-laden Venice Blvd. in Culver City, Los Angeles, as if entering another dimension. Tea is still served here in samovars heated from the coals of a fire on the roof of the museum. To get a sense of the collection, see the museum's "Jubilee Catalogue," celebrating their first ten years and simply entitled *The Museum of Jurassic Technology* (Los Angeles: Society for the Diffusion of Useful Information Press, 2002); and also Leonard Feinstein's DVD *Inhaling the Spore: A Journey Through the Museum of Jurassic Technology* (2004).

49. All citations are from pamphlets advertising the museum.

50. Cassie Horner, "Museum Curator Celebrates the Spirit of Whimsy," *Vermont Standard* (Thursday, February 13, 2003): 9C.

51. Worden, *Mütter Museum of the College of Physicians of Philadelphia*, 7.

52. Farnese de Andrade and Rodrigo Naves, *Farnese de Andrade* (São Paulo: Cosac & Naify, 2002).

53. Rosamond Purcell and Stephen Jay Gould, *Crossing Over: Where Art and Science Meet* (New York: Three Rivers Press, 2000), 82.

54. Walter Benjamin, *Illuminations* (New York: Schocken Books, 1969).

CHAPTER 4

1. James Lockhart, *Nahuas and Spaniards: Postconquest Central Mexican History and Philology* (Stanford: Stanford University Press, 1991), 13. See also Elizabeth Hill Boone and Tom Cummins, eds., *Native Traditions in the Postconquest World* (Washington, D.C.: Dumbarton Oaks Research Library and Collection, 1998).

2. Lockhart, *Nahuas and Spaniards*, 17.

3. According to hermetic symbolism, the life road taken, and by extension a pilgrimage or the *via Crucis*, can serve as a religious mnemonic. Religious "reminders" and promises are pinned along the route. According to this hermetic tradition, fortified cities were star-shaped to mirror the shape of God. See, for example, "Figure Opus Magnum: Ladder," in Alexander Roob, *The Hermetic Museum: Alchemy and Mysticism* (Köln: Taschen, 1997), 336. In the New World, highly performative traditions of pilgrimage overlaid indigenous religious routes and served as a cultural mnemonic.

4. David I. Kertzer, *Ritual, Politics, and Power* (New Haven: Yale University Press, 1988), 66.

5. Serge Gruzinski, *Images at War: Mexico from Columbus to Blade Runner* (1492–2009), translated by Heather McLean (Durham, NC: Duke University Press, 2001), 50.

6. In the 1980s, critic Angel Rama coined this term to describe the Spanish writing technologies that made up the colonial administration (from petty bureaucrats, to the clergy, to the colonial elite) and that overlayered oral indigenous forms of knowledge with western writing. See Angel Rama, *La ciudad letrada* (Hanover, NH: Ediciones del Norte, 1984); and the translation *The Lettered City: (Post-Contemporary Interventions)* by John Chasteen (Durham, NC: Duke University Press, 1996).

7. While in classical times the art of memory served as a form of artificial memory, there to help orators remember their speeches, in the early modern Church the principles of artificial memory would stimulate the intense visualization of similitudes and affinities between things in order to avoid the pitfalls of a multitude of vices.

8. A note of caution: It is impossible and erroneous to speak of a unified Church since Catholicism was deeply divided and often at odds with regard to the rise of increasingly syncretic practices. In areas where the Franciscans led the evangelization campaigns, they emphasized religious "purity" of practice and dogma, whereas the Jesuits actively participated in the creation of religious syncretism, which they saw as an expedient (and maybe somewhat inevitable) way of promoting the Christianization of native populations. Jacques Lafaye goes so far as to argue that "the triumphant advance of the eighteenth-century Mexican creoles merged with the apotheosis of the Society," given that the Jesuits' cause, in fact, became so intertwined, almost collapsed into, a creole proto-nationalist agenda. See Jacques Lafaye, *Quetzalcoatl and Guadalupe: The Formation of Mexican National Consciousness, 1531–1813*, translated by Benjamin Keen (Chicago: University of Chicago Press, 1976), 99.

9. See the chapter "Dagon Is Their Ark and Christ Their Baal," in my *Between Two Waters: Narratives of Transculturation in Latin America* (College Station: Texas A&M University Press, 2006).

10. Paradoxically, intent on evangelization, priests created many of the most valuable documents we

have pertaining to pre-Columbian tradition and history. Schools such as that at Tlatelolco underline the contradiction and tension in the Crown's efforts to protect common Indians from abuses by mestizos and others, segregating them into pueblos de indios, and the desire to assimilate the Indian aristocracy through intermarriage with Spaniards as well as through education (i.e., through the foundation of institutions such as the Colegio). The texts produced at these institutions are interestingly transcultural, based on pre-Conquest Náhuatl thought at the same time as they incorporate Spanish culture. As such they serve as the foundational narratives of what was to become Mexican nationalism in the nineteenth century.

11. See Lois Parkinson Zamora and Monika Kaup, eds., *The New World Baroque* (Durham, NC: Duke University Press, forthcoming).

12. Alejo Carpentier, "The Baroque and the Marvelous Real," in *Magical Realism: Theory, History, Community*, edited by Lois Parkinson Zamora and Wendy Faris (Durham, NC: Duke University Press, 1995), 100. The original essay, "Lo barroco y lo real maravilloso," appeared in *La novela latinoamericana en vísperas de un nuevo siglo y otros ensayos* (México, DF: Siglo XXI, 1981), 126.

13. Quoted by John Tierney in his review of Kertzer, *Ritual, Politics, and Power*, "The Value of Rituals," in *New York Times Book Review* (Sunday, August 15, 2004): 16.

14. See the discussion of this national ritual in Kertzer, *Ritual, Politics, and Power*, 1.

15. For a useful history of the influence of the Virgin Mary and her many incarnations (no pun intended!) in Spain and the Americas, see Linda B. Hall, *Mary, Mother and Warrior: The Virgin in Spain and the Americas* (Austin: University of Texas Press, 2004).

16. Vivian Schelling, *Through the Kaleidoscope: The Experience of Modernity in Latin America* (London: Verso, 2000), 2–3.

17. W. J. T. Mitchell, *What Do Pictures Want? The Lives and Loves of Images* (Chicago; London: University of Chicago Press, 2005), 8.

18. As Mitchell states, echoing Freud's question of women's desire, "Pictures want equal rights with language, not to be turned into language." Ibid., 8.

19. Parkinson Zamora, *The Inordinate Eye*, 13.

20. Vivian Schelling, *Through the Kaleidoscope: The Experience of Modernity in Latin America* (London: Verso, 2000), 14.

21. Parkinson Zamora, *The Inordinate Eye*, 12.

22. Luis Millones, "Los Santos patronos. De la ciudad indígena a la ciudad indiana," in *Más allá de la ciudad letrada: Crónicas y espacios urbanos*, edited by Boris Muñoz and Silvia Spitta (Pittsburgh: Biblioteca de América, Instituto Internacional de Literatura Iberoamericana, 2003), 283.

23. Parkinson Zamora, *The Inordinate Eye*, 15.

24. See Diana Taylor's important reclaiming of these practices in *The Archive and the Repertoire: Performing Cultural Memory in the Americas* (Durham, NC: Duke University Press, 2003).

25. Serge Gruzinski, *Images at War: Mexico from Columbus to Blade Runner (1492–2009)*, translated by Heather McLean (Durham, NC: Duke University Press, 2001), 50.

26. Ibid., 50, 51.

27. In his presentation at Dartmouth at the conference "Los Angeles/la frontera/Mexico City" in July 1999, Carlos Martin showed how Mexican-Americans change their lived environment radically through the use of fences, ironwork around windows and doors, and gardens and home life facing the street.

28. Bernal Díaz del Castillo, *Historia verdadera de la conquista de la Nueva España*, edited by Miguel León-Portilla (Madrid: Historia 16, 1984), 71.

29. The abstraction of indigenous arts is increasingly being understood by art historians as a negation of the visual and a favoring of the tactile. I thank my colleague Mary Coffey for this observation.

30. Bernal Díaz del Castillo, *Historia verdadera*, 131, 132.

31. Hans Belting, *Likeness and Presence: A History of the Image before the Era of Art*, translated by Edmund Jephcott (Chicago: University of Chicago Press, 1994), 1.

32. See my chapter on the Cuzco School in *Between Two Waters* for a description of this type of "miracle" in the Andes.

33. Richard Nebel, *Santa María Tonantzin, Virgen de Guadalupe: Continuidad y transformación religiosa en México*, translated by Carlos Warnholtz Bustillos (México: Fondo de Cultura Económica, 1995), 235. See also John F. Moffitt, *Our Lady of Guadalupe: The Painting, the Legend, and the Reality* (Jefferson, North Carolina, and London: McFarland & Company, Inc., 2006). While popular tradition has it that

Malinche was the mother of the "first" mestizo, that is not quite accurate, since Bernal Díaz and other chroniclers report that Gonzalo Guerrero, shipwrecked off the coast of the Yucatán, had gone native and had mestizo children long before the arrival of Cortés to Mexico.

34. Quotes from the *Nican mopohua* translated by Fr. Martinus Cawley, in Jacqueline Orsini Dunnington, *Viva Guadalupe! The Virgin in New Mexican Popular Art* (Santa Fe: Museum of New Mexico Press, 1997), 3.

35. Quoted in Dunnington, *Viva Guadalupe!*, 6. The source of the quote is unacknowledged in the text.

36. Francisco de la Maza, *El Guadalupanismo mexicano*, 70.

37. Indeed, J. J. Benítez, an extremely popular writer of over twenty books on UFOs and other such phenomena, has also tackled the mystery of the Guadalupan apparitions. Pulling yet another scientist out of the bag, the *Guadalupan Encyclopedia*'s reproduction of the reflection of "an Indian" (i.e., Juan Diego) in the Virgin of Guadalupe's eyes is now expanded to a whole host of other characters, including Archbishop Zumárraga himself. Basing himself on a "study" by Dr. Aste Tonsmann, he lists these reflections in Zumárraga's eyes as "an Indian displaying his cloak or tilma before a Franciscan upon whose face one sees a tear fall, a very young peasant, his hand on his beard and with a look of consternation, an Indian with his torso uncovered in an attitude of prayer, a woman with very curly hair (probably a black woman servant of the bishop), a man, a woman, and some children with their heads half-shaven, and other religious people in Franciscan robes, that is . . . the same episode retold in Náhuatl by an indigenous writer of the first part of the XVI century!" ["un indio en el acto de desplegar su 'tilma' o túnica ante un franciscano; al propio franciscano en cuyo rostro se ve deslizarse una lágrima; un paisano muy joven, la mano puesta sobre la barba con ademán de consternación; un indio con el torso desnudo en actitud casi orante; una mujer de pelo crespo, probablemente una negra de la servidumbre del obispo; un varón, una mujer y unos niños con la cabeza medio rapada y otros religiosos más en hábito franciscano, es decir. . . . ¡el mismo episodio relatado en lengua náhuatl por un escritor indígena en la primera mitad del siglo XVI . . ."] J. J. Benítez, *El misterio de la Virgen de Guadalupe: Sensacionales descubrimientos en los ojos de la Virgen mexicana* (Barcelona: Planeta, 1982), 14.

38. See Jesús Galera Lamadrid, *Nican mopohua: Breve análisis literario e histórico* (México City: Editorial Jus, 1991). This edition includes the Nahua text and four different translations into Spanish from 1666, 1926, and two from 1978. For an edited version in verse, see Miguel León-Portilla in *Tonantzin Guadalupe: Pensamiento náhuatl y mensaje cristiano en el "Nican mopohua"* (México City: Fondo de Cultura Económica, 2000).

39. See Rama, *La ciudad letrada*.

40. The hyperbolic statements and reckless manipulation of "facts" that characterize the scholarship surrounding Guadalupe vary greatly also with respect to estimates of the number of pilgrims that visit the Guadalupan church. While some critics estimate that twenty-five million pilgrims visit the Villa/Tepeyac annually, and six million on December 12, the Mexican church estimates that 25,000 visit it each month.

41. Dunnington, *Viva Guadalupe!*, 14.

42. Ibid., 15.

43. Guillermo Ortiz de Montellano, translator and ed., *Nican mopohua* (México: Universidad Iberoamericana, 1990), 14.

44. "Dedication" of the *Enciclopedia Guadalupana*, Xavier Escalada, S.J. (México: Enciclopedia Guadalupana A.C., 1995), no page number.

45. *Enciclopedia Guadalupana*, 359.

46. See J. Garcia Icazbalceta, *Investigación histórica y documental sobre la aparición de la Virgen de Guadalupe* (México, DF: Ediciones Fuente Cultural, 1958), 123.

47. de la Maza, *El guadalupanismo mexicano*, 15.

48. Historian Jacques Lafaye calls it a "Basilica," whereas other historians call this building an "ermita," or shrine.

49. de la Maza, *El guadalupanismo mexicano*, 15.

50. Lafaye, *Quetzalcoatl and Guadalupe*, 240.

51. See J. Garcia Icazbalceta, *Investigación histórica y documental sobre la aparición de la Virgen de Guadalupe* (México, DF: Ediciones Fuente Cultural, 1958), 117.

52. According to some critics, an original painting (which the tilma copied)—based on the small

sculpture of Guadalupe supposedly brought to Mexico by Archbishop Zumárraga—may have initially given rise to the cult.

53. "Gachupín" was the term used to designate Spaniards born in the New World. It soon acquired denigrating overtones.

54. de la Maza, *El guadalupanismo mexicano*, 72–73.

55. Lafaye, *Quetzalcoatl and Guadalupe*, 243. See also de la Maza, *El Guadalupanismo mexicano*, 55.

56. de la Maza, *El guadalupanismo mexicano*, 56.

57. Nebel, *Santa María Tonantzin*, 238.

58. de la Maza, *El guadalupanismo mexicano*, 59.

59. Ibid., 69.

60. Quoted in Ibid., 73.

61. *Enciclopedia Guadalupana*, 670.

62. It was known as the "ermita de indios."

63. de la Maza, *El guadalupanismo mexicano*, 13.

64. *Enciclopedia Guadalupana*, 122.

65. de la Maza, *El guadalupanismo mexicano*, 74.

66. Edmundo O'Gorman, *Destierro de sombras* (México: UNAM, 1986), 54.

67. The imprinting of the tilma has several different versions: in some, this happened at Tepeyac; in others, it happened at Zumárraga's when Juan Diego opened his tilma and the roses of Castille fell out.

68. O'Gorman, *Destierro de sombras*, 55.

69. Ortiz de Montellano, ed., *Nican mopohua*, 14.

70. Jaime Cuadriello, "Visiones en Patmos Tenochtitlán. La mujer águila," *Artes de México* 29 (1995): 23.

71. León-Portilla, *Tonantzin Guadalupe*, 68.

72. With respect to the aesthetic form of the *Nican mopohua*, scholars are deeply divided. In their 1998 collaborative reprinting and translation of the text, Lisa Sousa, C. M. Stafford Poole, and James Lockhart detail how closely Lasso de la Vega's text mimics Sánchez's account. They argue that although it is a foundational account written in Náhuatl, the story is European in "form and substance" and follows standard European apparition narratives. Inexplicably, without ever mentioning Lafaye's seminal study, they arrive at his same conclusion, namely, that the "nature and popularity of the Guadalupan legend thus seem to have been strongly affected by two texts that Mexican-born Spanish ecclesiastics published in the late 1640s." They suspect that Lasso may have copied extant Náhuatl texts, which were readily available at the time, in order to lend his text Náhuatl expressiveness. While Sánchez's text does not have the *Nican mopohua*'s strings of honorific vocatives at the beginning and ending of speeches, the frequent examples of polite small talk, or the metaphorical double phrases, these stylistic features do not add anything of substance to the tale, and sources for them were readily available, whether in refined Náhuatl conversation or in well-known Náhuatl texts of ecclesiastical provenance. Such collections as the *Bancroft Dialogues*, the *Huehuetlatolli* of Fray Juan Bautista, Book Six of the *Florentine Codex*, or various sets of biblical/moralistic plays, all of which were in some form or other circulating in Mexico at this time, contain models for virtually every example of Náhuatl rhetoric used in the Guadalupan texts. See C. M. Stafford Poole, *Our Lady of Guadalupe: The Origins and Sources of a Mexican National Symbol, 1531–1797* (Tucson: University of Arizona Press, 1995), 28.

The scholar Miguel León-Portilla, in his *Tonantzin Guadalupe* (notice that he puts her Náhuatl name first), traces the ancient Nahua tradition of the classical "cantares mexicanos" throughout the text, and comes to a diametrically opposed view. The *Nican mopohua*, according to him, shows the persistence of the classical Nahua symbolic universe and the way in which wise scholars communicated with one another ["Es ciertamente un hecho . . . que en el Nican mopohua perdura no poco del universo de símbolos característicos del náhuatl clásico, a través del cual los tlamantinime o sabios se comunicaban entre sí y transmitían a otros su pensamiento"]. León-Portilla, *Tonantzin Guadalupe*, 51.

73. The 1983 novel *Famous All Over Town* was marketed as a "Chicano" novel and received great acclaim. It was awarded a distinguished fiction prize by the American Academy and Institute of Arts and Letters in 1984. An uproar ensued when critics found out that Danny Santiago was a pen name for seventy-three-year-old Daniel James. The author, a playwright blacklisted in the 1950s, was an Anglo-American who had done volunteer work in Mexican-American communities in Los Angeles in the 1950s and 1960s—hence he knew the culture quite well and was able to mimic it in his novel. The question then

arises whether his not being a Chicano should make any difference, particularly given the fact that no one noticed any inauthenticity in the novel before his identity was revealed.

74. Psalms 147:20 (King James translation).

CHAPTER 5

1. Jacqueline Orsini Dunnington, *Viva Guadalupe! The Virgin in New Mexican Popular Art* (Santa Fe: Museum of New Mexico Press, 1997), 22.

2. There were also early Guadalupan churches founded in Santa Fe (1808), Velarde (1817), Villanueva (1818–1826), Ocaté (1900), Cañada de los Alamos (1922), La Madera (1918), Cerro (1940), Gallina (1954), Clovis, Peña Blanca, Los Chávez, Sabinoso, San Juan, Sapello, Tecolotito, Canyon, Des Moines, El Macho, Encino, Glorieta, Guachupangue, Guadalupita, Pojoaque, and Taos.

3. Her influence ranges much earlier and much further south: in Ecuador, the town of Guápulo was founded to honor her (ca. 1581), and in Perú, the town of Guadalupe was founded around 1560. In Latin America, of 240 colonial period shrines, 30 percent were established by 1599, 62 percent were founded between 1492 and 1799, and 38 percent are modern (1800–1980). There were relatively few shrines founded in the nineteenth century, but "the twentieth century has been a time of substantial shrine-formative activity." See Mary Lee Nolan, "The European Roots of Latin American Pilgrimage," in *Pilgrimages in Latin America*, edited by N. Ross Crumrine and Alan Morinis (New York: Greenwood Press, 1991), 25.

4. The most important celebration of the Virgin of Guadalupe is that of the Tewa Pueblo Indians and takes place at Tortugas, a small village south of Las Cruces.

5. "The Spanish image of Guadalupe is an ancient wood carving dressed in rich brocade cloaks that give it the triangular shape much favored at the time. She is very different from the Tepeyac painting, not only because of her Iberian-Byzantine features, but also because she carries the Child Jesus in her left arm and holds a royal scepter in her right hand, displaying a gold crown on her head. The Guadalupe, whose origin, according to legend, is placed about the 6th century, was found on the shore of the Guadalupe River (hidden river in Arabic) in the Villuercas mountain range, around 1326," http://www.hispaniconline.com/hh03/mainpages/religion/mary_mexico.html.

6. Victor Turner and Edith Turner, *Image and Pilgrimage in Christian Culture: Anthropological Perspectives* (New York: Columbia University Press, 1978), 44.

7. Dunnington, *Viva Guadalupe!*, 14.

8. While some dark Virgins today were darkened when they were hidden in caves or buried to protect them from invaders at different times in Europe, many were originally sculpted out of black wood or black stone. According to Fulcanelli, in hermetic symbolism, black Madonnas "represent the Virgin earth, which the artist must choose as the subject of his work. It is the Prima Materia in its mineral state." See Fulcanelli, *Le mystère des Cathédrales* (Paris, 1964), quoted in Alexander Roob, *The Hermetic Museum: Alchemy and Mysticism* (Köln: Taschen, 1997), 238.

9. See, for example, Norma Alarcón, "Chicana's Feminist Literature: A Re-Vision through Malintzín, Or, Malintzín: Putting Flesh Back on the Objects," in *This Bridge Called My Back: Writings by Radical Women of Color*, edited by Cherríe Moraga and Gloria Anzaldúa (Watertown: Persephone Press, 1981); and "Traduttora, Traditora: A Paradigmatic Figure of Chicana Feminism," *Cultural Critique* 13 (1990).

10. Sandra Cisneros, "Guadalupe the Sex Goddess," in *Goddess of the Americas/La diosa de las Américas: Writings on the Virgin of Guadalupe*, edited by Ana Castillo (New York: Riverhead Books, 1996).

11. Engraving in *Third Woman* 4, no. 1–2 (1989).

12. See Joel Merino, *Tepeyac en Nueva York* (Puebla: Benemérita Universidad Autónoma de Puebla, 2002).

13. Turner and Turner, *Image and Pilgrimage*, 57.

14. Nolan, "The European Roots of Latin American Pilgrimage," 32–33. A stunning collection of relics embedded in weapons and jewelry used to anchor religious and political power can be seen in Vienna's Imperial and Ecclesiastical Treasury. Among many other amazing artificialia they include a fourth-century agate bowl from Constantinople believed to be the Holy Grail (which is said to have held Christ's blood from the Cross) and various ornate reliquaries containing a particle of the Cross, a chip of wood from Christ's crib, a piece of the tablecloth from the Last Supper, a piece of Christ's loincloth, the shinbone of St. Elizabeth of Thuringia, and links from the prison chains of Saints Peter, Paul, and John. There is also an ostensory with a nail from Christ's Cross, and Veronika's famous handkerchief (the Sudarium)

upon which Christ wiped his sweat on his way to the Cross, leaving the imprint of his face. The Imperial insignias of the Holy Roman Empire include the imperial crown, the holy lance, the imperial orb, and a particle of the "true" Cross. See Manfred Leithe-Jasper and Rudolf Distelberger, *The Kunsthistorisches Museum Vienna: The Imperial and Ecclesiastical Treasury* (Munich: Scala Publishers, 2003).

15. Third-order signs are signs that are a replica of the "truly significant Icon found in the Church." They are therefore themselves a sign of the divine. See Kay F. Turner, "The Cultural Semiotics of Religious Icons: La Virgen de San Juan de los Lagos," *Semiotica* 47, 1/4 (1983): 317–361, 348.

16. Kay F. Turner, "The Cultural Semiotics of Religious Icons," 341.

17. Ibid., 350.

18. Turner and Turner, *Image and Pilgrimage*, 11.

19. Turner, "The Cultural Semiotics of Religious Icons," 353.

20. Alan Morinis and N. Ross Crumrine, "La peregrinación: The Latin American Pilgrimage," in *Pilgrimages in Latin America*, edited by N. Ross Crumrine and Alan Morinis (New York: Greenwood Press, 1991), 9.

21. Turner and Turner, *Image and Pilgrimage*, 39.

22. For an insightful distinction between coyotes, pateros, pollos, etc., see David Spener, "Narrativas del mal: El coyote mexicano en el drama del cruce fronterizo," in Boris Muñoz and Silvia Spitta, editors, *Más allá de la ciudad letrada: Crónicas y espacios urbanos* (Pittsburgh: Iberoamericana, 2003), 379–410.

23. Reports of December 12 celebrations are increasingly occurring in rural areas remote from large urban centers, but where migrant workers are present.

24. Paolo Apolito, *The Internet and the Madonna: Religious Visionary Experience on the Web*, translated by Antony Shugaar (Chicago: University of Chicago Press, 2005), 2.

25. Kay F. Turner argues that religious icons function on three levels: as icon, as index, and as symbol. For those bearing a Virgin on a litter, and those following the litter in a procession, the image is an index of "heaven's sacred royalty, paid due respect by being carried like a queen." She is an icon for those awaiting her arrival for whom this moment, particularly the eye contact they may make with the image, is "charged with the emotion of a personal encounter." Additionally, the image is a dominant symbol (or langue), knowable only as parole or "partially as structures: the single image creates a semantic field of many referents—not a single referent." Turner, "The Cultural Semiotics of Religious Icons," 355.

26. B. V. Olguín, "Tattoos, Abjection, and the Political Unconscious," *Cultural Critique* (Fall 1997, no. 37): 159–214, 168.

27. As Olguín notes, the denomination *Pintos* stems from the bilingual play merging "*penitencia* (or penitentiary), as well as the Chicano colloquial past participle *pintao* (e.g., as in *estar pintado*), which means to be painted, tainted, or otherwise marked (e.g., by skin pigmentation or a courtroom conviction). The Protestant notion of the perpetually suffering and sometimes repentant human being (i.e., the penitent) is in part preserved in the translation: once a Pinto always a Pinto. The only difference is that *Pintos* are not repentant" (166).

28. Tomás Ybarra-Frausto, "Rasquachismo: A Chicano Sensibility," in *Chicano Art: Resistance to Affirmation, 1965–1985*. Edited by Richard Griswold del Castillo et al. (Los Angeles: Wight Gallery, 1991), 155–162.

29. Olguín, "Tattoos, Abjection, and the Political Unconscious," 168.

30. Ibid., 163.

31. Margo DeMello, *Bodies of Inscription: A Cultural History of the Modern Tattoo Community* (Durham and London: Duke University Press, 2000), 84–85, 137–194.

32. Important too were Japanese tattoos. For an interesting discussion of these as well as an excellent history of tattooing worldwide, see Arnold Rubin, ed., *Marks of Civilization: Artistic Transformations of the Human Body* (Los Angeles: Museum of Cultural History, 1988).

33. As DeMello explains, the Modern Primitives movement originated in the S/M communities of the 1960s. Modern Primitive "referred to a host of sexual, sartorial, and cultural practices involving ritualistic body modifications like cutting, piercing, and tattooing." Going beyond these, tattoos were seen as "vehicles for personal transformation, a basis for greater spiritual awareness, and a way for participants to reconnect with their physical bodies" (174).

34. Tattoos went officially middle-class with the publication of *TattooTime* in 1982 by Ed Hardy. Hardy, the editor and publisher, is a tattoo artist with a B.F.A. from the San Francisco Art Institute. With high-quality photos and serious articles, the journal's emphasis is on the art, history, and culture of tattooing

and is aimed at an educated readership. This journal has contributed to the "current elitism surrounding middle-class tattooing" (DeMello, *Bodies of Inscription*, 103).

35. Ibid., 140.

36. Ibid., 161, 166, 167.

37. Ibid., 173.

38. Jane Caplan, "Introduction," in *Written on the Body: The Tattoo in European and American History*, edited by Jane Caplan (Princeton, NJ: Princeton University Press, 2000), xv.

39. Caplan, "Introduction," xvii.

40. Stephan Oettermann, "On Display: Tattooed Entertainers in America and Germany," in Caplan, *Written on the Body: The Tattoo in European and American History*, 198.

41. Oettermann, "On Display," 198. Today's Modern Primitives revive the connections with shipwrecked Europeans in the New World: they go native as a way of aligning themselves with a more ritualistic way of life, thus acquiring meaning in a world that they find consumerist and flat. This new aesthetics and ethics has resulted in the adoption of native tattoos as a new fashion. Ironically, for these new tribes, "non-Western tattoos and belief systems [are] liberated from 'primitive' peoples and can now be properly positioned as aspects of fine art." DeMello, *Bodies of Inscription*, 174–184, 181. For a Levinasian reading of tattoos, see Nikki Sullivan, *Tattooed Bodies: Subjectivity, Textuality, Ethics, and Pleasure* (Westport, CT; London: Praeger, 2001).

42. Oettermann, "On Display," 199, 200.

43. Carmella Padilla, *Low 'n Slow: Lowriding in New Mexico* (Santa Fe: Museum of New Mexico Press, 1999), 16.

44. Ibid. The Smithsonian exhibit of *Dave's Dream* was followed by an exhibition dedicated to hot rods and lowriders at the Institute of Contemporary Art in Boston. Customized cars filled the relatively small space of the museum, and alongside them were exhibited lowrider-inspired paintings (Robert Williams, "Snuff Fink," "Blue Collar Bravado Born of a Torque Wrench"); photography (Craig McDean, "I Love Fast Cars"; Alex Harris, "Chamisal, New Mexico, looking north from Juan Domínguez's 1957 Chevrolet Impala"); and cartoons (Coop's), as well as the feminist installations of Sylvie Fleury (where the artist chromes objects from high fashion and transforms regular car parts such as tires and engines through chroming to look like high fashion) and the wordscapes of Fiona Banner that critique the all-too-easy equation of masculinity with cars and speed.

45. See Rubén Ortiz Torres's video *Custom Mambo* (exhibited at the ICA in Boston, 2000). The Border Patrol uses the term "DWM" in order "to describe their rationale for stopping and searching Latino drivers near the Mexican border." See "Driving While Mexican vs. the 4th Amendment," in *Puro Border*, 57–58.

46. Olguín, "Tattoos, Abjection, and the Political Unconscious," 187.

47. Given the tradition of customized cars, Clinton R. Sanders titled his book on tattoos *Customizing the Body: The Art and Culture of Tattooing* (Philadelphia: Temple University Press, 1989).

48. Padilla, *Low 'n Slow*, 16–17.

49. Ibid., 16.

50. Pat Ganahl traces the transformation of early hot-rod cars in Southern California in the 1920s and early 30s (a blue-collar phenomenon) to the creation of stylish customized cars in the late '30s and from there to their disappearance and morphing into lowriders in the late '50s and '60s, while *Low 'n Slow* argues that they were a Chicano creation in the '40s. See "The Hot Rod Culture," in *Customized: Art Inspired by Hot Rods, Lowriders, and American Car Culture*, edited by Nora Donnelly (Boston: Harry N. Abrams, Inc., and the Institute of Contemporary Art, 2000), 13–14.

51. Rubén Ortiz Torres, "Cathedrals on Wheels," in Donnelly, *Customized: Art Inspired by Hot Rods, Lowriders, and American Car Culture*, 37.

52. Padilla, *Low 'n Slow*, 19.

53. Ganahl, "The Hot Rod Culture," 13.

54. Padilla, *Low 'n Slow*, 19.

55. Rubén Ortiz Torres, "Cathedrals on Wheels," 37. Serving perhaps to differentiate lowrider culture in New Mexico and East LA, thus explaining the different dating of their origin, in LA they are Baroque agglomerations; in Southern California, cultural symbols are used by lowriders as a grab bag in Disney fashion. Anything and everything is taken and combined with anything and everything else: "Heroes and iconography from religious and pop worlds share the lowrider pantheon with those from all the

nations of Southern Califas. We find on the cars the inevitable . . . Teenage Mutant Ninja Turtles, Jesus Christ, Native American motifs, Bart Simpson . . . Tweetie and Speedy Gonzalez, Afrocentrism, the Mexican Legend of the Volcanoes, Emiliano Zapata, local homeboys, Disney characters, leprechauns and shamrocks, and so forth" (Ibid.). As with the pintos' transformation of prison tattoos into an art form that has made its way into mainstream culture, lowrider aesthetics too have inspired contemporary painters and installation artists beyond traditional lowriding communities. Ortiz Torres's own work draws on lowriders for inspiration. In his recent installation "The Garden of Earthly Delights," he turns a tractor lawnmower into a performance piece by painting it magenta, and customizing it so that it "dances" (Fisher Gallery, U.S.C., 2002).

56. Quoted in D. A. Brading, *Mexican Phoenix. Our Lady of Guadalupe: Image and Tradition Across Five Centuries* (Cambridge: Cambridge University Press, 2001), xvii.

57. Miroslava Flores, "Tribute to 'La Virgen de Guadalupe' in Beverly Hills and New York, http://aztlan.net/tributetonantzin.htm.

58. Cristina Breen, "Pilgrimage Through North Carolina Ends on Sacred Mexican Holiday," http://www.tepeyac.org/r14.html.

59. Brian Caulfield, "Show of Faith," *Catholic New York*, December 16, 1999, http://cny.org/archive/ft/ft121699.htm (accessed May 3, 2006).

60. Morinis and Crumrine, "La peregrinación: The Latin American Pilgrimage," 5.

61. See Rubén Martínez's description of this miracle in *Crossing Over: A Mexican Family on the Migrant Trail* (New York: Henry Holt, 2001), 302.

62. CNN's 1997 report of this miraculous apparition with a short video clip is still up on the Internet. See http://www.cnn.com/WORLD/9706/22/mexico.virgin/index.html, accessed October 30, 2007, and Chris Kline, "Water stain or sign from God? Mexican faithful flock to subway station," on the same website.

63. For images taken of this apparition, see http://www.visionsofjesuschrist.com/weeping162.htm.

64. Pamela Ferdinand, "Believers See Image of Mary in Window," *Valley News*, Friday, June 27, 2003.

65. http://www.cbsnews.com/stories/2005/04/22/earlyshow/main690089.shtml.

66. Carole Ashley, "Weeping Virgin of Las Vegas. Journal of a Miracle," *Share International* July/August 1999, http://www.share-international.org/archives/signs-miracles/sm_caweeping.htm.

67. Crumrine and Morinis, "La peregrinación: The Latin American Pilgrimage," 9.

68. Ibid.

69. Ibid., 11.

70. As Stafford Poole writes, "The hold that the devotion of Our Lady of Guadalupe has on the Mexican people is universally recognized. It permeates their lives; her picture is to be found throughout the republic. No visitor to the shrine at Tepeyac can fail to be impressed by the depth of faith that it arouses. Nor is this confined to Mexico, for the Empress of the Americas is venerated throughout the Western Hemisphere. Though immigrants have brought her to the United States, the devotion extends far beyond any single ethnic group. More than one predominantly Anglo parish in this country carries the name of the Dark Virgin, and her feast, 12 December, is observed in all dioceses in the United States. In the annals of Catholic Marian devotion Guadalupe has few, if any, equals." *Our Lady of Guadalupe: The Origins and Sources of a Mexican National Symbol, 1531–1797* (Tucson: University of Arizona Press, 1995), 1.

71. The tradition of having posadas has even arrived at Dartmouth College, Harvard University, and other places in New England.

72. See José Vasconcelos, *La raza cósmica: misión de la raza iberoamericana*. Paris: Agencia Mundial de Librería, 192–.

CHAPTER 6

1. deBuys, William, *Enchantment and Exploitation: The Life and Hard Times of a New Mexico Mountain Range* (Albuquerque: University of New Mexico Press, 1985).

2. "The Aura of the Southwest," *New York Times*, Sunday, October 27, 2002. The article promotes New Age resorts such as that at Sedona, where you can "look inward at yourself and outward at Arizona's multihued landscape." The vacation here is a psychic quest and includes "aura cleansings" at resorts that charge $250 a night.

3. Other critics write that Taos and Santa Fe became America's Orient for Eastern aesthetes. Laurie

Beth Kalb, *Crafting Devotions: Tradition in Contemporary New Mexico Santos* (Albuquerque: University of New Mexico Press, 1994), 96.

4. See the Mabel Dodge Luhan House website, http://www.mabeldodgeluhan.com/.

5. See Ilan Stavans's "Introduction" to Ricardo Feierstein's *Mestizo: A Novel* (Albuquerque: University of New Mexico Press, 2000), v; and W. G. Sebald, *The Emigrants*, translated by Michael Hulse (London: Harvill Press, 1997), 24.

6. See the Georgia O'Keeffe page at the website Ellen's Place, http://www.ellensplace.net/okeeffe1.html.

7. Ibid.

8. Lois Palken Rudnick, *Utopian Vistas: The Mabel Dodge Luhan House and American Counterculture* (Albuquerque: University of New Mexico Press, 1996), 6.

9. Quoted in Ibid.

10. Ibid.,5.

11. Ibid., 119.

12. See http://www.spanishcolonial.org.

13. See the catalogue that accompanies the important exhibition "Taos Artists and Their Patrons." Dean A. Porter, et al., *Taos Artists and Their Patrons, 1898–1950* (South Bend: University of Notre Dame Press, 1999).

14. See the Millicent Rogers Museum website, http://millicentrogers.org.

15. James Clifford, "On Ethnographic Allegory," in *Writing Culture: The Poetics and Politics of Ethnography*, edited by James Clifford and George E. Marcus (Berkeley: University of California Press, 1986), 112–113.

16. Alexander H. Girard, "Foreword," in *Folk Art from the Global Village: The Girard Collection of the Museum of International Folk Art* (Santa Fe: Museum of New Mexico Press, 1995), 7.

17. Ibid.

18. *Folk Art from the Global Village: The Girard Collection of the Museum of International Folk Art* (Santa Fe: Museum of New Mexico Press, 1995), 53.

19. New Mexico Arts website, http://www.nmarts.org.

20. Autry National Center, Southwest Museum of the American Indian, http://www.autry-museum.org.

21. Miguel León-Portilla, "Aztlán: From Myth to Reality," translated by Rose Verony, in *The Road to Aztlán: Art from the Mythic Homeland* (Los Angeles County Museum, 2001), 23. See also the works of Carl Lumholtz, Manuel Gamio, Emil W. Haury, Carl Sauer, J. Charles Kelley, and Charles C. DiPeso.

22. Ibid., 30.

23. *Chicano Art: Resistance and Affirmation*, edited by Richard Griswold del Castillo, Teresa McKenna, and Yvonne Yarbro-Bejarano (Los Angeles: Wight Art Gallery, University of California, 1991).

24. I thank Judy Baca for telling me the history of this counter-exhibition, "The Other Road to Aztlán."

25. *Santa Fe El Norte*, Wednesday, August 21, 2002.

26. http://www.den-cabrini-shrine.org.

27. The *Boston Globe* ran a story (Thursday, September 19, 2002) about this shrine. Trying to dramatize the widespread effects of the drought that has plagued the Southwest, the headline read: "In pinch, nuns tap city for holy water." Perhaps not quite coincidentally, this spring was found on property thought to be barren, and which Mother Cabrini had therefore bought quite cheaply to serve as a summer camp for an orphanage. A shrewd businesswoman, the *Globe* tells us, Mother Cabrini went on to found more than 60 schools, orphanages, and hospitals. The nuns today are trying to raise $250,000 to supply the shrine with city water so that the holy water is preserved for the pilgrims.

28. Enrique R. Lamadrid, "Santa Madre Tierra—The Holy Mother Earth of Chimayó," in *Pilgrimage to Chimayó: Contemporary Portrait of a Living Tradition*, edited by Sam Howarth and Enrique R. Lamadrid (Santa Fe: Museum of New Mexico Press, 1999).

29. Ibid., 16.

30. Ibid., 18.

31. While I was there, the priest was actually throwing everything into a cardboard box and trying to give some of the toys (little cars, dolls, glasses, cigarette packs, beads, etc.) to the visitors. When a little girl refused to take something he was handing her, he said (unfortunately): "Ah! Of course. You are a girl, and women are only interested in money."

32. Teresa Gisbert, "Prologue," in Martha J. Egan, *Relicarios: Devotional Miniatures from the Americas* (Santa Fe: Museum of New Mexico Press, 1993), viii.

33. Alan Morinis and N. Ross Crumrine, "La peregrinación: The Latin American Pilgrimage," in *Pilgrimages in Latin America*, edited by N. Ross Crumrine and Alan Morinis (New York: Greenwood Press, 1991), 7.

34. Ibid., 17.

35. Lamadrid, "Santa Madre Tierra," 21.

36. Henry F. Dobyns, "Do-It-Yourself Religion: The Diffusion of Folk Catholicism on Mexico's Northern Frontier 1821–1846," in Crumrine and Morinis, *Pilgrimages in Latin America*, 53–68.

37. Marta Weigle, *The Penitentes of the Southwest* (Santa Fe: Ancient City Press, 1970), 15–17. See also Alberto López Pulido, *The Sacred World of the Penitentes* (Washington and London: Smithsonian Institution Press, 2000); Lorayne Ann Horka-Follick, *Los Hermanos Penitentes: A Vestige of Medievalism in Southwestern United States* (Los Angeles: Westernlore Press, 1969); Martha Weigle, *Brothers of Light, Brothers of Blood: The Penitentes of the Southwest* (Albuquerque: University of New Mexico Press, 1976); David J. Weber, *The Mexican Frontier, 1821–1846: The American Southwest under Mexico* (Albuquerque: University of New Mexico Press, 1982); Chris Wilson, *The Myth of Santa Fe: Creating a Modern Regional Tradition* (Albuquerque: University of New Mexico Press, 1997); *En divina luz: The Penitente Moradas of New Mexico*, photographs by Craig Varjabedian, essay by Michel Wallis (Albuquerque: University of New Mexico Press, 1994).

38. Weigle, *The Penitentes of the Southwest*, 18.

39. Ibid.

40. Ibid., 16.

41. Viewed and viewing themselves as translators of the divine, or painters of the memory of God, local santeros acquired great prestige in both artistic and psychic terms. Indeed, to this day, their privileged position parallels Native Americans' psychic privileges in the popular imaginary. In turn, many santeros claim that divine inspiration grants their works an aura absent from commercially produced objects, despite the fact that many of them produce religious artifacts for both churches and home altars and for the tourist and fine art markets.

42. Enrique R. Lamadrid, "Luz y sombra: The Poetics of Mestizo Identity," in *Nuevo México Profundo: Rituals of an Indo-Hispano Homeland*, photographs by Miguel Gandert (Santa Fe: Museum of New Mexico Press, 2000), 1.

43. Quoted in Ibid., 2.

44. *The Book of New Mexico* symptomatically begins in the following way: "The children had carried their supper out to the banco that ran along the west wall, to watch the sun set behind the Valley ranges." Mary Austin, *Starry Adventure. Book 1. The Book of New Mexico* (Boston: Houghton Mifflin, 1931), 3.

45. Increasingly, U.S. or European New Agers seeking shamans are transferring this U.S.-specific way of viewing Indians to Latin America and endowing particular individuals with psychic powers, to the utter ridicule of most Latin Americans.

CHAPTER 7

1. This misplacement not only continues unabated but has also increased exponentially since the neoconservative movement took hold of this country. When I teach classes on the US-Mexico border, most of my students confess complete ignorance of the Treaty of Guadalupe-Hidalgo (1848), despite coming from some of the best schools in the United States. Efforts to erase the Hispanic colonial legacy of this country from school curricula are only intensifying. A recent (April 25, 2008) e-mail from David Carrasco alerted scholars of Latino Studies about legislation in Arizona making its way through the legal system to ban MEChA and Mexican-American Studies outright in the interests of homeland security. It reads: "Arizona legislation will outlaw MEChA and Mexican-American Studies. The Appropriations Committee of the Arizona House of Representatives has approved provisions to a 'Homeland Security' measure that would essentially destroy the Movimiento Estudiantil Chicano de Aztlán (MEChA) and Mexican-American study programs in the state's public schools, colleges, and universities. The anti-Mexican provisions to SB1108 were approved yesterday and the bill is now scheduled for a vote by the full House. The provisions would withhold funding to schools whose courses 'denigrate American values and the teachings of European based civilization.' One section of SB1108 would bar public schools,

238

community colleges, and universities from allowing organizations to operate on campus if it is 'based in whole or in part on race-based criteria,' a provision Rep. Russell Pearce said is aimed at MEChA. Pearce is a Republican and the Chairman of the Appropriations Committee out of Mesa, Arizona. According to Chairman Pearce, SB1108 would also bar teaching practices that 'overtly encourage dissent from American values' such as Raza Studies at the Tucson Unified School District. In addition, SB1108 mandates the State Superintendent of Public Instruction to confiscate books and teaching materials that are deemed anti-American. Chairman Pearce said some of the teaching materials amount to 'sedition' by suggesting that the current border between the United States and Mexico disappear with La Raza taking over the American Southwest. One book that would be confiscated mentioned by Pearce is *Occupied America—A History of Chicanos* by Professor Rodolfo Acuña." See also http://antiracismdsa.blogspot.com/2008/04/arizona-republicans-seek-to-ban-mecha.html.

2. Sheila Ortiz Taylor and Sandra Ortiz Taylor, *Imaginary Parents: A Family Autobiography* (Albuquerque: University of New Mexico Press, 1996). Cited hereafter in text.

3. Juan Bruce-Novoa, back-cover review of *Imaginary Parents*.

4. Telephone conversation with Sandra Ortiz Taylor, summer 2001.

5. An early version of this chapter, "Un altar a la presencia: Los objetos hallados, la fotografía, la memoria y la identidad latina en EEUU," appeared in *Hibridismos culturales: La literatura y cultura de los latinos en los Estados Unidos*, ed. Alberto Sandoval-Sánchez and Frances Aparicio, *Revista Iberoamericana* LXXI–212 (2005): 745–762.

6. While their name should be Taylor Ortiz, the sisters have inverted the order. As Sheila Ortiz Taylor explained in an e-mail, "I was born Sheila Lea Taylor. I took Ortiz as my middle name around 1980, as did Sandra. I published under that name: Sheila Ortiz Taylor; 1982 was the first time. I legally changed it about 10 years ago to Sheila Ortiz-Taylor because the Ortiz kept disappearing. I wanted to glue it on. But I continue to publish under Ortiz Taylor. My mother never spoke Spanish, nor did her 12 brothers and sisters, because they grew up in a time when Mexican-Americans were disrespected and even abused. My father spoke Spanish; he learned it as a second language early in life. He knew she didn't speak Spanish and thought it was a loss. He tried to help her learn Spanish, but she resisted him. It had become a power play. But she had grown up hearing her mother and aunts speaking Spanish in the kitchen. My own theory is that she simply absorbed it subconsciously" (Thursday, June 28, 2007). I thank the anonymous reader from the University of Texas Press for asking for this clarification.

7. For a very thorough discussion of this text regarding the connection between photography and memory, see Timothy Dow Adams, "Case History: Sheila Ortiz Taylor and Sandra Ortiz Taylor," in *Light Writings and Life Writing: Photography in Autobiography* (Chapel Hill: University of North Carolina Press, 2000), 57–78.

8. See Juan Bruce-Novoa, "Sheila Ortiz Taylor's *Faultline*: A Third-Woman Utopia," in *Confluencia* 6, no. 2 (Spring 1991): 75–87; and also Karen Christian, "Will the 'Real Chicano' Please Stand Up? The Challenge of John Retchy and Sheila Ortiz Taylor to Chicano Essentialism," *Americas Review* 20, no. 2 (1992): 89–104.

9. In this manner, and because the photographs are used within the miniature installations, the Ortiz Taylors corroborate Elizabeth Edwards's assertion that photographs obtain their privileged status as "conduits of memory" precisely when they become "refracted through the photograph's materiality." Elizabeth Edwards, "Photographs as Objects of Memory," in *Material Memories: Design and Evocation*, edited by Marius Kwint, Christopher Breward, and Jeremy Aynsley (Oxford: Berg, 1999), 221. See also Gaston Bachelard's classical study, *The Poetics of Space*, translated by Maria Jolas (Boston: Beacon Press, 1994).

10. Edwards, "Photographs as Objects of Memory, 222.

11. Ibid., 222, 225.

12. Jeremy Seabrook reports an interview he had with Mrs. Taylor, nearly ninety, who, as she leafs through the family photographs in a shoe box tells him: "There's my Harry; he died . . . after just six years of marriage. . . . My father said I could go home, but I wanted to show him I could survive. These pictures are the proof that I did it. I don't want them to fall into the hands of strangers, people who'd just think it was a pile of rubbish and throw it out with the rest of my bits and pieces. 'My life is in that box.'" Jeremy Seabrook, "My Life Is in That Box," in *Family Snaps: The Meaning of Domestic Photography*, edited by Jo Spence and Patricia Holland (London: Virago, 1991), 179.

13. An interesting reflection on this process is Marianne Hirsch's concept of "postmemory": "to describe the relationship of children of survivors of cultural or collective trauma to the experiences of

their parents, experiences that they 'remember' only as the stories and images with which they grew up, but that are so powerful, so monumental, as to constitute memories in their own right." Marianne Hirsch, "Projected Memory: Holocaust Photographs in Personal and Public Fantasy," in *Acts of Memory: Cultural Recall in the Present*, edited by Mieke Bal, Jonathan Crewe, and Leo Spitzer (Hanover, NH: University Press of New England, 1999), 8.

14. Lorie Novak, *Collected Visions*, http://cvisions.cat.nyu.edu/.

15. Susan Stewart, *On Longing: Narratives of the Miniature, the Gigantic, the Souvenir, the Collection* (Durham, NC: Duke University Press, 1993), 49.

16. Stafford reflects on the function of household cabinets of wonders. "Sorting and resorting a heterogeneous mountain of historical mementoes," she writes, "became a means for family members to witness and talk about generational continuities or discontinuities. One era's familiar objects turn alien in another epoch. Memories, if they are to persist, have to be incorporated into the stuff of contemporary stories. The display of oddities as a component of ordinary household furnishings could have offered . . . any tightly knit group—opportunities for rethinking, making sense of, and telling themselves and their guests how they and *this* particular cluster of artifacts fit into what otherwise would only be the vast, impersonal scheme of things [. . .]. Long before there was a museum setting as such, the mutable *Wunderschrank* invited the sensory structuring of common experience. Like other smart tools, such furniture-to-think-with not only had a socializing effect but also contributed to the ongoing formation of human intelligence." Barbara Maria Stafford, "Revealing Technologies/Magical Domains," in *Devices of Wonder: From the World in a Box to Images on a Screen*, edited by Barbara Maria Stafford and Frances Terpak (Los Angeles: Getty Research Institute, 2001), 11.

17. Emphasis mine. May 22, 2001, e-mail from Sheila Ortiz Taylor.

18. Emphasis mine. See Toni Morrison's moving essay, "The Site of Memory," in *Out There: Marginalization and Contemporary Cultures*, edited by Russell Ferguson, Martha Gever, Trin T. Minh-ha, and Cornel West (New York: New Museum of Contemporary Art, 1990), 302.

19. Seabrook, "My Life Is in That Box," 184.

20. Sheila Ortiz Taylor, May 22, 2001, e-mail.

21. In their visit to Dartmouth, Sheila and Sandra Ortiz Taylor explained their father's relationship to their mother in these terms. Her refusal to speak Spanish (or to learn it from him) and, at the same time, her ability to "suddenly" understand the language when visiting Mexico after his death signal her refusal of colonialism and exoticization that made for quite violent family relations.

22. See Laura E. Pérez's chapter "Altar, Alter," in *Chicana Art: The Politics of Spiritual and Aesthetic Altarities* (Durham, NC: Duke University Press, 2007). This important book unfortunately came out as *Misplaced* was already in press.

23. Susan Stewart, quoted by Edwards, "Photographs as Objects of Memory," 230.

24. See Fazal Sheikh's photographs in *A Sense of Common Ground* (1996) and his work on Afghanistan in *The Victor Weeps* (1998).

25. E-mail from Sheila Ortiz Taylor (Thursday, June 14, 2001).

26. This derogatory term was used in the U.S. Southwest in the nineteenth century to refer to Mexicans. There was even an early discriminatory California statute, the Greaser Act of 1855.

27. Tomás Ybarra-Frausto, "Notes from Losaida: A Foreword," in *Velvet Barrios: Popular Culture and Chicana/o Sexualities*, edited by Alicia Gaspar de Alba (New York: Palgrave, 2003), xv.

28. Dan R. Goddard, "Fotoseptiembre: Various Locations," *Artlies* (Fall 2000): 106.

29. Sandra Ortiz Taylor brought my attention to the connection between her work and that of contemporary Mexican artists who have revived and reinvented the tradition. See "Collective Memory: Foto-Esculturas from Mexico City," the pamphlet accompanying the exhibit held in 1999 in Mexico City and at the Russell Hill Rogers Gallery in San Antonio, Texas (August 24–October 28, 2000), curated by Pamela Scheinman. The Latino side of the exhibit was curated by Kathy Armstrong-Gillis.

30. See also Pérez, *Chicana Art*.

31. Roland Barthes, *Camera Lucida: Reflections on Photography* (New York: Hill and Wang, 1981), 9.

32. Edwards, "Photographs as Objects of Memory," 234.

33. As we saw earlier, Erving Goffman, in his study of "total" institutions (such as jails, psychiatric wards, monasteries, military institutions, etc.), points out that one of the main things that characterize them and that they all share is the process of total "deculturation" of the individual (of his/her identity and being). Deculturation happens as a consequence of the relative isolation of total institutions from

the rest of the world and because, upon entry, the individual is stripped of his/her "identity kit" (cosmetics, clothes, photographs, etc.), which each person uses to individualize him- or herself. These personal identity kits are replaced by a standard uniform. See Erving Goffman, *Asylums* (New York: Doubleday-Anchor, 1961), 20.

34. Ybarra-Frausto, "Notes from Losaida," xvi–xvii.

CHAPTER 8

An early version of this chapter appeared as "Sandra Ramos: La vida no cabe en una maleta," in *Imaginarios Femeninos en Latinoamérica*, ed. Alicia Ortega and Susana Rosano, special issue of *Revista Iberoamericana* LXXI–210 (2005): 35–53; an even earlier talk was posted by Sandra Ramos on her website, http://www.art-havana.com/sandra/. All translations are mine unless otherwise stated.

1. The entire poem "The New Colossus" reads as follows:

> Not like the brazen giant of Greek fame,
> with conquering limbs astride from land to land;
> Here at our sea-washed, sunset gates shall stand
> a mighty woman with a torch, whose flame
> is the imprisoned lightning, and her name
> Mother of Exiles. From her beacon-hand
> Glows world-wide welcome; her mild eyes command
> The air-bridged harbor that twin cities frame,
> "Keep, ancient lands, your storied pomp!" cries she
> with silent lips. "Give me your tired, your poor,
> Your huddled masses yearning to breathe free,
> The wretched refuse of your teeming shores,
> Send these, the homeless, tempest-tost to me,
> I lift my lamp beside the golden door!"

2. Louis DeSipio, "Cuban Miami: Seeking Identity in a Political Borderland," *Latin American Research Review* 38, no. 2 (2003), 207.

3. Ibid., 214.

4. See the impressive compilation of Cuban exile narratives of Daniel C. Maratos and Marnesba D. Hill, *Escritores de la diáspora cubana: Manual biobliográfico* (Washington, D.C.: Library of Congress, 1986).

5. Ruth Behar, ed., *Bridges to Cuba/Puentes a Cuba* (Ann Arbor: University of Michigan Press, 1995), 9.

6. As DeSipio writes, Robert M. Levine in *Cuban Miami* argues that the Miami Cuban community's anger about the Democrats' treatment of Elián drove Cuban-Americans even more solidly than usual into the Republican camp, helping to elect George Bush in a close national and Florida election ("Cuban Miami," 215).

7. Ibid., 214.

8. I saw a class of schoolchildren at a museum and was shocked to learn from one of the guards that the girls were 14 and 15 years old, but they looked 9 or 10.

9. Gerardo Mosquera, "New Cuban Art Y2K," in *Art Cuba: The New Generation*, edited by Holly Block (New York: Harry N. Abrams, 2001), 13.

10. Eugenio Valdéz Figueroa, "Trajectories of a Rumor: Cuban Art in the Postwar Period," in *Art Cuba: The New Generation*, edited by Holly Block (New York: Harry N. Abrams, 2001), 21.

11. Conversation with the artist in Havana, December 2000.

12. Saskia Sassen, *Guests and Aliens* (New York: New Press, 1999); and *Losing Control? Sovereignty in an Age of Globalization* (New York: Columbia University Press, 1996). See also Roger Rouse's seminal essay, "Mexican Migration and the Social Space of Postmodernism," in *Between Two Words: Mexican Immigrants in the United States*, edited by David G. Gutiérrez (Wilmington, DE: Scholarly Resources, 1996), 247–263.

13. Luis Rafael Sánchez, *La guagua aérea*. San Juan, PR: Editorial Cultural, 1994.

14. Alberto Sandoval-Sánchez, "Puerto Rican Identity Up in the Air: Air Migration, Its Cultural Representations, and Me 'Cruzando el Charco,'" in *Puerto Rican Jam: Essays on Culture and Politics*, edited by

Frances Negrón-Muntaner and Ramón Grosfoguel (Minneapolis: University of Minnesota Press, 1997), 189–208.

15. Lourdes Casal, "La Habana 1968," in *Palabras juntan revolución* (La Habana: Casa de las Américas, 1981), 49.

16. Lourdes Casal, *Palabras juntan revolución* (La Habana: Casa de las Américas, 1981), 61.

17. Ibid., 31.

18. Eduardo Machado, "A Return to Cuba, A Search for Himself," *New York Times*, Sunday, October 21, 2001.

19. Ibid.

20. Brison, "Trauma Narrative and the Remaking of the Self," in *Acts of Memory: Cultural Recall in the Present*, edited by Mieke Bal, Jonathan Crewe, and Leo Spitzer (Hanover, NH: University Press of New England, 1999), 39.

21. Susan Brison concludes, "I take these comments seriously, as more than mere façons de parler, in part because, after enduring a near-fatal murder attempt and sexual assault, I could no longer find in myself the self I once was." Ibid. See also Susan Brison, *Aftermath: Violence and the Remaking of a Self* (Princeton: Princeton University Press, 2002); *Trauma: Explorations in Memory*, edited by Cathy Caruth (Baltimore: Johns Hopkins University Press, 1995); Marianne Hirsch, *Family Frames: Photography, Narrative, and Postmemory* (Cambridge, MA: Harvard University Press, 1997); Ruth Leys, *Trauma: A Genealogy* (Chicago: University of Chicago Press, 2000); and Irene Kacandes, *Talk Fiction: Literature and the Talk Explosion* (Lincoln: University of Nebraska Press, 2001).

22. Brison, "Trauma Narrative," 41.

23. Casal, *Palabras juntan revolución*, 98.

24. Gustavo Pérez Firmat, *Cincuenta lecciones de exilio y desexilio* (Miami: Ediciones Universal, 2000), 7.

25. See Leslie Camhi, "Art; Her Body, Herself," in *New York Times*, June 20, 2004. http://query.nytimes.com/gst/fullpage.html?res=9502E1DD1E30F933A15755C0A9629C8B63&sec=travel&pagewanted=print. For an essay that sums up Ana Mendieta's desperate need to merge with Cuba, see Todd Dvorak, "Ana Mendieta: siempre en la búsqueda de la pertenencia," *La Opinión*, Los Angeles, April 10, 2005, http://www.cubanet.org/CNews/y05/apr05/11011.htm.

26. Pérez Firmat, *Cincuenta lecciones de exilio y desexilio*, 9–10.

27. Ibid.

28. Sandra Ramos, e-mail, August 30, 2003.

29. The payer of promises is an individual who attempts to reflect upon a way of life where primitive and marginal cultural traits persist. He resists, he is marginal, he is the materialization of the other ["pretende reflexionar sobre la subsistencia de modos de vida y patrones culturales de fuerte carácter primitivo y marginal como los Pagadores de promesas a San Lázaro . . . y mantenerse como tradición incluso en un país cuya ideología oficial ha sido el socialismo. . . . El pagador de promesas es un individuo que se resiste, es un marginal, es la materialización de lo otro"]. All the above quotes are taken from the exhibition notes accompanying Ramos's works. Sandra Ramos: Obra Plástica, 1989–1999. CD-ROM in the author's collection.

EPILOGUE

1. All citations in this section are from the museum's pamphlet "Feather Headdress."

2. See the web report "Found Objects. What archaeologists can gain from markets, or lose by ignoring them," by Jeremy Lott. January 2004, http://www.reason.com/news/show/28995.html (accessed November 4, 2007). Even *Archaeology: A Publication of the Archaeological Institute of America* on the Internet reports that Iraqi curators prepared in anticipation of massive plundering. http://www.archaeology.org/0305/etc/iraq.html (accessed November 7, 2007).

3. Simón Marchán Fiz, "Los placeres del parecido entre las brumas de la ficción," in *Cristóbal Toral: Pinturas, acuarelas y dibujos, 1967–1996* (Lima: Museo de Arte de Lima, Exposion Itinerante en Iberoamérica, 1997–1998), 53–69, 61.

4. For an important source on connecting violence, torture, and dehumanization during the Third Reich, see Jean Améry's *At the Mind's Limits: Contemplations by a Survivor on Auschwitz and Its Realities*, translated by Sidney Rosenfeld and Stella P. Rosenfeld (Bloomington and Indianapolis: Indiana Univer-

sity Press, 1980). In this shattering autobiography, a "phenomenological description of the existence of the victim" (xiii), Améry theorizes that the materialization of Nazi ideology was the direct result of and stood in direct relation to the dehumanization of camp victims and their transformation into refuse. As he notes, "But only in torture does the transformation of the person into flesh become complete. Frail in the face of violence, yelling out in pain, awaiting no help, capable of no resistance, the tortured person is only a body, and nothing else beside that" (33).

5. See Sergio González Rodríguez, *Huesos en el desierto* (Barcelona: Anagrama, 2002); and María Socorro Tabuenca Córdoba, "*Baile de fanstamas* en Ciudad Juárez al final/principio del milenio," in *Más allá de la ciudad letrada: Crónicas y espacios urbanos* (Pittsburgh: Biblioteca de América, IILL, 2003), edited by Boris Muñoz and Silvia Spitta, 411–438; Ursula Biemann's short documentary *Performing the Border* (1999); and Lourdes Portillo's documentary *Señorita Extraviada* (2001).

6. See *Trash*, edited by John Knechtel (Cambridge: MIT Press, 2007).

7. http://www.wola.org/index.php?option=com_frontpage&Itemid=1. See also Roselyn Costantino, "Feminicide, Impunity, and Citizenship: The Old and New in the Struggle for Justice in Guatemala," *Chicana/Latina Studies* 6, no. 1 (Fall 2006): 108–120.

8. Daniela Rossell, *Ricas y famosas* (Madrid, España: Turner Publicaciones, 2002). I repeatedly wrote the photographer for permission to reproduce some of her photos to no avail.

9. Photographed by *Time*'s fall 2004 issue, "Luxury Fever: How Long Will it Last?"

10. Patricia McLaughlin, "Let Them Eat Alligator! Luxury Spending Is Booming. Is $1,000 Too Much for an Omelet?" *Valley News* (Sunday, September 19, 2004): C2.

11. For a beautiful meditation on kitsch and collecting, see Celeste Olalguiaga, *The Artificial Kingdom: A Treasury of the Kitsch Experience with Remarkable Objects of Art and Nature, Extraordinary Events, Eccentric Biography, and Original Theory plus Many Wonderful Illustrations Selected by the Author* (New York: Pantheon, 1998).

12. Benjamin, *Illuminations*, 239.

13. Julio Cortázar, *Final del juego*, edited by Jaime Alazraki (Madrid: Anaya & Mario Muchnik, 1995).

14. Benjamin, *Illuminations*, 239.

15. John Prest, *The Garden of Eden: The Botanic Garden and the Re-Creation of Paradise* (New Haven, CT; London: Yale University Press, 1981), 6.

16. Ibid., 10.

17. Indeed, the West tends to view South America and particularly the Amazon as a precious, immense Garden of Eden. The Amazon forest, for example, is being held up as the "lungs of the earth," and Brazilian farmers' slash burning is being protested. Brazilians, in return, retort that Europeans destroyed their forests and habitat, so why now insist on a pristine environment in Latin America? Despite the superficiality of these arguments back and forth, Catholic priests, heirs to liberation theology, have begun recently to engage in what is being called "liberation ecology," aware that environmental depredation affects the poor most. Even Pope Benedict, instrumental in destroying the liberation theology movement in the 1960s and 70s in Latin America and a rabid anti-leftist, is speaking out in favor of the environment and environmental justice. His 2007 New Year's Day speech is being widely quoted: "Respect for nature is closely linked to the need to establish, between individuals and between nations, relationships that are attentive to the dignity of the person and capable of satisfying his or her authentic needs. The destruction of the environment, its improper or selfish use, and the violent hoarding of the earth's resources cause grievances, conflicts, and wars precisely because they are the consequence of an inhumane concept of development." Marilyn Berlin Snell, "Bulldozers & Blasphemy: In Latin America, Catholics Are Standing Up to Those Who Covet Their Gold and Timber," *Sierra* (September/October, 2007): 36–76.

WORKS CITED

Adams, Timothy Dow. "Case History: Sheila Ortiz Taylor and Sandra Ortiz Taylor." In *Light Writings and Life Writing: Photography in Autobiography*, 57–78. Chapel Hill: University of North Carolina Press, 2000.

Alarcón, Norma. "Chicana's Feminist Literature: A Re-Vision through Malintzín, Or, Malintzín: Putting Flesh Back on the Objects." In *This Bridge Called My Back: Writings by Radical Women of Color*, edited by Cherríe Moraga and Gloria Anzaldúa. Watertown: Persephone Press, 1981.

———. "Traduttora, Traditora: A Paradigmatic Figure of Chicana Feminism." *Cultural Critique* 13 (1990).

Alegría, Claribel. *Fugues*. Translated by D. J. Flakoll. Willimantic, CT: Curbstone Press, 1993.

Améry, Jean. *At the Mind's Limits: Contemplations by a Survivor on Auschwitz and Its Realities*. Translated by Sidney Rosenfeld and Stella P. Rosenfeld. Bloomington and Indianapolis: Indiana University Press, 1980.

Andrade, Farnese de, and Rodrigo Naves. *Farnese de Andrade*. São Paulo: Cosac & Naify, 2002.

Aparicio, Frances R., and Susana Chávez-Silverman, eds. *Tropicalizations: Transcultural Representations of Latinidad*. Hanover, NH: Dartmouth College Press, 1997.

Apolito, Paolo. *The Internet and the Madonna: Religious Visionary Experience on the Web*. Translated by Antony Shugaar. Chicago: University of Chicago Press, 2005.

Appadurai, Arjun. "Introduction: Commodities and the Politics of Value." In *The Social Life of Things: Commodities in Cultural Perspective*, edited by Arjun Appadurai, 3–63. Cambridge: Cambridge University Press, 1986.

Arciniegas, Germán. *Cuando América completó la tierra*. Bogotá: Villegas Editores, 2001.

Ashley, Carole. "Weeping Virgin of Las Vegas. Journal of a Miracle." *Share International* July/August 1999. http://www.share-international.org/archives/signs-miracles/sm_caweeping.htm (accessed April 24, 2006).

Austin, Mary. *Starry Adventure*. Book 1. *The Book of New Mexico*. Boston: Houghton Mifflin, 1931.

Autry National Center. Southwest Museum of the American Indian. http://www.autry-museum.org (accessed May 2, 2006).

Baarsen, Reinier. "The Cabinet as Gesamtkunstwerk: Philipp Hainhofer and His Followers." In *17th-Century Cabinets*, translated by John Rudge, 11–21. Amsterdam: Waanders Publishers, Rijksmuseum, 2000.

Bachelard, Gaston. *The Poetics of Space*. Translated by Maria Jolas. Boston: Beacon Press, 1994.

Barras de Aragón, Francisco de las. "Una historia del Perú contenida en un cuadro al óleo de 1799." *Boletín de la Real Sociedad Española* 12 (1912): 224–285.

Barthes, Roland. *Camera Lucida: Reflections on Photography*. New York: Hill and Wang, 1981.

Baudrillard, Jean. *The System of Objects*. Translated by James Benedict. London: Verso, 1996.

Becoming Animal: Contemporary Art in the Animal Kingdom. Edited by Nato Thompson with Joseph Thompson and Christoph Cox. North Adams, MA: MASSMoCA, 2005.

Behar, Ruth. *Bridges to Cuba/Puentes a Cuba*. Ann Arbor: University of Michigan Press, 1995.

Belting, Hans. *Likeness and Presence: A History of the Image before the Era of Art*. Translated by Edmund Jephcott. Chicago: University of Chicago Press, 1994.

Bemberg, Maria Luisa. *I Don't Want to Talk About It* [*De eso no se habla*]. Aura Films, 1995.

Benedict, Barbara M. *Curiosity: A Cultural History of Early Modern Inquiry*. Chicago: University of Chicago Press, 2001.

Benítez, J. J. *El misterio de la Virgen de Guadalupe: Sensacionales descubrimientos en los ojos de la Virgen mexicana*. Barcelona: Planeta, 1982.

Benjamin, Walter. *Illuminations*. Translated by Harry Zohn. New York: Schocken Books, 1969.

Bergson, Henri. *Matter and Memory*. Translated by Nancy Margaret Paul and W. Scott Palmer. New York: Zone, 1988.

Blanchard, Laura. "Remembering Gretchen Worden." Northwest South Philly. http://www.southphilly-blocks.org/photos_essays/gretchens_creche/ (accessed May 1, 2006).

Blom, Philipp. *To Have and to Hold: An Intimate History of Collectors and Collecting.* Woodstock and New York: Overlook Press, 2004.

Bodyworlds: The Anatomical Exhibition of Real Human Bodies. Institute for Plastination. http://www.bodyworlds.com/en/pages/home.asp (accessed April 24, 2006).

Boone, Elizabeth Hill, and Tom Cummins, eds. *Native Traditions in the Postconquest World.* Washington, D.C.: Dumbarton Oaks Research Library and Collection, 1998.

Borges, Jorge Luis. *Elogio de la sombra, Obras Completas: 1952–1972.* Barcelona: Emecé Editors, 1996.

———. *In Praise of Darkness.* Translated by Norman Thomas di Giovanni. New York: E. P. Dutton and Co., Inc., 1974.

Brading, D. A. *Mexican Phoenix. Our Lady of Guadalupe: Image and Tradition Across Five Centuries.* Cambridge: Cambridge University Press, 2001.

Breen, Cristina. "Pilgrimage Through N.C. Ends in NYC on Sacred Mexican Holiday." http://www.tepeyac.org/r14.html (accessed March 9, 2008).

Brison, Susan. *Aftermath: Violence and the Remaking of a Self.* Princeton: Princeton University Press, 2002.

———. "Trauma Narrative and the Remaking of the Self." In *Acts of Memory: Cultural Recall in the Present,* edited by Mieke Bal, Jonathan Crewe, and Leo Spitzer, 39–54. Hanover, NH: University Press of New England, 1999.

Brown, Bill, ed. *Things.* Chicago: University of Chicago Press, 2004.

Browning, Tod. *Freaks.* Metro-Goldwyn Mayer, 1932.

Bruce-Novoa, Juan. "Sheila Ortiz Taylor's *Faultline*: A Third-Woman Utopia." *Confluencia* 6, no. 2 (Spring 1991): 75–87.

Brüning, Jochen. "Der Teil und das Ganze—Motive einer Austellung." In *Theater der Natur und Kunst: Theatrum Naturae et Artis,* 20–30. Berlin: Humboldt-Universität, 2000.

Buffon, Georges Louis Leclerc. *Histoire naturelle, générale et particulière.* Paris: De l'imprimerie royale, 1749.

———. *Histoire naturelle, générale et particulière avec la description du cabinet du roy.* 2nd ed. Paris: De l'imprimerie royale, MDCCL: 1750 Seconde Edition.

Cabinets of Curiosities: Four Artists, Four Visions: Martha Glowacki, Mark Lorenzi, Natasha Nicholson, Mary Alice Wimmer. Exhibition organized by Natasha Nicholson, with essays by Joseph Goldyne and Thomas H. Garver. Madison, WI: Elvehjem Museum of Art, 2000.

Calatayud, María de los Ángeles, ed. *Catálogo de documentos del Real Gabinete de Historia Natural (1752–1786).* Madrid: Consejo Superior de Investigaciones Científicas, Museo Nacional de Ciencias Naturales, 1987.

———. *Catálogo de las expediciones y viajes científicos españoles a América y Filipinas (Siglos XVIII y XIX).* Madrid: Museo Nacional de Ciencias Naturales, 1984.

———. *Diario de Don Francisco de Paula Martínez y Sáez. Miembro de la Comisión Científica del Pacífico (1862–1865).* Madrid: Consejo Superior de Investigaciones Científicas, 1994.

———. *Pedro Franco Dávila: Primer Director del Real Gabinete de Historia Natural Fundado por Carlos III.* Madrid: Consejo Superior de Investigaciones Científicas, Museo Nacional de Ciencias Naturales, 1988.

Caplan, Jane, ed. *Written on the Body: The Tattoo in European and American History.* Princeton, NJ: Princeton University Press, 2000.

Carpentier, Alejo. "The Baroque and the Marvelous Real." In *Magical Realism: Theory, History, Community,* edited by Lois Zamora and Wendy Faris, 89–108. Durham, NC: Duke University Press, 1995. Originally published as "Lo barroco y lo real maravilloso," in *La novela latinoamericana en vísperas de un nuevo siglo y otros ensayos* (México, DF: Siglo XXI, 1981).

———. *El reino de este mundo.* México: E.D.I.A.P.S.A., 1949.

Caruth, Cathy, ed. *Trauma: Explorations in Memory.* Baltimore: Johns Hopkins University Press, 1995.

Casal, Lourdes. *Palabras juntan revolución.* La Habana: Casa de las Américas, 1981.

Cash, Marie Romero. *Living Shrines: Home Altars of New Mexico.* Photographs by Siegfried Halus. Santa Fe: Museum of New Mexico Press, 1998.

Castillo, Abel Romeo. *Don Pedro Franco Dávila (1711–1786)*. Guayaquil: Editorial Casa de la Cultura Ecuatoriana, 1966.

———. *Pedro Franco Dávila: El sabio guayaquileño olvidado*. Guayaquil: Ediciones Casa de la Cultura, 1952.

Caulfield, Brian. "Show of Faith." *Catholic New York*, December 16, 1999. http://cny.org/archive/ft/ft121699.htm (accessed May 3, 2006).

Cavafy, C. P. *The Essential Cavafy*. Translated from the Greek by Edmund Keeley and Dimitri Gondicas. Selected and with an Introduction by Edmund Keeley. New Jersey: Ecco Press, 1995.

Cerny, Charlene, and Suzanne Seriff, eds. *Recycled, Re-Seen: Folk Art From the Global Scrap Heap*. New York: Harry N. Abrams, 1996.

Christian, Karen. "Will the 'Real Chicano' Please Stand Up? The Challenge of John Retchy and Sheila Ortiz Taylor to Chicano Essentialism." *Americas Review* 20, no. 2 (1992): 89–104.

Cisneros, Sandra. "Guadalupe the Sex Goddess." In *Goddess of the Americas/La diosa de las Américas: Writings on the Virgin of Guadalupe*, edited by Ana Castillo. New York: Riverhead Books, 1996.

Clavigero, Francisco. *Historia antigua de México*. Edited by R. P. Mariano Cuevas. México: Editorial Porrúa, 1964.

Clifford, James. "On Ethnographic Allegory." In *Writing Culture: The Poetics and Politics of Ethnography*, edited by James Clifford and George E. Marcus. Berkeley: University of California Press, 1986.

———. *The Predicament of Culture: Twentieth-Century Ethnography, Literature, and Art*. Cambridge: Harvard University Press, 1988.

Cohen, Bernard. *The New World as a Source of Science for Europe. Actes du IXeme Congrès International d'Histoire des Sciences*. Barcelona-Madrid: Asociación para la historia de ciencia española, 1959.

Cortázar, Julio. *Final del juego*. Edited by Jaime Alazraki. Madrid: Anaya & Mario Muchnik, 1995.

Costantino, Roselyn. "Feminicide, Impunity, and Citizenship: The Old and New in the Struggle for Justice in Guatemala." *Chicana/Latina Studies* 6, no. 1 (Fall 2006): 108–120.

Crary, Jonathan. *Techniques of the Observer: On Vision and Modernity in the Nineteenth Century*. Boston, Cambridge: MIT Press, 1992.

Crosthwaite, Luis Humberto, John William Byrd, and Bobby Byrd, eds. *Puro Border: Dispatches, Snapshots, and Graffiti from La Frontera*. El Paso: Cinco Puntos Press, 2003.

Cuadriello, Jaime. "Visiones en Patmos Tenochtitlán. La mujer águila." In *Artes de México* 29 (1995): 10–23.

Curious in Our Way: The Culture of Nature in Philadelphia, 1740–1840. Conference, November 18–21, 2004.

Daston, Lorraine. "Neugierde als Empfindung und Epistemologie in der frühmodernen Wissenschaft." In *Macrocosmos in Microcosmo: Die Welt in der Stube. Zur Geschichte des Sammelns 1450–1800*, edited by Andreas Grote, 35–59. Berlin: Leske and Budrich, Opladen, 1994.

Daston, Lorraine, and Katharine Park. *Wonders and the Order of Nature: 1150–1750*. New York: Zone Books, 2001.

deBuys, William. *Enchantment and Exploitation: The Life and Hard Times of a New Mexico Mountain Range*. Albuquerque: University of New Mexico Press, 1985.

de la Maza, Francisco. *El guadalupanismo mexicano*. 1953. México: Fondo de Cultura Económica, 1986.

DeMello, Margo. *Bodies of Inscription: A Cultural History of the Modern Tattoo Community*. Durham, NC, and London: Duke University Press, 2000.

de Orellana, Margarita, ed. *Retablos y exvotos*. Mexico: Museo Franz Mayer and Artes de México, 2000.

DeSipio, Louis. "Cuban Miami: Seeking Identity in a Political Borderland." *Latin American Research Review* 38, no. 2 (2003): 207–219.

Desnoes, Edmundo. *Memorias del subdesarrollo*. México: J. Mortiz, 1980.

de Solano, Francisco. *Antonio de Ulloa y la Nueva España*. México: Universidad Nacional Autónoma de México, 1987.

Diamond, Jared M. *Guns, Germs, and Steel: The Fates of Human Societies*. New York: Norton, 2005.

Díaz del Castillo, Bernal. *Historia verdadera de la conquista de la Nueva España*. Edited by Miguel León-Portilla. Madrid: Historia 16, 1984.

Didion, Joan. *The Year of Magical Thinking*. New York: Alfred A. Knopf, 2005.

Dion, Mark. *Polar Bear (Ursus maritimus) 1992–2002*. Köln: Verlag der Buchhandlung Walther König, 2003.

————. "Tate Thames Dig 1999." Tate Museum, http://www.tate.org.uk/servlet/ViewWork?cgroupid=999 999961&workid=27353 (accessed April 24, 2006).

Dobyns, Henry F. "Do-It-Yourself Religion: The Diffusion of Folk Catholicism on Mexico's Northern Frontier 1821–1846." In *Pilgrimages in Latin America*, edited by N. Ross Crumrine and Alan Morinis, 53–68. New York: Greenwood Press, 1991.

Domosh, Mona. *Invented Cities: The Creation of Landscape in Nineteenth-Century New York & Boston*. New Haven: Yale University Press, 1996.

Douglas, Mary. *Purity and Danger*. New York: Routledge, 2003.

Duncan, Kate C. *1001 Curious Things: Ye Olde Curiosity Shop and Native American Art*. Seattle: University of Washington Press, 2000.

Dunnington, Jacqueline Orsini. *Guadalupe: Our Lady of New Mexico*. Santa Fe: Museum of New Mexico Press, 1999.

————. *Viva Guadalupe! The Virgin in New Mexican Popular Art*. Santa Fe: Museum of New Mexico Press, 1997.

Durand, Jorge, and Douglas S. Massey. *Miracles on the Border: Retablos of Mexican Immigrants to the United States*. Tucson and London: University of Arizona Press, 1995.

Dussel, Enrique. *El encubrimiento del Otro: Hacia el origen del mito de la modernidad*. Madrid: Ediciones Abya-yala, 1994. Translated by Michael D. Barber as *The Invention of the Americas: Eclipse of "the Other" and the Myth of Modernity*. New York: Continuum, 1995.

Dyson, Freeman. "A New Newton." *New York Review of Books* 50, no. 11 (July 3, 2003): 4–6.

Edwards, Elizabeth. "Photographs as Objects of Memory." In *Material Memories: Design and Evocation*, edited by Marius Kwint, Christopher Breward, and Jeremy Aynsley, 221–236. Oxford: Berg, 1999.

Egan, Martha J. *Milagros: Votive Offerings from the Americas*. Albuquerque: University of New Mexico Press, 1991.

————. *Relicarios: Devotional Miniatures from the Americas*. Santa Fe: Museum of New Mexico Press, 1993.

Elliott, J. H. *The Old World and the New: 1492–1650*. London: Cambridge University Press, 1970.

————. "Snakes in Paradise." *New York Review of Books* 50, no. 18 (November 20, 2003): 40–42.

Enciclopedia Universal Ilustrada Europeo Americana. Barcelona: Espasa, 1924.

En divina luz: The Penitente Moradas of New Mexico. Photographs by Craig Varjabedian, essay by Michel Wallis. Albuquerque: University of New Mexico Press, 1994.

Escalada, Xavier, S.J. *Enciclopedia Guadalupana*. México: Enciclopedia Guadalupana A.C., 1995.

Espinosa, Gastón and Mario T. Garcia. *Mexican American Religions: Spirituality, Activism, and Culture*. Durham & London: Duke University Press, 2008.

Evans, R. Tripp. *Romancing the Maya: Mexican Antiquity in the American Imaginary, 1820–1915*. Austin: University of Texas Press, 2004.

Fabian, Johannes. *Time and the Other: How Anthropology Makes Its Object*. New York: Columbia University Press, 1983.

Feest, Christian. "Mexico and South America in the European *Wunderkammer*." In *The Origins of Museums: The Cabinet of Curiosities in Sixteenth-and Seventeenth-Century Europe*, edited by Oliver Impey and Arthur MacGregor, 237–244. Oxford: Clarendon Press, 1985.

Flores, Juan. "The Latino Imaginary: Dimensions of Community and Identity." In *Tropicalizations: Transcultural Representations of Latinidad*, edited by Frances R. Aparicio and Susana Chávez-Silverman, 183–193. Hanover, NH: Dartmouth College Press, 1997.

Flores Galindo, Alberto. *Buscando un Inca: Identidad y utopía en los Andes*. Lima, Perú: Editorial Horizonte, 1988.

————. *La ciudad sumergida: Aristocracia y plebe en Lima, 1760–1830*. Lima, Perú: Editorial Horizonte, 1991.

Floriscano, Enrique, and Virginia García Acosta, eds. *Mestizajes tecnológicos y cambios culturales en México*. México: Centro de Investigaciones y Estudios Superiores en Antropología Social, 2004.

Foucault, Michel. *The Order of Things: An Archaeology of the Human Sciences*. New York: Vintage, 1973.

Freed, Robin. "'In Business for Myself': P. T. Barnum and the Museum of Spectacle." University of Virginia. http://xroads.virginia.edu/~MA02/freed/Barnum/museumessay.html (accessed April 24, 2006).

Freedberg, David. *The Eye of the Lynx: Galileo, His Friends, and the Beginnings of Natural History*. Chicago and London: University of Chicago Press, 2002.

Galaor, Isabel, et al., eds. *Las minas hispanoamericanas a mediados del siglo XVIII: Informes enviados al Real Gabinete de Historia Natural de Madrid*. Frankfurt am Main: Vervuert-Iberoamericana, 1998.

Galdós, Benito Pérez. *Obras inéditas*. Edited by Alberto Ghiraldo. Madrid: Renacimiento, 1923.

Galeano, Eduardo. *El descubrimiento de América que todavía no fue y otros escritos*. Barcelona: Editorial Laia, 1986.

———. *Memoria del fuego*. Madrid: Siglo Veintiuno de España Editores, 1982–1986.

———. *Memory of Fire*. Translated by Cedric Belfrage. New York: Pantheon Books, 1985–1988.

———. *Open Veins of Latin America: Five Centuries of the Pillage of a Continent*, translated by Cedric Belfrage. New York: Monthly Review Press, 1973.

Galera Lamadrid, Jesús. *Nican mopohua: Breve análisis literario e histórico* (México City: Editorial Jus, 1991).

Gallagher, Edward J. "*America* by Johannes Stradanus (1523–1605)." Department of English, Lehigh University. http://www.lehigh.edu/~ejg1/ed/strad1.html (accessed April 23, 2006).

Ganahl, Pat. "The Hot Rod Culture." In *Customized: Art Inspired by Hot Rods, Lowriders, and American Car Culture*, edited by Nora Donnelly, 13–16. Boston: Harry N. Abrams, Inc., and the Institute of Contemporary Art, 2000.

García Márquez, Gabriel. *Cien años de soledad*. Buenos Aires: Editorial Sudamericana, 1973, 1.

———. *One Hundred Years of Solitude*. Translated by Gregory Rabassa. New York: Harper & Row, 1970.

García Sáiz, María Concepción. *Las castas mexicanas: Un Género Pictórico Americano*. México: Olivetti, 1989.

Georgia O'Keeffe Biography, Images. Ellen's Place. http://www.ellensplace.net/okeeffe1.html (accessed April 24, 2006).

Gibbons, Kaye. *On the Occasion of My Last Afternoon*. New York: Avon Books, 1998.

Girard, Alexander H. "Foreword." In *Folk Art from the Global Village: The Girard Collection of the Museum of International Folk Art*, 6–7. Santa Fe: Museum of New Mexico Press, 1995.

Gisbert, Teresa. "Prologue." In Martha J. Egan, *Relicarios: Devotional Miniatures from the Americas*, vii–ix. Santa Fe: Museum of New Mexico Press, 1993.

Goddard, Dan R. "Fotoseptiembre: Various Locations." *Artlies* (Fall 2000): 106–108.

Goffman, Erving. *Asylums*. New York: Doubleday-Anchor, 1961.

Gold, Hazel. "A Tomb with a View: The Museum in Galdós' *Novelas contemporáneas*." MLN 103, no. 2 (March 1988): 312–334.

Gómez-Peña, Guillermo, Enrique Chagoya, and Felicia Rice. *Codex Espangliensis*. San Francisco: City Lights Books, 2000.

González-Crussi, F. *Suspended Animation: Six Essays on the Preservation of Bodily Parts*. San Diego: Harvest, Harcourt Brace, 1995.

González Muñoz, María del Carmen. "Estudio preliminar." In Juan Lopez de Velasco, *Geografía y descripción universal de las Indias*. Madrid: Biblioteca de Autores españoles, 1971.

González Rodríguez, Sergio. *Huesos en el desierto*. Barcelona: Anagrama, 2002.

Goodwin, Katherine R. "The World in Your Hands: Recent Cartographic Acquisitions." Special Collections Division, University of Texas at Arlington Libraries. http://libraries.uta.edu/SpecColl/cros00/cartacq.htm (accessed April 23, 2006).

Gould, Stephen Jay. *The Mismeasure of Man*. New York: W. W. Norton, 1981.

Gould, Stephen Jay, and Rosamond Purcell. *Crossing Over: Where Art and Science Meet*. New York: Three Rivers Press, 2000.

Grafton, Anthony. *Rome Reborn: The Vatican Library and Renaissance Culture*. Washington: Library of Congress, in association with Biblioteca Apostólica Vaticana, 1993.

Greenblatt, Stephen. *Marvelous Possessions: The Wonder of the New World*. Chicago: University of Chicago Press, 1991.

Griswold del Castillo, Richard, Teresa McKenna, and Yvonne Yarbro-Bejarano, eds. *Chicano Art: Resistance and Affirmation*. Los Angeles: Wight Art Gallery, University of California, 1991.

Gross, Terry. Interview with Rosamond Purcell. *Fresh Air*. February 2, 2004. http://www.npr.org/templates/story/story.php?storyId=1628953 (accessed November 4, 2007).

Grote, Andreas. *Macrocosmos in Microcosmo: Die Welt in der Stube. Zur Geschichte des Sammelns 1450–1800*. Berlin: Leske and Budrich, Opladen, 1994.

Gruzinski, Serge. *Images at War: Mexico from Columbus to Blade Runner (1492–2009)*. Translated by Heather McLean. Durham, NC: Duke University Press, 2001.

Gundestrup, Bente, and Tine Wanning. National Museum of Denmark. "The King's Kunstkammer: Presenting Systems of Knowledge," http://www.archimuse.com/mw2004/papers/gundestrup/gundestrup.html.

Günther von Hagens' Körperwelten: Die Faszination des Echten. http://www.bodyworlds.com/index.html (accessed November 4, 2007).

Hall, Linda B. *Mary, Mother and Warrior: The Virgin in Spain and the Americas*. Austin: University of Texas Press, 2004.

Hernández, Ester. *The Virgin of Guadalupe Defending the Rights of Xicanos* [Virgen de Guadalupe defendiendo los derechos de los Xicanos]. Engraving in *Third Woman* 4, no. 1–2 (1989).

Hernández, Francisco. *Antigüedades de la Nueva España*. Edited by Ascención H. de León-Portilla. Madrid: Historia 16, 1986.

———. *Historia natural de la Nueva España*. 1615. México, DF: Universidad Nacional de México, 1959.

Hirsch, Marianne. *Family Frames: Photography, Narrative, and Postmemory*. Cambridge, MA: Harvard University Press, 1997.

———. "Projected Memory: Holocaust Photographs in Personal and Public Fantasy." In *Acts of Memory: Cultural Recall in the Present*, edited by Mieke Bal, Jonathan Crewe, and Leo Spitzer, 3–23. Hanover, NH: University Press of New England, 1999.

Hirsch, Marianne, and Leo Spitzer. *Ghosts of Home: The Afterlife of Czernowitz in Jewish Memory*, forthcoming.

Hirst, K. Kris. "The Roots of NAGPRA." About.com Archaeology. http://www.archaeology.about.com/cs/ethicsandlaw/a/russell.html (accessed April 24, 2006).

Horka-Follick, Lorayne Ann. *Los Hermanos Penitentes: A Vestige of Medievalism in Southwestern United States*. Los Angeles: Westernlore Press, 1969.

Hulme, Peter. *Colonial Encounters: Europe and the Native Caribbean, 1492–1797*. London; New York: Methuen, 1986.

Hulten, Pontus. "Zur Ausstellung." In *Wunderkammer des Abendlandes: Museum und Sammlung im Spiegel der Zeit*, 10. Germany: Kunst– und Ausstellungshalle der Bundesrepublik Deutschland und Autoren, 1994.

Humboldt, Alexander von. *Essai politique sur le royaume de la Nouvelle Espagne*. Paris, 1811. Translated by John Black as *Political Essay on the Kingdom of New Spain*. London: Longman, Hurst, Rees, et al., 1811.

Ianni, Octavio. "A ideia do Brasil moderno." In *Through the Kaleidoscope: The Experience of Modernity in Latin America*, edited by Vivian Schelling. London: Verso, 2000.

Icazbalceta, J. García. *Investigación histórica y documental sobre la aparición de la Virgen de Guadalupe*. México, DF: Ediciones Fuente Cultural, 1958.

Images from Milton. Visions of Jesus Christ. http://www.visionsofjesuschrist.com/weeping162.htm (accessed April 24, 2006).

Impey, Oliver, and Arthur MacGregor. *The Origins of Museums: The Cabinets of Curiosities in Sixteenth- and Seventeenth-Century Europe*. Oxford: Clarendon Press, 1985.

Inhaling the Spore: A Journey Through the Museum of Jurassic Technology. DVD. Leonard Feinstein, 2004.

Ishikawa, Chiyo, ed. *1492–1819: Spain in the Age of Exploration*. Seattle: Seattle Art Museum; University of Nebraska Press, 2004.

Jacobs, Jane. *Cities and the Wealth of Nations: Principles of Economic Life*. New York: Random House, 1984.

Jay, Ricky. *Dice: Deception, Fate & Rotten Luck*. Photography by Rosamond Purcell. Italy: Quantuck Lane Press, 2003.

———. *Jay's Journal of Anomalies: Conjurers, Cheats, Hustlers, Hoaxsters, Pranksters, Impostors, Pretenders, Sideshow Showmen, Armless Calligraphers, Mechanical Marvels, Popular Entertainments*. New York: Farrar, Straus & Giroux, 2001.

Juárez, José. *Ofrenda*. Mexico: Dolores Olmedo, 1983.

Kacandes, Irene. *Talk Fiction: Literature and the Talk Explosion*. Lincoln: University of Nebraska Press, 2001.

Kalb, Laurie Beth. *Crafting Devotions: Tradition in Contemporary New Mexico Santos*. Albuquerque: University of New Mexico Press, 1994.

Katzew, Ilona. "Casta Painting: Identity and Social Stratification in Colonial Mexico," http://www .gc.maricopa.edu/laberinto/fall1997/casta1997.htm (accessed September 13, 2007).

———. *Casta Painting: Images of Race in Eighteenth-Century Mexico*. New Haven: Yale University Press, 2004.

Kellogg, Susan. "Depicting Mestizaje: Gendered Images of Ethnorace in Colonial Mexican Texts." *Journal of Women's History* 12, no. 3 (2000): 69–92.

Kertzer, David I. *Ritual, Politics, and Power*. New Haven: Yale University Press, 1988.

Kirshenblatt-Gimblett, Barbara. *Destination Culture: Tourism, Museums, and Heritage*. Berkeley: University of California Press, 1998.

Kopilli Ketzalli petition website. Montezuma's Feather Crown Petition. http://www.deliberate.com/aztec/ en/aztec_en.html (accessed April 23, 2006).

Kopytoff, Igor. "The Cultural Biography of Things." In *The Social Life of Things: Commodities in Cultural Perspective*, edited by Arjun Appadurai, 64–91. Cambridge: Cambridge University Press, 1986.

Kubler, George. *The Shape of Time: Remarks on the History of Things*. New Haven: Yale University Press, 1962.

Krauss, Rosalind. *The Optical Unconscious*. Boston, Cambridge: MIT Press, 1993.

Kunhardt, Philip B., et al. *P. T. Barnum: America's Greatest Showman*. New York: Alfred A. Knopf, 1995.

The Kunsthistorisches Museum Vienna: The Imperial and Ecclesiastical Treasury. Edited by Manfred Leithe-Jasper and Rudolf Distelberger. London and Munich: Scala Books, 2003.

Lafaye, Jacques. *Quetzalcoatl and Guadalupe: The Formation of Mexican National Consciousness, 1531–1813*. Translated by Benjamin Keen. Chicago: University of Chicago Press, 1976.

Lamadrid, Enrique R. "Luz y sombra: The Poetics of Mestizo Identity." In *Nuevo México Profundo: Rituals of an Indo-Hispano Homeland*, photographs by Miguel Gandert, 1–11. Santa Fe: Museum of New Mexico Press, 2000.

———. "Santa Madre Tierra—The Holy Mother Earth of Chimayó." In *Pilgrimage to Chimayó: Contemporary Portrait of a Living Tradition*, edited by Sam Howarth and Enrique R. Lamadrid, 13–25. Santa Fe: Museum of New Mexico Press, 1999.

Lamb, Jonathan. *Preserving the Self in the South Seas, 1680–1840*. Chicago: University of Chicago Press, 2001.

Lautréamont, Comte de. *Les Chants de Maldoror* (Chant VI). http://www.gutenberg.org/etext/12005.

León, Luis E. *La Llorona's Children: Religion, Life, and Death in the US-Mexican Borderlands*. Berkeley: University of California Press, 2004.

León-Portilla, Miguel. "Aztlán: From Myth to Reality." Translated by Rose Verony. In *The Road to Aztlán: Art from the Mythic Homeland*, edited by Virginia Fields and Victor Zamudio-Taylor, 20–33. Los Angeles: Los Angeles County Museum of Art, 2001.

———. *Tonantzin Guadalupe: Pensamiento náhuatl y mensaje cristiano en el "Nican mopohua."* México: Fondo de Cultura Económica, 2000.

Lester, John. "Meet Joseph Paul Jernigan." Massachusetts General Hospital Neurology Service. http:// neuro-www.mgh.harvard.edu/creepy.html (accessed April 24, 2006).

Lewontin, Richard. "Dishonesty in Science." *New York Review of Books* 51, no. 18 (November 18, 2004): 38–40.

Leys, Ruth. *Trauma: A Genealogy*. Chicago: University of Chicago Press, 2000.

Lockhart, James. *Nahuas and Spaniards: Postconquest Central Mexican History and Philology*. Stanford: Stanford University Press, 1991.

López, José Ramón. "La fábula del tiempo" [The Fable of Time]. In *Richard Ross: Historia natural*, 7–12. Madrid: Museo de Ciencias Naturales, 1994.

López Pulido, Alberto. *The Sacred World of the Penitentes*. Washington and London: Smithsonian Institution Press, 2000.

Lowood, Henry. "The New World and the European Catalog of Nature." In *America in European Consciousness, 1493–1750*, edited by Karen Ordahl Kupperman, 295–323. Chapel Hill and London: North Carolina Press, 1995.

Ludmer, Josefina. "Las tretas del débil." In *La sartén por el mango: encuentro de escritoras latinoamericanas*, edited by Patricia Elena González and Eliana Ortega. Río Piedras, PR: Ediciones Huracán, 1985.

Mabel Dodge Luhan House. http://www.mabeldodgeluhan.com/ (accessed April 24, 2006).

MacDonald, Sharon. "Exhibitions of Power and Powers of Exhibition: An Introduction to the Politics of

Display." In *The Politics of Display: Museums, Science, Culture*, edited by Sharon MacDonald, 1–24. New York: Routledge, 1998.

Machado, Eduardo. "A Return to Cuba, A Search for Himself." *New York Times*, Sunday, October 21, 2001.

Machado, Maria Helena. "The Nature of Tropical Nature: Brazil Through the Eyes of William James." *ReVista* 3, no. 1 (Fall 2004/Winter 2005): 13–15.

Maratos, Daniel C., and Marnesba D. Hill. *Escritores de la diáspora cubana: Manual biobliográfico*. Washington, D.C.: Library of Congress, 1986.

Marchán Fiz, Simón. "Los placeres del parecido entre las brumas de la ficción." In *Cristóbal Toral: Pinturas, acuarelas y dibujos, 1967–1996*, 53–69. Lima: Museo de Arte de Lima, Exposición Itinerante en Iberoamérica, 1997–1998.

Martin, Carlos. Presentation at Los Angeles/la frontera/Mexico City conference, Dartmouth College, July 1999.

Martin, Valerie. *Property*. New York: Nan A. Talese, 2003.

Martínez, Rubén. *Crossing Over: A Mexican Family on the Migrant Trail*. New York: Henry Holt, 2001.

Martin-Márquez, Susan. "Anatomy of a Black Legend: Bodies of Cultural Discourse and Madrid's National Museum of Anthropology." *Journal of Spanish Cultural Studies* 4, no. 2 (2003): 205–222.

Maseko, Zola. *The Life and Times of Sara Baartman: "The Hottentot Venus."* First Run/Icarus Films, 1998.

Mauries, Patrick. *Cabinets of Curiosities*. London: Thames and Hudson, 2002.

Mavor, Carol. "Collecting Loss." *Cultural Studies* 11, no. 1 (1997): 111–137.

McEachran, John D. Syllabus for "Museums and Their Functions." Texas A&M University. wfscnet.tamu .edu/COURSES/wfsc421.htm (accessed November 4, 2007).

McLaughlin, Patricia. "Let Them Eat Alligator! Luxury Spending Is Booming. Is $1,000 Too Much for an Omelet?" *Valley News*, Sunday, September 19, 2004, page C2.

Merino, Joel. *Tepeyac en Nueva York*. Puebla: Benemérita Universidad Autónoma de Puebla, 2002.

Mexico: Our Lady of Guadalupe: Nuestra Señora de Guadalupe. *Hispanic Online*. http://www .hispaniconline.com/hh03/mainpages/religion/mary_mexico.html (accessed April 24, 2006).

Mignolo, Walter, ed. *Capitalismo y geopolítica del conocimiento: El eurocentrismo y la filosofía de la liberación en el debate intelectual contemporáneo*. Buenos Aires: Ediciones del Signo, 2003.

———. *The Darker Side of the Renaissance: Literacy, Territoriality, and Colonization*. Ann Arbor: University of Michigan Press, 1995.

———. *Local Histories/Global Designs: Coloniality, Subaltern Knowledges, and Border Thinking*. Princeton: Princeton University Press, 2000.

Millicent Rogers Museum. http://millicentrogers.org (accessed April 24, 2006).

Millones, Luis. "Los Santos patronos. De la ciudad indígena a la ciudad Indiana." In *Más allá de la ciudad letrada: Crónicas y espacios urbanos*, edited by Boris Muñoz and Silvia Spitta, 267–286. Pittsburgh: Biblioteca de América, Instituto Internacional de Literatura Iberoamericana, 2003.

Mitchell, Michael, ed. *Monsters: Human Freaks in America's Gilded Age*. Toronto: ECW Press, 2002.

Mitchell, W. J. T. *The Last Dinosaur Book: The Life and Times of a Cultural Icon*. Chicago: University of Chicago Press, 1998.

———. *What Do Pictures Want? The Lives and Loves of Images*. Chicago and London: University of Chicago Press, 2005.

Moffitt, John F. *Our Lady of Guadalupe: The Painting, the Legend, and the Reality*. Jefferson, N.C.; and London: McFarland & Company, Inc., 2006.

Monsiváis, Carlos. "La Virgen de Guadalupe y el arte (necesariamente) popular." *El mito guadalupano*, Rius. México: Grijalbo, 1996.

Morán, J. Miguel, and Fernando Checa. *El coleccionismo en España: De la cámara de maravillas a la galería de pinturas*. Madrid: Cátedra, 1985.

Moraña, Mabel. *Relecturas del barroco de Indias*. Hanover, NH: Ediciones del Norte, 1994.

———. *Viaje al silencio: exploraciones del discurso barroco*. México, DF: Facultad de Filosofía y Letras, UNAM, 1998.

Moreiras, Alberto. *The Exhaustion of Difference: The Politics of Latin American Cultural Studies*. Durham, NC: Duke University Press, 2001.

Morinis, Alan, and N. Ross Crumrine. "La peregrinación: The Latin American Pilgrimage." In *Pilgrim-

ages in Latin America, edited by N. Ross Crumrine and Alan Morinis, 1–19. New York: Greenwood Press, 1991.

Morrison, Toni. "The Site of Memory." In *Out There: Marginalization and Contemporary Cultures*, edited by Russell Ferguson, Martha Gever, Trin T. Minh-ha, and Cornel West, 289–305. New York: New Museum of Contemporary Art, 1990.

Mosquera, Gerardo. "New Cuban Art Y2K." In *Art Cuba: The New Generation*, edited by Holly Block, 13–15. New York: Harry N. Abrams, 2001.

Mount Holyoke College. "The Collector: MHC Museum Hosts Rosamond Purcell Exhibition." *College Street Journal*, January 30, 2004. http://www.mtholyoke.edu/offices/comm/csj/013004/purcell.shtml (accessed November 4, 2007).

Mukerji, C. *From Graven Images: Patterns of Modern Materialism*. New York: Columbia University Press, 1983.

The Museum of Jurassic Technology. Los Angeles: Society for the Diffusion of Useful Information Press, 2002.

Museum of Spanish Colonial Art. http://www.spanishcolonial.org/ (accessed May 3, 2006).

Mütter Museum. "Virtual Tour." College of Physicians of Philadelphia. http://www.collphyphil.org/virt_tour/museum_5.htm (accessed April 24, 2006).

Nebel, Richard. *Santa María Tonantzin, Virgen de Guadalupe: Continuidad y transformación religiosa en México*. 1992. Translated by Carlos Warnholtz Bustillos. México: Fondo de Cultura Económica, 1995.

Neruda, Pablo. *Confieso que he vivido. Memorias*. Buenos Aires: Losada, 1974.

New Mexico Arts. http://www.nmarts.org/ (accessed May 3, 2006).

New World Orders: Casta Painting and Colonial Latin America. Exhibition organized by the Americas Society Art Gallery, September 26–December 22, 1996.

Nican mopohua. Translated and edited by Guillermo Ortiz de Montellano. México: Universidad Iberoamericana, 1990.

Nolan, Mary Lee. "The European Roots of Latin American Pilgrimage." In *Pilgrimages in Latin America*, edited by N. Ross Crumrine and Alan Morinis, 19–52. New York: Greenwood Press, 1991.

Novak, Lorie. *Collected Visions*. http://cvisions.cat.nyu.edu (accessed May 3, 2006).

"Objects and Memory: Engendering Private and Public Archives." Conference, Columbia University, March 23, 2007. http://www.columbia.edu/cu/irwag/events/main/memory/index.html (accessed September 26, 2007).

Oettermann, Stephan. "On Display: Tattooed Entertainers in America and Germany." In *Written on the Body: The Tattoo in European and American History*, edited by Jane Caplan, 193–211. Princeton: Princeton University Press, 2000.

O'Gorman, Edmundo. *Destierro de sombras*. México: UNAM, 1986.

———. *La invención de América; el universalismo de la cultura de Occidente*. México: Fondo de Cultura Económica, 1958.

Olalquiaga, Celeste. *The Artificial Kingdom: A Treasury of the Kitsch Experience*. New York: Pantheon, 1998.

Olguín, B. V. "Tattoos, Abjection, and the Political Unconscious." *Cultural Critique* (Fall 1997, no. 37): 159–214.

Ortiz de Montellano, Guillermo, ed. and trans. *Nican mopohua*. México: Universidad Iberoamericana, 1990.

Ortiz Taylor, Sheila. *OutRageous*. Duluth, MN: Spinsters Ink, 2006.

Ortiz Taylor, Sheila, and Sandra Ortiz Taylor. *Imaginary Parents: A Family Autobiography*. Albuquerque: University of New Mexico Press, 1996.

Ortiz Torres, Rubén. "Cathedrals on Wheels." In *Customized: Art Inspired by Hot Rods, Lowriders, and American Car Culture*, edited by Nora Donnelly, 37–38. Boston: Harry N. Abrams, Inc., and the Institute of Contemporary Art, 2000.

———. *Custom Mambo*. Video installation, Institute of Contemporary Art, Boston, 2000.

———. *The Garden of Earthly Delights*. Installation, Fisher Gallery, University of Southern California, 2002.

Padilla, Carmella. *Low 'n Slow: Lowriding in New Mexico*. Santa Fe: Museum of New Mexico Press, 1999.

Pané, Fray Ramón. *Relación acerca de las antigüedades de los indios: (el primer tratado escrito en América).* Edited by José Juan Arrom. México: Siglo Veintiuno, 1988.

Paz, Octavio. *El laberinto de la soledad.* Madrid: Cátedra, 1993. Translated by Lysander Kemp as *The Labyrinth of Solitude: Life and Thought in Mexico.* New York: Grove Press, 1962.

Pelayo, Francisco. *Del diluvio al megaterio; Los orígenes de la paleontología en España.* Madrid: Consejo Superior de Investigaciones Científicas, 1996.

Pérez Firmat, Gustavo. *Cincuenta lecciones de exilio y desexilio.* Miami: Ediciones Universal, 2000.

Pérez, Laura E. *Chicana Art: The Politics of Spiritual and Aesthetic Altarities.* Durham & London: Duke University Press, 2007.

Performing the Border: Gender, Bodies & Technology at the Crosspoint of Private Desire & Public Space. Videorecording. Ursula Biemann, 1999.

Pinero, José María López. *El megaterio de bru y el presidente Jefferson: Relación insospechada en los albores de la paleontología.* Valencia: Universidad de Valencia, 1957.

Porter, Dean A., et al. *Taos Artists and Their Patrons, 1898–1950.* South Bend: University of Notre Dame Press, 1999.

Pratt, Mary Louise. *Imperial Eyes: Travel Writing and Transculturation.* New York: Routledge, 1992.

Prest, John. *The Garden of Eden: The Botanic Garden and the Re-Creation of Paradise.* New Haven and London: Yale University Press, 1981.

Puig-Samper, Miguel Angel, and Sandra Rebok. "Virtuti et merito. El reconocimiento oficial de Alexander von Humboldt en España." *HiN: Alexander von Humboldt im Netz* V, no. 8 (2004). http://www.uni-potsdam.de/u/romanistik/humboldt/hin/hin8/rebok-ps.htm (accessed June 25, 2007).

Purcell, Rosamond. *Half-Life.* Boston: David R. Godine, 1980.

———. *Naturalezas.* With texts and photographs by Rosamond Purcell. Translation from the English by Isabel Brias. Madrid: Museo Nacional de Ciencias Naturales, 1991.

———. *Owl's Head.* New York: Quantuck Lane Press, 2003.

———. "Rosamond Purcell: Two Rooms." Tufts University Art Gallery. http://ase.tufts.edu/gallery/shows/purcell.html (accessed April 24, 2006).

———. *Special Cases: Natural Anomalies and Historical Monsters.* San Francisco, CA: Chronicle Books, 1997.

———. *Swift as a Shadow: Extinct and Endangered Animals.* Text by the Staff of Naturalis, Nationaal Natuurhistorisch Museum, Leiden. Boston and New York: Houghton Mifflin, 1999.

Purcell, Rosamond, and Stephen Jay Gould. *Crossing Over: Where Art and Science Meet.* New York: Three Rivers Press, 2000.

———. *Finders, Keepers: Eight Collectors.* New York and London: W. W. Norton, 1992.

———. *Illuminations: A Bestiary.* New York: W. W. Norton, 1986.

Rabasa, José. *Inventing America: Spanish Historiography and the Formation of Eurocentrism.* Norman: University of Oklahoma Press, 1993.

Rafael Sánchez, Luis. *La guagua aérea.* San Juan, PR: Editorial Cultural, 1994.

Rama, Angel. *La ciudad letrada.* Hanover, NH: Ediciones del Norte, 1984. Translated by John Chasteen as *The Lettered City (Post-Contemporary Interventions).* Durham, NC: Duke University Press, 1996.

Ramirez, Yasmin. "New World Orders: Casta Paintings and Colonial Latin America at the Americas Society." *ArtNet,* December 2, 1996. http://www.artnet.com/magazine_pre2000/features/ramirez/ramirez12-02-96.asp (accessed May 3, 2006).

Ramos, Sandra. *Obra Plástica, 1989–1999.* CD-ROM. In author's collection.

Raskin, Marcus G. "Reconstruction and Its Knowledge Method." In *New Ways of Knowing: The Sciences, Society, and Reconstructive Knowledge,* edited by Marcus G. Raskin and Herbert J. Bernstein. New Jersey: Rowman and Littlefield, 1987.

Rathje, W. J. "Why the Taliban are destroying Buddhas." CNN report, March 22, 2001. www.usatoday.com/news/science/archaeology/2001-03-22-afghan-buddhas.htm.

Rodríguez, Richard. *Brown: The Last Discovery of America.* New York: Viking, 2002.

Roob, Alexander. *The Hermetic Museum: Alchemy and Mysticism.* Köln: Taschen, 1997.

Rossell, Daniela. *Ricas y famosas.* Madrid, España: Turner Publicaciones, 2002.

Rothman, David. "The Murderer's Gift: The Life and Eternal Cyberlife of Paul Jernigan." *NetWorld.* Reprinted at http://www.davidrothman.com/murderer.html (accessed April 24, 2006).

Rouse, Roger. "Mexican Migration and the Social Space of Postmodernism." In *Between Two Words:*

Mexican Immigrants in the United States, edited by David G. Gutiérrez, 247–263. Wilmington, DE: Scholarly Resources, 1996.

Rowland, Ingrid D. "Through a Glass, Darkly." *New York Review of Books* 49, no. 3 (February 28, 2002): 10–14.

Royal Treasures. Lisbon: Palácio Nacional da Ajuda, Instituto Português do Patrimonio Cultural, 1992.

Rubin, Arnold, ed. *Marks of Civilization: Artistic Transformations of the Human Body.* Los Angeles: Museum of Cultural History, 1988.

Rudnick, Lois Palken. *Utopian Vistas: The Mabel Dodge Luhan House and American Counterculture.* Albuquerque: University of New Mexico Press, 1996.

Ruiz Gómez, Leticia. "The Prado Museum: A Spanish Perspective." In *The Majesty of Spain: Royal Collections from the Museo del Prado and the Patrimonio Nacional.* Jackson, MS: Mississippi Commission for International Cultural Exchange, 2001.

Ruiz-Navarro, Patricia. "Religious-Political Movements of Mexicans Across the Mexico-U.S. Border. Being *guadalupano.*" Unpublished paper.

Rushdie, Salman. *Imaginary Homelands: Essays and Criticism 1981–1991.* New York: Penguin, 1991.

Salvo, Dana. *Home Altars of Mexico.* Albuquerque: University of New Mexico Press, 1997.

Sánchez, Miguel. *Imagen de la Virgen María Madre de Dios de Guadalupe, milagrosamente aparecida en la ciudad de México* [. . .] . México: Imprenta de la viuda de Bernardo Calderón, 1648.

Sanders, Clinton R. *Customizing the Body: The Art and Culture of Tattooing.* Philadelphia: Temple University Press, 1989.

Sandoval-Sánchez, Alberto. *José, Can You See? Latinos On and Off Broadway.* Madison: University of Wisconsin Press, 1999.

———. "Puerto Rican Identity Up in the Air: Air Migration, Its Cultural Representations, and Me 'Cruzando el Charco.'" In *Puerto Rican Jam: Essays on Culture and Politics,* edited by Frances Negrón-Muntaner and Ramón Grosfoguel, 189–208. Minneapolis: University of Minnesota Press, 1997.

Santiago, Danny. *Famous All Over Town.* New York: Simon and Schuster, 1983.

Sassen, Saskia. *Guests and Aliens.* New York: New Press, 1999.

———. *Losing Control? Sovereignty in an Age of Globalization.* New York: Columbia University Press, 1996.

Schedel, Hartmann. *Liber cronicarum.* Nuremberg: Anton Koberger, 1493.

Scheinman, Pamela, and Kathy Armstrong-Gillis, curators. "Collective Memory: Foto-Esculturas from Mexico City." Russell Hill Rogers Gallery, San Antonio, Texas, August 24–October 28, 2000.

Schelling, Vivian. *Through the Kaleidoscope: The Experience of Modernity in Latin America.* London: Verso, 2000.

Seabrook, Jeremy. "My Life Is in That Box." In *Family Snaps: The Meaning of Domestic Photography,* edited by Jo Spence and Patricia Holland, 171–185. London: Virago, 1991.

Sebald, W. G. *The Emigrants.* Translated by Michael Hulse. London: Harvill Press, 1997.

———. *On the Natural History of Destruction.* Translated by Anthea Bell. New York: Random House, 2003.

———. *The Rings of Saturn.* Translated by Michael Hulse. New York: New Directions, 1998.

Seeds of Change: A Quincentennial Commemoration, edited by Herman J. Viola and Carolyn Margolis. Washington, D.C.: Smithsonian Institution Press, 1991.

Sheehy, Colleen J., ed. *Cabinet of Curiosities: Mark Dion and the University as Installation.* Minneapolis and London: University of Minnesota Press in cooperation with the Weisman Art Museum, 2006.

Sheikh, Fazal. *A Sense of Common Ground.* Zurich: Scalo, 1996.

———. *The Victor Weeps.* Zurich: Scalo, 1988.

Simic, Charles. *Dime-Store Alchemy. The Art of Joseph Cornell.* New York: New York Review of Books, 1992.

———. *The Victor Weeps: Afghanistan.* Zurich: Scalo, 1998.

Snell, Marilyn Berlin. "Bulldozers & Blasphemy: In Latin America, Catholics Are Standing Up to Those Who Covet Their Gold and Timber." *Sierra* (September/October 2007): 36–76.

Sommer, Doris. *Proceed with Caution, When Engaged by Minority Writing in the Americas.* Cambridge: Harvard University Press, 1999.

Sommers, Laurie Kay. "Inventing Latinismo: The Creation of 'Hispanic' Panethnicity in the United States." *Journal of American Folklore* 104, no. 411 (1991): 32–53.

————. "Latinismo and Ethnic Nationalism in Cultural Performance." *Studies in Latin American Popular Culture* 10 (1991): 75–86.

————. "Symbol and Style in *Cinco de Mayo*." *Journal of American Folklore* 98, no. 390 (1985): 476–482.

Sontag, Susan. *On Photography*. New York: Farrar, Straus & Giroux, 1977.

————. *Regarding the Pain of Others*. New York: Farrar, Straus & Giroux, 2003.

Spence, Jo, and Patricia Holland, eds. *Family Snaps: The Meaning of Domestic Photography*. London: Virago, 1991.

Spence, Jonathan D. *The Memory Palace of Mateo Ricci*. New York: Penguin, 1985.

Spener, David. "Narrativas del mal: El coyote mexicano en el drama del cruce fronterizo." In *Más allá de la ciudad letrada: Crónicas y espacios urbanos*, edited by Boris Muñoz and Silvia Spitta, 379–410. Pittsburgh: Iberoamericana, 2003.

Spitta, Silvia. *Between Two Waters: Narratives of Transculturation in Latin America*. 2nd ed. College Station: Texas A&M University Press, 2006.

Spitta, Silvia, and Boris Muñoz, eds. *Más allá de la ciudad Letrada; Crónicas y espacios urbanos*. Pittsburgh: Biblioteca de América, Instituto Internacional de Literatura Iberoamericana, 2003.

Spitzer, Leo. *Hotel Bolivia: The Culture of Memory in a Refuge from Nazism*. New York: Hill and Wang, 1998.

Stafford, Barbara Maria. "Revealing Technologies/Magical Domains." In *Devices of Wonder: From the World in a Box to Images on a Screen*, edited by Barbara Maria Stafford and Frances Terpak, 1–142. Los Angeles: Getty Research Institute, 2001.

Stafford Poole, C. M. *Our Lady of Guadalupe: The Origins and Sources of a Mexican National Symbol, 1531–1797*. Tucson: University of Arizona Press, 1995.

Stallybrass, Peter. "Worn Worlds: Clothes, Mourning, and the Life of Things." *Yale Review* 81, no. 2 (April 1993): 35–50.

Stavans, Ilan. "Introduction." In *Mestizo: A Novel*, by Ricardo Feierstein. Albuquerque: University of New Mexico Press, 2000.

Stewart, Susan. *On Longing: Narratives of the Miniature, the Gigantic, the Souvenir, the Collection*. Durham, NC: Duke University Press, 1993.

Strauss, Walter L., and Marjon van der Meulen. *The Rembrandt Documents*. New York: Abaris, 1979.

Sullivan, Nikki. *Tattooed Bodies: Subjectivity, Textuality, Ethics, and Pleasure*. Westport, CT, and London: Praeger, 2001.

Tabuenca Córdoba, María Socorro. "*Baile de fanstamas* en Ciudad Juárez al final/principio del milenio." In *Más allá de la ciudad letrada: Crónicas y espacios urbanos*, edited by Boris Muñoz and Silvia Spitta, 411–438. Pittsburgh: Biblioteca de América, IILL, 2003.

Taylor, Diana. *The Archive and the Repertoire: Performing Cultural Memory in the Americas*. Durham, NC: Duke University Press, 2003.

Thompson, Barbara. *Fred Wilson: So Much Trouble in the World—Believe It or Not!* Hanover and London: Hood Museum of Art, distributed by University Press of New England, 2006.

Thompson, Krista A. "Exhibiting 'Others' in the West." Emory University Department of English. http://www.english.emory.edu/Bahri/Exhibition.html (accessed April 24, 2006).

Torre Villar, Ernesto de la. *Breve historia del libro en México*. México: UNAM, 1999.

Trash. Edited by John Knechtel. Cambridge: MIT Press, 2007.

Turner, Kay F. *Beautiful Necessity: The Art and Meaning of Women's Altars*. New York: Thames & Hudson, 1999.

————. "The Cultural Semiotics of Religious Icons: La Virgen de San Juan de los Lagos." *Semiotica* 47, 1/4 (1983): 317–361.

Turner, Victor, and Edith Turner. *Image and Pilgrimage in Christian Culture: Anthropological Perspectives*. New York: Columbia University Press, 1978.

Ulloa, Antonio de. *Noticias americanas: Entretenimientos phísicos-históricos, sobre la América Meridional, y la Septentrional Oriental. Comparación general de los territorios, climas, y producciones en las tres especies, vegetales, animales, y minerales: Con relación particular de las petrificaciones de cuerpos marinos de los indios naturales de aquellos países, sus costumbres, y usos: De las Antigüedades: Discurso sobre la lengua, y sobre el modo en que pasaron los primeros pobladores*. Madrid: Imprenta de Don Francisco Manuel de Mena, 1772.

Valdéz Figueroa, Eugenio. "Trajectories of a Rumor: Cuban Art in the Postwar Period." In *Art Cuba: The New Generation*, edited by Holly Block, 17–23. New York: Harry N. Abrams, 2001.

Vasconcelos, José. *La raza cósmica: misión de la raza iberoamericana.* Paris: Agencia Mundial de Librería, 192–.

Velázquez, María del Carmen, ed. *Theatro Americano.* México: Editorial Trillas, 1992.

Viola, Herman J., and Carolyn Margolis, eds. *Seeds of Change: Five Hundred Years Since Columbus. A Quincentennial Celebration.* Washington, D.C.: Smithsonian Institution Press, 1991.

Waggoner, Ben. "Carl Linnaeus (1707–1778)." University of California Berkeley Museum of Paleontology. http://www.ucmp.berkeley.edu/history/linnaeus.html (accessed April 23, 2006).

Weber, David J. *The Mexican Frontier, 1821–1846: The American Southwest under Mexico.* Albuquerque: University of New Mexico Press, 1982.

Wechsler, Lawrence. *Mr. Wilson's Cabinet of Wonder: Pronged Ants, Horned Humans, Mice on Toast, and Other Marvels of Jurassic Technology.* New York: Vintage, 1995.

Weigle, Marta. *Brothers of Light, Brothers of Blood: The Penitentes of the Southwest.* Albuquerque: University of New Mexico Press, 1976.

———. *The Penitentes of the Southwest.* Santa Fe: Ancient City Press, 1970.

Westerman, Frank. *El Negro: Eine verstörende Begegnung.* Translated from the Dutch by Stefan Häring and Verena Kiefer. Berlin: Ch. Links Verlag, 2005.

Wilgus, Jack, and Beverley Wilgus. "The Magic Mirror of Life: An Appreciation of the Camera Obscura." http://brightbytes.com/cosite/collection.html (accessed April 23, 2006).

Wilson, Chris. *The Myth of Santa Fe: Creating a Modern Regional Tradition.* Albuquerque: University of New Mexico Press, 1997.

Wolf, Eric. *Europe and the People Without History.* Berkeley: University of California Press, 1982.

Wood, William, ed. *Natural History. General and Particular by the Count de Buffon.* London, 1812.

Worden, Gretchen. *Mütter Museum of the College of Physicians of Philadelphia.* New York: Blast Books, 2002.

Wunderkammer des Abendlandes: Museum und Sammlung im Spiegel der Zeit. Edited by Annesofie Becker and Arno Victor Nielsen. Bonn: Kunst- und Ausstellungshalle der Bundesrepublik Deutschland und Autoren, 1994.

Yates, Frances A. *The Art of Memory.* Chicago: University of Chicago Press, 1984.

Ybarra-Frausto, Tomás. "Notes from Losaida: A Foreword." In *Velvet Barrios: Popular Culture and Chicana/o Sexualities*, edited by Alicia Gaspar de Alba. New York: Palgrave, 2003.

———. "Rasquachismo: A Chicano Sensibility." In *Chicano Art: Resistance to Affirmation, 1965–1985*, edited by Richard Griswold del Castillo, et al., 155–162. Los Angeles: Wight Gallery, 1991.

Zamora, Lois Parkinson. *The Inordinate Eye: New World Baroque and Latin American Fiction.* Chicago: University of Chicago Press, 2006.

Zamora, Lois Parkinson, and Monika Kaup, eds. *The New World Baroque.* Durham, NC: Duke University Press, forthcoming.

Zamora, Margarita. *Reading Columbus.* Berkeley: University of California Press, 1993.

Zavala, Iris. *Colonialism and Culture: Hispanic Modernisms and the Social Imaginary.* Bloomington: Indiana University Press, 1992.

———, ed. *Discursos sobre la "invención" de América.* Amsterdam; Atlanta, GA: Rodopi, 1992.

INDEX

Note: Italicized page numbers indicate figures.

Abeyta, Bernardo, 153, 157
academies of science, 51, 221n23, 224n68
Academy of Natural Sciences (Philadelphia), 224n68
Academy of Sciences (Paris), 51
accumulation: Baudrillard on, 27; frenzy for, 38, 215n34; of memory, 171; of photographs, 167, 178–179. *See also* cabinets of wonders (*Wunderkammern*); consumer objects and commodities
Ackerman, Michael, 227n23
Acosta, José de, 55
Acosta, Zeta, 166
Acuña, Rodolfo, 238–239n1
Adams, Ansel, 139, 143
advertising and promotion: of arts markets, 139–140, 143; Barnum as precursor to, 73; Kodak moment of, 167. *See also* consumer objects and commodities; tourism
aesthetics: of Chicano artists, 144; of decontextualization, 90; of display, 30, 32, 213n15; of mestizaje, 148–149; of Modern Primitives, 235n41; of New World Baroque, 99–100; of *rasquachismo*, 127, 130
African peoples: as taxidermied specimens, 68, 201; zoo's exhibition of living, 74, 75, 226n15
Agassiz, Louis, 65
"Age of the Marvelous" (exhibition), x
Aguilera-Hellweg, Max, 78, *78*, 80, 227n24
Alarcón, Norma, 119
Albán, Vicente, *12*
Albertus Magnus, 5
Alegría, Claribel, 180
Alhazen of Basra, 217n55
Altamirano, Ignacio Manuel, 132
altars and shrines: author's, *19*; Chicago apparition of Virgin as, 135, *136*; foto-esculturas as, 178–179; Ground Zero, *20*; Latin American space marked by, 106; lowriders as, 128, *129*, 130–131, *142*; at Metro Hidalgo, *135*; miniature installations as, 174–175; periods of creation, 233n3; personal, 18, *19*; as personal expressions of gratitude, *18*; from recycled things, 124, *127*; at taxi stands, *18*, 124; of Weeping Guadalupe, 135–136. *See also* Virgin of Guadalupe
altepetl concept, 97

alterity: of American objects in Europe, 27, 29; assumptions of, 75
Alvarez, Julia, 50
American Museum (New York City): Barnum's cosmorama of, *73*; beginnings of, 69, 71; living human oddities exhibited in, *71, 77*; science and spectacle linked in, 72–73; science support linked to, 50, 66. *See also* Barnum, P. T.
American Museum of Natural History (New York City), 63
American Philosophical Society, 65, 213n12, 217–218n61, 223–224n59
Améry, Jean, 210n19, 243n4
anatomical theaters, 36, *36*, 76, 214n18, 227n23
Anatomical Theatre (Leiden), 76
Anderson, Claude, 149
Anderson, Elizabeth, 149
Andrade, Farnese de, 92, *92–93*, *93*
Anguía, Richard, 178
Antonio Maceo Brigade, 191. *See also* Bridges Project
Anzaldúa, Gloria, 119
Apolito, Paolo, 121, 123, 124, 125
Appadurai, Arjun, 90, 211n38, 212n4
Applegate, Frank, 148
Aragón, José Rafael, 154, 158
Aragón, Miguel, 154
Arawak people, 68
Archaeology Museum (Mexico City), 150
Argentina, large bones from, 50–51, 63–64
Aristotle, 217n55
Arizona, attempt to ban MEChA in, 238–239n1
Armand, Octavio, 194
art and artworks: depiction of, *30*; as folklore, 140; high vs. native, 92–93; indigenous objects distinguished from, 63; perspective in, 42, 216n50; science distinguished from, 6, 52, 93–94; science linked to, 79–82. *See also* aesthetics; Baroque; New World Baroque; recycling and recycled things; sculpture; surrealism; *specific artists*
artifacts: artworks distinguished from, 63; objects transformed into, 5, 7–8; surrealism and, 23, 90, 209n9
Art Institute of Chicago, *146*
art of memory: anchors in, 90, 163–164, 168–169; artificial memory in, 20, 169, 229n7; convergence of printing and, 36; development of,

20, 214n20; forgetting in, 172–173; mnemonic techniques in, 20; total recall in, 170–171. *See also* memory and memories

Asociación Tepeyac (New York City), 117–120, 131–134

assimilation: of displaced objects, 27–28; impossibility of, 56; via intermarriage, 230n10; of shipwreck survivor, 128

Astaire, Fred, 173

atlas, 37, 215n25. *See also* globes

augmented vision technologies, 42–44, 216n48, 217n53, 217n55

Augustus the Strong, 206

aura: absence of, 150; of Guadalupe, 120, 136; of miniatures, 174; reclaiming of, 200, 206; of santeros' works, 238n41; of Southwest, 139–140, 237n2

Austin, Mary: arts society co-founded by, 148–149; *The Land of Little Rain*, 148; New Mexico stay of, 143; Spanish terms of, 160, 238n44; *Starry Adventure: The Book of New Mexico*, 148, 238n44

Austria. *See* Vienna (Austria)

autobiographies, 71, 164, 172–173, 177. See also *Imaginary Parents*; memory and memories

Autry, Gene, 150

Aztlán: as borderland, 16; revival of notion, 190; use of term, 151–152. *See also* Chicano movement

Baartmann, Saarjite, 68, 201

Baca, Judy, *119*

Baca, Susana, *20*

Bachichi man (Ota Benga), *74, 75*, 226n15

Balmis, Francisco Javier, 50

Bambara culture, 29

Banner, Fiona, 235n44

Bardenstein, Carol, ix

Barnum, P. T.: beliefs of, 72; circus of, 75; collections of, 8, 69, 71; cosmorama of, *73*; invented monsters of, 72, 91; living human oddities exhibited by, *71, 77*, 127–128; "most beautiful" baby shows of, 73; science support linked to, 50, 66; "uncivilized races" exhibited by, 71–72, *74, 75*, 226n10. *See also* American Museum (New York City)

Barnum Museum (Connecticut), 72–73, 75

Baroque: absent in Southwest U.S., 156, *156*, 158; horror vacui (empty spaces) of, 97, 213n15; lowriders' inclusiveness as, 130; overarching and inclusive impulses of, 30, 33, 36, 97; tension of Enlightenment with, 43. *See also* New World Baroque

Barthes, Roland, 163, 168, 178

Bartram's Garden (Philadelphia), 207

Baudrillard, Jean, 27

Bautista, Juan, 232n73

Becoming Animal (exhibition), 87–88

Behar, Ruth, 181, 183, 194, 197

Belting, Hans, 106–107, 108, 109

Bemberg, Maria Luisa, 226n9

Benedict XIV, 116

Benedict XVI, 243n17

Benedict, Barbara M., 29–30

Benga, Ota, *74, 75*, 226n15

Benítez, J. J., 109, 231n37

Benjamin, Walter: angel of history of, 83, 94; on aura, 174; on collecting and collections, 27, 215n31; on looking at art, 207; on progress, 204; on quantity and quality, 206

Bergson, Henri, 22–23, 24

Bernardino, Juan, 107, 114

Bernstein, Herbert, 23

Bible, 37, 112–113

Bibliothéque Nationale (Paris), *8*, 46, 223n48

body markings, 128. *See also* tattoos

Bodyworlds exhibit, 79, 227n23

Boghosian, Varujan, ix–x

Bolivia (Potosí), silver production in, 51, 219n12

Bonfil Batalla, Guillermo, 158, 159

border crossings: blessings for, *122*, 123; circular moves in, 172–173; of disappearing Mexican legacy, 172–173; in 1848, 164, 238–239n1; by Guadalupe, 121–122, *122*, 123–125, 131–134, 176; misplacement of objects in, 22, 179; by Pancho Villa, 176–177; as porous vs. one-way, 190–191. *See also* borderlands; boundaries; Hispanic colonial period

borderlands: back-and-forth movements across, 172–173; communitas created in, 123–124; southwest (Aztlán) as, 17–18; violence against women in, 204–205. *See also* border crossings; boundaries; Hispanic colonial period

Border Patrol, 133, 135–136, 235n45

Border Security and Immigration Improvement Act, 133

Borges, Jorge Luis: "The Analytical Language of John Wilkins," *7*, 6; as blind librarian, 84, *85*; "Las cosas" [Plain Things], 1, 3, 18; memory master of, 170

Boston Globe, 237n27

botanical gardens: as democratic spaces, 207–208; function of, 215n22; objects moved from cabinets to, 53–54. *See also* museums (art, general, and natural history); zoos

Botanical Gardens (Madrid), 53–54

boundaries: definition of, 9–10; upsetting of, 90, 91. *See also* border crossings; borderlands

Brady, Mathew, *72*

Bravo, Francisco, 55

Brawley, Ernest, 165

Brazil: legacy of slavery in, 218n63; in technology/nature binary, 46, 93

Breton, André, 209n9

Brett, Dorothy, 143

Bridges Project, 182–183, 191–193, 197

Bridgman, Laura, 77

Brison, Susan, 194, 242n21

British Empire, rise of, 49

British Museum, 73, 221n27

Brooklyn Musum, 149

Brown, Bill, 23

brown, politics of, 17

Browning, Tod, 226n9

Bru, Juan Bautista: Jefferson's correspondence with, 7–8, 63–64, 66, 224n67; on New World species, 62

Bruce-Novoa, Juan, 165

Brueghel, Jan, II, 38, 39

Brueghel, Jan the Elder (Velvet), 37–38, 39

Brüning, Jochen, 215n22

Bry, Theodor de, 127

Buckminster, William, 80, 82–84

Buck-Morss, Susan, 23

Buddhas (Hazara), 42

Buffon, Count (George-Louis Leclerc): classification system of, 40–41, 53; Dávila's relationship with, 52; degeneracy theory of, 62, 64, 224n68; Histoire Naturelle, 50, 53; on observation, 79, 207, 216n41, 216n45; perspective in writings of, 223n51

burial sites, 68–69, 225n2

Burrus, Ernest J., 114

Bush, George W., 183, 241n6

Bustamante, Francisco de, 110–111, 113

butterflies, 86, 87–88, 87

Butterfly Pavilion (Vienna), 62–63

"Cabinet des Illusions" (Paris), 127

cabinets of wonders (Wunderkammern): aesthetics of display in, 30–31, 32, 213n15; author's interest in, x; as cornerstones of modern museums, 32, 221n27; depictions of, 28, 29, 30, 31, 39; disappearance on owner's death, 218–219n3; disarray of, 6; dispersed into museums, 40, 40–42, 44, 52–53, 221n23; European subjects privileged in, 37–38, 39, 42, 44–46; family or household oriented, 240n16; hierarchies in, 62; human bodies in, 32, 34; intellectual impetus underlying, 213n13; Internet version of, 217n55; legacy of, 216–217n52; magical messiness of, 94; as means of control, 27, 212n2; overarching and inclusive impulses in, 29–32, 37–39; persistence of, 75–79; precursors to, 213n14; as public education space,

52–53; re-creations of, 81–82, 90; Roman with clock (Kabinettschränke), 28; shift from marvelous to scientific in, 41–42, 206–207; visual privileging in, 42–43; as whole world and encyclopedic, 36–37; worldliness and wealth evidenced in, 38. See also American Museum (New York City); classification; post-apocalyptic cabinets of wonders; Real Gabinete de Historia Natural de Madrid

Cabrera, Miguel, 12

Cabrini, Frances Xavier, 152, 154, 237n27. See also Mother Cabrini Shrine

Cabris, Jean Baptiste, 127

Calatayud Arinero, María de los Ángeles: on Dávila, 52–53, 221n24; as museum curator, 46; on Real Gabinete, 54, 66; on Spanish scientific failures, 224–225n72

Californios: apparition of Guadalupe and, 134–135; erasure of, 172–173; genealogy of, 166, 176–177; identification as, 165. See also Hispanic colonial period; Los Angeles (Calif.); Museum of Jurassic Technology (Los Angeles); Southwest (U.S.)

Calloway, Colin, 159

camera obscura, 43, 217n55

Camillo, Giulio, 214nn20–21

Campani, Pietro Tommaso, 28, 29

cannibalism: alleged by indigenous people, 46, 62; of subject by object, 91–92, 206–207, 226–227n22

capitalism, 212n4. See also consumer objects and commodities

"CARA, Chicano Art" (exhibition), 152

Caribbean region, chronicle of, 55. See also Cuba

Carpentier, Alejo, 99, 209n9

Carrasco, David, 238–239n1

Carrera Guadalupana (relay race), 132–134

Carroll, Lewis, 196

cars: history of customized, 235n50; hubcaps for, 124, 126. See also lowriders (cars)

Cartese, Gugliemo, 28, 29

cartography, visual regime of, 43–44. See also atlas; globes

Casa de Geografía (Madrid), 51, 52. See also Real Gabinete de Historia Natural de Madrid

Casal, Lourdes, 191–194, 197

caste paintings: Quadro compared with, 62–63; racial hierarchies in, 10–11, 12, 13, 14; rediscovery of, 224n60; Virgin of Guadalupe and, 100, 101

Castillo, Abel Romeo, 221n24

Castillo, Ana, 119

Castro, Anton, 218–219n3

Castro, Fidel, 185

Cather, Willa, 143, 158

Catholic Church: alms collection of, 110–111; differences and divisions in, 229n8; evangelization campaigns of, 97, 99–100, 111, 229n8; Guadalupe cult harnessed by, 98, 100; idols replaced by Guadalupe, 106–107

Catholicism: ecclesiastical performance of, 105–106; folk type of, 157, 160; mobility of images and relics in, 120–121; postmodern images of, 124–125; radical reappropriation of, 115–116; sight as visualization of divine in, 98–100; Virgin of, 103. *See also* contagion with the sacred; crosses; *Penitentes*; pilgrimages

Catlin, George, 72

Cavafy, C. P., 161–162

Ceballos, Sandra, 185

celebrations and festivals: Easter, *131*, *155*; Guadalupe's Day, 118, 119, 131, 132–134, 234n23; International Day of the Migrant, 119; lowriders and, 130–131; of Tewa Pueblo Indians, 233n4

Cervantes, Miguel de, 7

Chagoya, Enrique, 117

chalk, 92–93

Chang and Eng, 71, *77*, 78

Charles III, 51–52, 64, 219n6

Charles IV, 50, 218n66

Charles Ratton Gallery (Paris), 90

Charleston Museum, 225n6

Chateau d'Oiron, 90

Chávez, Carlos, 143

Chávez, Ignacio, 50

Chicago: apparition of Virgin in, 135, *136*; dinosaur skeleton in, 66

Chicago World's Fair (1933), 83

Chicano movement: aesthetics of *rasquachismo* and, 126, 130; in autobiography, 177; Hispanic culture affirmed by, 151–152, 179, 190; imaginary homeland of, 18; MEChA and, 238–239n1; murals and, 15, *16*, 150; opening for mestizo politics and aesthetics of, 144; tattoos as symbol of, *124*, 125–127. *See also* New Mexico/New Mestizo effect

Chile, Spanish expeditions to, 49–50

Chimayó (N.Mex.): Guadalupan images sold in, *125*; pilgrimages to, 125, 130, 131, *154*, *155*, 156, *159*; sacred geography of, 153–154, 157

China, memory theater in, 214n20

chronicles: *Liber cronicarum* (Nuremberg Chronicle), 36, 215n24; New World, 55–56, 219n11

Cipac de Aquino, Marcos, Guadalupe painting by, 108, 109, 110, 113, 118

circuses, 75. *See also* Barnum, P. T.

Cisneros, Sandra, 120

cities and urban areas: indigenous peoples in, 62; "lettered" (concept), 98, 105, 106, 109, 112, 115, 229n6; as wealth-creating, 61

citizenship, destabilization of, 191

Ciudad Juárez (Mexico), violence against women in, 204–205

classification: alternative to, 6–7; as alternative to chaos, 216n38; in cabinets of wonders, 30, 32, 53, 61–62; fine-tuning of, 38–40, 200; first modern system of, 38–40; incongruities in, 6–7; Náhuatl terminology in, 222n32; objects moved due to, 53–54; other peoples reorganized by, 96–97; people and nature on same level in, 68; of people on intelligence scale, 47; of races, 10–11, *12*, *13*, 14; resemblances in, 223n51; threats to, 40–41; as tool of empire, 53–57, *58–59*, *60*, 61–62, 221n27, 222n32; visual regime in, 43–44. *See also* hierarchies; taxonomies

Clavigero, Francisco, 222n41

Clavijo y Fajardo, José, 50

Clearwater (Fla.), apparition of Virgin in, 135, *136*

Clifford, James, 21, 149, 215n31

Clofullia, Madame, 71

Codex Boturini, 151

Coffey, Mary, 230n29

Cohen, Philip, *168*, *171*, *173*, *174*, *175*

Colegio de Santa Cruz de Tlatelolco, 113, 114

collecting: bankruptcies from, 38, 52, 71, 215n32; on eBay, 216–217n52; of facts, 215–216n35; frenzied nature of, 37–38; inversion of, 81–83, 228n31, 228n33; obsession of, 22, 38, 51–52, 53, 139–140, 163, 205, 220n18; parodies of, 140, *141*; persistence of, 163–164; popularity of, 90, 215n30; possessive individualism distinguished from, 215n31; puzzlement at, 220n21; worldwide network for, 52–53. *See also* consumer objects and commodities; re-collecting

collections: accumulations compared with, 167; as always incomplete, 38, 53; of books, 215n31; changed consciousness of, 27–29, 212–213n5; cultures as, 22; individual identity evidenced in, 163–164; for lay people and scientists, 215n22; love as basis for, 91; Neruda on, 25–26; out-of-control acquisition of, 37–38. *See also* cabinets of wonders (*Wunderkammern*)

"Collective Memory" (exhibition), 240–241n29

College of Physicians. *See* Mütter Museum (Philadelphia)

Collier, John, 143

Colombia (Nueva Granada), Spanish expeditions to, 49, 50

colonialism. *See* conquest and colonialism; Hispanic colonial period

Colorado Springs Museum of Fine Arts, Taylor Museum of Southwestern Study, 138, 158

Colored Baptist Ministers, 75

Columbus, Christopher: as first "modern,"

218n62; geographic misplacement of Americas by, 7; living exhibits of, 68; location of meeting with monarchs, 118; rhetoric of, 65; voyage of 1492, 5, 53

commerce, science as interdependent with, 56–57, 61, 65. *See also* advertising and promotion; consumer objects and commodities

communitas and community: creation of, 106, 123–124; dissociation from, 191; lowriders in context of, 131. See also *Penitentes*

Como agua para chocolate [*Like Water for Chocolate*], 177

Condamine, Charles-Marie de la, 51

conquest and colonialism: bypassed discussion of, 7; epistemology linked to, 23; indigenous cultures destroyed in, 42; justification for, 61; racial hierarchies in, 10–11, 12, 14; religion, science, and technology underlying, 84; as scientific and economic enterprise, 56–57, 61, 65, 69; signifiers of, 29; social stratification and marginalization in, 96–97, 98, 201, 204; surveying and surveillance linked to, 68; tattoos encountered in, 127; technologies of power in, 9; Virgin of Guadalupe in, 15–16. *See also* empire; imperialism; migrants and migration; misplacement

consumer objects and commodities: butterflies as, *87*; capitalism linked to, 212n4; Guadalupe images on, 124, *126*; island of things, 187; material covetousness, 186; mirage, 188; museum sales of, 87; photographs as, 167; proliferation of, 206; recovery of, 87–88; recycling of, 81–83, 228n31, 228n33; religious images as, 121; transformed into family history, 177–179. *See also* advertising and promotion; commerce

contagion with the sacred, 104, 120–121

Coop (cartoonist), 235n44

copyright issues, 57

Córdova, Benito, 129

Corrigan, Kathleen, 223–224n59

Cortázar, Julio, 206–207, 226–227n22

Cortés, Hernán: Aztec lover of (Malinche), 107, 159, 230–231n33; dance about, 159; Guadalupan cult and, 15, 100, 103, 118; iconoclastic fury of, 106; objects acquired by, 199

cosmic race (raza cósmica), 15, 17, 137, 151

cosmography, 36–37

cosmorama, *73*

Cospi, Fernando, 48

Council of Trent, 98–99

Counter-Reformation, 96–99. *See also* Baroque

Covarrubias family, 135–136

coyote, use of term, 11, 123, 167, 172–173

crosses: border crossers' deaths marked by, 136;

Ground Zero, *21*; indigenous altars replaced with, 97; landscape sacralized by, 144, *146*, *151*; Latin American space marked by, 106; moradas marked by, 157–158; O'Keeffe's fascination with, 147, 151–152; pilgrims with, 147, *155*, *159*; recreating Christ's journey to, 133–134; returning to original sites, 153–154; violence depicted with, *15*. *See also* altars and shrines; *Penitentes*

crowd control, 73

Crumrine, N. Ross, 137, 157

Cuba: artistic negotiations in, 185–186; "bridge" to, 191–193, 197; community and citizenship destabilization in, 191; as consumer wasteland, 164; erasure of, 182; flag of, 187–188, 191; obsession with exile and, 182–190, 195, 197; Peter Pan generation of, 193–194; political action in, *184*, 185; Rupestrian sculptures in, 193–195; socialist project of, 183, 185, 187–88, 197; writing, rewriting, and naming of, 195. *See also* Ramos, Sandra

Cuban-American community: cultural cachet of, 182–183; objects representing, x; public perception of, 181–182; success of, 195

Cuban Diaspora: alternative perspective on, 183–190; narratives of trauma compared to, 194

Cuéllar, Juan de, 50

cultural legibility concept, 99, 112

cultures: asymmetries in, 103; continuity of, 152; destroyed in conquest, 42; divisions of, 14; effects of misplacement of plants on, 221n29; showcasing differences of, 73, 75; of theft, 200–201. *See also* transculturation

curiosities: fascination with, 52; juxtapositions of, 77–78; as resistant to curiosity, 27, 28, 30; shops of, *4*, 68–69; specimens privileged over, 44. *See also* cabinets of wonders *(Wunderkammern)*

curiosity: definitions of, 27, 29–30; as imperialist and aggressive, 29–30; as subservient to commercialization of nature, 56–57; use of term, 5. *See also* marvel and the marvelous; wonder

"Curious in Our Way" (conference), 213n12, 217–218n61, 223–224n59

Custom Mambo (video), 235n45

Cuvier, Georges, 64

Dartmouth College: Orozco's murals at, 14, *14*; Ortiz Taylor sisters at, 165, 173, 240n21; Ripley's connection to, 83–84. *See also* Hood Museum of Art (Dartmouth College)

Dasburg, Andrew, 143, *145*

"Dave's Dream," 128, *129*, 235n44

Dávila, Pedro Franco: archival process of Real Gabinete, 54–57; background of, 220n18; cabinet of wonders of, 51–52; circle of, 52–53;

classification system of, 53; Spanish encyclopedia on, 221n24

death: crosses marking, 136; objects as mediating,
19; objects in remembering, 19, 175; O'Keeffe
on, 139; and photographs, 178–179

deBuys, William, 139, 147

deculturation concept, 14, 241n32

deficiency theory, 62, 64–65, 224n68

degeneration theory: critique of notion, 64–65,
224n68; eugenics and, 11; fear of, 62. *See also*
caste paintings; mestizaje

Delgado, Angel, 185

DeMello, Margo, 234–235n33

Denmark, Royal Kunstkammer of, 38, *40*

Denver (Colo.), as sacred geography, 153

Denver Art Museum, 144, *145*

Descartes, René, 5

DeSipio, Louis, 181–182, *183*, 241n6

"Devices of Wonder" (exhibition), 42–43, 217n53

Díaz, Porfirio, 15

Díaz del Castillo, Bernal, 106, 110, 127, 230–
231n33

Didion, Joan, 20

Diego, Juan: Aztec connection of, 107; beatification of, 113–114, 152; "onomastic esoterism"
and, 108; reflection of, 110, 231n37; St. John
linked to, 112–113; tilma (cloak) of, *102*, *103*,
107–108, *109*–110, 111, 113, 115; Virgin's appearance to, 100, 107–108, 114–115

dinosaurs: extinction of, 207; fascination with,
50–51, 63–64, 66, 87; reconstructions of, *64*, *66*

Dion, Mark: cabinets of wonders by, x, 8; natural
history and, 65; subject/object repositioned
by, 91

Dion, Mark, works of: *An Account of Six Disas-
trous Years in the Library for Animals*, 88, *89*;
The Library for the Birds of Massachusetts, 88;
The Library for the Birds of New York, 88, *88*;
Polar Bear, 87; *Raiding Neptune's Vault*, 87;
Tate Thames Dig, 88; "Toys 'R' U.S. (When
Dinosaurs Ruled the Earth)," *64*

dioramas: containment and, 67, 92; continued
need for, 28; living people in, 57, 68–69, *71*,
72, *74*; visual privileged in, 216n41; voyeuristic nature of, 212n3. *See also* miniatures and
miniaturization

dirt, as matter out of place, 9–10, 20

discrimination: attempt to ban MEChA, 238–
239n1; DWM (Driving While Mexican) and,
235n45; of Greaser Act, 240n26. *See also* lowriders (cars); stereotypes

disorder: balance between order and, 18–19,
215n31; fear of, 40–41, 53

domestic workers, *119*

double consciousness concept, 104

Douglas, Mary, 9

Dresden (Germany), cabinets of wonders of, 206,
226n22

Duchamp, Marcel, 6, *7*, 88, 209n7

Dupláa, Christina, *21*

Durkheim, Emile, 98

Dusserl, Enrique, 218n62

DWM (Driving While Mexican), 235n45

East India Marine Society, 225n6

eBay, 43

Ecija, Diego de, 111

economy. *See* commerce; consumer objects and
commodities

Ecuador, Guadalupanism in, 233n3

Edwards, Elizabeth, 166–167, 179, 239n9

Egypt, pyramids of, 42

Ehrenberg, Felipe, 178

El Escorial (Spain), 51, 52, 219n11

Elizabeth I, 43, *45*

Elliott, J. H., 45, 46, 218n62

El Paso del Norte, Guadalupan mission in, 123

empire: discovery translated into, 37; as scientific
and economic enterprise, 56–57, 61; technologies of augmented vision enlisted in, 43–44,
45; wealth needed for, 51, 219n12. *See also* conquest and colonialism; imperialism

enacted spaces. *See* pilgrimages; place; sacred
space/landscape/geographies

Enciclopedia Guadalupana (1895), 109–110

encyclopedias, 36–37, 110

Enlightenment: augmented vision technologies
of, 42–43; caste paintings in context of, 11;
technology/nature binary of, 45–46

epistemology: cabinets and museums as spaces
for, 52–53, 220n21; changes in order of things,
3–5; collecting of facts distinguished from,
215–216n35; as colonial, 9, 29, 37, 46, 201;
condensed into I/eye, 42; critique of, 23–24;
disruptions of, 90–94; inception of modernity, 6–8, 212–213n5; indigenous, 51, 57–59, 63,
98–99; institutional filtering of, 57–60; public
interest in, 52, 217–218n61; as seeing, 98; sight
equated with, 37, *39*; for strange things, 30

Eslava, Bruno, 178

Espacio Aglutinador, 185–186

Ethnological Society (New York City), 75

eugenics, 11. *See also* caste paintings; degeneration theory; mestizaje

Eurocentrism: effects of, 49, 96–97; as heuristic
device and visual hierarchy, 44–46; in history,
218n62; Jefferson's critique of, 7, 62, 64–65,
224n68; of science, 41, 224n66. *See also* classification; hierarchies; taxonomies

evangelization campaigns: of Franciscans vs.

Jesuits, 111, 229n8; images privileged in, 99–100; religious syncretism in, 96–97

Evans, R. Tripp, 226n10

exhibitions: "Age of the Marvelous," x; Becoming Animal, 87–88; Bodyworlds, 78–79, 227n23; butterflies, *86, 87*; "Cabinet des Illusions," 128; "Collective Memory," 240–241n29; "Devices of Wonder," 42–43, 217n53; "El frente Bauhaus," 185; "El objeto esculturado," 185; "Garden of Eden on Wheels," *91*; of *Homo sapiens*, 88; household objects, *91*, 171, 240n16; "Market at Tenochtitlán," 150; "Multiple Visions," 150; "Other Roads to Aztlán," 152; "The Road to Aztlán," 152, 160; "Stuffing Birds, Pressing Plants, Shaping Knowledge," 213n12, 217–218n61, 223–24n59; "University of Man," 84; "When the President Is the Patient," 78; *Wunderkammer des Abendlandes*, 213n13

exiles/non-exiles and exile: alcohol and, 186, 196; community and citizenship destabilization in, 191; destabilization of citizenship in, 191; migrants compared with, 190–191; nostalgia and rupture of, 181, 193–195; from perspective of those remaining behind, 183–185, 195, 197; Ramos's *Buzos* and, *196*; redefinition of, 164; rupture of self in, 191–194; trauma of, 187; U.S. as "Mother" of, 181, 241n1

extinction, 85, 87, 207

Extremadura, Guadalupe cult in, 100, *102*, 103

eye/I, 23, 24, 42, 43–44. *See also* memory and memories; observation; sight; visual, the

Fabian, Johannes, 218n62

Fairbanks Museum of Natural History (St. Johnsbury, Vt.), *76*

family: consumer objects transformed into history of, 177–719; generation gap in, 171–172; language conflict in, 174, 177, 239n6, 240n21; means of articulating individual, 175–177. See also *Imaginary Parents* (Ortiz Taylor sisters)

Family Snaps (Spence and Holland), 167–168

feather headdress: as misplaced object, 3, *4, 5, 6*, 28; provenance of, 83, 199–201

Fechin, Nicolai, 143

feng shui, 18

Ferdinand, 118

Ferdinand (archduke), 200

Ferguson, Harvey, 143

fiction and films: aliens in, 7; on freaks, 226n9; misplaced objects in, 3; museums in, 220n21; on object's cannibalism, 226–227n22; questions of authenticity in, 232–233n74; Spanish terms in, 160; Tony Luhan depicted in, 143

Fifth Havana Biennial (1994), 186

films. *See* fiction and films; *specific films*

Findlen, P., 212n2

Fiz, Marchán, 201, 204

Fleury, Sylvie, 235n44

Flores Galindo, Alberto, 224n63

Florida, apparition of Virgin in, 135, *136*

folk and religious art, 149, 158. *See also* santeros

folk Catholicism, 157, 160. See also *Penitentes*

Ford, David Fairbanks, x, *90, 91*

fossils and bones: from Argentina, 50–51, 63–64; collecting of, 25, 26; Jefferson's collection of, 66, 224n71; object/subject interpenetration of (Solnhofen fossil), 22–23, 94. *See also* dinosaurs; Gould, Stephen Jay

Foster, George, 215–216n35

foto-esculturas, 178–179, 240–241n29

Foucault, Michel: Eurocentrism of, 45; on Hispanic writers, 6–7; on "historia" of plants and animals, 223n51; on order of things, 3, 5, 201; on representation, 201

foundational myths: of Aztec culture, 107; of indigenous artists and Guadalupe, 107; of Mexican nationalism, 100, *102*, 103, 108–116, 118, 132

found objects: re-collecting of, 168, 171. *See also* recycling and recycled things

Francken, Frans, II, 37, 38, *39*

Franco, Francisco, 121

Franklin, Benjamin, 65, 217–218n61

freaks: appreciation for, x; Barnum's, 71–72, 128; movie about, 226n19; tattooed survivor as, 128

Freaks (film), 225–226n9

Frederick, 52

Frederick William III, 127

Frederik III, 38, *40*

"frente Bauhaus, El" (exhibition), 185

Freud, Sigmund, 228n38

Frisco Native American Museum and Natural History Center Shop (N.C.), *63*

Fulcanelli, 233n8

Fusco, Coco, 88, *89, 90*

gachupín, use of term, 111, 232n53

Galdós, Benito Pérez, 220n21

Galeano, Eduardo, 46, 48

Galilei, Galileo, 42, 216n48

Ganahl, Pat, 235n50

Gandert, Miguel, *151*, 158–160

García, Bartolomé, 111

García Márquez, Gabriel, 2, 3

Garden of Eden: recreation of, 207–208; South America as, 243n17. *See also* botanical gardens; natural history

"Garden of Eden on Wheels" (exhibition), *91*

Gene Autry Western Heritage Museum (Los Angeles), 150

Germany: cabinets of wonders in, 28, 30; painting in Hamburger Kunsthalle, *44*

Getty Museum, 42–43, 217n53

ghosting concept, 80

Gibbons, Kaye, 163, 168

Gijón, Miguel, 221n23

Gilpin, Laura, 143

Girard, Alexander, 149–150

Girard, Susan, 149–150

Gisbert, Teresa, 154

Gleick, James, 217n54

globalization, Guadalupan mobility in, 121, 123. *See also* borderlands; exiles/non-exiles and exile; Internet; migrants and migration

global warming, 85, 87, 207, 243n17

globes, 43–44, *45*, 217n59. *See also* atlas

Gods Must Be Crazy, The, 3

Goffman, Erving, 13, 240–241n32

"going native," 128, 230–231n33, 235n41

Gold, Hazel, 220n21

Gómez-Peña, Guillermo, 88, *89*, 90, 117, 120

González, Elián, 182, 241n6

González, Laurence, 165

González-Crussi, F., 214n18

González Muñoz, María del Carmen, 55

Goodwin, Katherine R., 217n59

Gould, Stephen Jay: on art and science, 94; *Crossing Over*, 80; *Finders, Keepers*, 80; *Illuminations*, 80, 85–86; on objects collected but not exhibited, 85–86; Purcell's collaboration with, x, 23, 80; on ranking and classification, 47, 61–62; on subject/object interpenetration, 22

Gracián, Baltasar, 48, 218–219n3

Graham, Martha, 143

Grand Ethnological Congress, 75

Grand Rapids (Mich.): pilgrims from, 152, 156; transformation of, 156–157

Granma, 185

Greaser Act (1855), 240n26

greaser stereotype, 177, 240n26

Greenblatt, Stephen, 5

Green Vault (Dresden), 206

Grew, Nehemiah, 85

Gross, Terry, 227n24

Grote, Andreas, 215n27

Ground Zero altar (New York City), *21*

Gruzinski, Serge, 98, 105

Guadalupanism: border crossings of, 121, *122*, 123–124, 176; centripetal pull of, 137; emergence of, 16; European secularization vs., 99; expansion and mobility of, 117–137; images at center of, 104–107; Mexico City as center of, *102*, *103*, 117–118, *135*; object and narratives underlying, 107–116; relay race as connection in, 131–133, *132*. *See also* miracles; miraculous objects; Virgin of Guadalupe

GuadalupeNation, Virgin transformed into, *102*, 103

Guadalupe's Day (December 12), 118, 119, 131, 132–134, 234n23

guagua aérea (flying bus), 190

Guatemala: Christ at Esquípulas in, 153–154; feminicide in, 205; Indians depicted in 1980s, 12–13

Guerrero, Gonzalo, 127, 230–231n33

Gutenberg, Johannes, 37

Gutiérrez, Ramón, 158–160

Hagens, Günther von, 227n23

Hardy, Ed, 235n34

Harris, Alex, 235n44

Hartley, Marsden, 143

Harvard Museum of Natural History, *64*, 81, *86*, *87*

Harwood Museum (Taos), 148

Hegel, Georg Wilhelm Friedrich, 45

Hermann, Giacomo, *28*

Hermanos Penitentes. See *Penitentes*

hermetic symbolism, 114, 229n3, 233n8

Hernández, Ester, 119

Hernández, Francisco, 55–56, 219n11, 222n32, 222n38

Herrgen, Christian, 50

Hidalgo y Costilla, Miguel, 15, 100, 111–112, 135

hierarchies: anti-colonial movements as threat to, 201, 204; in conquest and colonialism, 96–97, 98, 201, 204; in cultural showcasing, 73, 75; European species as top of, 41; racial, 10–11, *12*, *13*, 14, 159–160; spatial organization disrupted, 88; ubiquitousness of, 223–224n59; upsetting of, 90–91; violence inherent in, 47, 61–62. *See also* classification; taxonomies; visual, the

Hiroshima tribute, *93*, 94

Hirsch, Marianne, 239–240n13

Hispanic colonial period: erasure of, 148, 164, 166, 238–239n1; geographical extent of, 153–154; misplacement and erasure of, 148, 164, 166, 238–239n1; Puritan influence on, 106; science central to, 104; takeovers in, 176–177; utopian projection of, 143. *See also* border crossings; borderlands; Southwest (U.S.); U.S.-Mexico border

Hitler, Adolf, 200

Holland, Patricia, 167

homeland security, 238–239n1

Hood Museum of Art (Dartmouth College): "Age of the Marvelous" exhibition of, x; life-cast heads at, *84*, 226n15; paintings in, *16*; Ripley's collection in, 84–85

Hopkins, Arthur, 144

Horkavy, Ken, *136*

Howarth, Sam, *154, 155, 159*

hubcaps, 124, *126*. *See also* lowriders (cars)

Hulme, Peter, 223n48

human body: anatomical studies of, 33, *36, 37,* 214n18; musculature and skeleton of, *37, 77–79*; oddities of, *71, 72, 77–79*; preservation of, 32, *34, 77,* 79, 93, 227n23; sections of, 227n23; as site of mestizaje (female), 16–17; skin of, 78, *78,* 227n24. *See also* body markings; race; tattoos

Humboldt, Alexander von, 50, 106, 218n66, 223n46

Hurston, Zora Neale, 169

Huxley, Aldous, 143

Hyman, Alexis, 91

hyphens: as colonization, 173; as connector and symbol of loss, 188; as continental bridge, 137; identity and, 190; between Mexico and U.S., 172

Ianni, Octavio, 218n63

icons and iconicity: adaptability of Guadalupan, 118–121; function of, 234n25; of *latinidad,* 17, 137; of lowriders, 130–131, 236n55; mobility and visibility of, 120–121; pilgrimages linked to, 152–156; saddle Virgins as, 128; third-order signs of, 234n15; with will of their own, 118. *See also* altars and shrines; miracles; miraculous objects; relics; religious syncretism

identity: assigned to immigrants, 191; Guadalupe as anchor of, 131–132; hyphenated, 190; objects and memories linked to, 18–20, 22; objects as anchors of, 163–64; objects as marking, 14–15; pilgrimages as celebration of, 156–157; proto-nationalist understanding of, 97–98; questioning location of, 227n24; stripped by institutions, 14, 241n32. *See also* identity kit; memory and memories

identity kit: concept of, 164; construction of, 173–174, 179; stripped by institutions, 14, 241n32

idolatries: church identification of, 98–99; ugliness of, 106. *See also* altars and shrines; icons and iconicity

I Don't Want to Talk about It [*De eso no se habla*], 226n9

images: as absence vs. presence, 103–107; attempt to control power of, 106–107; desire and, 104; as equal to language, 230n18; as ixiptla, 105–106; status of, 98, 103–104

Imaginary Parents (Ortiz Taylor sisters): as altarbook, 178–179; collaboration of, 164; different memories of parents and children in, 170–172; double move in, 168–169, 174; as influence, ix–x, 21; Latino and Hollywood images in, 173–174; Ramos's empty suitcases compared with, 189–190; structure and form of, 166–167, 174–175, 177–178; whip and whipping in, 176–177; writing of, 165–166. *See also* Ortiz Taylor, Sandra; Ortiz Taylor, Sheila

imagination: coyote and, 11, 123, 172–173; memory and narrative linked to, 168–179; ship metaphor in, 161–162

immigrants. *See* migrants and migration

Imperato, Ferrante, 29, *31*

imperialism: accumulation linked to, 37–38; aggressive curiosity linked to, 29–30; technologies of augmented vision enlisted in, 43–44, *45. See also* conquest and colonialism; empire

impermanence, 228n31

Indian Market (Taos): founding of, 149; guidelines of, 150; packaging of, 139–140, 143

indigenization and indigenism: call for repatriation of objects, 200–201; clothing as index of marginality, 14; in colonial hierarchies, 61–62; concept of, 147–149; dichotomy created in, 159–160; exhibitions of living people, 68, *71, 72, 74,* 226n10; image-as-presence for, 104–105; "magic technology" to impress, 223n48; natural history linked to history of, 62–64; painting style as evidence of, 144, 145; photographic evidence of, 160; post-Conquest histories of, 96; sacred space as counter to, 151; Virgin of Guadalupe as protectress, 100, 103–104. *See also* identity; mestizaje; Native Americans; New Mexico/New Mestizo effect

indigenous artists and arts: abstraction of, 230n29; in churches, 96–97; image and text combined in, 105; religious orders' promotion of, 110–111; Virgin of Guadalupe as foundational act in, 107

individualism: car as symbol of, 130–131; collecting vs. possessive type of, 215n31; collections as evidence of, 163–164; tattoos as symbol of, 127–128

installations. *See* Andrade, Farnese de; Dion, Mark; Duchamp, Marcel; Ortiz Taylor, Sandra; Purcell, Rosamond W.; Ramos, Sandra; Wilson, Fred

Institute for Policy Studies (Washington, D.C.), 23

Institute of Contemporary Art (Boston), 235nn44–45

institutions. *See* total institutions

International Day of the Migrant (December 18), 119

Internet: community and citizenship destabilization via, 191; Guadalupan sites on, 121, 123, 124, 132–134; legacy of Wunderkammern for, 216–217n52

Iowa, burial site in, 225n2

Iraq National Museum, 200–201
Iriordo, Josu, 133
Isabella, 68, 118
ixiptla, image as, 105–106
Ixtlilxochitl, Alva, 152

J. Paul Getty Museum, 42–43, 217n53
Jackson, Andrew, 78
Jackson, Chevalier, 77
Jacobs, Jane, 61
James, Daniel, 232–233n74
Jamnitzer, Abraham, 33
Jansen, Hans, 216n48
Jansen, Zacharias, 216n48
Jaramillo, Dave, 128, 129, 130
Jaramillo, Irene Maria, 128, 129
Jardin du Roi (Paris), 207
Jaurena, Carlos, 178
Jay, Ricky, 76, 76, 217n53, 227n26
Jefferson, Thomas: Bru's correspondence with, 7–8, 63–64, 66, 224n67; collections of, 66, 224n71; Eurocentrism critiqued by, 7, 62, 64–65, 224n68; Real Gabinete linked to, 7–8, 50–51, 63–64
Jesus Christ: Denver statue of, 152; stages of the cross remembered, 133; tattooed image of, 126
Jetter, Alexis, x
Jiménez, Nicario, 15
John (saint), 112–113
John Paul II (pope): Juan Diego beatified by, 113–114; on Virgin of Guadalupe, 117, 118; Virgin of Guadalupe statue blessed by, 152, 156–157
Jo Jo the Russian Dog Face Boy, 71
Jones, Robert Edmond, 143, 144
Jung, Carl, 143

Kahlo, Frida, 126
Karlin, Dorothy, x
Katzman, Steven, 78
Kenseth, Joy, x
Kentucky, mastodon of, 64
Kepler, Johannes, 217n55
Kertzer, David I., 98
Khosian people, 68
Kino (priest), 123
Kircher, Atanasius, 48
kitsch, 21, 206, 220n21
Klee, Paul, 94
knowledge. See epistemology
knowledges reconstruction project, 23–24
Kodak moment, 167
kopillu ketzalli (Mexican indigenous group), 200, 201
Kossmann, Mayvor, x
Kubler, George, 3, 5, 22, 209n10

Kuhn, Richard, 110
Kunsthistorisches Museum (Vienna): Imperial and Ecclesiastical Treasury collection of, 206, 207, 214n16, 233–234n14; objects of, 28, 29
Kupferminc, Mirta, 17, 17

Lafaye, Jacques: on creole proto-nationalist agenda, 229n8; on indigenous artists, 110–111; on "onomastic esoterism," 108; on Sánchez, 111–112, 115
Lamadrid, Enrique R., 154, 158–160
Lamb, Jonathan, 43
languages: family conflicts over, 174, 177, 239n6, 240n21; pictures as equal to, 230n18; shift from Spanish to English focus, 49; Spanish terms in English fiction, 160. See also Náhuatl language; narratives
Lasso de la Vega, Luis, 114–116, 232n73
Lastanosa, Vicencio Juan, 48, 218–219n3
Las Trampas church, 156
Las Vegas, Weeping Guadalupe in, 135–136
latinidad: construction of, 173–174, 179; promotion of, 165; role of pilgrimage and community in, 121; use of term, 210–211n25; and Virgin of Guadalupe, 16, 137
Latinization: celebrations fostering, 132–134; construction of, 21, 179; of consumer objects, 191; evidence of, 124, 125, 126–127; and Guadalupe, 132–133; role of exported sacred landscape in, 140, 143. See also lowriders (cars)
Latinos/as: refusal to identify as, 165; use of terms, 210–211n25
Latino Studies, 238–239n1
Lautréamont, le Comte de (Isidore-Lucien Ducasse), 7, 209n9
La Villa/Tepeyac (Mexico): events connecting New York to, 131–134; Guadalupan Basilica in, 100, 102, 103, 107, 109, 111, 118–119; and Guadalupan images, 124, 126; as New Jerusalem, 112; pilgrimages to, 131–132, 231n40; and Virgin of Guadalupe, 100, 102, 103, 104, 107–108, 110–111, 120. See also Guadalupanism; miracles
Lawrence, D. H., 143, 144
Lazarus (saint), 196
Lazarus, Emma, 181, 182, 183, 241n1
Leclerc, George-Louis. See Buffon, Count (George-Louis Leclerc)
Leeuwenhoek, Antonie van, 216n48
Leibniz, Gottfried Wilhelm, 43
León, Luis E., 117
Leonardo da Vinci, 43
León-Portilla, Miguel, 114, 115, 151, 232n73
Lequanda, José Ignacio, 58–62, 223n51
Léry, Jean de, 46

lettered city *(ciudad letrada)* concept, 98, 105, 106, 109, 112, 115, 229n6

Levanti, Antonio, 214n18

Levine, Robert M., 241n6

Lewis, Edith, 143

Lewis and Clark expedition, 50, 65, 66, 219n4

liberation ecology concept, 243n17

Liber cronicarum (Nuremberg Chronicle, Schedel), 36, 215n24

Lienzo de Tlaxcala (indigenous post-Conquest history), 96

Linnaeus, Carolus (Carl von Linné), 40, 216n38

Lippard, Lucy, 158–160

Lippershey, Hans, 42, 216n48

literacy/illiteracy, definitions of, 99–100

Locke, John, 194

Lockhart, James, 97–98, 232n73

London Zoo, 88, 90

López, Alma, 119, 120

López, José Ramón, 48, 67, 212n3, 212–213n5

López, Tomás, 43

López, Yolanda M., *119*

Lord of the Rings, The, 3

Los Angeles (Calif.): Guadalupanism in, 117; lowriders in, 236n55; Museum of Latin American Art (MoLAA), x. *See also* Museum of Jurassic Technology (Los Angeles)

Los Angeles County Museum, 152

Los Unidos Car Club, *129*

Louis XVIII, 127

Louisiana Exposition (1904), 84, *84*

Lovato, Charles, 138

lowriders (cars): as colonial religious carretas, *142*; cultural role of, 128, *129*, 130–131; exhibitions of, 128, *129*, 130, 235nn44–45; in New Mexico vs. East LA, 235n55; T-shirts for, *125*; Virgin of Guadalupe depicted on, 128, *129*

Lucasie family, 71, *71*

Ludmer, Josefina, 9

Luhan, Antonio (Tony), 143, 160

Luhan, Mabel Dodge, x–xi, 143, 148, 160. *See also* Mabel Dodge Luhan House (Taos)

luxury trade, 206

Lytle, Nancy, *89*

Mabel Dodge Luhan House (Taos): author's visit to, x–xi; biography of, 147–148; description of, 141; star visitors to, 143–144, 147

Macbeth, 144

MacDonald, Sharon, 212n2

Machado, Eduardo, 193–194

Machado, Maria Helena, 46, 61

Macpherson, C. B., 215n31

Madrid (Spain): Botanical Gardens, 53–54; Casa de Geografía, 51, 52; Museo Arqueológico Nacional, 53; Museo de América in, 12, 54, *101*; Museo del Prado, *30*, 38, *39*, 53, 221n28; Museo Etnológico Nacional, 53; National Museum of Anthropology, 68. *See also* Museo de Ciencias Naturales (Madrid); Real Gabinete de Historia Natural de Madrid

Magellan, Joel, 133

Main Street Museum (White River Junction, Vt.), x, 8, *90*, 90–91

Malaspina, Alejandro, 49

Man, Cornelis de, *44*

Mann, Charles, *126*

maquiladora workers, 204–205

Maratta, Carlo, 28, *29*

Marin, John, 143

"Market at Tenochtitlán" (display), 150

Marshall, John, 77

Martin, Carlos, 230n27

Martínez, Francisco de Paula, 65–66

Martínez, José, 158

Martínez, María, 148, 159

Martínez, Marion C., 124, *127*, 140

Martínez, Victor, *126*

marvel and the marvelous: changing status of, 206–207; critique of contrived, 209n9; use of terms, 5. *See also* curiosity; wonder

Marx, Karl, 23

Massachusetts, apparition of Virgin in, 135

Massachusetts Museum of Contemporary Art, 87

mastodon *(Megatherium americanum),* 63–64, *64,* 66

Mastroianni, Marcelo, 226n9

matachines, 158–159

Matamoros International Bridge, 133

Mavor, Carol, 163

Maxon, Joseph, 217n59

Mayer, Caspar, *74*

Maza, Francisco de la, 111, 112

McDean, Craig, 235n44

McLaughlin, Patricia, 206

MEChA (Movimiento Estudiantil Chicano de Aztlán), 238–239n1

medicine: natural history museum for, 77–79; photography of surgeries, 227n24; plants useful in, 57. *See also* anatomical theaters; human body

memory and memories: artificial vs. involuntary personal, 169; in classical times vs. early modern Church, 229n7; coyote trickster of, 11, 123, 167, 172–173; and family stories and photographs, 167–168, 240n13; identity and objects linked to, 17–21, 22; narratives and imagination linked in, 168–179; objects as anchors of, 90, 163–164, 168–169; objects imprinted with, 22, 57; photographs as anchors of, 167–168;

in pilgrimage tradition, 229n3. *See also* art of memory; consumer objects and commodities; identity; sacred space/landscape/geographies

memory theaters, 36–37, 214n20

Mena, Luis de, *101*

Mendieta, Ana, 195

Mercator, Gerhard, 37, 215n25

Mesoamerican geography. *See* sacred space/landscape/geographies

mestizaje: boundary definition in, 9–10; commonalities and exclusions of, 12–13; concept of, 9; cult and nationalism interconnected with, 109–116; degeneration and, 64–65, 224n68; eastern elites' imagining of, 143–152; female body as site of, 15–16; and Guadalupan Basilica, 103; location of, 227n24; matter out of place and, 9–10, 20; New World Baroque origins in, 99–100; objects as marking and framing, 14–15; as reality and aesthetic agenda, 147–149; representation of, 14, 62, 224n63; scientific type of, 222n32; transculturation distinguished from, ix; as unrepresentable, 14–16; Virgin of Guadalupe as exemplar of, ix, 15–16, 99–100, 137. *See also* caste paintings; classification; identity kit

mestizo imaginary, church narrative in script for, 98, 100. *See also* New Mexico/New Mestizo effect

Metropolitan Museum (New York City), 63

Mexican-American Studies, 238–239n1

Mexican nationalism: cult and mestijaze interconnected with, 109–116; foundational documents in, 230n10; Guadalupe as foundational in, 100, *102*, 103, 108–116, 118, 132

Mexican Revolution (1910), 118, 150

Mexicans and Mexican Americans: continuous presence of, 164, 238–239n1; derogatory terms for, 177, 240n26; Hispanic culture reconfigured by, 152; land losses of, 176–177; lived environment changed by, 230n27; public perception of, 181, 182–183; refusal to identify as, 165; right-wing attacks on, 166, 238–239n1

Mexico City: Guadalupan images in, *102*, 103; Guadalupe as patroness of, 117–118; Metro Hidalgo Virgin Apparition Shrine in, *135*. *See also* La Villa/Tepeyac (Mexico)

Meyer, Pedro, *122*

Michael (saint), 108

Michigan. *See* St. Francis Xavier parish (Grand Rapids, Mich.)

microscopes, 42, 216n48

Mier, Servando Teresa de, 113–114

Mignolo, Walter, 46, 218n62

migrants and migration: circular moves of, 172–173; community and citizenship desta-

bilization in, 191; current level of, 16–17; destabilization of citizenship in, 191; exiles compared with, 190–191; Guadalupe carried across borders by, 121, *122*, 123–124, 133–137; identity-in-migration and, 156–157; mestizaje linked to, 13–15; mis- and displacement of, 201, 204–206; misplacement of people in, 9–16, 201, 204–205; prayers for, 117; public discourse on, 181–182; undocumented workers, 120, 133–134; as uprooting of people, 16, *17*; Virgin of Guadalupe as symbol of, 120. *See also* exiles/non-exiles and exile; globalization; workers

military, 13, 210n20

Millicent Rogers Museum (Taos), 148, 159

Millones, Luis, 104–105

Milton (Mass.), apparition of Virgin in, 135

mind and matter. *See* subject/object binary; subject/object interpenetration

mines and mining, 51, 56–57, 219n12, 220n15

miniatures and miniaturization: as altars, 178–179; aura of, 174–175; of Bible, 36; cultures represented as, 149–150; expansive nature of, 43–44; of globes, 217n59; nostalgia and, 181, 193–195; remembered objects as, 168–179; Stewart on, 24, 36, 42, 43, 217n60. *See also* dioramas; *Imaginary Parents* (Ortiz Taylor sisters)

miracles: apparitions of Virgin, 135, *136*; narratives of, 107–116, 134–135; role of relics and icons in, 120–121. *See also* Chimayó (N.Mex.); miraculous objects

miraculous objects: devotion to, 134–135; interpretation of, 108–109; Juan Diego's tilma (cloak) as, *102*, 103, 107–111, 113, 115; paintings as, 100, 107, 110–111. *See also* Chimayó (N.Mex.); relics

Miró, Joan, *21*

misplacement: across borders, 22, 179; catastrophic events underlying, 21–22; concept of, 3, 5, 21; in conquest and colonialism, 96–97; double nature of, 41–42; of Hispanic colonial period, 148, 164, 166, 238–239n1; of New World in Europe, 6–8, 27–29; of people in migrations and movements, 9–18, 201, 204–205; of plants, 221n29; strange objects converted to technologies of power in, 9; in travel and tourism, 88, 90–91; violence linked to, 204–205. *See also* cabinets of wonders (*Wunderkammern*); classification; epistemology; Eurocentrism; exiles/non-exiles and exile; Guadalupanism; icons and iconicity; migrants and migration; modernity; natural history; post-apocalyptic cabinets of wonders; Virgin of Guadalupe

Mission Church of Nuestra Señora de Guadalupe (Halona [now Zuni] Pueblo), 118

Mitchell, W. J. T., 64, 94, 103, 211n37, 230n18

modernist art: artifact and art distinguished, 63; "encounter with totem" in, 143; salvage ethnology and, 149. *See also* recycling and recycled things

modernity: Americas as constitutive of object of inquiry in, 42, 45; art/science distinction in, 6; birth of, 218n62; colonial inequality underpinning, 96–97, 98, 201, 204; definitions of, 103–104; displacements of, 147; Eurocentric accounts of, 49; role of objects in shaping, x, 5, 7, 9

Modern Latin American Art Museum, 187–188

Modern Primitives: aesthetics and ethics of, 235n41; origins of, 234–235n33; and tattoo renaissance, 126–127

Molina, Luis de, 222n41

Moll, Carl Erenvert von, 50

Monastery of Guadalupe (Spain), 118

Monsiváis, Carlos, 107

Montezuma: dance about, 159; expedition of, 151; and feather headdress, 3, *4*, 5, 6, 29, 84, 199–201

Montúfar (bishop), 110–111

Moraga, Cherríe, 119

Moraña, Mabel, 213n15

Morinis, Alan, 137, 157

Morrison, Toni, 169

Mosquera, Gerardo, 185

Mother Cabrini Shrine, 152

Mo-Ti, 217n55

Movimiento Estudiantil Chicano de Aztlán (mecha), 238–239n1

Mukerji, C., 212n4

"Multiple Visions" (exhibition), 150

murals and muralism, 15, *16*, 150

Museo Arqueológico Nacional (Madrid), 53

Museo de América (Madrid), *12*, 54, *101*

Museo de Ciencias Naturales (Madrid): background of, 212–213n5; Don Francisco de Paula's diary in, 65–66; human skeletons in, *81*; mastodon of, *64*; objects in, 54, *85*; pictorial account of Perú in, 58–59, *58–59*, 60, 61–62, 223n51; Purcell's work and, x, 80–81; Ross's exhibit and, 212n3; scientific archive of, 46

Museo Etnológico Nacional (Madrid), 53

museological practices: constructing meanings in, 5; critique of, 8; framing in, 75; reorganization of, 27–28. *See also* politics of display; provenance

Museo Nacional del Virreinato (Tepotzotlán, Mexico), *13*, 200

Museum of Ethnology (Vienna), 4, 5, 199–201

Museum of International Folk Art (Santa Fe), 149–150

Museum of Jurassic Technology (Los Angeles): entrance to, 229n48; exhibits in, *91*, 91–92; fame of, 91–92; focus of, x, 8; hierarchies upset in, 92

Museum of Latin American Art (Los Angeles, molaa), x

Museum of Man (Musée de l'Homme, Paris), 67, 68

Museum of Modern Art (New York City), 75, 88

museums (art, general, and natural history): of art, 92, 225n6; artistic interventions in, 80–81; beginnings of, 69, 71; captions in, 87; continued importance of, 28, 163–164; critique of, 8; earliest U.S., 225n6; emergence of, 6, 212–213n5; household objects in, 171; identity crisis of, 68; illogic of preservation in, 85, 87; as knowledge filters, 57–60; living people exhibited in, 68; Native American and natural history linked in, 61–63; objects collected but not exhibited in, 83, 84–85, 87, 92; persistence of, 76–79; precursors to, 27, 38, 212n2; as structuring devices, 5, 220n21; untouchable objects of, 207; as women's public space, 73. *See also* botanical gardens; museological practices; provenance; zoos; *specific institutions*

Music Center of Los Angeles, *119*

Mutis, José Celestino, 56–57, 224–225n72

Mütter, Thomas Dent, 77

Mütter Museum (Philadelphia): audience response to, 77–78; description of, 77; exhibitions of, 77, 78–79; objects, *77*; reversal of observation in, 79; virtual tour of, 226n17

nafta (North American Free Trade Agreement), 205

nagpra (Native American Graves Protection and Repatriation Act, 1990), 68, 225n2

Nahua people: early text on, 56; image as ixiptla for, 105–106; images and written signs of, 99; symbolic universe of, 232n73

Náhuatl language: in classification system, 222n32; in Southwest terminology, 152; Spanish influence on, 97; Virgin of Guadalupe account in, 108–110, 113–116

names and naming: of Cuba, 195; cultural continuity in, 152; cultural dichotomy in, 159–160; of lowrider organizations, 131; of mixed couples, 62–63; of objects, 54–55; personal rationale for, 239n6; of previously unknown objects, 97; of Virgin of Guadalupe, 117–118

narratives: of car transformed into lowrider, 131; emergence of Virgin in, 97–98; memories created via, 167–168, 240n13; memory and imagination linked in, 168–179; of miracles (Guadalupanism), 107–116, 134–136; objects as pre-texts in, 164; objects as vehicles of, 18, *19*. *See also* exiles/non-exiles and exile; migrants and migration

national imaginary: Anglocentric, 16–17, 157, 166; creole, 115; household objects as grounding, 171; Latino, 210–211n25

nationality: as consumer fetish, 191; definitions of, 221n24; rituals of cohesion in, 100, *102*, 103. *See also* Mexican nationalism; proto-nationalism

National Museum of the American Indian (New York City), 133

National Museum of Anthropology (Madrid), 68, 201

Native American Graves Protection and Repatriation Act. *See* NAGPRA

Native Americans: as Barnum's freaks, 71–72, *72*, *74*; natural history linked to history of, 63–64; as both stereotyped and revered, 160; Virgin of Guadalupe as protectress of, 118

natural history: biggest, rarest specimens of, *32*; collected in Americas, 221n27; commercialization of, 56–57, 60–61; communitas created in, 123–124; construction of, 5, 209n5; curiosity in development of, 213n12; deficiency theory of, 62, 64–65, 224n68; dioramas of, 212n3; dis- and misplacement of, 221n29; early texts of New World, 55–56; extinction and, 87, 207; filtering knowledge about, 57–60; first reconstruction of fossilized mammal, 63–64; humans undistinguished from, 87–88; image as absence vs. presence in, 103–107; indigenization and, 51, 68–69; as other, 218n62; paradise of, 42, 44–46, 49, 61–64; public education of, 72–73; recycling of texts, 82–83; resemblances in, 223n51; uncanny logic of, 87; visual culture of, 213n12

nature: American culture as part of, 62–63; classification of, 38; commercialization of, 56–57; consumer objects reclaimed by, 81–83, 228n31, 228n33; environmental concerns about, 243n17; observation of, 41; perfectibility of, *32*; preservation of, 206–208

Nazi ideology, 210n19, 243n4

Nebel, Richard, 115

nepantla (land in-between), 152

Neruda, Pablo, 25–26

New Age ideas, 126–127, 236n2, 238n45

New Mexico (state): annexation of, 158; cultural continuity of, 152–160; Guadalupanism in, 118; Guadalupe as patroness of, 117–118; as land of enchantment, 143–152; lowriding capital in, 130, 236n55; marketing of, 139–140, 143; as sacred geography, 141, 152–160; slogan and license plate of, 139, *140*. *See also* Chimayó (N.Mex.); Santa Fe (N.Mex.); Taos (N.Mex.)

New Mexico Arts Society, 150

New Mexico Museum of Art, 144, *145*

New Mexico/New Mestizo effect: concept of, 140, 143; expansion across U.S., 147–148; land of enchantment in, 143–152; sacred geography of, 152–160

Newton, Isaac, 43, 217n54

New World Baroque: church policies underlying, 98–99; as contestatory aesthetic, 99–100; indigenous decoration of churches as, 96. *See also* Zamora, Lois Parkinson

New York City: American Museum of Natural History, 63; Asociación Tepeyac, 117–120, 132–134; Ethnological Society, 73; Ground Zero altar, *21*; Ground Zero Cross in, *21*; Guadalupan celebrations in, 131–134; luxury trade in, 206; Metropolitan Museum, 63; Museum of Modern Art, 73, 87; National Museum of the American Indian, 133; Nuyorican experience of, 190. *See also* American Museum (New York City)

New York Library Society, 226n10

New York Times, 139, 237n2

Nican mopohua (Náhuatl text): aesthetic form of, 232n73; authenticity of, 113–115; description of, 108–110

Nolan, Lee, 120

North American Free Trade Agreement. *See* NAFTA

nostalgia. *See* miniatures and miniaturization

Novak, Lorie, 167

Nubian people, *74*

Nuestra Señora de Guadalupe Church (Altar, Sonora), 123

Nueva Granada. *See* Colombia (Nueva Granada)

Nuevo Mexico profundo, 157, 158–160

Nuevo México Profundo (Lamadrid et al.), 158–160

Nuremberg Chronicle (*Liber cronicarum*, Schedel), 37, 215n24

objects: Borges on, 1, 3; as cannibalizing subject, 92, 206–207, 226–227n22; collected but not exhibited, 83, 84–85, 87, 92; complex totality of, 22, 94; as dead and alive, 93; and definition of self, 215n31; democratization of, 94; diverted from specified paths, 211n38; documentation of, 54–55; elusive nature of, 23; García Márquez on, 2, 3; as images, 211n37; in-between (unclassifiable), 40; introduced in conquest and colonialism, 96–97; narratives interconnected with, 107–116, 176;

not-searched-for-but-found, ix–x; personal history imprinted on, 175–177; power of, 18; remembered and imagined, 168–179; repatriation of, 200–201; rift in understanding caused by, 5; spatial organization of, 88; as staring back, 93, 120; telescoping and microscoping process of, 57; unequal exchange of, 9. *See also* consumer objects and commodities; curiosities; identity; memory and memories; miraculous objects; photographs; subject/object binary; subject/object interpenetration

"objeto esculturado, El" (exhibition), 185

observation: Buffon's emphasis on, 41, 216n41; in chronicles of New World, 55–56, 219n11; religion and science linked to, 216n45; reversals of, 78, 80, 92; role of, 41, 216n41, 216n45. *See also* eye/I; sight; visual, the

obsessions: books, 82–83; collecting, 22, 38, 51–52, 53, 139–140, 163, 205, 220n18; Cuba and exile, 181–183, 186–189, 195, 197; disorder, 41; globalization, 121–123

O'Gorman, Edmundo, 114, 218n62

O'Gorman, Juan, 143

O'Hare International Airport (Chicago), *66*

O'Keeffe, Georgia: on death, 139; New Mexico stay of, 143–144; Southwest's influence on, 143–147, 151–152

O'Keeffe, Georgia, works of: *Black Cross, New Mexico, 1929, 146*; *Cow's Skull—Red, White, and Blue*, 144; *Fragment of the Rancho de Taos Church*, 144; *The Lawrence Tree*, 144; *Ram's Head with Hollyhock*, 144

Olguín, B. V., 126, 234n27

onomastic esoterism concept, 108

Oppenheimer, Méret, 7

order: anti-colonial movements as threat to, 201, 204; balance between disorder and, 18–19, 215n31; demand for, 41; incongruities in, 6–8, 27–28; memories linked to, 20, 22; reversal and reordering of, 88, 90–91, 92–93; subversion of, 38. *See also* classification; hierarchies; taxonomies

Orleck, Annelise, x

Orozco, Jose Clemente, 14, *14*

Ortiz, Estrella, 152

Ortiz, Miguel, 176

Ortiz de Montellano, Guillermo, 115

Ortiz Taylor, Sandra: adult persona of, 172, 174; background of, 165; context of work, 178; Dartmouth visit of, 165, 173, 240n21; as influence, ix–x, 21; Mexico visit of, 173, 177; naming of, 239n6

Ortiz Taylor, Sandra, works of: *Catch the Wave, 168, 168*; *El músico y la dama* [The Musi-

cian and the Lady], *173*; *Night Closet, 171, 174*; *Ofrenda for a Maja* [Offering for a Diva], *174*; *Recuerdo para los abuelitos* [In Memory of Our Grandparents], *175*. See also *Imaginary Parents* (Ortiz Taylor sisters)

Ortiz Taylor, Sheila: adult persona of, 172, 174; background of, 165; Dartmouth visit of, 165, 173, 240n21; on "heaping up" evidence, 170; as influence, ix–x, 21; on memory, 168–169; Mexico visit of, 173, 177; naming of, 239n6; on Pancho Villa's whip, 176

Ortiz Taylor, Sheila, works of: *Coachella*, 165; *Faultline*, 165; *Outrageous*, 165; *Slow Dancing at Miss Polly's*, 165; *Southbound*, 165; *Spring Forward/Fall Back*, 165. See also *Imaginary Parents* (Ortiz Taylor sisters)

Ortiz Torres, Rubén, 131, 235n45, 236n55

"Other Roads to Aztlán" (exhibition), 152

Our Lady of the Rosary of Talpa, 158

Our Lady of the Underpass, 135, *136*

Oviedo, Gonzalo Fernández de, 55

Owings, Nathaniel, 149

Owl's Head junkyard (Maine), 82–84

Oxford University, Tradescant Hall, 76

Padilla, Carmella, 128

Palácio Nacional da Ajuda (Portugal), 214n16

Pané, Ramón, 55

Paracas National Reserve (Perú), *208*

Paris (France): Academy of Sciences, 51; Bibliothéque Nationale, 8, 46, 223n48; "Cabinet des Illusions," 128; Charles Ratton Gallery, 88; Jardin du Roi, 207; Museum of Man (Musée de l'Homme), 67, 68; Royal Garden and Cabinet, 40–41, 53

Parsons, Jack, 124, *125, 140*

Peabody Essex Museum (Salem, Mass.), 225n6

Peale, Charles Wilson: *The Artist and His Museum* (self-portrait), *70*, 223n59; natural history museums of, 69, 71, 225n6

Pearce, Russell, 238–239n1

Pearson, Maria, 68, 225n2

Pelayo, Francisco, 224n67

Pelli, Cesar, 206

Pelton, Agnes, 143

Penitentes: crosses of, 151–152; description of, 157–158; pilgrimages of, 147, 155, 159

Pennsylvania Academy of Fine Arts (Philadelphia), *70*, 223–224n59

Pérez Firmat, Gustavo, 195

performance art: of caste paintings, 73; by Delgado, 185; by Ortiz Torres, 236n55; *Performance of the Couple in the Cage, 88, 89*

performative sites: cabinets of wonders as, 32, 36; pilgrimages as, 106, 131–132; role of relics

and icons in, 120–121, 233–234n14; tattoos and
lowriders as, 130–131

Perú: aristocratic lineage in, 62, 224n63; bio-
reserve of, *208*; Guadalupanism in, 233n3;
mercury mine in, 220n15; pictorial and text
account of, *58–59, 60*, 61–62, 223n51; Spanish
expeditions to, 49–50

Peter I, 32

Peter the Great Museum of Anthropology and
Ethnography (Kunstkammera, St. Petersburg), *34*, 214n17

Philadelphia: Academy of Natural Sciences,
224n68; Bartram's Garden, 207; museums
in, 71, 209n7; Pennsylvania Academy of
Fine Arts, *70*, 223–224n59. *See also* Mütter
Museum (Philadelphia)

Philadelphia Museum, 71

Philadelphia Museum of Art, 209n7

Philip II (king of Spain), 51, 52, 219n11

Philippines, Spanish expedition to, 49

photographs: as anchors of memory, 167–168;
elusive nature of, 23; memories created via,
167–168, 240n13; narratives linked to, 167, 176;
as objects, 166–167; poor vs. rich women as
subjects of, 205–206; as pre-texts, 164; privileged status of, 239n9; sculpture combined
with, 178–179; of surgeries, 227n24

Picasso, Pablo, 90

pilgrimages: as anchor of national identity, 131–
132; as celebration of social identity, 156–157;
cultural context of, 157; function of, 97–98, 121;
Guadalupan sites in Spain, 118; Guadalupan
sites in U.S., 134–137; hermetic symbolism of,
229n3; as indigenous performance, 106; of
lowriders, 131; miraculous image linked to,
104, 107; sacred geographies of, 152–160; sta-
tistics on, 231n40. *See also* rituals

Pineda, Cecile, 165

Pino, Pedro, 159

pintos (Chicanas/os in prison): and tattoos,
125–127, 236n55; use of term, 234n27

pirates and piracy, 53, 221n27

place: loss of anchors to, 191–194; memories
linked to, 20, 22; pilgrimages linked to, 134–
137; proto-nationalist understanding of, 98.
See also sacred space/landscape/geographies

plunder, 27, 46, 200–201, 214n16, 242n2

Po, Pietro del, 28, *29*

polar bears, 87–88

politics: of brown, 17; crisis of representation
in, 191; repatriation of objects and, 200–201;
unstable moments in, 23

politics of display: critiques of, 28, 75, 88; works
that make visible, 6, *7*, 88. *See also* museological practices

Polon, Joshua, x, *91*

polysyndeton (rhetorical figure), 38, 82, 220n21

Porta, Giovanni Battista Della, 43

post-apocalyptic cabinets of wonders: art and
science juxtaposed in, 79–80; art and science
melded in, 94; Bodyworlds exhibit as, 78–79;
consumer detritus in, 87–88; fascination with,
75; as frame to undo frame, 91; of objects
collected but not exhibited, 84–85, 87, 92;
past cabinets in dialogue with, 80, 81, 226n16;
reordering of order in, 92–93. *See also* global
warming; natural history; recycling and
recycled things

postmemory concept, 240n13

Potosí. *See* Bolivia (Potosí)

Prado Museum (Madrid), *30*, 38, *39*, 53, 221n28

Pratt, Mary Louise, 209n5, 216n45, 218n66, 225n1

Premio Nacional de Arte Cubano, 186

Prest, John, 208

Prida, Dolores, 197

printing technology, 36

proto-nationalism concept, 97–98, 106, 111,
229n8

Proust, Marcel, 170

provenance: absence of, 228n34; denial of, 84;
mis- and replacement of, 85, 199–201

Puebla (Mexico), 21

Pueblo Indians: dichotomy between Hispanic
peoples and, 159–160; Guadalupanism among,
118; mystique of, 139; use of term, 159

Pueblo Revolts (1680, 1696), 156, 158, 159

Puig-Samper, Miguel Angel, 66

Purcell, Rosamond W.: cabinets of wonders by,
x, 8, 29; on containment, 67, 92; Gould's collaboration with, x, 22, 80; Jay's work and,
227n26; on nature of collecting and decaying
objects, 76, 80, 91–93; on objects collected
but not exhibited, 84–85; photographs by, *34,
60, 80*, 85, *94*; recycled objects and, 81–83,
227–228n31, 228n33; subject/object repositioned by, 89, 92

Purcell, Rosamond W., works of: *Adam and Eve*,
x, 80; *Crossing Over*, 79, 94; *Dice*, 76; *Finders,
Keepers*, 80; *Half-Life*, 80; *Illuminations*, 80,
84–85; *Owl's Head*, 67, 80, 82, 92–93; *Special
Cases*, 80; *Swift as a Shadow*, 84; *Two Rooms*,
83, 228n31; *Worm Museum*, 81–82

*Quadro de Historial Natural, civil y geográfico del
Reyno del Perú* (Thiebaut), *58–59, 60*, 61–62,
223n51

questionnaires, 222n42; on mining potential,
56–57; scientific and religious linked, 54–55;
surveillance and, 68, 124, 127

Quintana, José, 152

race: hierarchies of, 10–11, *12, 13*, 14, 159–160; mixed, 62, 224n63; rewriting history of, 148; terminology and stereotypes of, 210–211n25; as unrepresentable, 12–16; of Virgin of Guadalupe, 100, *101, 102*, 103, *104*, 233n8. *See also* caste paintings; cosmic race (raza cósmica); degeneration theory

Raketa (artist group), *91*

Rama, Angel, lettered city concept of, 98, 105, 106, 109, 112, 115, 229n6

Ramírez, Yasmin, 224n60

Ramos, Sandra: as Alice in Wonderland, 195–197; background of, 186; on community destabilization, 191; as influence, x, 21; on loss incurred from exile, 164, 186–190; political context and critique of, 183, 185–186, 196–197; on rupture, 193

Ramos, Sandra, works of: *Ahogarse en lágrimas* [To Drown in Tears], 189; *Aurorreconocimiento del pez* [Self-Knowledge of Fish], *189*; *La balsa* [The Raft], *184*; *El bote* [The Boat], *186*; *Brazos* [Arms], *188*; *Buzos* [Scuba Divers], *196*; *Camina sobre el agua hombre de poca fe* [Walk on Water Man of Little Faith], *197*; *El canto de la sirena* [The Siren's Song], *188*; *Criaturas de isla* [Island Creatures], *188*; *Espejismos* [Mirages], *187*; "Exilio," 192–193; *Inmersiones y enterramientos* [Immersions and Burials] (series), 186; *La maldita circunstancia del agua por todas partes* [The Damned Circumstance of Being Surrounded by Water Everywhere], *197, 198*; *Máquina para ahogar las penas* [Machine to Drown Sorrows], 186, *196*; *Mi diaria vocación de suicida* [My Daily Vocation as a Suicide], *197*; *Migrations II*, *187–188*; *Los ojos de Dios* [God's Eyes], 186, *187*; *Los problemas del peso* [Weight Problems], *183*; *Promesas*, 197, 242n29; *Quizás hasta deba partirme en dos* [Maybe I Should Even Split Myself in Two], *193*; *Rostros que desaparecen para siempre* [Faces That Disappear for Good], *189*; *El silencio de los corderos* [The Silence of the Lambs], *184, 185*; *La vida no cabe en una maleta* [Life Does Not Fit in a Suitcase], x, *189*; *Y cuando todos se han ido llega la soledad . . .* [And When Everyone Has Left Comes Loneliness . . .], 189, *189*

Raskin, Marcus, 23

rasquachismo, aesthetics of, 126, 130

Rathje, W. J., 42

rationality: challenges to, 6–7; claims of, 28, 32, 44; development of, 52–53, 223n51; questions about, x, 103–104; rethinking of, 23–24, 49

Rauh, Ida, 143

raza cósmica (cosmic race), 15, 17, 137, 151

Raza Studies, 238–239n1

Real Gabinete de Historia Natural de Madrid: archival process of, 54–57; as case study, 49; caste paintings in, 12; changing support for, 50–51; expeditions sponsored by, 49–50; founding of, 51–52; Jefferson's involvement with, 7–8, 50–51, 63–64; as knowledge filter, 57–60; large bones sent to, 50–51, 64; legacy of, 64–66, 224n68; minerals in, 219–220n14; opened to public, 52; relocation and dispersal of, 53–54; renaming of, 52–53; Stardanus's "America" image and, 46

re-collecting: collaborative process of, 164–165; concept of, 164–165; of found objects, 168, 171; as go-between-ing, 172–173

Reconquista period (Spain), 118, 119

recycling and recycled things: aesthetics of *rasquachismo* in, 127, 130; Andrade's uses of, 92, 92–93, *93*; cultural shift and interests in, 94; decomposition of, 90; dredged and exhibited, 87–88; Guadalupe shrine from, 124, *127*, 140; misplacement in, 171; Purcell's uses of, 82–84, 93–94, 228n31, 228n33; reclaiming aura of object in, 206; as transforming guts into heart, 179

Reformation, 98, 99

Reina y Medina, Manuela, 220n18

relics: embedded in objects, 233–234n14; mobility of, 120–121; power of, 154–156. *See also* icons and iconicity

religious images: attempt to control power of, 106–107; black material used for, 233n8; Catholic and indigenous combined in, 105–106; church policies on, 98–99; as embodied and alive, 104–105; indigenous production of, 99–100; on lowriders (automobiles), *125, 126*; mobility of, 120–121; proliferation of, 104, 120; role in Mexican nationalism, 100, *102, 103*; tattoos as, *124*, 125–127; on tokens for journey, *122*; on T-shirts, *125*. *See also* icons and iconicity

religious syncretism: alternative approach to, 105–106; examples of, 13, 97–100, 111, 116, 229n8; problems with concept, 9; social life of saints in, 104

Rembrandt van Rijn, 38, 215n32

Retchy, John, 165

Ribera I Argomanis, José de, 113

Ricas y famosas [Rich and Famous] (exhibition and book), 205–206

Ricci, Mateo, 214n20

Rice, Felicia, 117

Rio, Dolores del, 173

Ripley, Robert, 83–84

Ripley's *Believe It or Not!*, 84

rituals: documentation of, 230n10; function of,

97–98; inside knowledge for eradication of, 98–99; of national cohesion, 100, *102*, 103; spirits embodied in, 104–105. *See also* pilgrimages
Rivera, Diego, 14
Rivera, Norberto, 133
"Road to Aztlán, The" (exhibition), 152, 160
Roentgen, Wilhelm, 215n29
Rogers, Ginger, 173
Rogers, Henry Huttleston, 148
Rogers, Millicent, 148, 159
Rönnebeck, Arnold, 143, *145*, 147
Roosevelt, Franklin Delano, 78
Ross, Richard, 80, 212n3
Rossell, Daniela, 205–206
Rouse, Roger, 190
Royal Garden and Cabinet (Paris), 40–41, 53
Royal Kunstkammer (Denmark), 40, *40*
Royal Society of London, 85
Rubenstein, Meridel, 128, *129*
Rubin, Arnold, 234n32
Rudhyar, Dane, 143
Rudnick, Lois Palken, 147
Ruiz Gómez, Leticia, 221n28
Rushdie, Salman, 170–171
Russell, Steve, 225n2
Rutherford, John, 127
Ruysch, Frederik: allegories and theatricality of, 32, 33, 79, 80; *Allegory of the Transitoriness of Life with "Music" as a Theme*, *35*, bodies preserved by, *34*, 79, 80–81, 92; heir of, 227n23; whereabouts of cabinet of, 214n17

Sacred Heart Auto League, 130
sacred space/landscape/geographies: Anglo vs. Latin American, 97; creation of, 137; crosses as marking, 144, *146*, 151; eastern elites' imaginary vs., 143–152; exported to other places, 140, 143; myth and allure vs. poverty and violence juxtaposed in, 147–148; New Mexico as, 152–160; relics as marking, 120–121
saints: relics of, 120–121, 154–155, 233–234n14; social life of, 104–105
Salinas, Raúl, 126, 129
salvage ethnology concept, 149
Sánchez, Miguel, 108, 111–113, 115, 232n73
Sanders, Clinton R., 235n47
Sandoval, Nicolás, 158
Sandoval-Sánchez, Alberto, *21*, 210–211n25
Santa Clara Pueblo Potters, 149, 159
Santa Fe (N.Mex.): as America's Orient, 236–237n3; art markets in, 139, 143; Museum of International Folk Art, 149–150; Náhuatl terms used in, 152; Spanish Colonial Arts Museum, 148–149
Santa Fe El Norte, 152, 156

santeros: privileged position of, 238n41; Virgin of Guadalupe by, *140*; work of, 143, 154, 158
Santiago, Danny, 232–233n74
Santo Niño de Atocha shrine, 154
Sassen, Saskia, 190
Satterfield, Jay, 214n19
Schedel, Hartmann, 36, 215n24
Scherer, Migael, 194
scholar/scientist circle, 52–53, 221n23
science: allegory and theatricality underlying, 32, *34*; art distinguished from, 6, 52, 93–94; art linked to, 23, 78–80; as central vs. marginal, 104; colonialism linked to, 28; commerce as interdependent with, 56–57, 61, 65; and curiosity, 213n12; depiction of, *30*; Eurocentrism of, 7, 41, 62, 64–65, 224n68; housing for branches of, 52; images as tool in, 103–104; and Juan Diego's tilma, 109–110, 231n37; manipulation of, 226n11; objects translated to specimens in, 41–42, 44; Spanish and American roles in, 46, 49, 50, 63–66, 218n66. *See also* classification; natural history; scholar/scientist circle; scientific inquiry; spectacles
scientific inquiry: Americas as object of, 42, 53–55, 221n27, 222n32; cabinets as spaces of, 52–53; specimens as focus of, 41–42, 44. *See also* observation; questionnaires
sculpture: human and nature forms combined in, 33; of lowrider interior/altar, *142*; of "native" woman, 62–63, *63*; of nostalgia and rupture, 193–195; parody of collectors in, 140, *141*; photographs combined with, 177–179
Seabrook, Jeremy, 167, 239n12
Sebald, W. G., 67, 87, 144
Shamnoag (Picurís Pueblo Indian), 153
Sheikh, Fazal, *122*, 123, 176
ships metaphor, 161–162
shipwrecks: of migrants, 182; of socialist project, 183, 185, 187–188, 197; survivors of, 128, 220n18, 230–231n33
shrines. *See* altars and shrines
Sicily, curiosity shop in, *4*
sight: belief linked to, 121; contagion with the sacred and, 104, 120–121; interplay of science and, 213n12; and ixiptla, 105–106; knowledge equated with, 37, 39; privileging of, 78; proliferation of images and, 120, 206; transformed into oversight, 68–69. *See also* eye/I; observation; visual, the
Silva, José Antonio, 152
Simonides of Ceos, 20–21
Siqueiros, David Alfaro, 14
Sloane, Hans, 221n27
smallpox vaccine, 50
Smithsonian Institution, 128, 235n44

Soane, John, 75–76

Social and Public Art Resource Center (SPARC) (Venice Beach), 119

Soldado, Juan, 137

Sontag, Susan, 176

Sousa, Lisa, 232n73

Southwest (U.S.): alterity of, 17–18; artistic creation of, 143–152; "aura" of, 139, 237n2; and Baroque, 156, 158; border's crossing in, 164, 238–239n1; documentation of arts and culture in, 151, 158–160; drought in, 237n27; fashion and, 149, 235n41; Guadalupan churches in, 118, 123, 233n2; kivas and moradas in, 157–158; lowrider circuit in, 128, 130–131; marketing of, 139–140, 143, 150–151; myth and allure vs. poverty and violence in, 147; Náhuatl terms used in, 152; obsessive collecting of arts of, 139–140; Spanish colonial period in, 148, 152–153, 164, 166, 238–239n1. See also Aztlán; Latinization

space. See pilgrimages; place; sacred space/landscape/geographies

Spain: decorated horses of, 129; empire as scientific and economic enterprise of, 56–57, 61; expeditions of, 49–50, 65–66; financial crisis of, 219n12; map of colonies of, 43; reinsertion into world order, 51; scientific role of, 46, 49, 50, 63–64, 65–66, 218n66; stereotypes of, 57; U.S. assistance from, 219n6; wealth needed for, 51, 56–57, 219n12. See also Madrid (Spain); Real Gabinete de Historia Natural de Madrid

Spanish Colonial Arts Museum (Santa Fe), 148

Spanish Colonial Arts Society, 148–149, 158

Spanish language, 160

Spanish Market (Santa Fe): guidelines of, 150; packaging of, 139–140, 143; sponsorship of, 149

SPARC (Social and Public Art Resource Center) (Venice Beach), 119

specimens: biggest and rarest, 32; objects transformed into, 41–42, 44; people as, 88, 90–91; real and fake juxtaposed, 82–83. See also taxidermied specimens and taxidermy

spectacles: altars/miniature installations compared with, 178–179; anatomical theaters as, 33, 36, 214n18; indigenous pilgrimages as, 106; lowriders as, 130–131; in Mütter Museum, 77–78; public education of natural history as, 72–73; spatial dynamics of, 36–37

Spence, Jonathan D., 214n20

Spitzer, Leo, 240n13

St. Francis Xavier parish (Grand Rapids, Mich.): identity transformation and, 156–157; pilgrims from, 152–153, 156

St. Louis World's Fair (1904), 74, 75, 83, 84

Stafford, Barbara Maria, 27, 213n14, 216–217n52, 240n16

Stafford Poole, C. M., 232n73, 236n70

Stalbent, Adriaen, 30

Stalin, Joseph, 200

Stallybrass, Peter, 18, 175

Standley, Joe, 69

Statue of Liberty, 117, 120, 181

Steichen, Edward, 75

Stein, Harvey, 80

Stephens, John Lloyd, 226n10

stereotypes: of Latinos/as, 210–211n25; of Mexican Americans, 165, 167, 173–174, 177, 182, 240n26; of Native Americans, 160; of Spanish greed, 57

Stern, Maurice, 143

Stewart, Susan: on family photographs, 167; on microscope, 42; on miniaturization, 23, 37, 43, 217n60

Stieglitz, Alfred, 7, 143, 144

Stokowski, Leopold, 143

Stradano, Giovanni, 8, 46, 223n48

Strand, Paul, 143

Strand, Rebecca, 143, 144

Strausbaugh, John, 227n23

"Stuffing Birds, Pressing Plants, Shaping Knowledge" (exhibition), 213n12, 217–218n61, 223–224n59

Suárez, Ezequiel, 185

subject/object binary: challenges to, 23; disrupting boundaries of, 79; reflections on, 199–208; refusal and undoing of, 92–94; repositioning in, 88, 90–91; unsettling of, 3, 5

subject/object interpenetration: concept of, 22; in fossil and rock, 22; in ritual dance, 104–105; transition in, 93–94

subjects: ghosting of, 80–81; mis- and displacement of, 9–16, 201, 204; object as cannibalizing, 92, 206–207, 226–227n22; objects distanced from, 216n50; poor vs. rich women as, 205–206; as privileged voyeurs in Kunstkammern, 37–38, 39, 42; privileging of European, 44–46; re-collecting, 16–21. See also subject/object interpenetration; subject/object binary

suitcases: of migrants and exiles, x, 187–190; miniature version of, 178; obsessions with, 17, 22; people in transit as, 201–204; reclaimed as objects, 82

surrealism, 7, 23, 90, 209n9

surveying and surveillance, 68, 124, 127. See also commerce; conquest and colonialism; Eurocentrism; natural history; science

"Sylvia" the Mummy, 69

Taliban, 42

Talpa (N.Mex.), 158

Taormina (Sicily), curiosity shop in, 4

Taos (N.Mex.): as America's Orient, 236–237n3;

art markets in, 139–140, 143; Harwood Museum, 148; as land of enchantment, 141–148; Millicent Rogers Museum, 149, 159. *See also* Mabel Dodge Luhan House (Taos)

Taos Artists Colony, 148

Taos Rebellion (1847), 158

Taos Society of Artists, 148, 150

Tapia, Luis, 140, *141, 142*

Tate Gallery, x

tattoos: "body altar" of, 130; history of, 125–128, 234n32; lowriders linked to, 130–131, 236n55; middle-class embrace of, 126–127, 234–235n34; native translated into fashion, 235n41; in S/M communities, 234–235n33; of Virgin of Guadalupe, 124, *124,* 125–126

TattooTime (journal), 234–235n34

taxidermied specimens and taxidermy: of birds, 88; in early museums, 225n6; of humans, 68–69, 201; of polar bears, 87–88; sadness evoked by, 207; wealthy women linked to, 205–206

taxonomies: Americas framed via, 9, 11–12, 14, 41, 68–69; cabinets utilizing, 53, 57; Eurocentrism of, 64; fear of fixed, 41; invention of, 38; rationality of, 6. *See also* caste paintings; classification; hierarchies; mestizaje

Taylor, Diana, 211n34, 230n24

Taylor, Elizabeth, 174

Taylor Museum of Southwestern Study (Colorado Springs Museum of Fine Arts), 138, 158

Tchitchoua, Nana, 91

technologies: of augmented vision, 42–44, 216n48, 217n53, 217n55; navigational ("magic"), 223n48; for viewing body sections, 227n23; of war and conquest, 96–97; of writing in colonial administration, 98, 229n6. *See also* Museum of Jurassic Technology (Los Angeles); surveying and surveillance

technology/nature binary, 45–46, 93

telescopes, 42, 216n48

Temple, Shirley, 174

Tenniel, John, 196

Tenochtitlán: fall of, 15, 16; foundational myth of, 107; Guadalupe/Tonantzin and, *102,* 103, *104,* 107–108, 112, 114, 115–116, 232n73; headwear of rulers in, 199; rituals of, 207; Virgin of Guadalupe linked to, 100, *102,* 103, *104,* 107–108, 112–113, 114, 115–116, 232n73. *See also* Mexico City

Tepeyac. *See* La Villa/Tepeyac (Mexico)

Tettnang Kunstkammer, 199–200

Tewa Pueblo Indians, 153–154, 233n4

Texas Giant Brothers, 71

Tezozomoc, Alvarado, 152

theater: of anatomy, 36, *36,* 76, 214n18, 227n23;

Barnum's spectacles as, 72–73; definitions of, 214nn20–221; of memory, 36, 214n20; settings of, 144. *See also* performative sites; spectacles

Theresa (saint), 121

Thiebaut, Luis, *58–59, 60,* 61–62, 223n51

Thompson, Barbara, *84,* 226n15

Thomson, Anna Leake, 71

Thumb family, 71, *71*

time: miniaturization and, 217n60; multilayered complex totality of, 22–23; shape in, 22, 209n10. *See also* subject/object interpenetration

Time magazine, *135*

Todas people, *74*

Tonantzin (Aztec goddess): Guadalupe and, *102,* 103, *104,* 107–108, 112–114, 115–116, 232n73; Virgin of Guadalupe as subsuming, 15–16

Tonsmann, Aste, 231n37

Toral, Cristóbal, 93, 201, *202–204*

Torre, Carlos de la, 25, 26

Torre Villar, Ernesto de la, 96

torture, at Abu Ghraib, 226n15

total institutions: identity stripped in, 14, 241n32; knowledge filtered by, 57–60; Nazi concentration camps as, 210n19

tourism: arts markets and, 139–140, 143; Mexico as pre-modern in, 172; utopian projection of, 143; violence of conquest in, 90–91. *See also* collecting

transatlantic movements: certainties destabilized in, 9; discoverer vs. Other in, 218n62; history of, 218n62; of New World objects, 6–8, 27–28; secularization and, 100; tattoos in, 128

transculturation: documents in, 230n10; gains and losses in, 172–173; mestizaje distinguished from, ix; objects and cultural narratives in, 22; questions of authorship in, 115; stages of, 97–98; two-way exchanges in, 151–152; as voluntary postmodernism, 179

translatinidad, Virgin of Guadalupe as index of, 17. *See also latinidad*

trashart. *See* recycling and recycled things

trauma: of border crossing, 135–136; of exile, 187–197

Treaty of Guadalupe Hidalgo (1848), 16, 177, 238–239n1

Tufts University, 228n31

Turner, Edith, 121, 123

Turner, Joseph, 23

Turner, Kay F., 121, 234n15, 234n25

Turner, Victor, 121, 123

2001: A Space Odyssey (film), 3

Ulloa, Antonio de, 37, 51, 219–220n14, 220n15

Ulrich of Montfort (count), 199–200

United Farm Workers, 119, 135

United States: anticommunism in, 181–182; as commercial not scientific lure, 224n66; as consumer paradise, x, 164, 182, 187, 191; Cuban embargo of, 185; first museums in, 225n6; historical amnesia of, 177; miracles in, 135, *136*; national imaginary of, 176; as nation of immigrants, 181–183; pilgrimages in, 134–137; racial divide in, 17; scientific role of, 50, 64–65; Spanish assistance for, 219n6; tattoo renaissance in, 127–128; visionary culture in, 124. *See also* Southwest (U.S.); U.S.-Mexico border; *specific states*

"University of Man" (exhibition), 84

U.S.-Mexico border: Border Patrol of, 133, 135–136, 235n45; daily tragedies along, 136, 182; U.S. militarization of, 123–124, 133, 165–166, 177; as zone of possibility, 190

Valadez, John, 9–10, *10–11*, 14

Valeriano, Antonio, 114–115

Vasconcelos, José, 14, *15*, 17, *137*, 150

Vega, Lasso de la, 108–110, 113–115

Velasco, Luis de, 222n41

Velázquez, Diego, 7, 201, *203*

Vermont Standard, 91

Verner, Samuel, 75

Vesalii, Andrea, 36, *36*, *37*, 79

Vespucci, Amerigo, *8*, 46, 223n48

Victoria, Guadalupe, 118

Vienna (Austria): Butterfly Pavilion, 62–63; Museum of Ethnology, *4*, 5, 199–201; Naturhistorisches Museum, *32*, 200; sculpture of "native" woman in, *63*. *See also* Kunsthistorisches Museum (Vienna)

Villa, Pancho, 176–177

Villanueva, Juan de, 221n28

Viramontes, Maria Helena, 119

Virgin Mary, 107, 112, 124, *134*, 176

Virgin of Guadalupe: anachronistic representations of, x–xi; apparitions of, 100, 107–108, 111–112, 114–115, 134–136, *136*; and border crossing, 15–16, 97–98, 107, 117–137, 176; changing images of, 118–121, 140, 233n5; Chicana feminists and, 119–120; depictions and altars of, *19*, *101*, *102*, *104*, 119, 122, *125*, 135, *136*, *140*, *141*, *142*; as evidence of Latinization, 22, 179; as mestizaje symbol, ix, 15–16, 99–100, *102*, *103*; Mexicanization and creolization of, 111–112; miracles of, 111–113, 134–136; native idols replaced by, 106; polysemous plasticity of (Virgin's "wheels"), 106, 115, 120–121, 124–125, 131–133; role in Mexican national foundations, 100, *102*, 103, 107–116, 118, 132–133; weeping figure of, 135–136. *See also* Guadalupanism

Virgin of Undocumented Workers, 120

Visible Human Project, 227n23

visionary culture, 124

visual, the: as empirical tool, 103–104; as privileged access to divinity, 98–99; privileging of, 41–42, 216n41, 216n50; technologies of, 42–44. *See also* eye/I; observation; sight

Viya, Manuel Joseph de la, 221n23

voyeurism: camera obscura as metaphor for, 43; of subjects in Kunstkammern, 37–38, *39*, 42

Wadsworth Atheneum (Hartford, Conn.), 225n6

Washington, George, 78, 219n6

Washington Office on Latin America (WOLA), 205

Waters, Frank, 143

Watsonville Canning and Frozen Food Company, 134–135

ways of knowing, 212n2. *See also* epistemology

Webster, Daniel, 83, 90

Wechsler, Lawrence, 90

Weeping Guadalupe, 135–136

Weigle, Marta, 158

Wells, Cady, 143

Weston, Edward, 143

"When the President Is the Patient" (exhibition), 78

White, Allon, 18, 175

Wijck, Jan van, *40*

Wilcox, Ann, 23

Wilgus, Beverly, 217n55

Wilgus, Jack, 217n55

Wilkins, John, 6

Williams, Robert, 235n44

Wilson, Chris, 158–160

Wilson, David, 91

Wilson, Fred: on artifacts and art, 63; installations of, 224n64; *So Much Trouble in the World*, *83*, 226n15; subject/object repositioned by, 90, 226n15; unexhibited objects as focus of, 84, 92

Wilson, Woodrow, 78

WOLA (Washington Office on Latin America), 205

Wolf, Eric, 218n62

women: mis- and displacement of, 201, 204; museums as public space for, 72; tattoos of, 127–128; violence against, 204–205

wonder: distinctions in collections, 149; harnessing of, 37; memory, imagination, and narrative as producing, 168; of nature, 206–208; as pre-logical, pre-reflexive phase, 5; scientist's overcoming, 41, 216n41; in surgery, 227n24; at technologies of war and conquest, 96–97. *See also* cabinets of wonders *(Wunderkammern)*; curiosity; marvel and the marvelous

Worden, Gretchen: as collector, 78–79, 226n18; directorship of, 227n23; on objects and observation, 93; on participation of specimens, 79, 80

Wordsworth, William, 57, 67

workers: apparition of Guadalupe during strike of, 134–135; Guadalupe as symbol of, 119, 135; maquiladora, 204–205; undocumented, 120, 133–134

Worm, Hans, 48

Worm, Ole, 29, *31*, 81–82, *81*

Wunderkammer des Abendlandes (exhibition), 213n13

Wunderkammern. See cabinets of wonders (*Wunderkammern*)

X-rays, 37, 215n29

Yarbro-Bejarano, Yvonne, 119

Yates, Frances A., 20, 214n20

Ybarra-Frausto, Tomás, 126, 177, 179

Yellow Bear (chief), 72

Ye Olde Curiosity Shop (Seattle), 68–69

Zamora, Lois Parkinson: on cultural legibility and literacy, 99, 112; on images, 103; on performativity, 106; on representational modes, 213n15; on visual culture, 112, 217n56

Zapata, Emiliano, 118, 205

Zavala, Iris, 218n62

zoos: function of, 215n22; *Homo sapiens* exhibit of, 88; human exhibited at, 75; subject/object repositioned by, 90. *See also* botanical gardens; museums (art, general, and natural history)

Zumárraga, Juan, 107, 113, 114, 231n37